Arthur Wardlaw's Letter.

Dearest Helen

I hear from Mr Adams that you desire to know the name of the Counsel who defended Robert Penfold.

It was Mr Tollemache, he has Chambers in Lincoln's Inn.

Ever devotedly yours,

Arthur Wardlaw

Over

To enable the reader to follow Mr. Undercliff's Summary, the materials of his judgment are here reproduced. (*See page* 134.)

The Forged Note.

£2000, 0, 0

London, February 10th 1864.

Three Months after Date, I promise to pay Robert Penfold or Order, the Sum of Two Thousand Pounds, value received.

John Wardlaw

The genuine handwriting of John Wardlaw.

I promise to pay
One Thousand Pounds
John Wardlaw

Over

FOUL PLAY.

A Novel.

BY

CHARLES READE AND DION BOUCICAULT.

WITH ILLUSTRATIONS BY GEORGE DU MAURIER.

BOSTON:
TICKNOR AND FIELDS.
1868.

AUTHORS' EDITION.

University Press: Welch, Bigelow, & Co.,
Cambridge.

FOUL PLAY.

CHAPTER I.

THERE are places which appear at first sight inaccessible to romance: and such a place was Mr. Wardlaw's dining-room in Russell Square. It was very large, had sickly green walls, picked out with aldermen, full length; heavy maroon curtains; mahogany chairs; a turkey carpet an inch thick: and was lighted with wax candles only.

In the centre, bristling and gleaming with silver and glass, was a round table, at which fourteen could have dined comfortably; and at opposite sides of this table sat two gentlemen, who looked as neat, grave, precise, and unromantic, as the place; Merchant Wardlaw, and his son.

Wardlaw senior was an elderly man, tall, thin, iron-gray, with a round head, a short, thick neck, a good, brown eye, a square jowl that betokened resolution, and a complexion so sallow as to be almost cadaverous. Hard as iron: but a certain stiff dignity and respectability sat upon him, and became him.

Arthur Wardlaw resembled his father in figure, but his mother in face. He had, and has, hay-colored hair, a forehead singularly white and delicate, pale blue eyes, largish ears, finely chiselled features, the under lip much shorter than the upper; his chin oval and pretty, but somewhat receding; his complexion beautiful. In short, what nineteen people out of twenty would call a handsome young man, and think they had described him.

Both the Wardlaws were in full dress, according to the invariable custom of the house; and sat in a dead silence, that seemed natural to the great, sober room.

This, however, was not for want of a topic; on the contrary, they had a matter of great importance to discuss, and in fact this was why they dined *tête-à-tête:* but their tongues were tied for the present; in the first place, there stood in the middle of the table an epergne, the size of a Putney laurel-tree; neither Wardlaw could well see the other, without craning out his neck like a rifleman from behind his tree: and then there were three live suppressors of confidential intercourse, two gorgeous footmen, and a sombre, sublime, and, in one word, episcopal, butler; all three went about as softly as cats after a robin, and conjured one plate away, and smoothly insinuated another, and seemed models of grave discretion: but were known to be all ears, and bound by a secret oath to carry down each crumb of dialogue to the servants' hall, for curious dissection, and boisterous ridicule.

At last, however, those three smug hypocrites retired, and, by good luck, transferred their suffocating epergne to the sideboard; so then father and son looked at one another with that conscious air which naturally precedes a topic of interest; and Wardlaw senior invited his son to try a certain decanter of rare old port, by way of preliminary.

While the young man fills his glass, hurl we in his antecedents.

At school till fifteen, and then clerk in his father's office till twenty-two, and showed an aptitude so remarkable, that John Wardlaw, who was getting tired, determined, sooner or later, to put the reins of government into his hands. But he conceived a desire that the future head of his office should be an university man. So he announced his resolution, and to Oxford went young Wardlaw, though he had not looked at Greek or Latin for seven years. He was, however, furnished with a private tutor, under whom he recovered lost ground rapidly. The Reverend Robert Penfold was a first-class man, and had the gift of teaching. The house of Wardlaw had peculiar claims on him, for he was the son of old Michael Penfold, Wardlaw's cashier; he learned from young Wardlaw the stake he was playing for, and, instead of merely giving him one hour's lecture per day, as he did to his other pupils, he used to come to his rooms at all hours, and force him to read, by reading with him. He also stood his friend in a serious emergency. Young Wardlaw, you must know, was blessed or cursed with Mimicry; his powers in that way really seemed to have no limit, for he could imitate any sound you liked with his voice, and any form with his pen or pencil. Now, we promise you, he was one man under his father's eye, and another down at Oxford; so, one night, this gentleman, being warm with wine, opens his window, and, seeing a group of undergraduates chattering and smoking in the quadrangle, imitates the peculiar grating tones of Mr. Champion, vice-president of the college, and gives them various reasons why they ought to disperse to their rooms and study. "But, perhaps," says he, in conclusion, "you are too blind drunk to read Bosh in crooked letters by candle-light? In that case —" And he then gave them some very naughty advice how to pass the evening; still in the exact tones of Mr. Champion, who was a very, very strict moralist; and this unexpected sally of wit caused shrieks of laughter, and mightily tickled all the hearers, except Champion *ipse*, who was listening and disapproving at another window. He complained to the president. Then the ingenious Wardlaw, not having come down to us in a direct line from Bayard, committed a great mistake, — he denied it.

It was brought home to him, and the president, who had laughed in his sleeve at the practical joke, looked very grave at the falsehood; Rustication was talked of and even Expulsion. Then Wardlaw came sorrowfully to Penfold, and said to him, "I must have been awfully cut, for I don't remember all that; I had been wining at Christchurch. I do remember slanging the fellows, but how can I tell what I said? I say, old fellow, it will be a bad job for me if they expel me, or even rusticate me; my father will never forgive me; I shall be his clerk, but never his partner; and then he will find out what a lot I owe down here. I'm done for! I'm done for!"

Penfold uttered not a word, but grasped his hand, and went off to the president, and said his pupil had wined at Christchurch, and could not be expected to remember minutely. Mimicry was, unfortunately, a habit with him. He then pleaded for the milder construction, with such zeal and eloquence, that the high-minded scholar he was addressing admitted that construction was *possible*, and therefore must be received. So the affair ended in a written apology to Mr. Champion, which had all the smoothness and neatness of a merchant's letter. Arthur Wardlaw was already a master in that style.

Six months after this, and one fortnight before the actual commencement of our tale, Arthur Wardlaw, well crammed by Penfold, went up for his final examination, throbbing with anxiety. He passed; and was so grateful to his tutor that, when the advowson of a small living near Oxford came into the market, he asked Wardlaw senior to lend Robert Penfold a sum of money, much more than was needed: and Wardlaw senior declined without a moment's hesitation.

This slight sketch will serve as a key to the dialogue it has postponed, and to subsequent incidents.

"Well, Arthur, and so you have really taken your degree?"

"No, sir; but I have passed my examination: the degreé follows as a matter of course, — that is a mere question of fees."

"Oh! Then now I have something to say to you. Try one more glass of the '47 port. Stop; you 'll excuse me; I am a man of business; I don't doubt your word; Heaven forbid! but, do you happen to have any document you can produce in further confirmation of what you state; namely, that you have passed your final examination at the University?"

"Certainly, sir"; replied young Wardlaw. "My Testamur."

"What is that?"

The young gentleman put his hand in his pocket, and produced his Testamur, or "We bear witness"; a short printed document in Latin, which may be thus translated: —

"*We bear witness that Arthur Wardlaw, of St. Luke's College, has answered our questions in humane letters.*

"GEORGE RICHARDSON,
"ARTHUR SMYTHE,
"EDWARD MERIVALE,
Examiners."

Wardlaw senior took it, laid it beside him on the table, inspected it with his double eye-glass, and, not knowing a word of Latin, was mightily impressed, and his respect for his son rose 40, or 45, per cent.

"Very well, sir"; said he. "Now listen to me. Perhaps it was an old man's fancy; but I have often seen in the world what a stamp these Universities put upon a man. To send you back from commerce to Latin and Greek, at two and twenty, was trying you rather hard; it was trying you doubly; your obedience, and your ability into the bargain. Well, sir, you have stood the trial, and I am proud of you. And so now it is my turn: from this day and from this hour, look on yourself as my partner in the old established house of Wardlaw. My balance-sheet shall be prepared immediately, and the partnership deed drawn. You will enter on a flourishing concern, sir; and you will virtually conduct it, in written communication with me; for I have had five and forty years of it: and then my liver, you know! Watson advises me strongly to leave my desk, and try country air, and rest from business and its cares."

He paused a moment; and the young man drew a long breath, like one who was in the act of being relieved of some terrible weight.

As for the old gentleman, he was not observing his son just then, but thinking of his own career; a certain expression of pain and regret came over his features; but he shook it off with manly dignity. "Come, come," said he, "this is the law of Nature, and must be submitted to with a good grace. Wardlaw junior, fill your glass." At the same time he stood up and said, stoutly, "The setting sun drinks to the rising sun"; but could not maintain that artificial style, and ended with, "God bless you, my boy, and may you stick to business; avoid speculation, as I have done; and so hand the concern down healthy to your son, as my father there (pointing to a picture) handed it down to me, and I to you."

His voice wavered slightly in uttering this benediction; but only for a moment: he then sat quietly down, and sipped his wine composedly.

Not so the other: his color came and went violently all the time his father was speaking, and, when he ceased, he sank into his chair with another sigh deeper than the last, and two half-hysterical tears came to his pale eyes.

But presently, feeling he was expected to say something, he struggled against all this mysterious emotion, and faltered out that he should not fear the responsibility, if he might have constant recourse to his father for advice.

"Why, of course," was the reply. "My country house is but a mile from the station: you can telegraph for me in any case of importance."

"When would you wish me to commence my new duties?"

"Let me see, it will take six weeks to prepare a balance-sheet, such as I could be content to submit to an incoming partner. Say two months."

Young Wardlaw's countenance fell.

"Meantime you shall travel on the continent and enjoy yourself."

"Thank you," said young Wardlaw, mechanically, and fell into a brown study.

The room now returned to what seemed its natural state. And its silence continued until it was broken from without.

A sharp knocking was heard at the street-door, and resounded across the marble hall.

The Wardlaws looked at one another in some little surprise.

"I have invited nobody," said the elder.

Some time elapsed, and then a footman made his appearance, and brought in a card.

"Mr. Christopher Adams."

Now that Mr. Christopher Adams should call on John Wardlaw, in his private room, at nine o'clock in the evening, seemed to that merchant irregular, presumptuous, and monstrous. "Tell him he will find me at my place of business to-morrow, as usual," said he, knitting his brows.

The footman went off with this message; and, soon after, raised voices were heard in the hall, and the episcopal butler entered the room with an injured countenance.

"He says he *must* see you; he is in great anxiety."

"Yes, I am in great anxiety," said a quavering voice at his elbow; and Mr. Adams actually pushed by the butler, and stood, hat in hand, in those sacred precincts. "Pray excuse me, sir," said he, "but it is very serious; I can't be easy in my mind till I have put you a question."

"This is very extraordinary conduct, sir," said Mr. Wardlaw. "Do you think I do business here, and at all hours?"

"O no, sir: it is my own business. I am come to ask you a very serious question. I could n't wait till morning with such a doubt on my mind."

"Well, sir, I repeat this is irregular and extraordinary; but as you are here, pray what is the matter?" He then dismissed the lingering butler with a look. Mr. Adams cast uneasy glances on young Wardlaw.

"O," said the elder, "you can speak before him. This is my partner; that is to say, he will be as soon as the balance-sheet can be prepared, and the deed drawn. Wardlaw junior, this is Mr. Adams, a very respectable bill discounter."

The two men bowed to each other, and Arthur Wardlaw sat down motionless.

"Sir, did you draw a note of hand to-day?" inquired Adams of the elder merchant.

"I dare say I did. Did you discount one signed by me?"

"Yes, sir, we did."

"Well, sir, you have only to present it at maturity. Wardlaw and Son will provide for it, I dare say." This with the lofty nonchalance of a rich man, who had never broken an engagement in his life.

"Ah, that I know they will if it is all right; but suppose it is not?"

"What d' ye mean?" asked Wardlaw, with some astonishment.

"O, nothing, sir! It bears your signature, that is good for twenty times the amount; and it is indorsed by your cashier. Only what makes me a little uneasy, your bills used to be always on your own forms, and so I told my partner; he discounted it. Gentlemen, I wish you would just look at it."

"Of course we will look at it. Show it Arthur first; his eyes are younger than mine."

Mr. Adams took out a large bill-book, extracted the note of hand, and passed it across the table to Wardlaw junior. He took it up with a sort of shiver, and bent his head very low over it; then handed it back in silence.

Adams took it to Wardlaw senior, and laid it before him, by the side of Arthur's Testamur.

The merchant inspected it with his glasses.

"The writing is mine, apparently."

"I am very glad of it," said the bill-broker, eagerly.

"Stop a bit," said Mr. Wardlaw. "Why, what is this? For two thousand pounds! and, as you say, not my form. I have signed no note for two thousand pounds this week. Dated yesterday. You have not cashed it, I hope?"

"I am sorry to say my partner has."

"Well, sir, not to keep you in suspense, the thing is not worth the stamp it is written on."

"Mr. Wardlaw! — Sir! — Good heavens! Then it is as I feared. It is a forgery."

"I should be puzzled to find any other name for it. You need not look so pale, Arthur. We can't help some clever scoundrel imitating our hands; and as for you, Adams, you ought to have been more cautious."

"But, sir, your cashier's name is Penfold," faltered the holder, clinging to a straw. "May he not have drawn — is the indorsement forged as well?"

Mr. Wardlaw examined the back of the bill, and looked puzzled. "No," said he. "My cashier's name is Michael Penfold, but this is indorsed 'Robert Penfold.' Do you hear, Arthur? Why, what is the matter with you? You look like a ghost. I say there is your tutor's name at the back of this forged note. This is very strange. Just look, and tell me who wrote these two words 'Robert Penfold?'"

Young Wardlaw took the document, and tried to examine it calmly, but it shook visibly in his hand, and a cold moisture gathered on his brow. His pale eyes roved to and fro in a very remarkable way; and he was so long before he said anything, that both the other persons present began to eye him with wonder.

At last he faltered out, "This 'Robert Penfold' seems to me very like his own handwriting. But then the rest of the writing is equally like yours, sir. I am sure Robert Penfold never did anything wrong. Mr. Adams, please oblige *me*. Let this go no further till I have seen him, and asked him whether he indorsed it."

"Now don't you be in a hurry," said the elder Wardlaw. "The first question is, who received the money!"

Mr. Adams replied that it was a respectable looking man, a young clergyman.

"Ah!" said Wardlaw, with a world of meaning.

"Father!" said young Wardlaw, imploringly, "for my sake, say no more to-night. Robert Penfold is incapable of a dishonest act."

"It becomes your years to think so, young man. But I have lived long enough to see what crimes respectable men are betrayed into in the hour of temptation. And, now I think of it, this Robert Penfold is in want of money. Did he not ask me for a loan of two thousand pounds? Was not that the very sum? Can't you answer me? Why, the application came through you."

Receiving no reply from his son, but a sort of agonized stare, he took out his pencil and wrote down Robert Penfold's address. This he handed the bill-broker, and gave him some advice in a whisper, which Mr. Christopher Adams received with a profusion of thanks, and bustled away, leaving Wardlaw senior excited and indignant, Wardlaw junior, ghastly pale, and almost stupefied.

Scarcely a word was spoken for some minutes, and then the younger man broke out suddenly: "Robert Penfold is the best friend I ever had; I should have been expelled, but for him, and I should never have earned that Testamur but for him."

The old merchant interrupted him. "You exaggerate: but, to tell the truth, I am sorry now I did not lend him the money you asked for. For, mark my words, in a moment of temptation, that miserable young man has forged my name, and will be convicted of the felony, and punished accordingly."

"No, no: O, God forbid!" shrieked young Wardlaw. "I could n't bear it. If he did, he must have intended to replace it. I must see him; I will see him directly." He got up all in a hurry, and was going to Penfold to warn him, and get him out of the way till the money should be replaced. But his father started up at the same moment and forbade him, in accents that he had never yet been able to resist.

"Sit down, sir, this instant," said the old man, with terrible sternness. "Sit down, I say, or you will never be a partner of mine. Justice must take its course. What business and what right have we to protect a felon? I would not take *your* part if you were one. Indeed it is too late now, for the detectives will be with him before you could reach him. I gave Adams his address."

At this last piece of information Wardlaw junior leaned his head on the table, and groaned aloud, and a cold perspiration gathered in beads upon his white forehead.

CHAPTER II.

THAT same evening sat over their tea, in Norfolk Street, Strand, another couple, who were also father and son; but, in this pair, the Wardlaws were reversed. Michael Penfold was a reverend, gentle creature, with white hair, blue eyes, and great timidity; why, if a stranger put to him a question, he used to look all round the room before he ventured to answer.

Robert, his son, was a young man, with a large brown eye, a mellow voice, square shoulders, and a prompt and vigorous manner. Cricketer. Scholar. Parson.

They were talking hopefully together over a living Robert was going to buy; it was near Oxford, he said, and would not prevent his continuing to take pupils. "But, father," said he, "it will be a place to take my wife to if I ever have one; and, meantime, I hope you will run down now and then, Saturday to Monday"

"That I will, Robert. Ah! how proud *she* would have been to hear you preach; it was always her dream, poor thing."

"Let us think she *can* hear me," said Robert. "And I have got *you* still; the proceeds of this living will help me to lodge you more comfortably."

"You are very good Robert; I would rather see you spend it upon yourself; but, dear me, what a manager you must be to dress so beautifully as you do, and send your old father presents as you do, and yet put by fourteen hundred pounds to buy this living."

"You are mistaken, sir, I have only saved four hundred; the odd thousand, — but that is a secret for the present."

"O, I am not inquisitive: I never was."

They then chatted about things of no importance whatever, and the old gentleman was just lighting his candle to go to bed, when a visitor was ushered into the room.

The Penfolds looked a little surprised, but not much. They had no street door all to themselves; no liveried dragons to interpose between them and unseasonable or unwelcome visitors.

The man was well dressed, with one exception; he wore a gold chain. He had a hooked nose, and a black, piercing eye. He stood at the door, and observed every person and thing in the room minutely, before he spoke a word.

Then he said, quietly, "Mr. Michael Penfold, I believe."

"At your service, sir."

"And Mr. Robert Penfold."

"I am Robert Penfold. What is your business?"

"Pray is the 'Robert Penfold' at the back of this note your writing?"

"Certainly it is; they would not cash it without that."

"O, you got the money, then?"

"Of course I did."

"You have not parted with it, have you?"

"No."

"All the better." He then turned to Michael, and looked at him earnestly a moment. "The fact is, sir," said he, "there is a little irregularity about this bill, which must be explained, or your son might be called on to refund the cash."

"Irregularity about — a bill?" cried Michael Penfold, in dismay. "Who is the drawer? Let me see it. O, dear me, something wrong about a bill indorsed by you, Robert?" and the old man began to shake piteously.

"Why, father," said Robert, "what are you afraid of? If the bill is irregular, I can but return the money. It is in the house."

"The best way will be for Mr. Robert Penfold to go at once with me to the bill-broker; he lives but a few doors off. And you, sir, must stay here, and be responsible for the funds, till we return."

Robert Penfold took his hat directly, and went off with this mysterious visitor.

They had not gone many steps, when Robert's companion stopped, and, getting in front of him, said, "We can settle this matter here." At the same time a policeman crossed the way, and joined them; and another man, who was in fact a policeman in plain clothes, emerged from a door-way, and stood at Robert Penfold's back.

The Detective, having thus surrounded him, threw off disguise. "My man," said he, "I ought to have done this job in your house. But I looked at the worthy old gentleman, and his gray hairs. I thought I'd spare him all I could. I have a warrant to arrest you for forgery!"

"Forgery! arrest me for forgery!" said Robert Penfold, with some amazement, but little emotion; for he hardly seemed to take it in, in all its horrible significance.

The next moment, however, he turned pale, and almost staggered under the blow.

"We had better go to Mr. Wardlaw," said he. "I entreat you to go to him with me."

"Can't be done," said the Detective. "Wardlaw has nothing to do with it. The bill is stopped. You are arrested by the gent that cashed it. Here is the warrant; will you go quietly with us, or must I put the darbies on?"

Robert was violently agitated. "There is no need to arrest me," he cried; "I shall not run from my accuser. Hands off, I say. I'm a clergyman of the Church of England, and you shall not lay hands on me."

But one of the policemen did lay hands on him. Then the Reverend Robert Penfold shook him furiously off, and, with one active bound, sprang into the middle of the road.

The officers went at him incautiously, and the head-detective, as he rushed forward, received a heavy blow on the neck and jaw, that sounded along the street, and sent him rolling in the mud; this was followed by a quick succession of staggering facers, administered right and left, on the eyes and noses of the subordinates. These, however, though bruised and bleeding, succeeded at last in grappling their man, and all came to the ground together, and there struggled furiously; every window in the street was open by this time, and at one the white hair and reverend face of Michael Penfold looked out on this desperate and unseemly struggle, with hands that beat the air in helpless agony, and inarticulate cries of terror.

The Detective got up and sat upon Robert Penfold's chest; and at last the three forced the handcuffs upon him, and took him in a cab to the station-house.

Next day, before the magistrate, Wardlaw senior proved the note was a forgery, and Mr. Adams's partner swore to the prisoner as the person who had presented and indorsed the note. The officers attended, two with black eyes a-piece, and one with his jaw bound up, and two sound teeth in his pocket, which had been driven from their sockets by the prisoner in his desperate attempt to escape. Their evidence hurt the prisoner, and the magistrate refused bail.

The Reverend Robert Penfold was committed to prison, to be tried at the Central Criminal Court on a charge of felony.

Wardlaw senior returned home, and told Wardlaw junior, who said not a word. He soon received a letter from Robert Penfold, which agitated him greatly, and he promised to go to the prison and see him.

But he never went.

He was very miserable, a prey to an inward struggle. He dared not offend his father on the eve of being made partner. Yet his heart bled for Robert Penfold.

He did what might perhaps have been expected from that pale eye and receding chin, — he temporized. He said to himself, "Before that horrible trial comes on, I shall be the house of Wardlaw, and able to draw a check for thousands. I'll buy off Adams at any price, and hush up the whole matter."

So he hoped, and hoped. But the accountant was slow, the public prosecutor unusually quick, and, to young Wardlaw's agony, the partnership deed was not ready when an imploring letter was put into his hands, urging him, by all that men hold sacred, to attend at the court as the prisoner's witness.

This letter almost drove young Wardlaw mad. He went to Adams, and entreated him not to carry the matter into court. But Adams was inexorable. He had got his money, but would be revenged for the fright.

Baffled here, young Wardlaw went down to Oxford and shut himself up in his own room, a prey to fear and remorse. He sported his oak, and never went out. All his exercise was that of a wild beast in its den, walking restlessly up and down.

But all his caution did not prevent the prisoner's solicitor from getting to him. One morning, at seven o'clock, a clerk slipped in at the heels of his scout, and, coming to young Wardlaw's bedside, awoke him out of an uneasy slumber by serving him with a subpœna to appear as Robert Penfold's witness.

This last stroke finished him. His bodily health gave way under his mental distress. Gastric fever set in, and he was lying tossing and raving in delirium, while Robert Penfold was being tried at the Central Criminal Court.

The trial occupied six hours, and could easily be made rather interesting. But, for various reasons, with which it would not be good taste to trouble the reader, we decide to skim it.

The indictment contained two counts; one for forging the note of hand, the other for uttering it, knowing it to be forged.

On the first count, the Crown was weak, and had to encounter the evidence of Undercliff, the distinguished Expert, who swore that the hand which wrote "Robert Penfold" was not, in his opinion, the hand that had written the body of the instrument. He gave many minute reasons, in support of this: and nothing of any weight was advanced contra. The judge directed the jury to acquit the prisoner on that count.

But, on the charge of uttering, the evidence was clear, and on the question of knowledge, it was, perhaps, a disadvantage to the prisoner that he was tried in England, and could not be heard in person, as he could have been in a foreign court; above all, his resistance to the officers eked out the presumption that he knew the note had been forged by some person or other, who was probably his accomplice.

The absence of his witness, Wardlaw junior, was severely commented on by his counsel; indeed, he appealed to the judge to commit the said Wardlaw for contempt of court. But Wardlaw senior was recalled, and swore that he had left his son in a burning fever, not expected to live: and declared, with genuine emotion, that nothing but a high sense of public duty had brought *him* hither from his dying son's bedside. He also told the court that Arthur's inability to clear his friend had really been the first cause of his illness, from which he was not expected to recover.

The jury consulted together a long time; and, at last, brought in a verdict of "GUILTY"; but recommended him to mercy, on grounds which might fairly have been alleged in favor of his innocence; but, if guilty, rather aggravated his crime.

Then an officer of the court inquired, in a sort of chant or recitativo, whether the prisoner had anything to say why judgment should not be given in accordance with the verdict.

It is easy to divest words of their meaning by false intonation; and prisoners in general receive this bit of singsong in dead silence. For why? the chant conveys no idea to their ears, and they would as soon think of *replying* to the notes of a cuckoo.

But the Reverend Robert Penfold was in a keen agony that sharpened all his senses; he caught the sense of the words in spite of the speaker, and clung wildly to the straw that monotonous machine held out. "My Lord! my Lord!" he cried, "I'll tell you the real reason why young Wardlaw is not here."

The judge put up his hand with a gesture that enforced silence: "Prisoner," said he, "I cannot go back to facts; the jury have dealt with them. Judgment can be arrested only on grounds of law. On these you can be heard. But if you have none to offer, you must be silent, and submit to your sentence." He then, without a pause, proceeded to point out the heinous character of the offence, but admitted there was one mitigating circumstance; and, in conclusion, he condemned the culprit to five years penal servitude.

At this the poor wretch uttered a cry of anguish that was fearful, and clutched the dock convulsively.

Now a prisoner rarely speaks to a judge without revolting him by bad law, or bad logic, or hot words. But this wild cry was innocent of all these, and went straight from the heart in the dock to the heart on the judgment-seat. And so his lordship's voice trembled for a moment, and then became firm again, but solemn and humane. "But," said he, "my experience tells me this is your first crime, and may possibly be your last. I shall therefore use my influence that you may not be associated with more hardened criminals, but may be sent out of this country to another, where you may begin life afresh, and in the course of years, efface this dreadful stain. Give me hopes of you; begin your repentance where now you stand, by blaming yourself, and no other man. No man constrained you to utter a forged note, and to receive the money; it was found in your possession. For such an act there can be no defence in law, morality, or religion."

These words overpowered the culprit. He burst out crying with great violence.

But it did not last long. He became strangely composed all of a sudden; and said, "God forgive all concerned in this — but one — but one."

He then bowed respectfully, and like a gentleman, to the judge and the jury, and walked out of the dock with the air of a man who had parted with emotion, and would march to the gallows now without flinching.

The counsel for the Crown required that the forged document should be impounded.

"I was about to make the same demand," said the prisoner's counsel.

The judge snubbed them both, and said it was a matter of course.

Robert Penfold spent a year in separate confinement, and then, to cure him of its salutary effect (if any), was sent on board the hulk "Vengeance," and was herded with the greatest miscreants in creation. They did not reduce him to their level, but they injured his mind: and, before half his sentence had expired, he sailed for a penal colony, a man with a hot coal in his bosom, a creature embittered, poisoned; hoping little, believing little, fearing little, and hating much.

He took with him the prayer-book his mother had given him when he was ordained deacon. But he seldom read beyond the fly-leaf; there the poor lady had written at large her mother's heart, and her pious soul aspiring heavenwards for her darling son. This, when all seemed darkest, he would sometimes run to with moist eyes: for he was sure of his mother's love, but almost doubted the justice of his God.

CHAPTER III.

Mr. Wardlaw went down to his son, and nursed him. He kept the newspapers from him, and on his fever abating, had him conveyed by easy stages to the seaside, and then sent him abroad.

The young man obeyed in gloomy silence. He never asked after Robert Penfold, now; never mentioned his name. He seemed, somehow, thankful to be controlled mind and body.

But, before he had been abroad a month, he wrote for leave to return home and to throw himself into business. There was, for once, a nervous impatience in his letters, and his father, who pitied him deeply, and was more than ever inclined to reward and indulge him, yielded readily enough; and, on his arrival, signed the partnership deed, and, Polonius-like, gave him much good counsel; then retired to his country seat.

At first he used to run up every three days, and examine the day-book and ledger, and advise his junior; but these visits soon became fewer, and at last he did little more than correspond occasionally.

Arthur Wardlaw held the reins, and easily paid his Oxford debts out of the assets of the firm. Not being happy in his mind he threw himself into commerce with feverish zeal, and very soon extended the operations of the house.

One of his first acts of authority was to send for Michael Penfold into his room. Now poor old Michael, ever since his son's misfortune, as he called it, had crept to his desk like a culprit, expecting every day to be discharged. When he received this summons he gave a sigh and went slowly to the young merchant.

Arthur Wardlaw looked up at his entrance, then looked down again, and said coldly, "Mr. Penfold, you have been a faithful servant to us many years; I raise your salary £ 50 a year, and you will keep the ledger."

The old man was dumbfoundered at first, and then began to give vent to his surprise and gratitude; but Wardlaw cut him short, almost fiercely. "There, there, there," said he, without raising his eyes, "let me hear no more about it, and, above all, never speak to me of that cursed business. It was no fault of yours, nor mine neither. There — go — I want no thanks. Do you hear? leave me, Mr. Penfold, if you please."

The old man bowed low and retired, wondering much at his employer's goodness, and a little at his irritability.

Wardlaw junior's whole soul was given to business night and day, and he soon became known for a very ambitious and rising merchant. But, by and by, ambition had to encounter a rival in his heart. He fell in love; deeply in love; and with a worthy object.

The young lady was the daughter of a distinguished officer, whose merits were universally recognized, but not rewarded in proportion. Wardlaw's suit was favorably received by the father, and the daughter gradually yielded to an attachment, the warmth, sincerity, and singleness of which were manifest; and the pair would have been married, but for the circumstance that her father (partly through Wardlaw's influence by the by) had obtained a lucrative post abroad which it suited his means to accept, at all events for a time. He was a widower, and his daughter could not let him go alone.

This temporary separation, if it postponed a marriage, led naturally to a solemn engagement; and Arthur Wardlaw enjoyed the happiness of writing and receiving affectionate letters by every foreign post. Love, worthily bestowed, shed its balm upon his heart, and, under its soft but powerful charm, he grew tranquil and complacent, and his character and temper seemed to improve. Such virtue is there in a pure attachment.

Meanwhile the extent of his operations alarmed old Penfold; but he soon reasoned that worthy down with overpowering conclusions and superior smiles.

He had been three years the ruling spirit of Wardlaw and Son, when some curious events took place in another hemisphere; and in these events, which we are now to relate, Arthur Wardlaw was more nearly interested than may appear at first sight.

Robert Penfold, in due course, applied to Lieutenant-General Rolleston for a ticket of leave. That functionary thought the application premature, the crime being so grave. He complained that the system had become too lax, and for his part he seldom gave a ticket of leave until some suitable occupation was provided for the applicant. "Will anybody take you as a clerk? If so, — I'll see about it."

Robert Penfold could find nobody to take him into a post of confidence all at once, and wrote the General an eloquent letter, begging hard to be allowed to labor with his hands.

Fortunately, General Rolleston's gardener had just turned him off; so he offered the post to his eloquent correspondent, remarking that he did not much mind employing a ticket of leave man himself, though he was resolved to protect his neighbors from their relapses.

The convict then came to General Rolleston, and begged leave to enter on his duties under the name of James Seaton. At that General Rolleston hem'd and haw'd, and took a note. But his final decision was as follows: "If you really mean to change your character, why the name you have disgraced might hang round your neck. Well, I'll give you every chance. But," said this old warrior, suddenly compressing his resolute lips just a little, "if you go a yard off the straight path *now*, look for no mercy, — Jemmy Seaton."

So the convict was re-christened at the tail of a threat, and let loose among the warrior's tulips.

His appearance was changed as effectually as his name. Even before he was Seatoned he had grown a silky mustache and beard of singular length and beauty; and what with these, and his working man's clothes, and his cheeks and neck tanned by the sun, our readers would never have recognized in this hale, bearded laborer the pale prisoner that had trembled, raged, wept, and submitted in the dock of the Central Criminal Court.

Our Universities cure men of doing things by halves, be the things mental or muscular; so Seaton gardened much more zealously than his plebeian predecessor: up at five, and did not leave till eight.

But he was unpopular in the kitchen, — because he was always out of it: taciturn and bitter, he shunned his fellow-servants.

Yet working among the flowers did him good; these his pretty companions and nurselings had no vices.

One day, as he was rolling the grass upon the lawn, he heard a soft rustle at some distance, and looking round, saw a young lady on the gravel path, whose calm but bright face, coming so suddenly, literally dazzled him. She had a clear cheek blooming with exercise, rich, brown hair, smooth, glossy, and abundant, and a very light hazel eye, of singular beauty and serenity. She glided along, tranquil as a goddess, smote him with beauty and perfume, and left him staring after her receding figure, which was, in its way, as captivating as her face.

She was walking up and down for exercise, briskly, but without effort. Once she passed within a few yards of him, and he touched his hat to her. She inclined her head gently, but her eyes did not rest an instant on her gardener; and so she passed and repassed, unconsciously sawing this solitary heart with soft but penetrating thrills.

At last she went indoors to luncheon, and the lawn seemed to miss the light music of her rustling dress, and the sunshine of her presence, and there was a painful void; but that passed, and a certain sense of happiness stole over James Seaton, — an unreasonable joy, that often runs before folly and trouble.

The young lady was Helen Rolleston, just returned home from a visit. She walked in the garden every day, and Seaton watched her, and peeped at her, unseen, behind trees and bushes. He fed his eyes and his heart upon her, and, by degrees, she became the sun of his solitary existence. It was madness; but its first effect was not unwholesome. The daily study of this creature, who, though by no means the angel he took her for, was at all events a pure and virtuous woman, soothed his sore heart, and counteracted the demoralizing influences of his late companions. Every day he drank deeper of an insane, but purifying and elevating passion.

He avoided the kitchen still more; and that, by the by, was unlucky; for there he could have learned something about Miss Helen Rolleston, that would have warned him to keep at the other end of the garden, whenever that charming face and form glided to and fro amongst the minor flowers.

A beautiful face fires our imagination, and we see higher virtue and intelligence in it, than we can detect in its owner's head or heart when we descend to calm inspection. James Seaton gazed on Miss Rolleston day after day, at so respectful a distance, that she became his goddess. If a day passed without his seeing her, he was dejected. When she was behind her time, he was restless, anxious, and his work distasteful; and then, when she came out at last, he thrilled all over, and the lawn, ay, the world itself, seemed to fill with sunshine. His adoration, timid by its own nature, was doubly so by reason of his fallen and hopeless condition. He cut nosegays for her; but gave them to her maid Wilson for her. He had not the courage to offer them to herself.

One evening, as he went home, a man addressed him familiarly, but in a low voice. Seaton looked at him attentively, and recognized him at last. It was a convict called Butt, who had come over in the ship with him. The man offered him a glass of ale; Seaton declined it. Butt, a very clever rogue, seemed hurt: so then Seaton assented reluctantly. Butt took him to a public-house in a narrow street, and into a private room. Seaton started as soon as he entered, for there sat two repulsive ruffians, and, by a look that passed rapidly between them and Butt, he saw plainly they were waiting for him. He felt nervous; the place was so uncouth and dark, the faces so villanous.

However, they invited him to sit down, roughly, but with an air of good fellowship; and very soon opened their business over their ale. We are all bound to assist our fellow-creatures, when it can be done without trouble; and what they asked of him was a simple act of courtesy, such as in their opinion no man worthy of the name could deny to his fellow. It was to give General Rolleston's watch-dog a piece of prepared meat upon a certain evening: and in return for this trifling civility, they were generous enough to offer him a full share of any light valuables they might find in the General's house.

Seaton trembled, and put his face in his hands a moment. "I cannot do it," said he.

"Why not?"

"He has been too good to me."

A coarse laugh of derision greeted this argument; it seemed so irrelevant to these pure egotists. Seaton, however, persisted, and on that one of the men got up and stood before the door, and drew his knife gently.

Seaton glanced his eyes round in search of a weapon, and turned pale.

"Do you mean to split on us, mate?" said one of the ruffians in front of him.

"No, I don't. But I won't rob my benefactor: you shall kill me first." And with that he darted to the fireplace, and in a moment the poker was high in air, and the way he squared his shoulders and stood ready to hit to the on, or cut to the off, was a caution.

"Come, drop that," said Butt, grimly; "and put up *your* knife, Bob. Can't a pal be out of a job, and yet not split on them that is in it!"

"Why should I split?" said Robert Penfold. "Has the law been a friend to me? But I won't rob my benefactor — and his daughter."

"That is square enough," said Butt. "Why, pals, there are other cribs to be cracked besides that old bloke's. Finish the ale, mate, and part friends."

"If you will promise me to 'crack some other crib,' and let that one alone."

A sullen assent was given, and Seaton drank their healths, and walked away. Butt followed him soon after, and affected to side with him, and intimated that he himself was capable of not robbing a man's house who had been good to him, or to a pal of his. Indeed this plausible person said so much, and his sullen comrades had said so little, that Seaton, rendered keen and anxious by love, invested his savings in a Colt's revolver and ammunition.

He did not stop there; after the hint about the watch-dog, he would not trust that faithful but too carnivorous animal; he brought his blankets into the little tool-house, and lay there every night in a sort of dog's sleep. This tool-house was erected in a little back garden, separated from the lawn only by some young trees in single file. Now Miss Rolleston's window looked out upon the lawn, so that Seaton's watchtower was not many yards from it; then, as the tool-house was only lighted from above he bored a hole in the wooden structure, and through this he watched, and slept, and watched. He used to sit studying theology by a farthing rushlight till the lady's bedtime, and then he watched for her shadow. If it appeared for a few moments on the blind, he gave a sigh of content, and went to sleep, but awaked every now and then to see that all was well.

After a few nights, his alarms naturally ceased, but his love increased, fed now from this new source, the sweet sense of being the secret protector of her he adored.

Meantime, Miss Rolleston's lady's maid, Wilson, fell in love with him after her fashion; she had taken a fancy to his face at once, and he had encouraged her a little, unintentionally; for he brought the nosegays to her, and listened complacently to her gossip, for the sake of the few words she let fall now and then about her young mistress. As he never exchanged two sentences at a time with any other servant, this flattered Sarah Wilson, and she soon began to meet and accost him oftener, and in cherrier-colored ribbons, than he could stand. So then he showed impatience, and then she, reading him by herself, suspected some vulgar rival.

Suspicion soon bred jealousy, jealousy vigilance, and vigilance, detection.

Her first discovery was, that, so long as she talked of Miss Helen Rolleston, she was always welcome; her second was, that Seaton slept in the tool-house.

She was not romantic enough to connect her two discoveries together. They lay apart in her mind, until circumstances we are about to relate supplied a connecting link.

One Thursday evening James Seaton's goddess sat alone with her papa, and — being a young lady of fair abilities, who had gone through her course of music and other studies, taught brainlessly, and who was now going through a course of monotonous pleasures, and had not accumulated any great store of mental resources — she was listless and languid, and would have yawned forty times in her papa's face, only she was too well-bred. She always turned her head away when it came, and either suppressed it, or else hid it with a lovely white hand. At last, as she was a good girl, she blushed at her behavior, and roused herself up, and said she, "Papa, shall I play you the new quadrilles?"

Papa gave a start and a shake, and said, with well-feigned vehemence, "Ay, do, my dear," and so composed himself — to listen; and Helen sat down and played the quadrilles.

The composer had taken immortal melodies, some gay, some sad, and had robbed them of their distinctive character, and hashed them till they were all one monotonous rattle. But General Rolleston was little the worse for all this. As Apollo saved Horace from hearing a poetaster's rhymes, so did Somnus, another beneficent little deity, rescue our warrior from his daughter's music.

She was neither angry nor surprised. A delicious smile illumined her face directly; she crept to him on tiptoe, and bestowed a kiss, light as a zephyr, on his gray head. And, in truth, the bending attitude of this supple figure, clad in snowy muslin, the virginal face and light hazel eye beaming love and reverence, and the airy kiss, had something angelic.

She took her candle, and glided up to her bedroom. And, the moment she got there, and could gratify her somnolence without offence, need we say she became wide-awake? She sat down, and wrote long letters to three other young ladies, gushing affection, asking questions of the kind nobody replies to, painting, with a young lady's colors, the male being to whom she was shortly to be married, wishing her dear friends a like demigod, if perchance earth contained two; and so to the last new bonnet and preacher.

She sat over her paper till one o'clock, and Seaton watched and adored her shadow.

When she had done writing, she opened her window and looked out upon the night. She lifted those wonderful hazel eyes towards the stars, and her watcher might well be pardoned if he saw in her a celestial being looking up from an earthly resting-place towards her native sky.

At two o'clock she was in bed, but not asleep. She lay calmly gazing at the Southern Cross, and other lovely stars shining with vivid, but chaste, fire in the purple vault of heaven.

While thus employed she heard a slight sound outside that made her turn her eyes towards a young tree near her window. Its top branches were waving a good deal, though there was not a breath stirring. This struck her as curious, very curious.

Whilst she wondered, suddenly an arm and a hand came in sight, and after them the whole figure of a man, going up the tree.

Helen sat up now, glaring with terror, and was so paralyzed she did not utter a sound. About a foot below her window was a lead flat that roofed the bay window below. It covered an area of several feet, and the man sprang on to it with perfect ease from the tree. Helen shrieked with terror. At that very instant there was a flash, a pistol-shot, and the man's arms went whirling, and he staggered and fell over the edge of the flat, and struck the grass below with a heavy thud. Shots and blows followed, and all the sounds of a bloody struggle rung in Helen's ears as she flung herself screaming from the bed and darted to the door. She ran and clung quivering to her sleepy maid, Wilson. The house was alarmed, lights flashed, footsteps pattered, there was universal commotion.

General Rolleston soon learned his daughter's story from Wilson, and aroused his male servants, one of whom was an old soldier. They searched the house first; but no entrance had been effected; so they went out on the lawn with blunderbuss and pistol.

They found a man lying on his back at the foot of the bay window.

They pounced on him, and, to their amazement, it was the gardener, James Seaton. Insensible.

General Rolleston was quite taken aback for a moment. Then he was sorry. But after a little reflection, he said very sternly, "Carry the blackguard in-doors; and run for an officer."

Seaton was taken into the hall, and laid flat on the floor.

All the servants gathered about him, brimful of curiosity, and the female ones began to speak altogether; but General Rolleston told them sharply to hold their tongues, and to retire behind the man. "Somebody sprinkle him with cold water," said he; "and be quiet, all of you, and keep out of sight, while I examine him." He stood before the insensible figure with his arms folded, amidst a dead silence, broken only by the stifled sobs of Sarah Wilson, and of a sociable housemaid who cried with her for company.

And now Seaton began to writhe and show signs of returning sense.

Next he moaned piteously, and sighed. But General Rolleston could not pity him; he waited grimly for returning consciousness, to subject him to a merciless interrogatory.

He waited just one second too long. He had to answer a question instead of putting one.

The judgment is the last faculty a man recovers when emerging from insensibility; and Seaton, seeing the General standing before him, stretched out his hands, and said, in a faint but earnest voice, before eleven witnesses, "Is she safe? O, is she safe?"

CHAPTER IV.

Sarah Wilson left off crying, and looked down on the ground with a very red face. General Rolleston was amazed. "Is she safe?" Is who safe?" said he. "He means my mistress," replied Wilson, rather brusquely; and flounced out of the hall.

"She is safe, no thanks to you," said General Rolleston. "What were you doing under her window at this time of night?" And the harsh tone in which this question was put showed Seaton he was suspected. This wounded him, and he replied, doggedly, "Lucky for you all I was there."

"That is no answer to my question," said the General, sternly.

"It is all the answer I shall give you."

"Then I shall hand you over to the officer, without another word."

"Do, sir, do," said Seaton, bitterly; but he added more gently, "you will be sorry for it when you come to your senses."

At this moment Wilson entered with a message. "If you please, sir, Miss Rolleston says the robber had no beard. Miss have never noticed Seaton's face, but his beard she have; and O! if you please, sir, she begged me to ask him, — Was it you that fired the pistol and shot the robber?"

The delivery of this ungrammatical message but rational query, was like a ray of light streaming into a dark place: it changed the whole aspect of things. As for Seaton, he received it as if Heaven was speaking to him through Wilson. His sullen air relaxed, the water stood in his eyes, he smiled affectionately, and said in a low, tender voice, "Tell her I heard some bad characters talking about this house, — that was a month ago, — so, ever since then, I have slept in the tool-house to watch. Yes, I shot the robber with my revolver, and I marked one or two more; but they were three to one; I think I must have got a blow on the head; for I felt nothing —"

Here he was interrupted by a violent scream from Wilson. She pointed downwards, with her eyes glaring; and a little blood was seen to be trickling slowly over Seaton's stocking and shoe.

"Wounded," said the General's servant, Tom, in the business-like accent of one who had seen a thousand wounds.

"O! never mind that," said Seaton. "It can't be very deep, for I don't feel it"; then, fixing his eyes on General Rolleston, he said, in a voice that broke down suddenly, "there stands the only man who has wounded me to-night, to hurt me."

The way General Rolleston received this point-blank reproach surprised some persons present, who had observed only the imperious and iron side of his character. He hung his head in silence a moment; then, being discontented with himself, he went into a passion with his servants for standing idle. "Run away, you women," said he, roughly. "Now, Tom, if you are good for anything, strip the man and stanch his wound. Andrew, a bottle of port, quick!"

Then, leaving him for a while in friendly hands, he went to his daughter, and asked her if she saw any objection to a bed being made up in the house for the wounded convict.

"O papa," said she, "why of course not. I am all gratitude. What is he like, Wilson? for it is a most provoking thing, I never noticed his face, only his beautiful beard glittering in the sunshine ever so far off. Poor young man! O yes, papa! send him to bed directly, and we will all nurse him. I never did any good in the world yet, and so why not begin at once?"

General Rolleston laughed at this squirt of enthusiasm from his staid daughter, and went off to give the requisite orders.

But Wilson followed him immediately and stopped him in the passage. "If you please, sir, I think you had better not. I have something to tell you." She then communicated to him by degrees her suspicion that James Seaton was in love with his daughter. He treated this with due ridicule at first; but she gave him one reason after another till she staggered him, and he went down stairs in a most mixed and puzzled frame of mind, inclined to laugh, inclined to be angry, inclined to be sorry.

The officer had just arrived, and was looking over some photographs to see if James Seaton was "one of his birds." Such, alas! was his expression.

At sight of this Rolleston colored up; but extricated himself from the double difficulty with some skill. "Hexam," said he, "this poor fellow has behaved like a man, and got himself wounded in my service. You are to take him to the infirmary; but mind, they must treat him like my own son, and nothing he asks for be denied him."

Seaton walked with feeble steps, and leaning on two men, to the infirmary; and General Rolleston ordered a cup of coffee, lighted a cigar, and sat cogitating over this strange business, and asking himself how he could get rid of this young madman, and yet befriend him. As for Sarah Wilson, she went to bed discontented, and wondering at her own bad judgment. She saw, too late, that, if she had held her tongue, Seaton would have been her patient and her prisoner; and as for Miss Rolleston, when it came to the point, why she would never have nursed him except by proxy, and the proxy would have been Sarah Wilson.

However, the blunder blind passion had led her into was partially repaired by Miss Rolleston herself. When she heard, next day, where Seaton was gone, she lifted up her hands in amazement. "What *could* papa be thinking of to send our benefactor to a hospital?" And, after meditating a while, she directed Wilson to cut a nosegay and carry it to Seaton. "He is a gardener," said she, innocently. "Of course he will miss his flowers sadly in that miserable place."

And she gave the same order every day with a constancy, that, you must know, formed part of this young lady's character. Soup, wine, and jellies were sent from the kitchen every other day with equal pertinacity.

Wilson concealed the true donor of all those things, and took the credit to herself. By this means she obtained the patient's gratitude, and he showed it so frankly, she hoped to steal his love as well.

But no! his fancy and his heart remained true to the cold beauty he had served so well, and she had forgotten him apparently.

This irritated Wilson at last, and she set to work to cure him with wholesome, but bitter medicine. She sat down beside him one day, and said, cheerfully, "We are all '*on the keyfeet*' just now. Miss Rolleston's beau is come on a visit."

The patient opened his eyes with astonishment.

"Miss Rolleston's beau?"

"Ay, her intended. What, did n't you know, she is engaged to be married?"

"She engaged to be married?" gasped Seaton.

Wilson watched him with a remorseless eye.

"Why, James," said she, after a while, "did you think the likes of her would go through the world without a mate?"

Seaton made no reply but a moan, and lay back like one dead, utterly crushed by this cruel blow.

A buxom middle-aged nurse now came up, and said, with a touch of severity, "Come, my good girl, no doubt you mean well, but you are doing ill. You had better leave him to us for the present."

On this hint Wilson bounced out, and left the patient to his misery.

At her next visit she laid a nosegay on his bed, and gossipped away, talking of everything in the world, except Miss Rolleston.

At last she came to a pause, and Seaton laid his hand on her arm directly, and looking piteously in her face spoke his first word.

"Does she love him?"

"What, still harping on *her?*" said Wilson. "Well, she does n't hate him, I suppose, or she would not marry him."

"For pity's sake don't trifle with me! Does she love him?"

"La, James, how can I tell? She may n't love him quite as much as I could love a man that took my fancy" (here she cast a languishing glance on Seaton); "but I see no difference between her and other young ladies. Miss is very fond of her papa, for one thing; and he favors the match. Ay, and she likes her partner well enough: she is brighter like, now he is in the house, and she reads all her friends' letters to him ever so lovingly; and I do notice she leans on him, out walking, a trifle more than there is any need for."

At this picture James Seaton writhed in his bed like some agonized creature under vivisection; but the woman, spurred by jealousy, and also by egotistical passion, had no mercy left for him.

"And why not?" continued she; "he is young, and handsome, and rich, and he dotes on her. If you are really her friend, you ought to be glad she is so well suited."

At this admonition the tears stood in Seaton's eyes, and after a while, he got strength to say, "I know I ought, I know it. If he is only worthy of her, as worthy as any man could be."

"That he is, James. Why, I 'll be bound you have heard of him. It is young Mr. Wardlaw."

Seaton started up in bed. "Who? Wardlaw? what Wardlaw?"

"What Wardlaw? why, the great London merchant, his son. Leastways he manages the whole concern now, I hear; the old gentleman, he is retired, by all accounts."

"CURSE HIM! CURSE HIM! CURSE HIM!" yelled James Seaton, with his eyes glaring fearfully, and both hands beating the air.

Sarah Wilson recoiled with alarm.

"That angel marry *him!*" shrieked Seaton. "Never, while I live: I'll throttle him with these hands first."

What more his ungovernable fury would have uttered was interrupted by a rush of nurses and attendants, and Wilson was bundled out of the place with little ceremony.

He contrived however to hurl a word after her, accompanied with a look of concentrated rage and resolution.

"NEVER, I TELL YOU, — WHILE I LIVE."

At her next visit to the hospital, Wilson was refused admission by order of the Head Surgeon. She left her flowers daily all the same.

After a few days she thought the matter might have cooled, and, having a piece of news to communicate to Seaton, with respect to Arthur Wardlaw, she asked to see that patient.

"Left the hospital this morning," was the reply.

"What, cured?"

"Why not? We have cured worse cases than his."

"Where has he gone to? Pray tell me."

"O, certainly." And inquiry was made. But the reply was, "Left no address."

Sarah Wilson, like many other women of high and low degree, had swift misgivings of mischief to come. She was taken with a fit of trembling, and had to sit down in the hall.

And, to tell the truth, she had cause to tremble; for that tongue of hers had launched two wild beasts, — Jealousy and Revenge.

When she got better she went home, and, coward-like, said not a word to living soul.

That day, Arthur Wardlaw dined with General Rolleston and Helen. They were to be alone for a certain reason; and he came half an hour before dinner. Helen thought he would, and was ready for him on the lawn.

They walked arm-in-arm, talking of the happiness before them, and regretting a temporary separation that was to intervene. He was her father's choice, and she loved her father devotedly; he was her male property; and young ladies like that sort of property, especially when they see nothing to dislike in it. He loved her passionately, and that was her due, and pleased her and drew a gentle affection, if not a passion, from her in return. Yes, that lovely forehead did come very near young Wardlaw's shoulder more than once or twice, as they strolled slowly up and down on the soft mossy turf.

And, on the other side of the hedge that bounded the lawn, a man lay crouched in the ditch, and saw it all with gleaming eyes.

Just before the affianced ones went in, Helen said, "I have a little favor to ask you, dear. The poor man, Seaton, who fought the robbers, and was wounded, — papa says he is a man of education, and wanted to be a clerk or something. *Could* you find him a place?"

"I think I can," said Wardlaw; "indeed, I am sure. A line to White and Co. will do it; they want a shipping clerk."

"O, how good you are!" said Helen; and lifted her face all beaming with thanks.

The opportunity was tempting; the lover fond: two faces met for a single moment, and one of the two burned for five minutes after.

The basilisk eyes saw the soft collision; but the owner of those eyes did not hear the words that earned him that torture. He lay still and bided his time.

General Rolleston's house stood clear of the town at the end of a short, but narrow and tortuous lane. This situation had tempted the burglars whom Seaton baffled; and now it tempted Seaton.

Wardlaw must pass that way on leaving General Rolleston's house.

At a bend of the lane two twin elms stood out a foot or two from the hedge. Seaton got behind these at about ten o'clock, and watched for him with a patience and immobility that boded ill.

His preparations for this encounter were singular. He had a close-shutting inkstand and a pen, and one sheet of paper, at the top of which he had written "Sydney," and the day of the month and year, leaving the rest blank. And he had the revolver with which he had shot the robber at Helen Rolleston's window; and a barrel of that arm was loaded with swan shot.

CHAPTER V.

THE moon went down; the stars shone out clearer.

Eleven o'clock boomed from a church clock in the town.

Wardlaw did not come, and Seaton did not move from his ambush.

Twelve o'clock boomed, and Wardlaw never came, and Seaton never moved.

Soon after midnight, General Rolleston's hall-door opened, and a figure appeared in a flood of light. Seaton's eyes gleamed at the light, for it was young Wardlaw, with a footman at his back holding a lighted lamp.

Wardlaw, however, seemed in no hurry to leave the house, and the reason soon appeared; he was joined by Helen Rolleston, and she was equipped for walking. The watcher saw her serene face shine in the light. The General himself came next; and, as they left the door, out came Tom with a blunderbuss, and brought up the rear. Seaton drew behind the trees, and postponed, but did not resign, his purpose.

Steps and murmurings came, and passed him, and receded.

The only words he caught distinctly came from Wardlaw, as he passed. "It is nearly high tide. I fear we must make haste."

Seaton followed the whole party at a short distance, feeling sure they would eventually separate and give him his opportunity with Wardlaw.

They went down to the harbor and took a boat; Seaton came nearer, and learned they were going on board the great steamer bound for England, that loomed so black, with monstrous eyes of fire.

They put off, and Seaton stood baffled.

Presently the black monster, with enormous eyes of fire, spouted her steam like a Leviathan, and then was still; next the smoke puffed, the heavy paddles revolved, and she rushed out of the harbor; and Seaton sat down upon the ground, and all seemed ended. Helen gone to England! Wardlaw gone with her! Love and revenge had alike eluded him. He looked up at the sky, and played with the pebbles at his feet, stupidly, stupidly. He wondered why he was born; why he consented to live a single minute after this. His angel and his demon gone home together! And he left here!

He wrote a few lines on the paper he had intended for Wardlaw, sprinkled them with sand, and put them in his bosom, then stretched himself out with a weary moan, like a dying dog, to wait the flow of the tide, and, with it, Death. Whether or not his resolution or his madness could have carried him so far cannot be known, for even as the water rippled in and, trickling under his back, chilled him to the bone, a silvery sound struck his ear. He started to his feet, and life and its joys rushed back upon him. It was the voice of the woman he loved so madly.

Helen Rolleston was on the water, coming ashore again in the little boat.

He crawled, like a lizard, among the boats ashore to catch a sight of her: he did see her, was near her, unseen himself. She landed with her father. So Wardlaw was gone to England without her. Seaton trembled with joy. Presently his goddess began to lament in the prettiest way. "Papa! Papa!" she sighed, "Why must friends part in this sad world? Poor Arthur is gone from me; and, by and by, I shall go from you, my own papa." And at that prospect she wept gently.

"Why, you foolish child!" said the old General, tenderly, "what matters a little parting, when we are all to meet again, in dear old England. Well then, there, have a cry; it will do you good." He patted her head tenderly, as she clung to his warlike breast; and she took him at his word; the tears ran swiftly and glistened in the very starlight.

But, O! how Seaton's heart yearned at all this.

What? must n't *he* say a word to comfort her; he who, at that moment, would have thought no more of dying to serve her, or to please her, than he would of throwing one of those pebbles into that slimy water.

Well, her pure tears somehow cooled his hot brain, and washed his soul, and left him wondering at himself and his misdeeds this night. His guardian angel seemed to go by and wave her dewy wings, and fan his hot passions as she passed.

He kneeled down and thanked God he had not met Arthur Wardlaw in that dark lane.

Then he went home to his humble lodgings, and there buried himself; and from that day seldom went out, except to seek employment. He soon obtained it as a copyist.

Meantime the police were on his track, employed by a person with a gentle disposition, but a tenacity of purpose truly remarkable.

Great was Seaton's uneasiness when one day he saw Hexham at the foot of his stair; greater still, when the officer's quick eye caught sight of him, and his light foot ascended the stairs directly. He felt sure Hexham had heard of his lurking about General Rolleston's premises. However, he prepared to defend himself to the uttermost.

Hexham came into his room without ceremony, and looking mighty grim. "Well, my lad, so we have got you, after all."

"What is my crime now?" asked Seaton, sullenly.

"James," said the officer, very solemnly, "it is an unheard-of crime this time. You have been — running — away — from a pretty girl. Now that is a mistake at all times; but, when she is as beautiful as a angel, and rich enough to slip a fiver into Dick Hexham's hands, and lay him on your track, what *is* the use? Letter for *you*, my man."

Seaton took the letter, with a puzzled air. It was written in a clear but feminine hand, and slightly scented.

The writer, in a few polished lines, excused herself for taking extraordinary means to find Mr. Seaton; but hoped he would consider that he had laid her under a deep obligation, and that gratitude *will* sometimes be importunate. She had the pleasure to inform him that the office of shipping clerk, at Messrs. White and Co.'s was at his service, and she hoped he would take it without an hour's further delay, for that she was assured that many persons had risen to wealth and consideration in the colony from such situations.

Then, as this wary but courteous young lady had no wish to enter into a correspondence with her ex-gardener, she added, —

"Mr. Seaton need not trouble himself to reply to this note. A simple 'yes' to Mr. Hexham will be enough, and will give sincere pleasure to Mr. Seaton's

"Obedient servant and well-wisher,
"HELEN ANNE ROLLESTON."

Seaton bowed his head over this letter in silent but deep emotion.

Hexam respected that emotion, and watched him with a sort of vague sympathy.

Seaton lifted his head, and the tears stood thick in his eyes. Said he, in a voice of exquisite softness, scarce above a whisper, "Tell her, 'yes' and 'God bless her.' Good by. I want to go on my knees, and pray God to bless her, as she deserves. Good by."

Hexam took the hint, and retired softly.

CHAPTER VI.

WHITE AND CO. stumbled on a treasure in James Seaton. Your colonial clerk is not so narrow and apathetic as your London clerk, whose two objects seem to be, to learn one department only, and not to do too much in that; but Seaton, a gentleman and a scholar, eclipsed even colonial clerks in this, that he omitted no opportunity of learning the whole business of White and Co., and was also animated by a feverish zeal, that now and then provoked laughter from clerks, but was agreeable, as well as surprising, to White and Co. Of that zeal, his incurable passion was partly the cause. Fortunes had been made with great rapidity in Sydney; and Seaton now conceived a wild hope of acquiring one, by some lucky hit, before Wardlaw could return to Helen Rolleston. And yet his common-sense said, if I was as rich as Crœsus, how could she ever mate with me, a stained man. And yet his burning heart said, don't listen to reason; listen only to me. Try.

And so he worked double tides; and, in virtue of his University education, had no snobbish notions about never putting his hand to manual labor: he would lay down his pen at any moment, and bear a hand to lift a chest, or roll a cask. Old White saw him thus multiply himself, and was so pleased that he raised his salary one third.

He never saw Helen Rolleston, except on Sunday. On that day he went to her church, and sat half behind a pillar, and feasted his eyes and his heart upon her. He lived sparingly, saved money, bought a strip of land, by payment of £10 deposit, and sold it in forty hours for £100 profit, and watched keenly for similar opportunities on a larger scale; and all for her. Struggling with a mountain: hoping against reason, and the world.

White and Co. were employed to ship a valuable cargo on board two vessels chartered by Wardlaw and Son; the Shannon and Proserpine.

Both these ships lay in Sydney harbor, and had taken in the bulk of their cargoes: but the supplement was the cream; for Wardlaw, in person, had warehoused eighteen cases of gold dust and ingots, and fifty of lead and smelted copper. They were all examined, and branded, by Mr. White, who had duplicate keys of the gold cases. But the contents as a matter of habit and prudence were not described outside; but were marked Proserpine and Shannon, respectively; the mate of the Proserpine, who was in Wardlaw's confidence, had written instructions to look carefully to the stowage of all these cases, and was in and out of the store one afternoon just before closing, and measured the cubic contents of the cases, with a view to stowage in the respective vessels. The last time he came he seemed rather the worse for liquor; and Seaton, who accompanied him, having stepped out for a minute for something or other, was rather surprised on his return to find the door closed, and it struck him Mr. Wylie (that was the mate's name) might be inside; the more so as the door closed very easily with a spring bolt, but it could only be opened by a key of peculiar construction. Seaton took out his key, opened the door, and called to the mate: but received no reply. However, he took the precaution to go round the store, and see whether Wylie, rendered somnolent by liquor, might not be lying oblivious among the cases; Wylie, however, was not to be seen, and Seaton finding himself alone did an unwise thing; he came and contemplated Wardlaw's cases of metal and specie. (Men will go too near the thing that causes their pain.) He eyed them with grief and with desire, and could not restrain a sigh at these material proofs of his rival's wealth: the wealth that probably had smoothed his way to General Rolleston's home, and to his daughter's heart; for wealth can pave the way to hearts, ay, even to hearts that cannot be downright bought. This revery, no doubt, lasted longer than he thought, for presently he heard the loud rattle of shutters going up below: it was closing time; he hastily closed and locked the iron shutters, and then went out and shut the door.

He had been gone about two hours, and that part of the street, so noisy in business hours, was hushed in silence, all but an occasional footstep on the flags outside, when something mysterious occurred in the warehouse, now as dark as pitch.

At an angle of the wall stood two large cases in a vertical position, with smaller cases lying at their feet: these two cases were about eight feet high, more or less. Well, behind these cases suddenly flashed a feeble light, and the next moment two brown and sinewy hands appeared on the edge of one of the cases, — the edge next the wall; the case vibrated and rocked a little, and the next moment there mounted on the top of it not a cat, nor a monkey, as might have been expected, but an animal that in truth resembles both these quadrupeds, viz. a sailor; and need we say that sailor was the mate of the Proserpine. He descended lightly from the top of the case behind which he had been jammed for hours, and lighted a dark lantern; and went softly groping about the store with it.

This was a mysterious act, and would perhaps have puzzled the proprietors of the store even more than it would a stranger: for a stranger would have said at once this is burglary, or else arson: but those acquainted with the place would have known that neither of those crimes was very practicable. This enterprising sailor could not burn down this particular store without roasting himself the first thing; and indeed he could not burn it down at all; for the roof was flat, and was in fact one gigantic iron tank, like the roof of Mr. Goding's brewery in London: and, by a neat contrivance of American origin, the whole tank could be turned in one moment to a shower bath, and drown a conflagration in thirty seconds or thereabouts. Nor could he rifle the place; the goods were greatly protected by their weight, and it was impossible to get out of the store without raising an alarm, and being searched.

But, not to fall into the error of writers who underrate their readers' curiosity and intelligence, and so deluge them with comments and explanations, we will now simply relate what Wylie did, leaving you to glean his motives as this tale advances. His jacket had large pockets, and he took out of them a bunch of eighteen bright steel keys, numbered, a set of new screw-drivers, a flask of rum, and two ship biscuits.

He unlocked the eighteen cases marked Proserpine, &c., and, peering in with his lantern, saw the gold dust and small ingots packed in parcels, and surrounded by Australian wool of the highest possible quality. It was a luscious sight.

He then proceeded to a heavier task; he unscrewed, one after another, eighteen of the cases marked Shannon, and the eighteen so selected, perhaps by private marks, proved to be packed close, and on a different system from the gold, viz. in pigs, or square blocks, three, or in some cases four, to each chest. Now, these two ways of packing the specie and the baser metal respectively, had the effect of producing a certain uniformity of weight in the thirty-six cases Wylie was inspecting: otherwise the gold cases would have been twice the weight of those that contained the baser metal; for lead is proverbially heavy, but under scientific tests is to gold as five to twelve, or thereabouts.

In his secret and mysterious labor Wylie was often interrupted. Whenever he heard a step on the pavement outside, he drew the slide of his lantern and hid the light. If he had examined the iron shutters, he would have seen that his light could never pierce through them into the street. But he was not aware of this. Notwithstanding these occasional interruptions, he worked so hard and continuously, that the perspiration poured down him ere he had unscrewed those eighteen chests containing the pigs of lead. However, it was done at last, and then he refreshed himself with a draught from his flask. The next thing was, he took the three pigs of lead out of one of the cases marked Shannon, &c., and numbered fifteen, and laid them very gently on the floor. Then he transferred to that empty case the mixed contents of a case branded Proserpine 1, &c., and this he did with the utmost care and nicety, lest gold dust spilled should tell tales. And so he went on and amused himself by shifting the contents of the whole eighteen cases marked Proserpine, &c., into eighteen cases marked Shannon, &c., and refilling them with the Shannon's lead. Frolicsome Mr. Wylie! Then he sat down on one of the cases Prosperined, and ate a biscuit and drank a little rum; not much: for at this part of his career he was a very sober man, though he could feign drunkenness, or indeed anything else.

The gold was all at his mercy, yet he did not pocket an ounce of it; not even a pennyweight to make a wedding-ring for Nancy Rouse. Mr. Wylie had a conscience. And a very original one it was; and, above all, he was very true to those he worked with. He carefully locked the gold cases up again, and resumed the screw-driver, for there was another heavy stroke of work to be done; and he went at it like a man. He carefully screwed down again, one after another, all those eighteen cases marked Shannon, which he had filled with gold dust, and then, heating a sailor's needle red-hot over his burning wick, he put his own secret marks on those eighteen cases, — marks that no eye but his own could detect. By this time, though a very powerful man, he felt much exhausted, and would gladly have snatched an hour's repose. But, consulting his watch by the light of his lantern, he found the sun had just risen. He retired to his place of concealment in the same cat-like way he had come out of it, — that is to say, he mounted on the high cases, and then slipped down behind them, into the angle of the wall.

As soon as the office opened, two sailors, whom he had carefully instructed overnight, came with a boat for the cases; the warehouse was opened in consequence, but they were informed that Wylie must be present at the delivery.

"O, he won't be long," said they; "told us he would meet us here."

There was a considerable delay, and a good deal of talking, and presently Wylie was at their backs, and put in his word.

Seaton was greatly surprised at finding him there, and asked him where he had sprung from.

"Me!" said Wylie, jocosely, "why, I hailed from Davy Jones's locker last."

"I never heard you come in," said Seaton, thoughtfully.

"Well, sir," replied Wylie, civilly, "a man does learn to go like a cat on board ship, that is the truth. I came in at the door like my betters; but I thought I heard you mention my name, so I made no noise. Well, here I am, any way, and, — Jack, how many trips can we take these thundering chests in? Let us see, eighteen for the Proserpine, and forty for the Shannon. Is that correct, sir?"

"Perfectly."

"Then, if you will deliver them, I 'll check the delivery aboard the lighter there; and then we 'll tow her alongside the ships."

Seaton called up two more clerks, and sent one to the boat, and one on board the barge. The barge was within hail; so the cases were checked as they passed out of the store, and checked again at the small boat, and also on board the lighter. When they were all cleared out, Wylie gave Seaton his receipt for them, and, having a steam-tug in attendance, towed the lighter alongside the Shannon first.

Seaton carried the receipt to his employer.

"But, sir," said he, "is this regular for an officer of the Proserpine to take the Shannon's cargo from us?"

"No, it is not regular," said the old gentleman; and he looked through a window, and summoned Mr. Hardcastle.

Hardcastle explained that the Proserpine shipped the gold, which was the more valuable consignment; and that he saw no harm in the officer, who was so highly trusted by the merchant (on this and on former occasions), taking out a few tons of lead and copper to the Shannon.

"Well, sir," said Seaton, "suppose I was to go out and see the chests stowed in those vessels?"

"I think you are making a fuss about nothing," said Hardcastle.

Mr. White was of the same opinion, but, being too wise to check zeal and caution, told Seaton he might go for his own satisfaction.

Seaton, with some difficulty, got a little boat and pulled across the harbor. He found the Shannon had shipped all the chests marked with her name; and the captain and mate of the Proserpine were beginning to ship theirs. He paddled under the Proserpine's stern.

Captain Hudson, a rough salt, sang out, and asked him roughly what he wanted there.

"O, it is all right," said the mate; "he is come for your receipt and Hewitt's. Be smart now, men; two on board, sixteen to come."

Seaton saw the chests marked Proserpine stowed in the Proserpine, and went ashore with Captain Hewitt's receipt of forty cases on board the Shannon, and Captain Hudson's of eighteen on board the Proserpine.

As he landed he met Lloyd's agent, and told him what a valuable freight he had just shipped. That gentleman merely remarked that both ships were underwritten in Sydney by the owners; but the freight was insured in London, no doubt.

There was still something about this business Seaton did not quite like; perhaps it was in the haste of the shipments, or in the manner of the mate. At all events, it was too slight and subtle to be communicated to others with any hope of convincing them; and, moreover, Seaton could not but own to himself that he hated Wardlaw, and was, perhaps, no fair judge of his acts, and even of the acts of his servants.

And soon a blow fell that drove the matter out of his head and his heart. Miss Helen Rolleston called at the office, and, standing within a few feet of him, handed Hardcastle a letter from Arthur Wardlaw, directing that the ladies' cabin on board the Shannon should be placed at her disposal.

Hardcastle bowed low to Beauty and Station, and promised her the best possible accommodation on board the Shannon, bound for England next week.

As she retired, she cast one quiet glance round the office in search of Seaton's beard. But he had reduced its admired luxuriance, and trimmed it to a narrow mercantile point. She did not know his other features from Adam, and little thought that young man, bent double over his paper, was her preserver and *protégé;* still less that he was at this moment cold as ice, and quivering with misery from head to foot, because her own lips had just told him she was going to England in the Shannon.

Heart-broken, but still loving nobly, Seaton dragged himself down to the harbor, and went slowly on board the Shannon to secure Miss Rolleston every comfort.

Then, sick at heart as he was, he made inquiries into the condition of the vessel which was to be trusted with so precious a freight; and the old boatman who was rowing him, hearing him make these inquiries, told him he himself was always about, and had noticed the Shannon's pumps were going every blessed night.

Seaton carried this intelligence directly to Lloyd's agent; he overhauled the ship, and ordered her into the graving dock for repairs.

Then Seaton, for White and Co., wrote to Miss Rolleston that the Shannon was not sea-worthy and could not sail for a month, at the least.

The lady simply acknowledged Messrs. White's communication, and Seaton breathed again.

Wardlaw had made Miss Rolleston promise him faithfully to sail that month in his ship the Shannon. Now she was a slave to her word, and constant of purpose; so when she found she could not sail in the Shannon, she called again on Messrs. White, and took her passage in the Proserpine, the essential thing to her mind was to sail when she had promised, and to go in a ship that belonged to her lover.

The Proserpine was to sail in ten days.

Seaton inquired into the state of the Proserpine. She was a good, sound vessel, and there was no excuse for detaining her.

Then he wrestled long and hard with the selfish part of his great love. Instead of turning sullen, h set himself to carry out Helen Rolleston's will. He went on board the Proserpine and chose her the best stern cabin.

General Rolleston had ordered Helen's cabin to be furnished, and the agent had put in the usual things, such as a standing bedstead with drawers beneath, chest of drawers, small table, two chairs, wash-stand, looking-glass, and swinging lamp.

But Seaton made several visits to the ship, and effected the following arrangements at his own cost. He provided a neat cocoa mat for her cabin-deck for comfort and foothold; he unshipped the regular six-paned stern windows, and put in single pane plate glass; he fitted venetian blinds, and hung two little rose-colored curtains to each of the windows; all so arranged as to be easily removed in case it should be necessary to ship dead lights in heavy weather. He glazed the door leading to her bath-room and quarter gallery with plate glass; he provided a light easy-chair, slung and fitted with grommets, to be hung on hooks screwed into the beams in the midship of the cabin. On this Helen could sit and read, and so become insensible to the motion of the ship. He fitted a small bookcase, with a button, which could be raised when a book might be wanted; he fixed a strike-bell in her maid's cabin, communicating with two strikers in Helen's cabin; he selected books, taking care that the voyages and travels were prosperous ones. No "Seaman's Recorder," "Life-boat Journal," or "Shipwrecks and Disasters in the British Navy."

Her cabin was the after-cabin on the starboard side, was entered through the cuddy, had a door communicating with the quarter gallery, two stern windows, and a dead-eye on deck. The maid's cabin was the port after-cabin; doors opened into cuddy and quarter gallery. And a fine trouble Miss Rolleston had to get a maid to accompany her; but at last a young woman offered to go with her for high wages, demurely suppressing the fact that she had just married one of the sailors, and would have gladly gone for nothing. Her name was Jane Holt, and her husband's Michael Donovan.

In one of Seaton's visits to the Proserpine he detected the mate and the captain talking together, and looking at him with unfriendly eyes, — scowling at him would hardly be too strong a word.

However, he was in no state of mind to care much how two animals in blue jackets received his acts of self-martyrdom. He was there to do the last kind offices of despairing love for the angel that had crossed his dark path, and illumined it for a moment, to leave it now forever.

At last the fatal evening came; her last in Sydney.

Then Seaton's fortitude, sustained no longer by the feverish stimulus of doing kindly acts for her, began to give way, and he desponded deeply.

At nine in the evening he crept upon General Rolleston's lawn, where he had first seen her. He sat down in sullen despair, upon the very spot.

Then he came nearer the house. There was a lamp in the dining-room; he looked in and saw her.

She was seated at her father's knee, looking up at him fondly; her hand was in his. The tears were in their eyes; she had no mother; he no son; they loved one another devotedly. This, their tender gesture, and their sad silence, spoke volumes to any one that had known sorrow. Poor Seaton sat down on the dewy grass outside, and wept, because she was weeping.

Her father sent her to bed early. Seaton watched, as he had often done before, till her light went out; and then he flung himself on the wet grass, and stared at the sky in utter misery.

The mind is often clearest in the middle of the night; and all of a sudden, he saw, as if written on the sky, that she was going to England expressly to marry Arthur Wardlaw.

At this revelation he started up, stung with hate as well as love, and his tortured mind rebelled furiously. He repeated his vow that this should never be; and soon a scheme came into his head to prevent it; but it was a project so wild and dangerous, that, even as his heated brain hatched it, his cooler judgment said, "Fly, madman, fly! or this love will *destroy* you!"

He listened to the voice of reason, and in another minute he was out of the premises. He fluttered to his lodgings.

When he got there he could not go in; he turned and fluttered about the streets, not knowing or caring whither; his mind was in a whirl; and, what with his bodily fever, and his boiling heart, passion began to overpower reason, that had held out so gallantly till now. He found himself at the harbor, staring with wild and bloodshot eyes at the Proserpine, he who, an hour ago, had seen that he had but one thing to do, — to try and forget young Wardlaw's bride. He groaned aloud, and ran wildly back into the town. He hurried up and down one narrow street, raging inwardly, like some wild beast in its den.

By and by, his mood changed, and he hung round a lamp-post, and fell to moaning and lamenting his hard fate, and hers.

A policeman came up, took him for a maudlin drunkard, and half-advised, half-admonished him to go home.

At that he gave a sort of fierce, despairing snarl, and ran into the next street, to be alone.

In this street he found a shop open, and lighted, though it was but five o'clock in the morning. It was a barber's, whose customers were working people. HAIR-CUTTING, SIXPENCE. EASY SHAVING, THREEPENCE. HOT COFFEE, FOURPENCE THE CUP. Seaton's eye fell upon this shop. He looked at it fixedly a moment from the opposite side of the way, and then hurried on.

He turned suddenly and came back. He crossed the road and entered the shop. The barber was leaning over the stove, removing a can of boiling water from the fire to the hob. He turned at the sound of Seaton's step, and revealed an ugly countenance, rendered sinister by a squint.

Seaton dropped into a chair, and said, "I want my beard taken off."

The man looked at him, if it could be called looking *at* him, and said, dryly, "O, do ye? How much am I to have for that job?"

"You know your own charge."

"Of course I do; threepence a chin."

"Very well. Be quick then."

"Stop a bit: that is my charge to working folk. I must have something more off you."

"Very well, man, I'll pay you double."

"My price to you is ten shillings."

"Why, what is that for?" asked Seaton, in some alarm; he thought, in his confusion, the man must have read his heart.

"I'll tell ye why," said the squinting barber. "No I won't; I'll show ye." He brought a small mirror, and suddenly clapped it before Seaton's eyes. Seaton started at his own image; wild, ghastly, and the eyes so bloodshot. The barber chuckled. This start was an extorted compliment to his own sagacity. "Now was n't I right?" said he; "did I ought to take the beard off such a mug as that — for less than ten shillings?"

"I see," groaned Seaton; "you think I have committed some crime. One man sees me weeping with misery; he calls me a drunkard; another sees me pale with the anguish of my breaking heart; he calls me a felon: may God's curse light on him and you, and all mankind!"

"All right," said the squinting barber, apathetically; my price is ten bob, whether or no."

Seaton felt in his pockets. "I have not got the money about me," said he.

"O, I'm not particular; leave your watch."

Seaton handed the squinting vampire his watch without another word, and let his head fall upon his breast.

The barber cut his beard close with the scissors, and made trivial remarks from time to time, but received no reply.

At last, Extortion having put him in a good humor, he said, "Don't be so down-hearted, my lad. You are not the first that has got into trouble, and had to change faces."

Seaton vouchsafed no reply.

The barber shaved him clean, and was astonished at the change, and congratulated him. "Nobody will ever know you"; said he, "and I'll tell you why; your mouth it is inclined to turn up a little; now a mustache it bends down, and that alters such a mouth as yours entirely. But, I'll tell you what, taking off this beard shows me something: *you are a gentleman!!* Make it a sovereign, sir."

Seaton staggered out of the place without a word.

"Sulky, eh?" muttered the barber. He gathered up some of the long hair he had cut off Seaton's chin with his scissors, admired it, and put it away in paper.

While thus employed, a regular customer looked in for his cup of coffee. It was the policeman who had taken Seaton for a convivial soul.

CHAPTER VII.

General Rolleston's servants made several trips to the Proserpine, carrying boxes, etc.

But Helen herself clung to the house till the last moment. "O papa!" she cried, "I need all my resolution, all my good faith, to keep my word with Arthur, and leave you. Why, why did I promise? Why am I such a slave to my word?"

"Because," said the old General, with a voice not so firm as usual, "I have always told you that a lady is not to be inferior to a gentleman in any virtue except courage. I've heard my mother say so often; and I've taught it to my Helen. And, my girl, where would be the merit of keeping our word, if we only kept it when it cost us nothing?"

He promised to come after, in three months at farthest, and the brave girl dried her tears, as well as she could, not to add to the sadness he fought against as gallantly as he had often fought the enemies of his country.

The Proserpine was to sail at two o'clock: at a little before one, a gentleman boarded her, and informed the captain that he was a missionary, the Rev. John Hazel, returning home, after a fever; and wished to take a berth in the Proserpine.

The mate looked him full in the face; and then told him there was very little accommodation for passengers, and it had all been secured by White and Co., for a young lady and her servants.

Mr. Hazel replied that his means were small, and moderate accommodation would serve him; but he must go to England without delay.

Captain Hudson put in his gracious word; "Then jump off the jetty at high tide and swim there; no room for black coats in my ship."

Mr. Hazel looked from one to the other piteously. "Show me some mercy, gentlemen; my very life depends on it."

"Very sorry, sir," said the mate; "but it is impossible. There's the Shannon, you can go in her."

"But she is under repairs; so I am told."

"Well, there are a hundred and fifty carpenters on to her; and she will come out of port in our wake."

"Now, sir," said Hudson, roughly, "bundle down the ship's side again if you please; this is a busy time. Hy! — rig the whip; here 's the lady coming off to us."

The missionary heaved a deep sigh, and went down into the boat that had brought him. But he was no sooner seated than he ordered the boatmen, somewhat peremptorily, to pull ashore as fast as they could row.

His boat met the Rollestons, father and daughter, coming out, and he turned his pale face, and eyed them as he passed. Helen Rolleston was struck with that sorrowful countenance, and whispered her father, "That poor clergyman has just left the ship." She made sure he had been taking leave of some beloved one, bound for England. General Rolleston looked round, but the boats had passed each other, and the wan face was no longer visible.

They were soon on board, and received with great obsequiousness. Helen was shown her cabin, and, observing the minute and zealous care that had been taken of her comfort, she said, "Somebody, who loves me, has been here," and turned her brimming eyes on her father. He looked quite puzzled; but said nothing.

Father and daughter were then left alone in the cabin, till the ship began to heave her anchor (she lay just at the mouth of the harbor), and then the boatswain was sent to give General Rolleston warning. Helen came up with him, pale and distressed. They exchanged a last embrace, and General Rolleston went down the ship's side. Helen hung over the bulwarks and waved her last adieu, though she could hardly see him for her tears.

At this moment a four-oared boat swept alongside; and Mr. Hazel came on board again. He presented Hudson a written order to give the Rev. John Hazel a passage in the small berth abreast the main hatches. It was signed "For White and Co., James Seaton"; and was indorsed with a stamped acknowledgment of the passage money, twenty-seven pounds.

Hudson, and Wylie the mate, put their heads together over this. The missionary saw them consulting, and told them he had mentioned their mysterious conduct to Messrs. White and Co., and that Mr. Seaton had promised to stop the ship if their authority was resisted. "And I have paid my passage money, and will not be turned out now except by force," said the reverend gentleman, quietly.

Wylie's head was turned away from Mr. Hazel's, and on its profile a most gloomy, vindictive look, so much so, that Mr. Hazel was startled when the man turned his front face to him with a jolly, genial air, and said, "Well, sir, the truth is, we seamen don't want passengers aboard ships of this class; they get in our way whenever it blows a capful. However, since you are here, make yourself as comfortable as you can."

"There, that is enough palaver," said the captain, in his offensive way. "Hoist the parson's traps aboard; and sheer off you. Anchor 's apeak."

He then gave his orders in stentorian roars; the anchor was hove up, catted, and fished; one sail went up after another, the Proserpine's head came round, and away she bore for England with a fair wind.

General Rolleston went slowly and heavily home, and often turned his head and looked wistfully at the ship putting out wing upon wing, and carrying off his child like a tiny prey.

To change the comparison, it was only a tender vine detached from a great sturdy elm: yet the tree, thus relieved of its delicate encumbrance, felt bare; and a soft thing was gone, that, seeking protection, had bestowed warmth; had nestled and curled between the world's cold wind and that stalwart stem.

As soon as he got home he lighted a cigar, and set to work to console himself by reflecting that it was but a temporary parting, since he had virtually resigned his post, and was only waiting in Sydney till he should have handed his papers in order over to his successor, and settled one or two private matters that could not take three months.

When he had smoked his cigar, and reasoned away his sense of desolation, Nature put out her hand, and took him by the breast, and drew him gently up stairs to take a look at his beloved daughter's bedroom, by way of seeing the last of her.

The room had one window looking south, and another west; the latter commanded a view of the sea. General Rolleston looked down at the floor, littered with odds and ends, — the dead leaves of dress that fall about a lady in the great process of packing, — and then gazed through the window at the flying Proserpine.

He sighed and lighted another cigar. Before he had half finished it, he stooped down and took up a little bow of ribbon that lay on the ground, and put it quietly in his bosom. In this act he was surprised by Sarah Wilson, who had come up to sweep all such waifs and strays into her own box.

"La, sir," said she, rather crossly, "why did n't you tell me, and I 'd have tidied the room: it is all huggermugger, with Miss a leaving."

And with this she went to the wash-hand-stand to begin. General Rolleston's eye followed her movements, and he observed the water in one of the basins was rather red. "What!" said he, "has she had an accident; cut her finger?"

"No, sir," said Wilson.

"Her nose been bleeding, then?"

"No, sir."

"Not from her finger, — nor — ? let me look."

He examined the basin narrowly, and his countenance fell. "Good heavens!" said he: "I wish I had seen this before; she should not have gone today. Was it the agitation of parting?"

"O no, sir," said Wilson; "don't go to fancy that. Why it is not the first time by a many."

"Not the first!" faltered Rolleston. "In Heaven's name, why was I never told of this?"

"Indeed, sir," said Wilson, eagerly, "you must not blame me, sir. It was as much as my place was worth to tell you. Miss is a young lady that will be obeyed; and she give me strict orders not to let you know: but she is gone now: and I always thought it was a pity she kept it so dark; but, as I was saying, sir, she *would* be obeyed."

"Kept what so dark?"

"Why, sir, her spitting of blood at times: and turning so thin by what she used to be, poor dear young lady."

General Rolleston groaned aloud. "And this she hid from me; from me!" He said no more, but kept looking bewildered and helpless, first at the basin, discolored by his daughter's blood, and then at the Proserpine, that was carrying her away, perhaps forever: and at the double sight, his iron features worked with cruel distress; anguish so mute and male, that the woman Wilson, though not good for much, sat down and shed genuine tears of pity.

But he summoned all his fortitude, told Wilson he could not say she was to blame, she had but obeyed her mistress's orders; and we must all obey orders. "But now," said he, "it is me you ought to obey: tell me, does any doctor attend her?"

"None ever comes here, sir. But, one day, she let fall that she went to Dr. Valentine, him that has the name for disorders of the chest."

In a very few minutes General Rolleston was at Doctor Valentine's house, and asked him bluntly what was the matter with his daughter.

"Disease of the lungs," said the doctor, simply.

The unhappy father then begged the doctor to give him his real opinion as to the degree of danger; and Dr. Valentine told him, with some feeling, that the case was not desperate, but was certainly alarming.

Remonstrated with for letting the girl undertake a sea voyage, he replied rather evasively at first; that the air of Sydney disagreed with his patient, and a sea voyage was more likely to do her good than harm, provided the weather was not downright tempestuous.

"And who is to insure me against that?" asked the afflicted father.

"Why, it is a good time of year," said Dr. Valentine; "and delay might have been fatal." Then, after a slight hesitation, "The fact is, sir," said he, "I gathered from her servant that a husband awaits Miss Rolleston in England; and I must tell you, what of course I did not tell her, that the sooner she enters the married state the better. In fact it is her one chance, in my opinion."

General Rolleston pressed the doctor's hand, and went away without another word.

Only he hurried his matters of business; and took his passage in the Shannon.

It was in something of a warrior's spirit that he prepared to follow his daughter and protect her; but often he sighed at the invisible, insidious nature of the foe, and wished it could have been a fair fight of bullets and bayonets, and his own the life at stake.

The Shannon was soon ready for sea.

But the gentleman who was to take General Rolleston's post, met with something better, and declined it.

General Rolleston, though chafing with impatience, had to give up going home in the Shannon. But an influential friend, Mr. Adolphus Savage, was informed of his difficulty, and obtained a year's leave of absence for him, and permission to put young Savage in as his *locum tenens;* which, by the by, is how politic men in general serve their friends.

The Shannon sailed, but not until an incident had occurred that must not be entirely passed over. Old Mr. White called on General Rolleston with a long face, and told him James Seaton had disappeared.

"Stolen anything?"

"Not a shilling. Indeed the last thing the poor fellow did was to give us a proof of his honesty. It seems a passenger paid him twenty-seven pounds for a berth in the Proserpine, just before she sailed. Well, sir, he might have put this in his pocket, and nobody been the wiser: but no, he entered the transaction, and the numbers of the notes, and left the notes themselves in an envelope addressed to me. What I am most afraid of is, that some harm has come to him, poor lad."

"What day did he disappear?"

"The 11th of November."

"The day my daughter sailed for England," said General Rolleston, thoughtfully.

"Was it, sir? Yes, I remember. She went in the Proserpine."

General Rolleston knitted his brows in silence for some time; then he said, "I'll set the Detectives on his track."

"Not to punish him, General. We do not want him punished."

"To punish him, protect him, or avenge him, as the case may require," was the reply, uttered very gravely.

Mr. White took his leave. General Rolleston rang the bell, and directed his servant to go for Hexham, the Detective.

He then rang the bell again, and sent for Sarah Wilson. He put some searching questions to this woman; and his interrogatory had hardly concluded when Hexham was announced. General Rolleston dismissed the girl, and looking now very grave indeed, asked the Detective whether he remembered James Seaton.

"That I do, sir."

"He has levanted."

"Taken *much*, sir?"

"Not a shilling."

"Gone to the diggings?"

"That you must find out."

"What day was he first missed, sir?"

"Eleventh of November. The very day Miss Rolleston left."

Hexham took out a little greasy note-book, and examined it. "Eleventh of November," said he, "then I almost think I have got a clew, sir; but I shall know more when I have had a word with two parties." With this he retired.

But he came again at night, and brought General Rolleston some positive information; with this, however, we shall not trouble the reader just here: for General Rolleston himself related it, and the person to whom he did relate it, and the attendant circumstances, gave it a peculiar interest.

Suffice it to say here, that General Rolleston went on board the Shannon, charged with curious information about James Seaton; and sailed for England in the wake of the Proserpine, and about two thousand miles astern.

CHAPTER VIII.

WARDLAW was at home before this, with his hands full of business; and it is time the reader should be let into one secret at least, which this merchant had contrived to conceal from the City of London, and from his own father, and from every human creature, except one poor, simple, devoted soul, called Michael Penfold.

There are men, who seem stupid, yet generally go right; there are also clever men, who appear to have the art of blundering wisely: "*sapienter descendunt in infernum*," as the ancients have it; and some of these latter will even lie on their backs, after a fall, and lift up their voices, and prove to you that in the nature of things they ought to have gone up, and their being down is monstrous; illusory.

Arthur Wardlaw was not quite so clever as all that; but still he misconducted the business of the firm with perfect ability from the first month he entered on it. Like those ambitious railways, which ruin a goodly trunk with excess of branches, not to say twigs, he set to work extending, and extending, and sent the sap of the healthy old concern a-flying to the ends of the earth.

He was not only too ambitious, and not cool enough; he was also unlucky, or under a curse, or something; for things, well conceived, broke down, in his hands, under petty accidents. And, besides, his new correspondents and agents hit him cruelly hard. Then what did he? Why, shot good money after bad, and lost both. He could not retrench, for his game was concealment; his father, was kept in the dark, and drew his four thousand a year, as usual, and, upon any hesitation, in that respect, would have called in an accountant and wound up the concern. But this tax upon the receipts, though inconvenient, was a trifle compared with the series of heavy engagements that were impending. The future was so black, that Wardlaw junior was sore tempted to realize twenty thousand pounds, which a man in his position could easily do, and fly the country. But this would have been to give up Helen Rolleston; and he loved her too well. His brain was naturally subtle and fertile in expedients; so he brought all its powers to bear on a double problem; how to marry Helen; and restore the concern he had mismanaged to its former state. For this, a large sum of money was needed, not less than £90,000.

The difficulties were great; but he entered on this project with two advantages. In the first place, he enjoyed excellent credit; in the second, he was not disposed to be scrupulous. He had been cheated several times; and nothing undermines feeble rectitude more than that. Such a man as Wardlaw is apt to establish a sort of account current with humanity.

"Several fellow-creatures have cheated me. Well, I must get as much back, by hook or by crook, from several fellow-creatures."

After much hard thought, he conceived his double master-stroke: and it was to execute this he went out to Australia.

We have seen that he persuaded Helen Rolleston to come to England and be married; but, as to the other part of his project, that is a matter for the reader to watch, as it develops itself.

His first act of business, on reaching England, was to insure the freights of the Proserpine and the Shannon.

He sent Michael Penfold to Lloyd's, with the requisite vouchers, including the receipts of the gold merchants. Penfold easily insured the Shannon, whose freight was valued at only six thousand pounds. The Proserpine, with her cargo, and a hundred and thirty thousand pounds of specie to boot, was another matter. Some underwriters had an objection to specie, being subject to theft as well as shipwreck; other underwriters, applied to by Penfold, acquiesced; others called on Wardlaw himself, to ask a few questions, and he replied to them courteously, but with a certain nonchalance, treating it as an affair which might be big to them, but was not of particular importance to a merchant doing business on his scale.

To one underwriter, Condell, with whom he was on somewhat intimate terms, he said, "I wish I could insure the Shannon, at her value; but that is impossible: the City of London could not do it. The Proserpine brings me some cases of specie, but my true treasure is on board the Shannon. She carries my bride, sir."

"O indeed! Miss Rolleston?"

"Ah, I remember; you have seen her. Then you will not be surprised at a proposal I shall make you. Underwrite the Shannon a million pounds, to be paid by you if harm befalls my Helen. You need not look so astonished; I was only joking; you gentlemen deal with none but substantial values; and, as for me, a million would no more compensate me for losing her, than for losing my own life."

The tears were in his pale eyes as he said these words; and Mr. Condell eyed him with sympathy. But he soon recovered himself, and was the man of business again. "O, the specie on board the Proserpine? Well, I was in Australia, you know, and bought that specie myself of the merchants whose names are attached to the receipts. I deposited the cases with White and Co., at Sydney. Penfold will show you the receipt. I instructed Joseph Wylie, mate of the Proserpine, and a trustworthy person, to see them stowed away in the Proserpine, by White and Co. Hudson is a good seaman; and the Proserpine a new ship, built by Mare. We have nothing to fear but the ordinary perils of the sea."

"So one would think," said Mr. Condell, and took his leave; but, at the door, he hesitated, and then, looking down a little sheepishly, said, "Mr. Wardlaw, may I offer you a piece of advice?"

"Certainly."

"Then, double the insurance on the Shannon, if you can."

With these words he slipped out, evidently to avoid questions he did not intend to answer.

Wardlaw stared after him, stupidly at first, and then stood up and put his hand to his head in a sort of amazement. Then he sat down again, ashy pale, and with the dew on his forehead, and muttered faintly, "Double — the insurance — of the — Shannon!"

Men who walk in crooked paths are very subject to such surprises; doomed, like Ahab, to be pierced, through the joints of their armor, by random shafts; by words uttered in one sense, but conscience interprets them in another.

It took a good many underwriters to insure the Proserpine's freight; but the business was done at last.

Then Wardlaw, who had feigned *insouciance* so admirably in that part of his interview with Condell, went, without losing an hour, and raised a large sum of money on the insured freight, to meet the bills that were coming due for the gold (for he had paid for most of it in paper at short dates), and also other bills that were approaching maturity. This done, he breathed again, safe for a month or two from everything short of a general panic, and full of hope from his coming master-stroke. But two months soon pass when a man has a flock of kites in the air. Pass? They fly. So now he looked out anxiously for his Australian ships; and went to Lloyd's every day to hear if either had been seen, or heard of by steamers, or by faster sailing vessels than themselves.

And, though Condell had underwritten the Proserpine to the tune of eight thousand pounds, yet still his mysterious words rang strangely in the merchant's ears, and made him so uneasy, that he employed a discreet person to sound Condell as to what he meant by "double the insurance of the Shannon."

It turned out to be the simplest affair in the world; Condell had secret information that the Shannon was in bad repairs, so he had advised his friend to insure her heavily. For the same reason, he declined to underwrite her freight himself.

With respect to those ships, our readers already know two things, of which Wardlaw himself, *nota bene*, had no idea; namely, that the Shannon had sailed last, instead of first, and that Miss Rolleston was not on board of her, but in the Proserpine, two thousand miles ahead.

To that, your superior knowledge, we; posters of the sea and land, are about to make a large addition, and relate things strange, but true. While that anxious and plotting merchant strains his eyes seaward, trying hard to read the future, we carry you, in a moment of time, across the Pacific, and board the leading vessel, the good ship Proserpine, homeward bound.

The ship left Sydney with a fair wind, but soon encountered adverse weather, and made slow progress, being close-hauled, which was her worst point of sailing. She pitched a good deal, and that had a very ill effect on Miss Rolleston. She was not sea-sick, but thoroughly out of sorts: and, in one week, became perceptibly paler and thinner than when she started.

The young clergyman, Mr. Hazel, watched her with respectful anxiety, and this did not escape her feminine observation. She noted quietly that those dark eyes of his followed her with a mournful tenderness, but withdrew their gaze when she looked at him. Clearly, he was interested in her, but had no desire to intrude upon her attention. He would bring up the squabs for her, and some of his own wraps, when she stayed on deck, and was prompt with his arm when the vessel lurched; and showed her those other little attentions, which are called for on board ship, but without a word. Yet, when she thanked him in the simplest and shortest way, his great eyes flashed with pleasure, and the color mounted to his very temples.

Engaged young ladies are, for various reasons, more sociable with the other sex, than those who are still on the universal mock-defensive: a ship, like a distant country, thaws even English reserve, and women in general are disposed to admit ecclesiastics to certain privileges. No wonder then that Miss Rolleston, after a few days, met Mr. Hazel half way; and they made acquaintance on board the Proserpine, in monosyllables at first; but, the ice once fairly broken, the intercourse of mind became rather rapid.

At first it was a mere intellectual exchange, but one very agreeable to Miss Rolleston; for a fine memory, and omnivorous reading from his very boyhood, with the habit of taking notes, and reviewing them, had made Mr. Hazel a walking dictionary, and a walking essayist if required.

But, when it came to something, which most of all the young lady had hoped from this temporary acquaintance, viz. religious instruction, she found him indeed as learned on that as on other topics, but cold, and devoid of unction: so much so, that one day she said to him, "I can hardly believe you have ever been a missionary." But at that he seemed so distressed, that she was sorry for him, and said, sweetly, "Excuse me, Mr. Hazel, my remark was in rather bad taste, I fear."

"Not at all," said he. "Of course I am unfit for missionary work, or I should not be here."

Miss Rolleston took a good look at him, but said nothing. However, his reply and her perusal of his countenance, satisfied her that he was a man with very little petty vanity and petty irritability.

One day they were discoursing of gratitude; and Mr. Hazel said he had a poor opinion of those persons, who speak of "the burden of gratitude," and make a fuss about being "laid under an obligation."

"As for me," said he, "I have owed such a debt, and found the sense of it very sweet."

"But perhaps you were always hoping to make a return," said Helen.

"That I was: hoping against hope."

"Do you think people are grateful, in general?"

"No, Miss Rolleston, I do not."

"Well, I think they are. To me at least. Why, I have experienced gratitude even in a convict. It was a poor man, who had been transported, for something or other, and he begged papa to take him for his gardener. Papa did, and he was so grateful that, do you know, he suspected our house was to be robbed, and he actually watched in the garden night after night: and, what do you think? the house *was* attacked by a whole gang; but poor Mr. Seaton confronted them and shot one, and was wounded cruelly; but he beat them off for us; and was not that gratitude?"

While she was speaking so earnestly, Mr. Hazel's blood seemed to run through his veins like heavenly fire, but he said nothing, and the lady resumed with gentle fervor, "Well, we got him a clerk's place in a shipping-office, and heard no more of him; but he did not forget us; my cabin here was fitted up with every comfort, and every delicacy. I thanked papa for it; but he looked so blank, I saw directly, he knew nothing about it; and now, I think of it, it was Mr. Seaton. I am positive it was. Poor fellow! And I should not even know him if I saw him."

Mr. Hazel observed, in a low voice, that Mr. Seaton's conduct did not seem wonderful to him. "Still," said he, "one is glad to find there is some good left even in a criminal."

"A criminal!" cried Helen Rolleston, firing up. "Pray, who says he was a criminal? Mr. Hazel, once for all, no friend of mine ever deserves such a name as that. A friend of mine may commit some great error or imprudence; but that is all. The poor grateful soul was never guilty of any downright wickedness: *that stands to reason.*"

Mr. Hazel did not encounter this feminine logic with his usual ability; he muttered something or other, with a trembling lip, and left her so abruptly, that she asked herself whether she had inadvertently said anything that could have offended him; and awaited an explanation. But none came. The topic was never revived by Mr. Hazel; and his manner, at their next meeting, showed he liked her none the worse that she stood up for her friends.

The wind steady from the west for two whole days, and the Proserpine showed her best sailing qualities, and ran four hundred and fifty miles in that time.

Then came a dead calm, and the sails flapped lazily, and the masts described an arc; and the sun broiled; and the sailors whistled; and the Captain drank; and the mate encouraged him.

During this calm, Miss Rolleston fell downright ill, and quitted the deck. Then Mr. Hazel was very sad: borrowed all the books in the ship, and read them, and took notes; and when he had done this, he was at leisure to read men, and so began to study Hiram Hudson, Joseph Wylie, and others, and take a few notes about them.

From these we select some that are better worth the reader's attention than anything we could relate in our own persons at this stagnant part of the story.

PASSAGES FROM MR. HAZEL'S DIARY.

"CHARACTERS ON BOARD THE PROSERPINE.

"There are two sailors, messmates, who have formed an antique friendship; their names are John Welch and Samuel Cooper. Welch is a very able seaman and a chatterbox. Cooper is a good sailor, but very silent; only what he does say is much to the purpose.

"The gabble of Welch is agreeable to the silent Cooper; and Welch admires Cooper's taciturnity.

"I asked Welch what made him like Cooper so much. And he said, 'Why, you see, sir, he is my messmate, for one thing, and a seaman that knows his work; and then he has been well eddycated, and he knows when to hold his tongue, does Sam.'

"I asked Cooper why he was so fond of Welch. He only grunted in an uneasy way at first; but when I pressed for a reply, he let out two words,— 'Capital company'; and got away from me.

"Their friendship, though often roughly expressed, is really a tender and touching sentiment. I think either of these sailors would bare his back and take a dozen lashes in place of his messmate. I too once thought I had made such a friend. Eheu!

"Both Cooper and Welch seem, by their talk, to consider the ship a living creature. Cooper chews. Welch only smokes, and often lets his pipe out: he is so voluble.

"Captain Hudson is quite a character: or, I might say, two characters; for he is one man when he is sober, and another when he is the worse for liquor: and that I am sorry to see is very often. Captain Hudson, sober, is a rough, bearish seaman, with a quick, experienced eye, that takes in every rope in the ship, as he walks up and down his quarter-deck. He either evades, or bluntly declines conversation, and gives his whole mind to sailing his ship.

"Captain Hudson, drunk, is a garrulous man, who seems to have drifted back into the past. He comes up to you and talks of his own accord, and always about himself, and what he did fifteen or twenty years since. He forgets whatever has occurred half an hour ago; and his eye, which was an eagle's is now a mole's. He no longer sees what his sailors are doing alow or aloft; to be sure he no longer cares; his present ship may take care of herself while he is talking of his past ones. But the surest indicia of inebriety in Hudson are these two. First, his nose is red. Secondly, he discourses upon a seaman's *duty to his employers.* Ebrius rings the changes on his 'duty to his employers' till drowsiness attacks his hearers. *Cicero de officiis* was all very well at a certain period of one's life: but *bibulus nauta de officiis* is rather too much.

"N. B. Except when his nose is red, not a word about his 'duty to his employers.' That phrase, like a fine lady, never ventures into the morning air. It is purely post-prandial, and sacred to occasions when he is utterly neglecting his duty to his employers, and to everybody else.

"All this is ridiculous enough but somewhat alarming. To think that *her* precious life should be intrusted to the care and skill of so unreliable a captain!

"Joseph Wylie, the mate, is less eccentric, but even more remarkable. He is one of those powerfully built fellows, whom Nature, one would think, constructed to gain all their ends by force and directness. But no such thing; he goes about as softly as a cat; is always popping up out of holes and corners; and I can see he watches me, and tries to hear what I say to her. He is civil to me when I speak to him; yet, I notice, he avoids me quietly. Altogether, there is something about him that puzzles me. Why was he so reluctant to let me on board as a passenger? Why did he tell a downright falsehood? For he said there was no room for me; yet, even now, there are two cabins vacant, and he has taken possession of them.

"The mate of this ship has several barrels of spirits in his cabin, or rather, cabins, and it is he who makes the captain drunk. I learned this from one of the boys. This looks ugly. I fear Wylie is a bad, designing man, who wishes to ruin the captain, and so get his place. But, meantime, the ship might be endangered by this drunkard's misconduct. I shall watch Wylie closely, and perhaps put the captain on his guard against this false friend.

"Last night, a breeze got up about sunset, and H. R. came on deck for half an hour. I welcomed her as calmly as I could; but I felt my voice tremble and my heart throb. She told me the voyage tired her much; but it was the last she should have to make. How strange, how hellish (God forgive me for saying so!) it seems that *she* should love *him.* But, does she love him? Can she love him? Could she love him if she kn͏ew all? Know him she shall before she marries him. For the present, be still, my heart.

"She soon went below and left me desolate. I wandered all about the ship, and, at last, I came upon the inseparables, Welch and Cooper. They were squatted on the deck, and Welch's tongue was going as usual. He was talking about this Wylie, and saying that, in all his ships, he had never known such a mate as this; why the captain was under his thumb. He then gave a string of captains, each of whom would have given his mate a round dozen at the gangway, if he had taken so much on him, as this one does.

"'Grog!' suggested Cooper, in extenuation.

"Welch admitted Wylie was liberal with that, and friendly enough with the men; but, still, he preferred to see a ship commanded by the captain, and not by a lubber like Wylie.

"I expressed some surprise at this term, and said I had envied Wylie's nerves in a gale of wind we encountered early in the voyage.

"The talking sailor explained, 'In course, he has been to sea afore this, and weathered many a gale.' But so has the cook. 'That don't make a man a sailor.' You ask him how to send down a to'-gallant yard or gammon a bowsprit, or even mark a lead line, and he 'll stare at ye, like Old Nick, when the angel caught him with the red-hot tongs, and questioned him out of the Church Catechism. Ask Sam there, if ye don't believe me. Sam, what do you think of this Wylie for a seaman?'

Cooper could not afford anything so precious, in his estimate of things, as a word; but he lifted a great brawny hand, and gave a snap with his finger and thumb, that disposed of the mate's pretensions to seamanship more expressively than words could have done it.

"The breeze has freshened, and the ship glides rapidly through the water, bearing us all homeward. Helen Rolleston has resumed her place upon the deck; and all seems bright again. I ask myself how we existed without the sight of her.

"This morning the wind shifted to the southwest; the captain surprised us by taking in sail. But his sober eye had seen something more than ours; for at noon it blew a gale, and by sunset it was deemed prudent to bring the ship's head to the wind, and we are now lying-to. The ship lurches, and the wind howls through the bare rigging; but she rides buoyantly, and no danger is apprehended.

"Last night, as I lay in my cabin, unable to sleep, I heard some heavy blows strike the ship's side repeatedly, causing quite a vibration. I felt alarmed, and went out to tell the captain. But I was obliged to go on my hands and knees, such was the force of the wind. Passing the mate's cabin, I heard sounds that made me listen acutely; and I then found the blows were being struck inside the ship. I got to the captain and told him. 'O,' said he, 'ten to one it 's the mate nailing down his chests, or the like.' But I assured him the blows struck the side of the ship, and, at my earnest request, he came out and listened. He swore a great oath, and said the lubber would be through the ship's side. He then tried the cabin-door, but it was locked.

"The sounds ceased directly.

"We called to the mate, but received no reply for a long time. At last Wylie came out of the gun-room, looking rather pale, and asked what was the matter.

"I told him he ought to know best, for the blows were heard where he had just come from.

"'Blows!' said he; 'I believe you. Why, a tierce of butter had got adrift, and was bumping up and down the hold like thunder.' He then asked us whether that was what we had disturbed him for, entered his cabin, and almost slammed the door in our faces.

"I remarked to the captain on his disrespectful conduct. The captain was civil, and said I was right; he was a cross-grained, unmanageable brute, and he wished he was out of the ship. 'But you see, sir, he has got the ear of the merchant ashore; and so I am obliged to hold a candle to the Devil, as the saying is.' He then fired a volley of oaths and abuse at the offender; and, not to encourage foul language, I retired to my cabin.

"The wind declined towards daybreak, and the ship recommenced her voyage at 8 A. M.; but under treble-reefed topsails and reefed courses.

"I caught the captain and mate talking together in the friendliest way possible. That Hudson is a humbug; there is some mystery between him and the mate.

"To-day H. R. was on deck for several hours, conversing sweetly, and looking like the angel she is. But happiness soon flies from me; a steamer came in sight, bound for Sydney. She signalled us to heave-to, and send a boat. This was done, and the boat brought back a letter for *her*. It seems they took us for the Shannon, in which ship she was expected.

"The letter was from *him*. How her cheek flushed and her eye beamed as she took it. And O the sadness, the agony, that stood beside her unheeded.

"I left the deck; I could not have contained myself. What a thing is wealth! By wealth, that wretch can stretch out his hand across the ocean, and put a letter into her hand under my very eye. Away goes all that I have gained by being near her, while he is far away. He is not in England now, — he is here. His odious presence has driven me from her. O that I could be a child again, or in my grave, to get away from this Hell of Love and Hate."

At this point, we beg leave to take the narrative into our own hands again.

Mr. Hazel actually left the deck to avoid the sight of Helen Rolleston's flushed cheek and beaming eyes, reading Arthur Wardlaw's letter.

And here we may as well observe that he retired not merely because the torture was hard to bear. He had some disclosures to make, on reaching England; but his good sense told him this was not the time, or the place, to make them, nor Helen Rolleston the person to whom, in the first instance, they ought to be made.

While he tries to relieve his swelling heart by putting its throbs on paper (and, in truth, this is some faint relief, for want of which many a less unhappy man than Hazel has gone mad), let us stay by the lady's side, and read her letter with her.

"RUSSELL SQUARE, Dec. 15, 1865.

"MY DEAR LOVE: Hearing that the Antelope steam-packet was going to Sydney, by way of Cape Horn, I have begged the captain, who is under some obligations to me, to keep a good look-out for the Shannon, homeward bound, and board her with these lines, weather permitting.

"Of course, the chances are you will not receive them at sea; but still you possibly may; and my heart is so full of you, I seize any excuse for overflowing; and then I picture to myself that bright face reading an unexpected letter in mid ocean, and so I taste beforehand the greatest pleasure my mind can conceive, — the delight of giving you pleasure, my own sweet Helen.

"News, I have very little. You know how deeply and devotedly you are beloved, — know it so well that I feel words are almost wasted in repeating it. Indeed, the time, I hope, is at hand when the word love will hardly be mentioned between us. For my part, I think it will be too visible in every act, and look, and word of mine, to need repetition. We do not speak much about the air we live in. We breathe it, and speak with it, not of it.

"I suppose all lovers are jealous. I think I should go mad if you were to give me a rival; but then I do not understand that ill-natured jealousy which would rob the beloved object of all affections but the one. I know my Helen loves her father, — loves him, perhaps, as well, or better, than she does me. Well, in spite of that, I love him too. Do you know, I never see that erect form, that model of courage and probity come into a room, but I say to myself, 'Here comes my benefactor; but for this man there would be no Helen in the world.' Well, dearest, an unexpected circumstance has given me a little military influence (these things do happen in the City); and I really believe that, what with his acknowledged merits (I am secretly informed a very high personage said, the other day, he had not received justice), and the influence I speak of, a post will shortly be offered to your father that will enable him to live, henceforth, in England, with comfort, I might say, affluence. Perhaps he might live with us. That depends upon himself.

"Looking forward to this, and my own still greater happiness, diverts my mind a while from the one ever-pressing anxiety. But, alas! it will return. By this time my Helen is on the seas, — the terrible, the treacherous, the cruel seas, that spare neither beauty nor virtue, nor the longing hearts at home. I have conducted this office for some years, and thought I knew care and anxiety. But I find I knew neither till now.

"I have two ships at sea, the Shannon and the Proserpine. The Proserpine carries eighteen chests of specie, worth a hundred and thirty thousand pounds. I don't care one straw whether she sinks or swims. But the Shannon carries my darling; and every gust at night awakens me, and every day I go into the great room at Lloyd's and watch the anemometer. O God! be merciful, and bring my angel safe to me! O God! be just, and strike her not for my offences!

"Besides the direct perils of the sea are some others you might escape by prudence. Pray avoid the night air, for my sake, who could not live if any evil befell you; and be careful in your diet. You were not looking so well as usual, when I left. Would I had words to make you know your own value. Then you would feel it a *duty* to be prudent.

"But I must not sadden you with my fears; let me turn to my hopes. How bright they are; what joy, what happiness, is sailing towards me, nearer and nearer every day. I ask myself what am I that such paradise should be mine.

"My love, when we are one, shall we share every thought, or shall I keep commerce, speculation, and its temptations away from your pure spirit?

Sometimes I think I should like to have neither thought nor occupation unshared by you; and that you would purify trade itself by your contact; at other times I say to myself, 'O, never soil that angel with your miserable business; but go home to her as if you were going from earth to heaven, for a few blissful hours.' But you shall decide this question, and every other.

"Must I close this letter? Must I say no more though I have scarcely begun?

"Yes, I will end, since, perhaps, you will never see it.

"When I have sealed it, I mean to hold it in my clasped hands, and so pray the Almighty to take it safe to you, and to bring you safe to him, who can never know peace nor joy till he sees you once more.

"Your devoted and anxious lover,

"ARTHUR WARDLAW."

Helen Rolleston read this letter more than once. She liked it none the less for being disconnected and unbusiness-like. She had seen her Arthur's business letters; models of courteous conciseness. She did not value such compositions. This one she did. She smiled over it, all beaming and blushing; she kissed it, and read it again, and sat with it in her lap.

But, by and by, her mood changed, and, when Mr. Hazel ventured upon deck again, he found her with her forehead sinking on her extended arm, and the lax hand of that same arm holding the letter. She was crying.

The whole drooping attitude was so lovely, so feminine, yet so sad, that Hazel stood irresolute, looking wistfully at her.

She caught sight of him, and, by a natural impulse, turned gently away, as if to hide her tears. But, the next moment, she altered her mind, and said, with a quiet dignity that came naturally to her at times, "Why should I hide my care from you, sir? Mr. Hazel, may I speak to you *as a clergyman?*"

"Certainly," said Mr. Hazel, in a somewhat faint voice.

She pointed to a seat and he sat down near her.

She was silent for some time; her lip quivered a little; she was struggling inwardly for that decent composure, which on certain occasions, distinguishes the lady from the mere woman; and it was with a pretty firm voice she said what follows: —

"I am going to tell you a little secret: one I have kept from my own father. It is, — that I have not very long to live."

Her hazel eye rested calmly on his face while she said these words quietly.

He received them with amazement, at first; amazement, that soon deepened into horror. "What do you mean?" he gasped. "What words are these?"

"Thank you for minding so much," said she, sweetly. "I will tell you. I have fits of coughing, not frequent, but violent; and then blood very often comes from my lungs. That is a bad sign, you know. I have been so for four months now, and I am a good deal wasted; my hand used to be very plump, look at it now. — Poor Arthur!"

She turned away her head to drop a gentle, unselfish tear or two; and Hazel stared with increasing alarm at the lovely but wasted hand she still held out to him, and glanced, too, at Arthur Wardlaw's letter, held slightly by the beloved fingers.

He said nothing, and, when she looked round again, he was pale and trembling. The revelation was so sudden.

"Pray be calm, sir," said she. "We need speak of this no more. But, now, I think, you will not be surprised that I come to you for religious advice and consolation, short as our acquaintance is."

"I am in no condition to give them," said Hazel, in great agitation. "I can think of nothing but how to save you. May Heaven help me, and give me wisdom for that."

"This is idle," said Helen Rolleston, gently, but firmly. "I have had the best advice for months, and I get worse; and, Mr. Hazel, I shall never be better. So, aid me to bow to the will of Heaven. Sir, I do not repine at leaving the world; but it does grieve me to think how my departure will affect those whose happiness is very, very dear to me."

She then looked at the letter, blushed, and hesitated a moment; but ended by giving it to him whom she had applied to as her religious adviser.

"Oblige me by reading that. And, when you have, I think you will grant me a favor I wish to ask you. Poor fellow! so full of hopes that I am doomed to disappoint."

She rose to hide her emotion, and left Arthur Wardlaw's letter in the hands of him who loved her, if possible, more devotedly than Arthur Wardlaw did; and she walked the deck pensively, little dreaming how strange a thing she had done.

As for Hazel, he was in a situation poignant with agony; only the heavy blow that had just fallen had stunned and benumbed him. He felt a natural repugnance to read this letter. But she had given him no choice. He read it. In reading it he felt a mortal sickness come over him, but he persevered; he read it carefully to the end, and he was examining the signature keenly, when Miss Rolleston rejoined him, and, taking the letter from him, placed it in her bosom before his eyes.

"He loves me; does he not?" said she, wistfully.

Hazel looked half-stupidly in her face for a moment; then, with a candor which was part of his character, replied, doggedly, "Yes, the man who wrote that letter loves you."

"Then you can pity him, and I may venture to ask you the favor to — It will be a bitter grief and disappointment to him. Will you break it to him as gently as you can; will you say that his Helen — Will you tell him what I have told you?"

"I decline."

This point-blank refusal surprised Helen Rolleston; all the more that it was uttered with a certain sullenness, and even asperity, she had never seen till then in this gentle clergyman.

It made her fear she had done wrong in asking it; and she looked ashamed and distressed.

However, the explanation soon followed.

"My business," said he, "is to prolong your precious life; and, making up your mind to die is not the way. You shall have no encouragement in such weakness from me. Pray let me be your physician."

"Thank you," said Helen, coldly; "I have my own physician."

"No doubt: but he shows me his incapacity, by allowing you to live on pastry and sweets; things that are utter poison to you. Disease of the lungs is curable, but not by drugs and unwholesome food."

"Mr. Hazel," said the lady, "we will drop the

subject, if you please. It has taken an uninteresting turn."

"To you, perhaps; but not to me."

"Excuse me, sir; if you took that real friendly interest in me and my condition I was vain enough to think you might, you would hardly have refused me the first favor I ever asked you; and, drawing herself up proudly, "need I say the last?"

"You are unjust," said Hazel, sadly; "unjust beyond endurance. I refuse you anything that is for your good? I, who would lay down my life with unmixed joy for you?"

"Mr. Hazel!" And she drew back from him with a haughty stare.

"Learn the truth why I cannot, and will not, talk to Arthur Wardlaw about you. For one thing, he is my enemy, and I am his."

"His enemy? my Arthur's!"

"His mortal enemy. And I am going to England to clear an innocent man, and expose Arthur Wardlaw's guilt."

"Indeed!" said Helen with lofty contempt. "And pray what has he done to *you?*"

"He had a benefactor, a friend; he entrapped him into cashing a note of hand, which he must have known, or suspected to be, forged; then basely deserted him at the trial, and blasted his friend's life forever."

"Arthur Wardlaw did that?"

"He did; and that very James Seaton was his victim."

Her delicate nostrils were expanded with wrath and her eyes flashed fire. "Mr. Hazel, you are a liar and a slanderer."

The man gave a kind of shudder, as if cold steel had passed through his heart. But his fortitude was great; he said, doggedly, "Time will show. Time, and a jury of our countrymen."

"I will be his witness. I will say, this is the malice of a rival. Yes, sir, you forget that you have let out the motive of this wicked slander. You love me yourself; Heaven forgive me for profaning the name of love!"

"Heaven forgive you for blaspheming the purest, fondest love, that ever one creature laid at the feet of another. Yes, Helen Rolleston, I love you; and will save you from the grave and from the villain Wardlaw; both from one and the other."

"O, said Helen," clenching her teeth, "I hope this is true; I hope you do love me, you wretch; then I may find a way to punish you for belying the absent, and stabbing me to the heart, through him."

Her throat swelled with a violent convulsion, and she could utter no more for a moment; and she put her white handkerchief to her lips, and drew it away discolored slightly with blood.

"Ah! you love me," she cried; "then know, for your comfort, that you have shortened my short life a day or two, by slandering *him* to my face, you monster. Look there at your love, and see what it has done for me."

She put the handkerchief under his eyes, with hate gleaming in her own.

Mr. Hazel turned ashy pale, and glared at it with horror; he could have seen his own shed, with stoical firmness; but a mortal sickness struck his heart at the sight of *her* blood. His hands rose and quivered in a peculiar way, his sight left him, and the strong man, but tender lover, staggered, and fell heavily on the deck, in a dead swoon, and lay at her feet, pale and motionless.

She uttered a scream, and sailors came running.

They lifted him, with rough sympathy; and Helen Rolleston retired to her cabin, panting with agitation. But she had little or no pity for the slanderer. She read Arthur Wardlaw's letter again, kissed it, wept over it, reproached herself for not having loved the writer enough; and vowed to repair that fault. "Poor slandered Arthur," said she; "from this hour I will love you as devotedly as you love me."

CHAPTER IX.

After this, Helen Rolleston and Mr. Hazel never spoke. She walked past him on the deck with cold and haughty contempt.

He quietly submitted to it; and never presumed to say one word to her again. Only, as his determination was equal to his delicacy, Miss Rolleston found, one day, a paper on her table, containing advice as to the treatment of disordered lungs, expressed with apparent coldness, and backed by a string of medical authorities, quoted memoriter.

She sent this back directly, indorsed with a line, in pencil, that she would try hard to live, now she had a friend to protect from calumny; but should use her own judgment as to the means.

Yet women will be women. She had carefully taken a copy of his advice, before she cast it out with scorn.

He replied, "Live, with whatever motive you please; only live."

To this she vouchsafed no answer; nor did this unhappy man trouble her again, until an occasion of a very different kind arose.

One fine night, he sat on the deck, with his back against the mainmast, in deep melancholy and listlessness, and fell, at last, into a doze, from which he was wakened by a peculiar sound below. It was a beautiful and stilly night; all sounds were magnified; and the father of all rats seemed to be gnawing the ship down below.

Hazel's curiosity was excited, and he went softly down the ladder to see what the sound really was. But that was not so easy, for it proved to be below decks; but he saw a light glimmering through a small scuttle abaft the mate's cabin, and the sounds were in the neighborhood of that light.

It now flashed upon Mr. Hazel that this was the very quarter where he had heard that mysterious knocking when the ship was lying-to in the gale.

Upon this a certain degree of vague suspicion began to mingle with his curiosity.

He stood still a moment, listening acutely; then took off his shoes very quietly, and moved with noiseless foot towards the scuttle.

The gnawing still continued.

He put his head through the scuttle, and peered into a dark, dismal place, whose very existence was new to him. It was, in fact, a vacant space between the cargo and the ship's run. This wooden cavern was very narrow, but not less than fifteen feet long. The candle was at the farther end, and between it and Hazel, a man was working, with his flank turned towards the spectator. This partly intercepted the light; but still it revealed in a fitful way the huge ribs of the ship, and her inner skin, that formed the right-hand partition, so to speak, of this black cavern; and close outside those gaunt timbers, was heard the wash of the sea.

There was something solemn in the close proximity of that tremendous element and the narrowness of the wooden barrier.

The bare place, and the gentle, monotonous wash of the liquid monster, on that calm night, conveyed to Mr. Hazel's mind a thought akin to David's.

"As the Lord liveth, and as thy soul liveth, there is but a step between me and death."

Judge whether that thought grew weaker or stronger, when, after straining his eyes for some time, to understand what was going on at that midnight hour, in that hidden place, he saw who was the workman, and what was his occupation.

It was Joseph Wylie, the mate. His profile was illuminated by the candle, and looked ghastly. He had in his hands an auger of enormous size, and with this he was drilling a great hole through the ship's side, just below the water-mark; an act, the effect of which would be to let the sea bodily into the ship and sink her, with every soul on board, to the bottom of the Pacific Ocean.

"I was stupefied; and my hairs stood on end, and my tongue clove to my jaws."

Thus does one of Virgil's characters describe the effect his mind produced upon his body, in a terrible situation.

Mr. Hazel had always ridiculed that trite line as a pure exaggeration; but he altered his opinion after that eventful night.

When he first saw what Wylie was doing, *obstupuit*, he was merely benumbed; but, as his mind realized the fiendish nature of the act, and its tremendous consequences, his hair actually bristled, and for a few minutes at least, he could not utter a word.

In that interval of stupor, matters took another turn. The auger went in up to the haft: then Wylie caught up with his left hand a wooden plug he had got ready, jerked the auger away, caught up a hammer, and swiftly inserted the plug.

Rapid as he was, a single jet of water came squirting viciously in. But Wylie lost no time; he tapped the plug smartly with his hammer several times, and then, lifting a mallet with both hands, rained heavy blows on it that drove it in, and shook the ship's side.

Then Hazel found his voice, and he uttered an ejaculation that made the mate look round; he glared at the man, who was glaring at him, and, staggering backward, trod on the light, and all was darkness and dead silence.

All but the wash of the sea outside, and that louder than ever.

But a short interval sufficed to restore one of the parties to his natural self-possession.

"Lord, sir," said Wylie, "how you startled me! You should not come upon a man at his work like that. We might have had an accident."

"What were you doing?" said Hazel, in a voice that quavered in spite of him.

"Repairing the ship. Found a crack or two in her inner skin. There, let me get a light, and I'll explain it to you, sir."

He groped his way out, and invited Mr. Hazel into his cabin. There he struck a light, and, with great civility, tendered an explanation. The ship, he said, had labored a good deal in the last gale, and he had discovered one or two flaws in her, which were of no immediate importance; but experience had taught him that in calm weather a ship ought to be kept tight. "As they say ashore, a stitch in time saves nine."

"But drilling holes in her is not the way," said Hazel, sternly.

The mate laughed. "Why, sir," said he, "what other way is there? We cannot stop an irregular crack; we can frame nothing to fit it. The way is to get ready a plug measured a trifle larger than the aperture you are going to make; then drill a round hole, and force in the plug. I know no other way than that; and I was a ship's carpenter for ten years before I was a mate."

This explanation, and the manner in which it was given, removed Mr. Hazel's apprehensions for the time being. "It was very alarming," said he; "but I suppose you know your business."

"Nobody better, sir," said Wylie. "Why, it is not one seaman in three that would trouble his head about a flaw in a ship's inner skin; but I'm a man that looks ahead. Will you have a glass of grog, sir, now you are here? I keep that under my eye, too; between ourselves, if the skipper had as much in his cabin as I have here, that might be worse for us all than a crack or two in the ship's inner skin."

Mr. Hazel declined to drink grog at that time in the morning, but wished him good night, and left him with a better opinion of him than he had ever had till then.

Wylie, when he was gone, drew a tumbler of neat spirits, drank half, and carried the rest back to his work.

Yet Wylie was a very sober man in a general way. Rum was his tool; not his master.

When Hazel came to think of it all next day, he did not feel quite so easy as he had done. The inner skin! But, when Wylie withdrew his auger, the water had squirted in furiously. He felt it hard to believe that this keen jet of water could be caused by a small quantity that had found its way between the skin of the ship and her copper, or her top booting; it seemed rather to be due to the direct pressure of the liquid monster outside.

He went to the captain that afternoon, and first told him what he had seen, offering no solution. The captain, on that occasion, was in an amphibious state; neither wet nor dry; and his reply was altogether exceptional. He received the communication with pompous civility; then swore a great oath, and said he would put the mate in irons: "Confound the lubber! he will be through the ship's bottom."

"But, stop a moment," said Mr. Hazel, "it is only fair you should also hear how he accounts for his proceeding."

The captain listened attentively to the explanation, and altered his tone. "O, that is a different matter," said he. "You need be under no alarm, sir; the thundering lubber knows what he is about, at that work. Why he has been a ship's carpenter all his life. Him a seaman! If anything ever happens to me, and Joe Wylie is set to navigate this ship, then you may say your prayers. He is n't fit to sail a wash-tub across a duck-pond. But I'll tell you what it is," added this worthy, with more pomposity than neatness of articulation, "here's respeckable passenger brought me a report; do my duty to m'employers, and — take a look at the well."

He accordingly chalked a plumb-line, and went and sounded the well.

There were eight inches of water. Hudson told him that was no more than all ships contained from various causes; "in fact," said he, "our pumps suck, and will not draw, at eight inches." Then suddenly grasping Mr. Hazel's hand, he said, in tearful accents, "Don't you trouble your head about Joe Wylie, or any such scum. I'm skipper of the Proserpine, and a man that does his duty to z'employers. Mr. Hazel, sir, I 'd come to my last anchor in that well this moment, if my duty to m'employers required it. B— my eyes if I would n't lie down there this minute, and never move to all eternity and a day after, if it was my duty to m'employers!"

"No doubt," said Hazel, dryly. "But I think you can serve your employers better *in other parts of the ship*." He then left him, with a piece of advice; "to keep his eye upon that Wylie."

Mr. Hazel kept his own eye on Wylie so constantly, that at eleven o'clock P. M. he saw that worthy go into the captain's cabin with a quart bottle of rum.

The coast was clear; the temptation great.

These men then were still deceiving him with a feigned antagonism. He listened at the keyhole, not without some compunction; which, however, became less and less as fragments of the dialogue reached his ear.

For a long time the only speaker was Hudson, and his discourse ran upon his own exploits at sea. But suddenly Wylie's voice broke in with an unmistakable tone of superiority. "Belay all that chat, and listen to me. It is time we settled something. I 'll hear what you have got to say; and then you 'll *do* what *I* say. Better keep your hands off the bottle a minute; you have had enough for the present; this is business. I know you are good for jaw; but what are you game to do for the governor's money? Anything?"

"More than you have ever seen or heard tell of, ye lubber," replied the irritated skipper. "Who has ever served his employers like Hiram Hudson?"

"Keep that song for your quarter-deck," retorted the mate, contemptuously. "No; on second thoughts, just tell me how you have served your employers, you old humbug. Give me chapter and verse to choose from. Come now, the Neptune?"

"Well, the Neptune; she caught fire a hundred leagues from land."

"How came she to do that?"

"That is my business. Well, I put her head before the wind, and ran for the Azores; and I stuck to her, sir, till she was as black as a coal, and we could n't stand on deck, but kept hopping like parched peas; and fire belching out of her portholes forward: then we took to the boats, and saved a few bales of silk by way of sample of her cargo, and got ashore; and she 'd have come ashore too next tide and told tales, but Somebody left a keg of gunpowder in the cabin, with a long fuse, and blew a hole in her old ribs, that the water came in, and down she went, hissing like ten thousand sarpints, and nobody the wiser."

"Who lighted the fuse, I wonder?" said Wylie.

"Did n't I tell ye it was 'Somebody'?" said Hudson. "Hand me the stiff." He replenished his glass, and, after taking a sip or two, asked Wylie if he had ever had the luck to be boarded by pirates.

"No," said Wylie. "Have you?"

"Ay; and they rescued me from a watery grave, as the lubbers call it. Ye see, I was employed by Downes and Co., down at the Havannah, and cleared for Vera Cruz with some boxes of old worn-out printers' type."

"To print psalm-books for the darkies, no doubt," suggested Wylie.

"Insured as specie," continued Hudson, ignoring the interruption. "Well, just at daybreak one morning, all of a sudden there was a rakish-looking craft on our weather-bow: lets fly a nine-pounder across our fore-foot, and was alongside before my men could tumble up from below. I got knocked into the sea by the boom and fell between the ships; and the pirate he got hold of me and poured hot grog down my throat to bring me to my senses."

"That is not what you use it for in general," said Wylie. "Civil sort of pirate, though."

"Pirate be d—d. That was my consort, rigged out with a black flag, and mounted with four nine-pounders on one side, and five dummies on the other. He blustered a bit, and swore, and took our type and our cabbages (I complained to Downes ashore about the vagabond taking the vegetables), and ordered us to leeward under all canvas, and we never saw him again, — not till he had shaved off his mustaches, and called on Downes to condole, and say the varmint had chased his ship fifty leagues out of her course; but he had got clear of him. Downes complimented me publicly. Says he, 'This skipper boarded the pirate single handed; only he jumped short, and fell between the two ships; and here he is by a miracle.' Then he takes out his handkerchief, and flops his head on my shoulder. 'His merciful preservation almost reconciles me to the loss of my gold,' says the thundering crocodile. Cleared $ 70,000, he did, out of the Marhattan Marine, and gave the pirate and me but £ 200 between us both."

"The Rose?" said Wylie.

"What a hurry you are in! Pass the grog. Well the Rose; she lay off Ushant. We canted her to wash the decks; lucky she had a careful commander; not like Kempenfelt, whose eye was in his pocket, and his fingers held the pen, so he went to the bottom, with Lord knows how many men. I noticed the squalls came very sudden; so I sent most of my men ashore, and got the boats ready in case of accident. A squall did strike her, and she was on her beam-ends in a moment: we pulled ashore with two bales of silk by way of salvage, and sample of what war n't in her hold when she settled down. We landed; and the Frenchmen were dancing about with excitement. 'Captain,' says one, 'you have much sang fraw.' 'Insured, munseer,' says I. 'Bone,' says he.

"Then there was the Antelope, lost in charge of a pilot off the Hooghly. I knew the water as well as he did. We were on the port tack, standing towards the shoal. Weather it, as we should have done next tack, and I should have failed in my duty to my employers. Anything but that! 'Look out!' said I. 'Pilot, she forereaches in stays.' Pilot was smoking: those Sandhead pilots smoke in bed and asleep. He takes his cigar out of his mouth for one moment. 'Ready about,' says he. 'Hands 'bout ship. Helms a-lee. Raise tacks and sheets.' Round she was coming like a top. Pilot smoking. Just as he was going to haul the mainsel Somebody tripped against him, and shoved the hot cigar in his eye. He sung out and swore, and there was no mainsel haul. Ship in irons, tide running hard on to the shoal, and before we could clear away for anchoring, bump! — there she was hard and fast. A stiff breeze got up at sunrise, and she broke up. Next day I was sipping my grog and reading the Bengal Courier, and it told the disastrous wreck of the brig Antelope, wrecked in charge of a pilot; 'but no lives lost, and the owners fully insured.' Then there was the bark Sally. Why, you saw her yourself distressed, on a lee shore."

"Yes," said Wylie. "I was in that tub, the Grampus, and we contrived to claw off the Scillies; yet you, in your smart Sally, got ashore. What luck!"

"Luck be blowed!" cried Hudson, angrily. "Somebody got into the chains to sound; and cut the weather halyards. Next tack the masts went over the side; and I had done my duty."

"Lives were lost that time, eh?" said Wylie, gravely.

"What is that to you?" replied Hudson, with the sudden ire of a drunken man. "Mind your own business. Pass me the bottle."

"Yes, lives was lost: and always will be lost in sea-going ships, where the skipper does his duty. There was a sight more lost at Trafalgar, owing to *every* man doing his duty. Lives lost, ye lubber! And why not mine? Because their time was come and mine was n't. For I'll tell you one thing, Joe Wylie, — if she takes fire and runs before the wind till she is as black as a coal, and belching flame through all her portholes, and then explodes, and goes aloft in ten thousand pieces no bigger than *my* hat, or *your* knowledge of navigation, Hudson is the last man to leave her: Duty! — If she goes on her beam ends and founders, Hudson sees the last of her, and reports it to his employers: Duty! — If she goes grinding on Scilly, Hudson is the last man to leave her bones. Duty! — Some day perhaps I shall be swamped myself along with the craft: I have escaped till now, *owing to not being insured;* but if ever my time should come, and you should get clear, promise me, Joe, to see the owners, and tell 'em Hudson did his duty."

Here a few tears quenched his noble ardor for a moment. But he soon recovered, and said, with some little heat, "You have got the bottle again. I never saw such a fellow to get hold of the bottle. Come, here's 'Duty to our employers!'" And now I'll tell you how we managed with the Carysbrook, and the Amelia."

This promise was followed by fresh narratives; in particular, of a vessel he had run upon the Florida reef at night, where wreckers had been retained in advance to look out for signals, and come on board and quarrel in pretence and set fire to the vessel, insured at thrice her value.

Hudson got quite excited with the memory of these exploits, and told each successive feat louder and louder.

But now it was Wylie's turn. "Well," said he, very gravely, "all this was child's play."

There was a pause that marked Hudson's astonishment. Then he broke out, "Child's play, ye lubber! If you had been there your gills would have been as white as your Sunday shirt; and a d—d deal whiter."

"Come, be civil," said Wylie, "I tell you, all the ways you have told me are too suspicious. Our governor is a high-flyer: he pays like a prince, and, in return, he must not be blown on, if it is ever so little. 'Wylie,' says he, 'a breath of suspicion would kill me.' 'Make it so much,' says I, 'and that breath shall never blow on you.' No, no, skipper; none of those ways will do for us; they have all been worked twice too often. It must be done in fair weather, and in a way — fill your glass and I'll fill mine — Capital rum this. You talk of my gills turning white; before long, we shall see whose keeps their color best, mine or yours, my Boy."

There was a silence, during which Hudson was probably asking himself what Wylie meant; for presently, he broke out in a loud, but somewhat quivering voice, "Why, you mad, drunken devil of a ship's carpenter, red-hot from hell, I see what you are at, now; you are going —"

"Hush!" cried Wylie, alarmed in his turn. "Is this the sort of thing to bellow out for the watch to hear? Whisper, now."

This was followed by the earnest mutterings of two voices. In vain did the listener send his very soul into his ear to hear. He could catch no single word. Yet he could tell, by the very tones of the speakers, that the dialogue was one of mystery and importance.

Here was a situation at once irritating and alarming; but there was no help for it. The best thing, now, seemed to be to withdraw unobserved, and wait for another opportunity. He did so; and he had not long retired, when the mate came out staggering, and flushed with liquor, and that was a thing that had never occurred before. He left the cabin door open, and went into his own room.

Soon after, sounds issued from the cabin, peculiar sounds, something between grunting and snoring.

Mr. Hazel came and entered the cabin. There he found the captain of the Proserpine in a position very unfavorable to longevity. His legs were crooked over the seat of his chair, and his head was on the ground. His handkerchief was tight round his neck, and the man himself dead drunk, and purple in the face.

Mr. Hazel instantly undid his stock, on which the gallant seaman muttered inarticulately. He then took his feet off the chair, and laid them on the ground, and put the empty bottle under the animal's neck.

But he had no sooner done all this, than he had a serious misgiving. Would not this man's death have been a blessing? Might not his life prove fatal?

The thought infuriated him, and he gave the prostrate figure a heavy kick that almost turned it over, and the words, "Duty to employers," gurgled out of its mouth directly.

It really seemed as if these sounds were independent of the mind, and resided at the tip of Hudson's tongue: so that a thorough good kick could, at any time, shake them out of his inanimate body.

Thus do things ludicrous, and things terrible, mingle in the real world; only to those who are in the arena, the ludicrous passes unnoticed, being overshadowed by its terrible neighbor.

And so it was with Hazel. He saw nothing absurd in all this; and in that prostrate, insensible hog, commanding the ship, forsooth, and carrying all their lives in his hands: he saw the mysterious and alarming only, saw them so, and felt them, that he lay awake all night thinking what he should do, and early next day he went into the mate's cabin, and said to him, "Mr. Wylie, in any other ship I should speak to the captain, and not to the mate; but here that would be no use, for you are the master, and he is your servant."

"Don't tell him so, sir, for he does n't think small beer of himself."

"I shall waste no more words on him. It is to you I speak, and you know I speak the truth. Here is a ship, in which, for certain reasons known to yourself, the captain is under the mate."

"Well, sir," said Wylie, good-humoredly, "it is no use trying to deceive a gentleman like you. Our skipper is an excellent seaman, but he has got a fault." Then Wylie imitated, with his hand, the action of a person filling his glass.

"And you are here to keep him sober, eh?"

Wylie nodded.

"Then why do you ply him with liquor?"

"I don't, sir."

"You do. I have seen you do it a dozen times: and last night you took rum into his room, and made him so drunk, he would have died where he lay if I had not loosed his handkerchief."

"I am sorry to hear that, sir; but he was sober when I left him. The fool must have got to the bottle the moment I was gone."

"But that bottle you put in his way; I saw you: and what was your object? to deaden his conscience with liquor, his and your own, while you made him your fiendish proposal. Man, man, do you believe in God, and in a judgment to come for the deeds done in the body, that you can plan in cold blood to destroy a vessel with nineteen souls on board, besides the live stock, the innocent animals that God pitied and spared, when he raised his hand in wrath over Nineveh of old?"

While the clergyman was speaking, with flashing eyes and commanding voice, the seaman turned ashy pale; and drew his shoulders together like a cat preparing to defend her life.

"I plan to destroy a vessel, sir! You never heard me say such a word; and don't you hint such a thing in the ship, or you will get yourself into trouble."

"That depends on you."

"How so, sir?"

"I have long suspected you."

"You need not tell me that, sir."

"But I have not communicated my suspicions. And now that they are certainties, I come first to you. In one word, will you forego your intention, since it is found out?"

"How can I forego what never was in my head?" said Wylie. "Cast away the ship! Why there's no land within two thousand miles. Founder a vessel in the Pacific! Do you think my life is not as sweet to me as yours is to you?"

Wylie eyed him keenly to see the effect of these words, and by a puzzled expression that came over his face, saw at once he had assumed a more exact knowledge than he really possessed.

Hazel replied that he had said nothing about foundering the ship; but there were many ways of destroying one. "For instance," said he, "I know how the Neptune was destroyed,—and so do you; how the Rose and the Antelope were cast away, and so do you."

At this enumeration, Wylie lost his color and self-possession for a moment; he saw Hazel had been listening. Hazel followed up his blow. "Promise me now, by all you hold sacred, to forego this villany; and I hold my tongue. Attempt to defy me, or to throw dust in my eyes, and I go instantly among the crew, and denounce both you and Hudson to them."

"Good Heavens!" cried Wylie in unfeigned terror. "Why the men would mutiny on the spot."

"I can't help that," said Hazel, firmly; and took a step towards the door.

"Stop a bit," said the mate. "Don't be in such a nation hurry: for, if you do, it will be bad for me, but worse for you." The above was said so gravely, and with such evident sincerity, that Mr. Hazel was struck, and showed it. Wylie followed up that trifling advantage. "Sit down a minute, sir, if you please, and listen to me. You never saw a mutiny on board ship, I'll be bound. It is a worse thing than any gale that ever blew: begins fair enough, sometimes; but how does it end? In breaking into the spirit-room, and drinking to madness, plundering the ship, ravishing the women, and cutting a throat or so for certain. You don't seem so fond of the picture, as you was of the idea. And then they might turn a deaf ear to you after all. Ship is well found in all stores; provisions served out freely; men in good humor; and I have got their ear. And now I'll tell you why it won't suit your little game to blacken me to the crew, upon the bare chance of a mutiny." He paused for a moment, then resumed in a lower tone, and revealed himself the extraordinary man he was.

"You see, sir," said he, "when a man is very ready to suspect me, I always suspect him. Now you was uncommon ready to suspect me. You did n't wait till you came on board; you began the game ashore. Oh! what, that makes you open one eye, does it? You thought I did n't know you again. Knew you, my man, the moment you came aboard. I never forget a face; and disguises don't pass on me."

It was now Hazel's turn to look anxious and discomposed.

"So, then, the moment I saw you suspected me I was down upon you. Well, you come aboard under false colors. We did n't want a chap like you in the ship; but you would come. 'What is the bloke after?' says I, and watches. You was so intent suspecting me of this, that, and t'other, that you unguarded yourself, and that is common too. I'm blowed if it is n't the lady you are after. With all my heart: only she might do better, and I don't *see* how she could do worse, unless she went to old Nick for a mate. Now, I'll tell you what it is, my man. I've been in trouble myself, and don't want to be hard on a poor devil, just because he sails under an alias, and lies as near the wind as he can, to weather on the beaks and the bobbies. But one good turn deserves another: keep your dirty suspicions to yourself; for if you dare to open your lips to the men, in five minutes, or less than that, you shall be in irons, and confined to your cabin; and we'll put you ashore at the first port that flies a British flag, and hand you over to the authorities, till one of her Majesty's cruisers sends in a boat for you."

At this threat Mr. Hazel hung his head in confusion and dismay.

"Come, get out of my cabin, Parson Alias," shouted the mate; "and belay your foul tongue in this ship, and don't make an enemy of Joe Wylie, a man that will eat you up else, and spit you out again, and never brag. Sheer off, I say, and be d—d to you."

Mr. Hazel, with a pale face and sick heart, looked aghast at this dangerous man, who could be fox, or tiger, as the occasion demanded.

Surprised, alarmed, outwitted, and out-menaced, he retired with disordered countenance, and uneven steps, and hid himself in his own cabin.

The more he weighed the whole situation, the more clearly did he see that he was utterly powerless in the hands of Wylie.

A skipper is an emperor; and Hudson had the power to iron him, and set him on shore at the nearest port. The right to do it was another matter; but even on that head, Wylie could furnish a plausible excuse for the act. Retribution, if it came at all, would not be severe, and would be three or four years coming: and who fears it much, when it is so dilatory, and so weak, and so doubtful into the bargain?

He succumbed in silence for two days; and then, in spite of Wylie's threat, he made one timid attempt to approach the subject with Welch and Cooper, but a sailor came up instantly, and sent them forward to reef topsails. And whenever he tried to enter into conversation with the pair, some sailor or other was sure to come up and listen.

Then he saw that he was spotted; or, as we say nowadays, picketed.

He was at his wits' end.

He tried his last throw. He wrote a few lines to Miss Rolleston, requesting an interview. Aware of the difficulties he had to encounter here, he stilled his heart by main force, and wrote in terms carefully measured. He begged her to believe he had no design to intrude upon her, without absolute necessity, and for her own good. Respect for her own wishes forbade this, and also his self-respect. "But," said he, "I have made a terrible discovery. The mate and the captain certainly intend to cast away this ship. No doubt they will try and not sacrifice their own lives and ours; but risk them they must, in the very nature of things. Before troubling you, I have tried all I could, in the way of persuasion and menace; but am defeated. So now it rests with you. You, alone, can save us all. I will tell you how, if you will restrain your repugnance, and accord me a short interview. Need I say that no other subject shall be introduced by me. In England, should we ever reach it, I may perhaps try to take measures to regain your good opinion; but here, I am aware, that is impossible; and I shall make no attempt in that direction upon my honor."

To this, came a prompt and feminine reply: —

"The ship is *his*. The captain and the mate are able men, appointed by *him*. Your suspicions of these poor men are calumnies, and of a piece with your other monstrous slanders.

"I really must insist on your holding no further communication of any sort with one, to whom your character is revealed and odious. H. R."

This letter benumbed his heart at first. A letter? It was a blow; a blow from her he loved, and she hated him!

His long-suffering love gave way at last. What folly and cruelty combined! He could no longer make allowances for the spite of a woman whose lover had been traduced. Rage and despair seized him; he bit his nails, and tore his hair with fury; and prayed Heaven to help him hate her as she deserved, "the blind, insolent idiot!" Yes, these bitter words actually came out of his mouth, in a torrent of fury.

But, to note down all he said, in his rage, would be useless; and might mislead, for this was a gust of fury; and, while it lasted, the long-suffering man was no longer himself.

As a proof how little this state of mind was natural to him, it stirred up all the bile in his body, and brought on a severe attack of yellow jaundice, accompanied by the settled dejection that marks that disorder.

Meantime the Proserpine glided on, with a fair wind, and a contented crew. She was well found in stores; and they were served out ungrudgingly.

Every face on board beamed with jollity, except poor Hazel's. He crept about, yellow as a guinea; a very scarecrow.

The surgeon, a humane man, urged him to drink sherry, and take strong exercise.

But persons afflicted with that distressing malady, are obstinately set against those things which tend to cure it; this is a feature of the disease. Mr. Hazel was no exception. And then his heart had received so many blows, it had no power left to resist the depressing effect of his disorder. He took no exercise; he ate little food. He lay, listless and dejected, about the deck, and let disease do what it pleased with him.

The surgeon shook his head, and told Hudson the parson was booked.

"And good riddance of bad rubbish!" was that worthy's gracious comment.

The ship now encountered an adverse gale, and, for three whole days, was under close-reefed topsails; she was always a wet ship under stress of weather; and she took in a good deal of water on this occasion. On the fourth day it fell calm, and Captain Hudson, having examined the well, and found three feet of water, ordered the men to the pumps.

After working through one watch, the well was sounded again, and the water was so much reduced that the gangs were taken off; and the ship being now becalmed, and the weather lovely, the men were allowed to dance upon deck to the boatswain's fiddle.

While this pastime went on, the sun, large and red, reached the horizon, and diffused a roseate light over the entire ocean.

Not one of the current descriptions of heaven approached the actual grandeur and beauty of the blue sky flecked with ruby and gold, and its liquid mirror that lay below, calm, dimpled, and glorified by that translucent, rosy tint.

While the eye was yet charmed with this enchanting bridal of the sea and sky, and the ear amused with the merry fiddle and the nimble feet, that tapped the sounding deck so deftly at every note, Cooper, who had been sounding the well, ran forward all of a sudden, and flung a thunderbolt in the midst.

"A LEAK!"

CHAPTER X.

THE fiddle ended in mid-tune, and the men crowded aft with anxious faces.

The captain sounded the well, and found three feet and a half water in it. He ordered all hands to the pumps.

They turned to with a good heart, and pumped, watch and watch, till daybreak.

Their exertions counteracted the leak, but did no more; the water in the well was neither more nor less perceptibly.

This was a relief to their minds, so far; but the situation was a very serious one. Suppose foul weather should come, and the vessel ship water from above as well!

Now, all those who were not on the pumps, set to work to find out the leak and stop it if possible. With candles in their hands, they crept about the ribs of the ship, narrowly inspecting every corner, and applying their ears to every suspected place, if haply they might hear the water coming in. The place where Hazel had found Wylie at work was examined, along with the rest; but neither there nor anywhere else could the leak be discovered. Yet the water was still coming in, and required unremitting labor to keep it under. It was then suggested by Wylie, and the opinion gradually gained ground, that some of the seams had opened in the late gale, and were letting in the water by small but numerous apertures.

Faces began to look cloudy; and Hazel, throwing off his lethargy, took his spell at the main pump with the rest.

When his gang was relieved he went away, bathed in perspiration, and, leaning over the well, sounded it.

While thus employed, the mate came behind him, with his cat-like step, and said, "See what has come on us with your forebodings! It is the unluckiest thing in the world to talk about losing a ship when she is at sea."

"You are a more dangerous man on board a ship than I am," was Hazel's prompt reply.

The well gave an increase of three inches.

Mr. Hazel now showed excellent qualities. He worked like a horse; and, finding the mate skulking, he reproached him before the men, and, stripping himself naked to the waist, invited him to do a man's duty. The mate, thus challenged, complied with a scowl.

They labored for their lives, and the quantity of water they discharged from the ship was astonishing; not less than a hundred and ten tons every hour.

They gained upon the leak — only two inches; but, in the struggle for life, this was an immense victory. It was the turn of the tide.

A slight breeze sprung up from the southwest, and the captain ordered the men from the buckets to make all sail on the ship, the pumps still going.

When this was done, he altered the ship's course, and put her right before the wind, steering for the island of Juan Fernandez, distant eleven hundred miles, or thereabouts.

Probably it was the best thing he could do, in that awful waste of water. But its effect on the seamen was bad. It was like giving in. They got a little disheartened and flurried; and the cold, passionless water seized the advantage. It is possible, too, that the motion of the ship through the sea, aided the leak.

"The Proserpine glided through the water all night, like some terror-stricken creature, and the incessant pumps seemed to be her poor heart, beating loud with breathless fear.

At daybreak she had gone a hundred and twenty miles. But this was balanced by a new and alarming feature. The water from the pumps no longer came up pure, but mixed with what appeared to be blood.

This got redder and redder, and struck terror into the more superstitious of the crew.

Even Cooper, whose heart was stout, leaned over the bulwarks, and eyed the red stream, gushing into the sea from the lee scuppers, and said aloud, "Ay, bleed to death, ye bitch! We sha'n't be long behind ye."

Hazel inquired, and found the ship had a quantity of dye-wood amongst her cargo; he told the men this, and tried to keep up their hearts by his words and his example.

He succeeded with some; but others shook their heads. And by and by, even while he was working double tides for them as well as for himself, ominous murmurs met his ear. "Parson aboard!" "Man aboard, with t' other world in his face!" And there were sinister glances to match.

He told this with some alarm, to Welch and Cooper. They promised to stand by him; and Welch told him it was all the mate's doing; he had gone amongst the men, and poisoned them.

The wounded vessel, with her ever-beating heart, had run three hundred miles on the new tack. She had almost ceased to bleed; but what was as bad, or worse, small fragments of her cargo and stores came up with the water, and their miscellaneous character showed how deeply the sea had now penetrated.

This, and their great fatigue, began to demoralize the sailors. The pumps and buckets were still plied, but it was no longer with the uniform manner of brave and hopeful men. Some stuck doggedly to their work, but others got flurried, and ran from one thing to another. Now and then a man would stop, and burst out crying; then to work again in a desperate way. One or two lost heart altogether, and had to be driven. Finally, one or two succumbed under the unremitting labor. Despair crept over others: their features began to change, so much so, that several countenances were hardly recognizable, and each, looking in the other's troubled face, saw his own fate pictured there.

Six feet water in the hold!

The captain, who had been sober beyond his time, now got dead drunk.

The mate took the command. On hearing this, Welch and Cooper left the pumps. Wylie ordered them back. They refused, and coolly lighted their pipes. A violent altercation took place, which was brought to a close by Welch.

"It is no use pumping the ship," said he. "She is doomed. D' ye think we are blind, my mate and me? You got the long-boat ready for yourself before ever the leak was sprung. Now get the cutter ready for my mate and me."

At these simple words Wylie lost color, and walked aft without a word.

Next day there were seven feet water in the hold, and quantities of bread coming up through the pumps.

Wylie ordered the men from the pumps to the boats. The jolly-boat was provisioned and lowered. While she was towing astern, the cutter was prepared, and the ship left to fill.

All this time Miss Rolleston had been kept in the dark, not as to the danger, but as to its extent. Great was her surprise when Mr. Hazel entered her cabin, and cast an ineffable look of pity on her.

She looked up surprised and then angry. "How dare you?" she began.

He waved his hand in a sorrowful but commanding way. "O, this is no time for prejudice or temper. The ship is sinking: we are going into the boats. Pray make your preparations. Here is a list I have written of the things you ought to take: we may be weeks at sea in an open boat."

Then, seeing her dumbfoundered, he caught up her carpet-bag, and threw her work-box into it for a beginning. He then laid hands upon some of her preserved meats, and marmalade, and carried them off to his own cabin.

His mind then flew back to his reading, and passed in rapid review, all the wants that men had endured in open boats.

He got hold of Welch, and told him to be sure and see there was plenty of spare canvas on board, and sailing needles, scissors, etc.: also three bags of biscuit, and, above all, a cask of water.

He himself ran all about the ship, including the mate's cabin, in search of certain tools he thought would be wanted.

Then to his own cabin, to fill his carpet-bag.

There was little time to spare; the ship was low in the water, and the men abandoning her. He flung the things into his bag, fastened and locked it, strapped up his blankets for her use, flung on his pea-jacket, and turned the handle of his door to run out.

The door did not open!

He pushed it. It did not yield!

He rushed at it. It was fast!

He uttered a cry of rage, and flung himself at it.

Horror! It was immovable.

CHAPTER XI.

The fearful, the sickening truth burst on him in all its awful significance.

Some miscreant or madman had locked the door, and so fastened him to the sinking ship, at a time when, in the bustle, the alarm, the selfishness, all would be apt to forget him, and leave him to his death.

He tried the door in every way, he hammered at it; he shouted, he raged, he screamed. In vain. Unfortunately the door of this cabin was of very unusual strength and thickness.

Then he took up one of those great augers he had found in the mate's cabin, and bored a hole in the door; through this hole he fired his pistol, and then screamed for help. "I am shut up in the cabin. I shall be drowned. O, for Christ's sake, save me! save me!" and a cold sweat of terror poured down his whole body.

What is that?

The soft rustle of a woman's dress.

O, how he thanked God for that music, and the hope it gave him!

It comes towards him; it stops, the key is turned, the dress rustles away, swift as a winged bird; he dashes at the door; it flies open.

Nobody was near. He recovered his courage in part, fetched out his bag and his tools, and ran across to the starboard side. There he found the captain lowering Miss Rolleston, with due care, into the cutter, and the young lady crying; not at being shipwrecked, if you please, but at being deserted by her maid. Jane Holt, at this trying moment, had deserted her mistress for her husband. This was natural; but, as is the rule with persons of that class, she had done this in the silliest and cruelest way. Had she given half an hour's notice of her intention, Donovan might have been on board the cutter with her and her mistress. But no; being a liar and a fool, she must hide her husband to the last moment, and then desert her mistress. The captain, then, was comforting Miss Rolleston, and telling her she should have her maid with her eventually, when Hazel came; he handed down his own bag, and threw the blankets into the stern-sheets. Then went down himself, and sat on the midship-thwart.

"Shove off," said the captain; and they fell astern.

But Cooper, with a boat-hook, hooked on to the long-boat; and the dying ship towed them both.

Five minutes more elapsed, and the captain did not come down, so Wylie hailed him.

There was no answer. Hudson had gone into the mate's cabin. Wylie waited a minute, then hailed again. "Hy! on deck there!"

"Hullo!" cried the captain, at last.

"Why did n't you come in the cutter?"

The captain crossed his arms, and leaned over the stern.

"Don't you know that Hiram Hudson is always the last to leave a sinking ship?"

"Well, you *are* the last," said Wylie. "So now come on board the long-boat at once. I dare not tow in her wake much longer, to be sucked in when she goes down."

"Come on board your craft and desert my own?" said Hudson, disdainfully. "Know my duty to m'employers better."

These words alarmed the mate. "Curse it all!" he cried; "the fool has been and got some more rum. Fifty guineas to the man that will shin up the tow-rope, and throw that madman into the sea, then we can pick him up. He swims like a cork."

A sailor instantly darted forward to the rope. But, unfortunately, Hudson heard this proposal, and it enraged him. He got to his cutlass. The sailor drew the boat under the ship's stern, but the drunken skipper flourished his cutlass furiously over his head. "Board *me!* ye pirates! the first that lays a finger on my bulwarks, off goes his hand at the wrist." Suiting the action to the word, he hacked at the tow-rope so vigorously that it gave way, and the boats fell astern.

Helen Rolleston uttered a shriek of dismay and pity. "O, save him!" she cried.

"Make sail!" cried Cooper; and, in a few seconds, they got all her canvas set upon the cutter.

It seemed a hopeless chase for these shells to sail after that dying monster with her cloud of canvas all drawing, alow and aloft.

"But it did not prove so. The gentle breeze was an advantage to light craft, and the dying Proserpine was full of water, and could only crawl.

After a few moments of great anxiety, the boats crept up, the cutter on her port, and the long-boat on her starboard-quarter.

Wylie ran forward, and, hailing Hudson, implored him, in the friendliest tones, to give himself a chance. Then tried him by his vanity, "Come, and command the boats, old fellow. How can we navigate them on the Pacific, without *you?*"

Hudson was now leaning over the taffrail utterly drunk. He made no reply to the mate, but merely waived his cutlass feebly in one hand, and his bottle in the other, and gurgled out "Duty to m'employers."

Then Cooper, without a word, double-reefed the cutter's mainsail, and told Welch to keep as close to the ship's quarter as he dare. Wylie instinctively did the same, and the three craft crawled on, in solemn and deadly silence, for nearly twenty minutes.

The wounded ship seemed to receive a death-blow. She stopped dead, and shook.

The next moment she pitched gently forward, and her bows went under the water, while her after-part rose into the air, and revealed to those in the cutter two splintered holes in her run, just below the water-line.

The next moment her stern settled down; the sea yawned horribly, the great waves of her own making rushed over her upper deck, and the lofty masts and sails, remaining erect, went down with sad majesty into the deep: and nothing remained but the bubbling and foaming of the voracious water, that had swallowed up the good ship and her cargo, and her drunken master.

All stood up in the boats, ready to save him. But either his cutlass sunk him, or the suction of so great a body drew him down. He was seen no more in this world.

A loud sigh broke from every living bosom that witnessed that terrible catastrophe.

It was beyond words: and none were uttered, except by Cooper, who spoke so seldom; yet now three words of terrible import burst from him, and, uttered in his loud, deep voice, rang like the sunk ship's knell over the still bubbling water,—

"SCUTTLED,—BY GOD!"

CHAPTER XII.

"HOLD your tongue," said Welch, with an oath.

Mr. Hazel looked at Miss Rolleston, and she at him. It was a momentary glance, and her eyes sank directly, and filled with patient tears.

For the first few minutes after the Proserpine went down, the survivors sat benumbed, as if awaiting their turn to be ingulfed.

They seemed so little, and the Proserpine so big; yet she was swallowed before their eyes, like a crumb. They lost, for a few moments, all idea of escaping.

But, true it is, that, "while there 's life there 's hope": and, as soon as their hearts began to beat again, their eyes roved round the horizon, and their elastic minds recoiled against despair.

This was rendered easier, by the wonderful beauty of the weather. There were men there, who had got down from a sinking ship, into boats heaving and tossing against her side in a gale of wind, and yet been saved: and here all was calm and delightful. To be sure, in those other shipwrecks, land had been near, and their greatest peril was over, when once the boats got clear of the distressed ship without capsizing. Here was no immediate peril; but certain death menaced them, at an uncertain distance.

Their situation was briefly this. Should it come on to blow a gale, these open boats, small and loaded, could not hope to live. Therefore they had two chances for life, and no more: they must either make land,—or be picked up at sea,—before the weather changed.

But how? The nearest known land was the group of islands called Juan Fernandez, and they lay somewhere to leeward; but distant, at least, nine hundred miles: and, should they prefer the other chance, then they must beat three hundred miles, and more to windward; for Hudson underrating the leak, as is supposed, had run the Proserpine fully that distance out of the track of trade.

Now the ocean is a highway—in law: but, in fact, it contains a few highways, and millions of by-ways; and, once a cockle-shell gets into those by-ways, small indeed is its chance of being seen and picked up by any sea-going vessel.

Wylie, who was leading, lowered his sail, and hesitated between the two courses we have indicated. However, on the cutter coming up with him, he ordered Cooper to keep her head north-east, and so run all night. He then made all the sail he could, in the same direction, and soon outsailed the cutter. When the sun went down, he was about a mile ahead of her.

Just before sunset, Mr. Hazel made a discovery that annoyed him very much. He found that Welch had put only one bag of biscuit, a ham, a keg of spirit, and a small barrel of water, on board the cutter.

He remonstrated with him sharply. Welch replied that it was all right; the cutter being small, he had put the rest of her provisions on board the long-boat.

"On board the long-boat!" said Hazel, with a look of wonder. "You have actually made our lives depend upon that scoundrel Wylie again. You deserve to be flung into the sea. You have no forethought yourself: yet you will not be guided by those that have it."

Welch hung his head a little at these reproaches. However, he replied, rather sullenly, that it was only for one night; they could signal the long-boat in the morning, and get the other bags, and the cask, out of her. But Mr. Hazel was not to be appeased. "The morning! Why, she sails three feet to our two. How do you know he won't run away from us? I never expect to get within ten miles of him again. We know him; and he knows we know him."

Cooper got up, and patted Mr. Hazel on the shoulder, soothingly. "Boat-hook aft," said he to Welch.

He then, by an ingenious use of the boat-hook, and some of the spare canvas, contrived to set out a studding-sail on the other side of the mast.

Hazel thanked him warmly. "But, O Cooper! Cooper!" said he, "I'd give all I have in the world if that bread and water were on board the cutter instead of the long-boat."

The cutter had now two wings, instead of one; the water bubbling loud under her bows marked her increased speed; and all fear of being greatly outsailed by her consort began to subside.

A slight sea-fret came on, and obscured the sea in part; but they had a good lantern and compass, and steered the course exactly, all night, according to Wylie's orders, changing the helmsman every four hours.

Mr. Hazel, without a word, put a rug round Miss Rolleston's shoulders, and another round her feet.

"O, not both, sir, please," said she.

"Am I to be disobeyed by everybody?" said he.

Then she submitted in silence, and in a certain obsequious way that was quite new, and well calculated to disarm anger.

Sooner or later, all slept, except the helmsman.

At daybreak, Mr. Hazel was wakened by a loud hail from a man in the bows.

All the sleepers started up.

"Long-boat not in sight!"

It was too true. The ocean was blank: not a sail, large or small, in sight.

ON SHIPBOARD.—See page 23.

Many voices spoke at once.

"He was carried on till he has capsized her."

"He has given us the slip."

Unwilling to believe so great a calamity, every eye peered and stared all over the sea. In vain. Not a streak that could be a boat's hull, not a speck that could be a sail.

The little cutter was alone upon the ocean. Alone, with scarcely two days' provisions, nine hundred miles from land, and four hundred miles to leeward of the nearest sea-road.

Hazel, seeing his worst forebodings realized, sat down in moody, bitter, and boding silence.

Of the other men some raged and cursed. Some wept aloud.

The lady, more patient, put her hands together, and prayed to Him who made the sea and all that therein is. Yet her case was the cruelest. For she was by nature more timid than the men, yet she must share their desperate peril. And then to be alone with all these men, and one of them had told her he loved her, and hated the man she was betrothed to! Shame tortured this delicate creature, as well as fear. Happy for her, that of late, and only of late, she had learned to pray in earnest. "Qui precari novit, premi potest, non potest opprimi."

It was now a race between starvation and drowning, and either way death stared them in the face.

CHAPTER XIII.

The long-boat was, at this moment, a hundred miles to windward of the cutter.

The fact is, that Wylie, the evening before, had been secretly perplexed as to the best course. He had decided to run for the island; but he was not easy under his own decision; and, at night, he got more and more discontented with it. Finally, at nine o'clock, P. M. he suddenly gave the order to luff, and tack: and by daybreak he was very near the place where the Proserpine went down: whereas the cutter, having run before the wind all night was, at least, a hundred miles to leeward of him.

Not to deceive the reader, or let him, for a moment, think we do business in monsters, we will weigh this act of Wylie's justly.

It was just a piece of iron egotism. He preferred, for himself, the chance of being picked up by a vessel. He thought it was about a hair's breadth better than running for an island, as to whose bearing he was not very clear, after all.

But he was not *sure* he was taking the best or safest course. The cutter might be saved, after all, and the long-boat lost.

Meantime he was not sorry of an excuse to shake off the cutter. She contained one man at least who knew he had scuttled the Proserpine; and therefore it was all-important to him to get to London before her, and receive the three thousand pounds, which was to be his reward for that abominable act.

But the way to get to London before Mr. Hazel, or else to the bottom of the Pacific before him, was to get back into the sea-road, at all hazards.

He was not aware that the cutter's water and biscuit were on board his boat; nor did he discover this till noon next day. And, on making this fearful discovery, he showed himself human: he cried out, with an oath, "What have I done? I have damned myself to all eternity!"

He then ordered the boat to be put before the wind again; but the men scowled, and not one stirred a finger; and he saw the futility of this, and did not persist: but groaned aloud: and then sat, staring wildly: finally, like a true sailor, he got to the rum, and stupefied his agitated conscience for a time.

While he lay drunk, at the bottom of the boat, his sailors carried out his last instructions, beating southward right in the wind's eye.

Five days they beat to windward, and never saw a sail. Then it fell dead calm; and so remained for three days more.

The men began to suffer greatly from cramps, owing to their number and confined position. During the calm, they rowed all day, and with this, and a light westerly breeze that sprung up, they got into the sea-road again: but having now sailed three hundred and fifty miles to the southward, they found a great change in the temperature: the nights were so cold they were fain to huddle together, to keep a little warmth in their bodies.

On the fifteenth day of their voyage it began to rain and blow, and then they were never a whole minute out of peril. Hand forever on the sheet, eye on the waves, to ease her at the right moment: and, with all this care, the spray eternally flying half way over her mast, and often a body of water making a clean breach over her, and the men bailing night and day with their very hats, or she could not have lived an hour.

At last, when they were almost dead with wet, cold, fatigue, and danger, a vessel came in sight, and crept slowly up, about two miles to windward of the distressed boat. With the heave of the waters they could see little more than her sails; but they ran up a bright bandana handkerchief to their mast-head; and the ship made them out. She hoisted Dutch colors, and — continued her course.

Then the poor abandoned creatures wept, and raved, and cursed, in their frenzy, glaring after that cruel, shameless man, who could do such an act, yet hoist a color, and show of what nation he was the native — and the disgrace.

But one of them said not a word. This was Wylie. He sat shivering, and remembered how he had abandoned the cutter, and all on board. Loud sighs broke from his laboring breast; but not a word. Yet one word was ever present to his mind; and seemed written in fire on the night of clouds, and howled in his ears by the wind — Retribution!

And now came a dirty night — to men on ships; a fearful night to men in boats. The sky black, the sea on fire with crested billows, that broke over them every minute; their light was washed out; their provisions drenched and spoiled: bail as they would, the boat was always filling. Up to their knees in water; cold as ice, blinded with spray, deafened with roaring billows, they tossed and tumbled in a fiery foaming hell of waters, and still, though despairing, clung to their lives, and bailed with their hats unceasingly.

Day broke, and the first sight it revealed to them was a brig to windward staggering along, and pitching under close-reefed topsails.

They started up, and waved their hats, and cried aloud. But the wind carried their voices to leeward, and the brig staggered on.

They ran up their little signal of distress; but still the ship staggered on.

Then the miserable men shook hands all round, and gave themselves up for lost.

But, at this moment, the brig hoisted a vivid flag all stripes and stars, and altered her course a point or two.

She crossed the boat's track a mile ahead, and her people looked over the bulwarks, and waved their hats to encourage those tossed and desperate men.

Having thus given them the weather-gage the brig hove-to for them.

They ran down to her, and crept under her lee; down came ropes to them, held by friendly hands, and friendly faces shone down at them: eager grasps seized each as he went up the ship's side, and so, in a very short time, they sent the woman up, and the rest being all sailors, and clever as cats, they were safe on board the whaling brig Maria, Captain Slocum, of Nantucket, U. S.

Their log, compass, and instruments were also saved.

The boat was cast adrift, and was soon after seen bottom upwards on the crest of a wave.

The good Samaritan in command of the Maria supplied them with dry clothes out of the ship's stores, good food, and medical attendance, which was much needed, their legs and feet being in a deplorable condition, and their own surgeon crippled.

A southeasterly gale induced the American skipper to give Cape Horn a wide berth, and the Maria soon found herself three degrees south of that perilous coast. There she encountered field-ice. In this labyrinth they dodged and worried for eighteen days, until a sudden chop in the wind gave the captain a chance, of which he promptly availed himself; and in forty hours they sighted Terra del Fuego.

During this time, the rescued crew having recovered from the effects of their hardships, fell in to the work of the ship, and took their turns with the Yankee seamen. The brig was short-handed; but now trimmed and handled by a full crew and the Proserpine's men, who were first-class seamen, and worked with a will, because work was no longer a duty, she exhibited a speed the captain had almost forgotten was in the craft. Now speed at sea means economy, for every day added to a voyage is so much off the profits. Slocum was part owner of the vessel, and shrewdly alive to the value of the seamen. When about three hundred miles south of Buenos Ayres, Wylie proposed that they should be landed there, from whence they might be transshipped to a vessel bound for home.

This was objected to by Slocum, on the ground that, by such a deviation from his course, he must lose three days, and the port-dues at Buenos Ayres were heavy.

Wylie undertook that the house of Wardlaw and Son should indemnify the brig for all expenses and losses incurred.

Still the American hesitated; at last he honestly told Wylie he wished to keep the men; he liked them, they liked him. He had sounded them, and they had no objection to join his ship, and sign articles for a three years' whaling voyage, provided they did not thereby forfeit the wages to which they would be entitled on reaching Liverpool. Wylie went forward and asked the men if they would take service with the Yankee captain. All but three expressed their desire to do so; these three had families in England, and refused. The mate gave the others a release, and an order on Wardlaw and Co. for their full wages for the voyage; then they signed articles with Captain Slocum, and entered the American Mercantile Navy.

Two days after this they sighted the high lands at the mouth of the Rio de la Plata at 10 P. M., and lay-to for a pilot. After three hours' delay they were boarded by a pilot-boat, and then began to creep into the port. The night was very dark, and a thin white fog lay on the water.

Wylie was sitting on the taffrail, and conversing with Slocum, when the look-out forward sung out, "Sail ho!"

Another voice almost simultaneously yelled out of the fog, "Port your helm!"

Suddenly out of the mist, and close aboard the Maria, appeared the hull and canvas of a large ship. The brig was crossing her course, and her great bowsprit barely missed the brig's mainsail. It stood for a moment over Wylie's head. He looked up, and there was the figure-head of the ship looming almost within his reach. It was a colossal green woman; one arm extended grasped a golden harp, the other was pressed to her head in the attitude of holding back her wild and flowing hair. The face seemed to glare down upon the two men: in another moment the monster, gliding on, just missing the brig, was lost in the fog.

"That was a narrow squeak," said Slocum.

Wylie made no answer, but looked into the darkness after the vessel.

He had recognized her figure-head.

It was the Shannon!

CHAPTER XIV.

Before the Maria sailed again, with the men who formed a part of Wylie's crew, he made them sign a declaration before the English Consul at Buenos Ayres. This document set forth the manner in which the Proserpine foundered; it was artfully made up of facts enough to deceive a careless listener; but, when Wylie read it over to them, he slurred over certain parts, which he took care, also, to express in language above the comprehension of such men. Of course, they assented eagerly to what they did not understand, and signed the statement conscientiously.

So Wylie and his three men were shipped on board the Boadicea, bound for Liverpool, in Old England, while the others sailed with Captain Slocum for Nantucket, in New England.

The Boadicea was a clipper laden with hides, and a miscellaneous cargo. For seventeen days she flew before a southerly gale, being on her best sailing point, and after one of the shortest passages she had ever made, she lay-to outside the bar, off the Mersey. It wanted but one hour to daylight, the tide was flowing; the pilot sprang aboard.

"What do you draw?" he asked of the master.

"Fifteen feet, barely," was the reply.

"That will do," and the vessel's head was laid for the river.

They passed a large bark, with her top-sails backed.

"Ay," remarked the pilot, "she has waited since the half-ebb; there ain't more than four hours in the twenty-four that such craft as that can get in."

"What is she? An American liner?" asked Wylie, peering through the gloom.

"No," said the pilot; "she 's an Australian ship. She 's the Shannon, from Sydney."

The mate started, looked at the man, then at the

vessel. Twice the Shannon had thus met him, as if to satisfy him that his object had been attained, and each time she seemed to him not an inanimate thing, but a silent accomplice. A chill of fear struck through the man's frame as he looked at her. Yes, there she lay, and in her hold were safely stowed £160,000 in gold, marked lead and copper.

Wylie had no luggage nor effects to detain him on board; he landed, and having bestowed his three companions in a sailors' boarding-house, he was hastening to the shipping agents of Wardlaw and Son to announce his arrival and the fate of the Proserpine. He had reached their offices in Water Street before he recollected that it was barely half past five o'clock, and, though broad daylight on that July morning, merchants' offices are not open at that hour. The sight of the Shannon had so bewildered him that he had not noticed that the shops were all shut, the streets deserted. Then a thought occurred to him, — why not be a bearer of his own news? He did not require to turn the idea twice over, but resolved, for many reasons, to adopt it. As he hurried to the railway-station, he tried to recollect the hour at which the early train started; but his confused and excited mind refused to perform the function of memory. The Shannon dazed him.

At the railway-station he found that a train had started at 4 A. M., and there was nothing until 7.30. This check sobered him a little, and he went back to the docks; he walked out to the farther end of that noble line of berths, and sat down on the verge with his legs dangling over the water. He waited an hour; it was six o'clock by the great dial at St. George's Dock. His eyes were fixed on the Shannon, which was moving slowly up the river; she came abreast to where he sat. The few sails requisite to give her steerage fell. Her anchor-chain rattled, and she swung round with the tide. The clock struck the half hour; a boat left the side of the vessel and made straight for the steps near where he was seated. A tall, noble-looking man sat in the stern-sheets beside the coxswain; he was put ashore, and, after exchanging a few words with the boat's crew, he mounted the steps which led him to Wylie's side, followed by one of the sailors, who carried a portmanteau.

He stood for a single moment on the quay, and stamped his foot on the broad stones; then heaving a deep sigh of satisfaction, he murmured, "Thank God!"

He turned towards Wylie.

"Can you tell me, my man, at what hour the first train starts for London?"

"There is a slow train at 7.30 and an express at 9."

"The express will serve me, and give me time for breakfast at the Adelphi. Thank you; good morning": and the gentleman passed on, followed by the sailor.

Wylie looked after him; he noted that erect military carriage and crisp, gray hair and thick white mustache; he had a vague idea that he had seen that face before, and the memory troubled him.

At 7.30 Wylie started for London; the military man followed him in the express at 9, and caught him up at Rugby; together they arrived at the station at Euston Square; it was a quarter to three. Wylie hailed a cab, but before he could struggle through the crowd to reach it a railway porter threw a portmanteau on its roof, and his military acquaintance took possession of it.

"All right," said the porter. "What address, sir?"

Wylie did not hear what the gentleman said, but the porter shouted it to the cabman, and then he did hear it.

"No. —, Russell Square."

It was the house of Arthur Wardlaw!

Wylie took off his hat, rubbed his frowsy hair, and gaped after the cab.

He entered another cab, and told the driver to go to "No. —, Fenchurch Street."

It was the office of Wardlaw and Son.

CHAPTER XV.

Our scene now changes from the wild ocean and its perils, to a snug room in Fenchurch Street; the inner office of Wardlaw and Son: a large apartment, panelled with fine old mellow Spanish oak; and all the furniture in keeping; the carpet, a thick Axminster of sober colors; the chairs, of oak and morocco, very substantial; a large office-table, with oaken legs like very columns, substantial; two Milner safes; a globe of unusual size, with a handsome tent over it, made of roan leather, figured; the walls hung with long oak boxes, about eight inches broad, containing rolled maps of high quality, and great dimensions; to consult which, oaken sceptres tipped with brass hooks stood ready: with these, the great maps could be drawn down and inspected; and, on being released, flew up into their wooden boxes again. Besides these were hung up a few drawings, representing outlines, and inner sections, of vessels: and, on a smaller table, lay models, almanacs, etc. The great office-table was covered with writing materials and papers, all but a square space enclosed with a little silver rail, and inside that space lay a purple morocco case about ten inches square; it was locked, and contained an exquisite portrait of Helen Rolleston.

This apartment was so situated, and the frames of the plate glass windows so well made and substantial, that, let a storm blow a thousand ships ashore, it could not be felt, nor heard, in Wardlaw's inner office.

But appearances are deceitful; and who can wall out a sea of troubles, and the tempests of the mind?

The inmate of that office was battling for his commercial existence, under accumulated difficulties and dangers. Like those who sailed the Proserpine's long-boat, upon that dirty night, which so nearly swamped her, his eye had now to be on every wave, and the sheet forever in his hand.

His measures had been ably taken; but, as will happen when clever men are driven into a corner, he had backed events rather too freely against time; had allowed too slight a margin for unforeseen delays. For instance, he had averaged the Shannon's previous performances, and had calculated on her arrival too nicely. She was a fortnight overdue, and that delay brought peril.

He had also counted upon getting news of the Proserpine. But not a word had reached Lloyd's as yet.

At this very crisis came the panic of '66. Overend and Gurney broke; and Wardlaw's experience led him to fear that, sooner or later, there would be a run on every bank in London. Now he had borrowed £80,000 at one bank, and £35,000 at another: and, without his ships, could not possibly pay a quarter of the money. If the banks in question were run upon, and obliged to call in all their resources, his credit must go; and this, in his precarious position, was ruin.

He had concealed his whole condition from his father, by false book-keeping. Indeed, he had only two confidants in the world; poor old Michael Penfold, and Helen Rolleston's portrait; and even to these two he made half confidences. He dared not tell either of them all he had done, and all he was going to do.

His redeeming feature was as bright as ever. He still loved Helen Rolleston with a chaste, constant, and ardent affection that did him honor. He loved money too well: but he loved Helen better. In all his troubles and worries, it was his one consolation, to unlock her portrait, and gaze on it, and purify his soul for a few minutes. Sometimes he would apologize to it, for an act of doubtful morality. "How can I risk the loss of you?" was his favorite excuse. No: he must have credit. He must have money. She must not suffer by his past imprudences. They must be repaired, at any cost — for her sake.

It was ten o'clock in the morning: Mr. Penfold was sorting the letters for his employer, when a buxom young woman rushed into the outer office, crying "O Mr. Penfold!" and sank into a chair, breathless.

"Dear heart! what is the matter now?" said the old gentleman.

"I have had a dream, sir: I dreamed I saw Joe Wylie out on the seas, in a boat; and the wind it was a blowing and the sea a roaring to that degree as Joe looked at me, and says he, 'Pray for me, Nancy Rouse.' "So I says, 'O dear, Joe, what is the matter? and whatever is become of the Proserpine?'

"'Gone to Hell!' says he: which he knows I object to foul language. 'Gone — *there* —' says he, 'and I am sailing in her wake. O pray for me, Nancy Rouse!' With that, I tries to pray in my dream, and screams instead, and wakes myself. O Mr. Penfold, do tell me, have you got any news of the Proserpine this morning?"

"What is that to you?" inquired Arthur Wardlaw, who had entered just in time to hear this last query.

"What is it to me!" cried Nancy, firing up; "it is more to me, perhaps, than it is to you, for that matter."

Penfold explained, timidly, "Sir, Mrs. Rouse is my landlady."

"Which I have never been to church with any man yet of the name of Rouse, leastways, not in my waking hours," edged in the lady.

"Miss Rouse, I should say," said Penfold, apologizing. "I beg pardon, but I thought Mrs. might sound better in a landlady. Please, sir, Mr. Wylie, the mate of the Proserpine, is her — her — sweetheart."

"Not he. Leastways, he is only on trial, after a manner."

"Of course, sir — only after a manner," added Penfold, sadly perplexed. "Miss Rouse is incapable of anything else. But, if you please m'm, I don't presume to know the exact relation"; — and then with great reserve — "but, you know you are anxious about him."

Miss Rouse sniffed, and threw her nose in the air, — as if to throw a doubt even on that view of the matter.

"Well, madam," says Wardlaw, "I am sorry to say I can give you no information. I share your anxiety, for I have got £160,000 of gold in the ship. You might inquire at Lloyd's. Direct her there, Mr. Penfold, and bring me my letters."

With this he entered his inner office, sat down, took out a golden key, opened the portrait of Helen, gazed at it, kissed it, uttered a deep sigh, and prepared to face the troubles of the day.

Penfold brought in a leathern case, like an enormous bill-book: it had thirty vertical compartments: and the names of various cities and seaports, with which Wardlaw and Son did business, were printed in gold letters on some of these compartments; on others, the names of persons; and on two compartments, the word "Miscellaneous." Michael brought this machine in, filled with a correspondence, enough to break a man's heart to look at.

This was one of the consequences of Wardlaw's position. He durst not let his correspondence be read, and filtered, in the outer office: he opened the whole mass; sent some back into the outer office: then touched a hand-bell, and a man emerged from the small apartment adjoining his own. This was Mr. Atkins, his shorthand writer. He dictated to this man some twenty letters, which were taken down in shorthand; the man retired to copy them, and write them out in duplicate from his own notes, and this reduced the number to seven: these Wardlaw sat down to write, himself, and lock up the copies.

While he was writing them, he received a visitor or two, whom he despatched as quickly as his letters.

He was writing his last letter, when he heard in the outer office a voice he thought he knew. He got up and listened. It was so. Of all the voices in the city, this was the one it most dismayed him to hear, in his office, at the present crisis.

He listened on, and satisfied himself that a fatal blow was coming. He then walked quietly to his table, seated himself, and prepared to receive the stroke with external composure.

Penfold announced, "Mr. Burtenshaw."

"Show him in," said Wardlaw, quietly.

Mr. Burtenshaw, one of the managers of Morland's bank, came in, and Wardlaw motioned him courteously to a chair, while he finished his letter, which took only a few moments.

While he was sealing it, he half turned to his visitor, and said, "No bad news? Morland's is safe, of course."

"Well," said Burtenshaw, "there is a run upon our bank, — a severe one. We could not hope to escape the effects of the panic.

He then, after an uneasy pause, and with apparent reluctance, added, "I am requested by the other directors to assure you it is their present extremity alone, that — in short, we are really compelled to beg you to repay the amount advanced to you by the bank."

Wardlaw showed no alarm, but great surprise. This was clever; for he felt great alarm, and no surprise.

"The £81,000," said he. "Why, that advance was upon the freight of the Proserpine. Forty-five thousand ounces of gold. She ought to be here by this time. She is in the Channel at this moment, no doubt."

"Excuse me; she is overdue, and the underwriters uneasy. I have made inquiries."

"At any rate, she is fully insured, and you hold the policies. Besides, the name of Wardlaw on your books should stand for bullion."

Burtenshaw shook his head. "Names are at a discount to-day, sir. We can't pay you down on the counter. Why, our depositors look cross at Bank of England notes."

To an inquiry, half ironical, whether the managers really expected him to find £81,000 cash, at a few hours' notice, Burtenshaw replied, sorrowfully, that they felt for his difficulty whilst deploring their own; but that, after all, it was a debt: and, in short, if he could find no means of paying it, they must suspend payment for a time, and issue a statement — and —

He hesitated to complete his sentence, and Wardlaw did it for him.

"And ascribe your suspension to my inability to refund this advance?" said he, bitterly.

"I am afraid that is the construction it will bear."

Wardlaw rose, to intimate he had no more to say.

Burtenshaw, however, was not disposed to go without some clear understanding. "May I say we shall hear from you, sir?"

"Yes."

And so they wished each other good morning; and Wardlaw sank into his chair.

In that quiet dialogue, ruin had been inflicted and received without any apparent agitation; ay, and worse than ruin — exposure.

Morland's suspension, on account of money lost by Wardlaw and Son, would at once bring old Wardlaw to London, and the affairs of the firm would be investigated, and the son's false system of book-keeping be discovered.

He sat stupefied a while, then put on his hat, and rushed to his solicitor; on the way, he fell in with a great talker, who told him there was a rumor the Shannon was lost in the Pacific.

At this he nearly fainted in the street; and his friend took him back to his office in a deplorable condition. All this time he had been feigning anxiety about the Proserpine, and concealing his real anxiety about the Shannon. To do him justice, he lost sight of everything in the world now but Helen. He sent old Penfold in hot haste to Lloyd's, to inquire for news of the ship; and then he sat down sick at heart; and all he could do now was to open her portrait, and gaze at it through eyes blinded with tears. Even a vague rumor, which he hoped might be false, had driven all his commercial manœuvres out of him, and made all other calamities seem small.

And so they all are small, compared with the death of the creature we love.

While he sat thus, in a stupor of fear and grief, he heard a well-known voice in the outer office; and, next after Burtenshaw's, it was the one that caused him the most apprehension. It was his father's.

Wardlaw senior rarely visited the office now; and this was not his hour. So Arthur knew something extraordinary had brought him up to town. And he could not doubt that it was the panic, and that he had been to Morland's, or would go there in course of the day; but, indeed, it was more probable that he had already heard something, and was come to investigate.

Wardlaw senior entered the room.

"Good morning, Arthur," said he. "I've got good news for you."

Arthur was quite startled by an announcement that accorded so little with his expectations.

"Good news — for *me?*" said he, in a faint, incredulous tone.

"Ay, glorious news! Have n't you been anxious about the Shannon? I have; more anxious than I would own."

Arthur started up. "The Shannon! God bless you, father."

"She lies at anchor in the Mersey," roared the old man, with all a father's pride at bringing such good news. "Why, the Rollestons will be in London at 2.15. See, here is his telegram."

At this moment, in ran Penfold, to tell them that the Shannon was up at Lloyd's, had anchored off Liverpool last night.

There was hearty shaking of hands, and Arthur Wardlaw was the happiest man in London — for a little while.

"Got the telegram at Elm-trees, this morning, and came up by the first express," said Wardlaw senior.

The telegram was from Sir Edward Rolleston. "*Reached Liverpool last night; will be at Euston, two-fifteen.*"

"Not a word from *her!*" said Arthur.

"O, there was no time to write; and ladies do not use the telegram." He added, slyly, "Perhaps she thought coming in person would do as well, or better, eh!"

"But why does he telegraph you instead of me?"

"I am sure I don't know. What does it matter? Yes, I do know. It was settled months ago that he and Helen should come to me at Elm-trees, so I was the proper person to telegraph. I'll go and meet them at the station; there is plenty of time. But, I say, Arthur, have you seen the papers? Bartley Brothers obliged to wind up. Maple and Cox, of Liverpool, gone; Atlantic trading. Terry and Brown, suspended, International credit gone. Old friends, some of these. Hopley and Timms, railway contractors, failed, sir; liabilities, seven hundred thousand pounds and more."

"Yes, sir," said Arthur, pompously: "1866 will long be remembered for its revelations of commercial morality."

The old gentleman, on this, asked his son, with excusable vanity, whether he had done ill in steering clear of speculation; he then congratulated him on having listened to good advice, and stuck to legitimate business. "I must say, Arthur," added he, "your books are models for any trading firm."

Arthur winced in secret, under this praise, for, it occurred to him, that in a few days his father would discover those books were all a sham, and the accounts a fabrication.

However, the unpleasant topic was soon interrupted, and effectually, too; for Michael looked in, with an air of satisfaction on his benevolent countenance, and said, "Gentlemen, such an arrival! Here is Miss Rouse's sweetheart, that she dreamed was drowned."

"What is the man to me?" said Arthur, peevishly. He did not recognize Wylie under that title.

"La, Mr. Arthur! why he is the mate of the Proserpine," said Penfold.

"What! Wylie! Joseph Wylie?" cried Arthur, in a sudden excitement, that contrasted strangely with his previous indifference.

"What is that?" cried Wardlaw senior; "the Proserpine; show him in at once."

Now this caused Arthur Wardlaw considerable anxiety; for obvious reasons he did not want his father and this sailor to exchange a word together. However, that was inevitable now: the door opened, and the bronzed face and sturdv figure of Wylie, clad in a rough pea-jacket, came slouching in.

Arthur went hastily to meet him, and gave him an expressive look of warning, even while he welcomed him in cordial accents.

"Glad to see you safe home," said Wardlaw senior.

"Thank ye, guv'nor," said Wylie. "Had a squeak for it, this time."

"Where is your ship?"

Wylie shook his head sorrowfully. "Bottom of the Pacific."

"Good heavens! What; is she lost?"

"That she is, sir: foundered at sea, 1,200 miles from the Horn, and more."

"And the freight? the gold?" put in Arthur, with well-feigned anxiety.

"Not an ounce saved," said Wylie, disconsolately. "A hundred and sixty thousand pounds gone to the bottom."

"Good heavens."

"Ye see, sir," said Wylie, "the ship encountered one gale after another, and labored a good deal, first and last; and we all say her seams must have opened; for we never could find the leak that sunk her," and he cast a meaning glance at Arthur Wardlaw.

"No matter how it happened," said the old merchant: "are we insured to the full; that is the first question?"

"To the last shilling."

"Well done, Arthur."

"But still it is most unlucky. Some weeks must elapse before the insurances can be realized, and a portion of the gold was paid for in bills at short date."

"The rest in cash?"

"Cash and merchandise."

"Then there is the proper margin. Draw on my private account, at the Bank of England."

These few simple words showed the struggling young merchant a way out of all his difficulties.

His heart leaped so, he dared not reply, lest he should excite the old gentleman's suspicions.

But, ere he could well draw his breath, for joy, came a freezer.

"Mr. Burtenshaw, sir."

"Bid him wait," said Arthur aloud, and cast a look of great anxiety on Penfold, which the poor old man, with all his simplicity, comprehended well enough.

"Burtenshaw, from Morland's. What does he want of us?" said Wardlaw senior, knitting his brows.

Arthur turned cold all over. "Perhaps to ask me not to draw out my balance. It is less than usual: but they are run upon; and, as you are good enough to let me draw on you, — by the by, perhaps you will sign a check before you go to the station."

"How much do you want?"

"I really don't know, till I have consulted Penfold: the gold was a large and advantageous purchase, sir."

"No doubt; no doubt. I'll give you my signature; and you can fill in the amount."

He drew a check in favor of Arthur Wardlaw, signed it, and left him to fill in the figures.

He then looked at his watch, and remarked they would barely have time to get to the station.

"Good Heavens!" cried Arthur; "and I can't go. I must learn the particulars of the loss of the Proserpine, and prepare the statement at once for the underwriters."

"Well, never mind. *I* can go."

"But what will she think of me? I ought to be the first to welcome her."

"I'll make your excuses."

"No, no; say nothing: after all, it was you who received the telegram: so you naturally meet her but you will bring her here, father: you won't whisk my darling down to Elm-trees, till you have blest me with the sight of her."

"I will not be so cruel, fond lover," said old Wardlaw, laughing, and took up his hat and gloves to go.

Arthur went to the door with him, in great anxiety, lest he should question Burtenshaw: but, peering into the outer office, he observed Burtenshaw was not there. Michael had caught his employer's anxious look, and conveyed the Banker into the small room, where the shorthand writer was at work. But Burtenshaw was one of a struggling firm; to him every minute was an hour: he had sat, fuming with impatience, so long as he heard talking in the inner office; and, the moment it ceased, he took the liberty of coming in: so that he opened the side door, just as Wardlaw senior was passing through the centre door.

Instantly Wardlaw junior whipped before him, to hide his figure from his retreating father.

Wylie — who all this time had been sitting silent, looking from one to the other, and quietly puzzling out the game, as well as he could — observed this movement, and grinned.

As for Arthur Wardlaw, he saw his father safe out, then gave a sigh of relief, and walked to his office table, and sat down, and began to fill in the check.

Burtenshaw drew near, and said, "I am instructed to say that fifty thousand pounds on account will be accepted."

Perhaps if this proposal had been made a few seconds sooner, the ingenious Arthur would have availed himself of it: but, as it was, he preferred to take the high and mighty tone. "I decline any concession," said he. "Mr. Penfold, take this check to the Bank of England. £81,647 10*s*. that is the amount, capital and interest, up to noon this day: hand the sum to Mr. Burtenshaw, taking his receipt, or, if he prefers it, pay it across his counter, to my credit. That will perhaps arrest the run."

Burtenshaw stammered out his thanks.

Wardlaw cut him short. "Good morning, sir," said he. "I have business of *importance*. Good day," and bowed him out.

"This is a Highflyer," thought Burtenshaw.

Wardlaw then opened the side door, and called his shorthand writer.

"Mr. Atkins, please step into the outer office, and don't let a soul come in to me. Mind, I am out for the day. Except to Miss Rolleston and her father."

He then closed all the doors, and sunk exhausted into a chair, muttering, "Thank Heaven! I have got rid of them all for an hour or two. *Now*, Wylie."

Wylie seemed in no hurry to enter upon the required subject.

Said he, evasively, "Why, guv'nor, it seems to me you are among the breakers here, yourself."

"Nothing of the sort, if you have managed your work cleverly. Come, tell me all, before we are interrupted again."

"Tell ye all about it! Why there's part on't, I am afraid to think on; let alone talk about it."

"Spare me your scruples, and give me your facts," said Wardlaw, coldly. "First of all, did you succeed in shifting the bullion as agreed?"

The sailor appeared relieved by this question.

"O, that is all right," said he. "I got the bullion safe aboard the Shannon, marked for lead."

"And the lead on board the Proserpine?"

"Ay, shipped as bullion."

"Without suspicion?"

"Not quite."

"Great Heaven! Who?"

"One clerk at the shipping agent's scented something queer, I think. James Seaton. *That was the name he went by.*"

"Could he prove anything?"

"Nothing. He knew nothing for certain; and what he guessed won't never be known in England now." And Wylie fidgeted in his chair.

Notwithstanding this assurance Wardlaw looked grave, and took a note of that clerk's name. Then he begged Wylie to go on. "Give me all the details," said he. "Leave *me* to judge their relative value. You scuttled the ship?"

"Don't say that! don't say that!" cried Wylie, in a low but eager voice. "Stone walls have ears." Then rather more loudly than was necessary, "Ship sprung a leak, that neither the captain, nor I, nor anybody could find, to stop. Me and my men, we all think her seams opened, with stress of weather." Then, lowering his voice again, "Try and see it as we do; and don't you ever use such a word as that what come out of your lips just now. We pumped her hard; but 't warn't no use. She filled, and we had to take to the boats."

"Stop a moment. Was there any suspicion excited?"

"Not among the crew: and, suppose there was, I could talk 'em all over, or buy 'em all over, what few of 'em is left. I've got 'em all with me in one house: and they are all square, don't you fear."

"Well, but you said 'among the *crew!*' Whom else can we have to fear?"

"Why, nobody. To be sure, one of the passengers was down on me; but what does that matter now?"

"It matters greatly,—it matters terribly. Who was this passenger?"

"He called himself the Reverend John Hazel. He suspected something or other; and what with listening here, and watching there, he judged the ship was never to see England, and I always fancied he told the lady."

"What, was there a lady there?"

"Ay, worse luck, sir; and a pretty girl she was: coming home to England to die of consumption; so our surgeon told me."

"Well, never mind her. The clergyman! This fills me with anxiety. A clerk suspecting us at Sydney, and a passenger suspecting us in the vessel. There are two witnesses against us already."

"No; only one."

"How do you make that out?"

"Why, White's clerk and the parson, they was one man."

Wardlaw stared in utter amazement.

"Don't ye believe me?" said Wylie. "I tell ye that there clerk boarded us under an alias. He had shaved off his beard; but, bless your heart, I knew him directly."

"He came to verify his suspicions," suggested Wardlaw, in a faint voice.

"Not he. He came for love of the sick girl, and nothing else; and you'll never see either him or her, if that is any comfort to you."

"Be good enough to conceal nothing. Facts must be faced."

"That is too true, sir. Well, we abandoned her, and took to the boats. I commanded one."

"And Hudson the other?"

"Hudson! No."

"Why, how was that? and what has become of him?"

"What has become of Hudson?" said Wylie, with a start. "There's a question! And not a drop to wet my lips, and warm my heart. Is this a tale to tell, dry? Can't ye spare a drop of brandy to a poor devil that has earned ye £150,000, and risked his life, and wrecked his soul, to do it?"

Wardlaw cast a glance of contempt on him, but got up, and speedily put a bottle of old brandy, a tumbler, and a caraffe of water, on the table before him.

Wylie drank a wine-glassful neat, and gave a sort of sigh of satisfaction. And then ensued a dialogue, in which, curiously enough, the brave man was agitated, and the timid man was cool and collected. But one reason was, the latter had not imagination enough to realize things unseen, though he had caused them.

Wylie told him how Hudson got to the bottle, and would not leave the ship. "I think I see him now, with his cutlass in one hand, and his rum bottle in the other, and the waves running over his poor, silly face, as she went down. Poor Hiram! he and I had made many a trip together, before we took to this."

And Wylie shuddered, and took another gulp at the brandy.

While he was drinking to drown the picture, Wardlaw was calmly reflecting on the bare fact. "Hum," said he, "we must use that circumstance. I'll get it into the journals. Heroic captain. Went down with the ship. Who can suspect Hudson in the teeth of such a fact? Now, pray go on, my good Wylie. The boats!"

"Well, sir, I had the surgeon, and ten men, and the lady's maid, on board the long-boat; and there was the parson, the sick lady, and five sailors aboard the cutter. We sailed together, till night, steering for Juan Fernandez, then a fog came on and we lost sight of the cutter, and I altered my mind and judged it best to beat to win'ard, and get into the track of ships. Which we did, and were nearly swamped in a sou'wester; but, by good luck, a Yankee whaler picked us up, and took us to Buenos Ayres, where we shipped for England, what was left of us, only four, besides myself; but I got the signatures of the others to my tale of the wreck. It is all as square as a die, I tell you."

"Well done. Well done. But, stop! the other boat, with that sham parson on board, who knows all. She will be picked up, too, perhaps."

"There is no chance of that. She was out of the

tracks of trade; and, I 'll tell ye the truth, sir." He poured out half a tumbler of brandy, and drank a part of it; and, now, for the first time, his hand trembled as he lifted the glass — "Some fool had put the main of her provisions aboard the long-boat; that is what sticks to me, and won't let me sleep. We took a chance, but we did n't give one. I think I told you there was a woman aboard the cutter, that sick girl, sir. O, but it was hard lines for her, poor thing! I see her face, pale and calm; O Lord, so pale and calm; every night of my life; she kneeled aboard the cutter with her white hands a clasped together, praying."

"Certainly, it is all very shocking," said Wardlaw; "but, then, you know, if they had escaped, they would have exposed us. Believe me, it is all for the best."

Wylie looked at him with wonder. "Ay," said he, after staring at him in wonder; "you can sit here at your ease, and doom a ship and risk her people's lives: but, if you had to do it, and see it, and then lie awake thinking of it, you 'd wish all the gold on earth had been in hell, before you put your hand to such a piece of work."

Wardlaw smiled a ghastly smile. "In short," said he, "you don't mean to take the three thousand pounds I pay you for this little job."

"O yes, I do; but, for all the gold in Victoria, I would n't do such a job again. And, you mark my words, sir, we shall get the money, and nobody will ever be the wiser." Wardlaw rubbed his hands complacently: his egotism, coupled with his want of imagination, nearly blinded him to everything but the pecuniary feature of the business. "But," continued Wylie, "we shall never thrive on it. We have sunk a good ship, and we have as good as murdered a poor dying girl."

"Hold your tongue, ye fool!" cried Wardlaw, losing his sang froid in a moment, for he heard somebody at the door.

It opened, and there stood a military figure in a travelling cap, — General Rolleston.

CHAPTER XVI.

As some eggs have actually two yolks, so Arthur Wardlaw had two hearts; and at sight of Helen's father, the baser one ceased to beat for a while.

He ran to General Rolleston, shook him warmly by the hand, and welcomed him to England with sparkling eyes.

It is pleasant to be so welcomed, and the stately soldier returned his grasp in kind.

"Is Helen with you, sir?" said Wardlaw, making a movement to go to the door: for he thought she must be outside in the cab.

"No, she is not," said General Rolleston.

"There, now," said Arthur, "that cruel father of mine has broken his promise, and carried her off to Elm-trees!"

At this moment Wardlaw senior returned, to tell Arthur he had been just too late to meet the Rollestons. "O, here he is!" said he; and there were fresh greetings.

"Well, but," said Arthur, "where is Helen!"

"I think it is I who ought to ask that question," said Rolleston, gravely. "I telegraphed you at Elm-trees, thinking of course she would come with you to meet me at the station. It does not much matter, a few hours; but her not coming makes me uneasy, for her health was declining when she left me. How is my child, Mr. Wardlaw? Pray tell me the truth."

Both the Wardlaws looked at one another, and at General Rolleston, and the elder Wardlaw said there was certainly some misunderstanding here. "We fully believed that your daughter was coming home with you in the Shannon."

"Come home with me? Why, of course not. She sailed three weeks before me. Good Heavens! Has she not arrived?"

"No," replied old Wardlaw "we have neither seen nor heard of her."

"Why, what ship did she sail in?" said Arthur.

"In the Proserpine."

CHAPTER XVII.

Arthur Wardlaw fixed on the speaker a gaze full of horror; his jaw fell; a livid pallor spread over his features; he echoed in a hoarse whisper, "the Proserpine!" and turned his scared eyes upon Wylie, who was himself leaning against the wall, his stalwart frame beginning to tremble.

"The sick girl," murmured Wylie, and a cold sweat gathered on his brow.

General Rolleston looked from one to another with strange misgivings, which soon deepened into a sense of some terrible calamity; for now a strong convulsion swelled Arthur Wardlaw's heart; his face worked fearfully; and with a sharp and sudden cry, he fell forward on the table, and his father's arm alone prevented him from sinking like a dead man on the floor. Yet though crushed and helpless, he was not insensible; that blessing was denied him.

General Rolleston implored an explanation.

Wylie, with downcast and averted face, began to stammer a few disconnected and unintelligible words; but old Wardlaw silenced him and said, with much feeling, "Let none but a father tell him. My poor, poor friend, — The Proserpine! How can I say it?"

"Lost at sea," groaned Wylie.

At these fatal words the old warrior's countenance grew rigid; his large, bony hands gripped the back of the chair on which he leaned, and were white with their own convulsive force; and he bowed his head under the blow, without one word.

His was an agony too great and mute to be spoken to; and there was silence in the room, broken only by the hysterical moans of the miserable plotter, who had drawn down this calamity on his own head. He was in no state to be left alone; and even the bereaved father found pity in his desolate heart for one who loved his lost child so well; and the two old men took him home between them, in a helpless and pitiable condition.

CHAPTER XVIII.

But this utter prostration of his confederate began to alarm Wylie, and rouse him to exertion. Certainly, he was very sorry for what he had done, and would have undone it and forfeited his £ 3,000 in a moment, if he could. But, as he could not undo the crime, he was all the more determined to reap the reward. Why, that £ 3,000, for aught he knew, was the price of his soul; and he was not the man to let his soul go gratis.

He finished the rest of the brandy, and went after

his men, to keep them true to him by promises; but the next day he came to the office in Fenchurch Street, and asked anxiously for Wardlaw. Wardlaw had not arrived. He waited, but the merchant never came; and Michael told him, with considerable anxiety, that this was the first time his young master had missed coming this five years.

In course of the day, several underwriters came in, with long faces, to verify the report which had now reached Lloyd's, that the Proserpine had foundered at sea.

"It is too true," said Michael; "and poor Mr. Wylie here has barely escaped with his life. He was mate of the ship, gentlemen."

Upon this, each visitor questioned Wylie, and Wylie returned the same smooth answer to all inquiries: one heavy gale after another had so tried the ship that her seams had opened, and let in more water than all the exertions of the crew and passengers could discharge; at last, they had taken to the boats; the long-boat had been picked up: the cutter had never been heard of since.

They nearly all asked after the ship's log.

"I have got it safe at home," said he. It was in his pocket all the time.

Some asked him where the other survivors were. He told them five had shipped on board the Maria, and three were with him at Poplar, one disabled by the hardships they had all endured.

One or two complained angrily of Mr. Wardlaw's absence at such a time.

"Well, good gentlemen," said Wylie, "I'll tell ye. Mr. Wardlaw's sweetheart was aboard the ship. He is a'most broken-hearted. He vallied her more than all the gold, that you may take your oath on."

This stroke, coming from a rough fellow in a pea-jacket, who looked as simple as he was cunning, silenced remonstrance, and went far to disarm suspicion; and so pleased Michael Penfold, that he said, "Mr. Wylie, you are interested in this business, would you mind going to Mr. Wardlaw's house, and asking what we are to do next? I'll give you his address, and a line, begging him to make an effort and see you. Business is the heart's best ointment. Eh, dear Mr. Wylie, I have known grief too; and I think I should have gone mad when they sent my poor son away, but for business, especially the summing-up of long columns, &c."

Wylie called at the house in Russell Square, and asked to see Mr. Wardlaw.

The servant shook his head. "You can't see him; he is very ill."

"Very ill," said Wylie. "I'm sorry for that. Well, but I sha'n't make him any worse; and Mr. Penfold says I must see him. It is very particular, I tell you. He won't thank you for refusing me, when he comes to hear of it."

He said this very seriously; and the servant, after a short hesitation, begged him to sit down in the passage a moment. He then went into the dining-room, and shortly reappeared, holding the door open. Out came, not Wardlaw junior, but Wardlaw senior.

"My son is in no condition to receive you," said he, gravely; "but I am at your service. What is your business?"

Wylie was taken off his guard, and stammered out something about the Shannon.

"The Shannon! What have you to do with her? You belonged to the Proserpine."

"Ay, sir; but I had his orders to ship forty chests of lead and smelted copper on board the Shannon."

"Well?"

"Ye see, sir," said Wylie, "Mr. Wardlaw was particular about them, and I feel responsible like, having shipped them aboard another vessel."

"Have you not the captain's receipt?"

"That I have, sir, at home. But you could hardly read it for salt water."

"Well," said Wardlaw senior, "I will direct our agent at Liverpool to look after them, and send them up at once to my cellars in Fenchurch Street. Forty chests of lead and copper, I think you said." And he took a note of this directly. Wylie was not a little discomfited at this unexpected turn things had taken; but he held his tongue now, for fear of making bad worse. Wardlaw senior went on to say that he should have to conduct the business of the firm for a time, in spite of his old age and failing health.

This announcement made Wylie perspire with anxiety, and his three thousand pounds seemed to melt away from him.

"But never mind," said old Wardlaw; "I am very glad you came. In fact, you are the very man I wanted to see. My poor afflicted friend has asked after you several times. Be good enough to follow me."

He led the way into the dining-room, and there sat the sad father in all the quiet dignity of calm, unfathomable sorrow.

Another gentleman stood upon the rug with his back to the fire, waiting for Mr. Wardlaw; this was the family physician, who had just come down from Arthur's bedroom, and had entered by another door through the drawing-room.

"Well, doctor," said Wardlaw, anxiously, "what is your report?"

"Not so good as I could wish; but nothing to excite immediate alarm. Overtaxed brain, sir; weakened and unable to support this calamity. However, we have reduced the fever; the symptoms of delirium have been checked, and I think we shall escape brain fever if he is kept quiet. I could not have said as much this morning."

The doctor then took his leave, with a promise to call next morning; and as soon as he was gone, Wardlaw turned to General Rolleston, and said, "Here *is* Wylie, sir. Come forward, my man, and speak to the General. He wants to know if you can point out to him on the chart the very spot where the Proserpine was lost?"

"Well, sir," said Wylie, "I think I could."

The great chart of the Pacific was then spread out upon the table, and rarely has a chart been examined as this was, with the bleeding heart as well as the straining eye.

The rough sailor became an oracle; the others hung upon his words, and followed his brown finger on the chart with fearful interest.

"Ye see, sir," said he, addressing the old merchant, for there was something on his mind that made him avoid speaking directly to General Rolleston, "When we came out of Sydney, the wind being south and by west, Hudson took the northerly course, instead of running through Cook's Straits. The weather freshened from the same quarter, so that, with one thing and another, by when we were a month out, she was five hundred miles or so nor'ard of her true course. But that was n't all; when the leak gained on us, Hudson ran the ship three hundred miles by my reckoning to the nor'east; and, I remember, the day before she foundered, he told me she was in latitude forty, and Easter Island bearing due north."

"Here is the spot, then," said General Rolleston, and placed his finger on the spot.

"Ay, sir," said Wylie, addressing the merchant; "but she ran about eighty-five miles after that, on a northerly course — no — wind on her starboard quarter, — and being deep in the water, she 'd make lee way, — say eighty-two miles, nor'east by east."

The General took eighty-two miles off the scale, with a pair of dividers, and set out that distance on the chart. He held the instrument fixed on the point thus obtained.

Wylie eyed the point, and after a moment's consideration, nodded his head.

"There, or thereabouts," he said, in a low voice, and looking at the merchant.

A pause ensued, and the two old men examined the speck pricked on the map, as if it were the waters covering the Proserpine.

"Now, sir," said Rolleston, "trace the course of the boats"; and he handed Wylie a pencil.

The sailor slowly averted his head, but stretched out his hand and took it, and traced two lines, the one short and straight, running nearly northeast. "That 's the way the cutter headed when we lost her in the night."

The other line ran parallel to the first for half an inch, then turning, bent backwards, and ran due south.

"This was *our* course," said Wylie.

General Rolleston looked up, and said, "Why did you desert the cutter?"

The mate looked at old Wardlaw, and, after some hesitation, replied, "After we lost sight of her, the men with me declared that we could not reach either Juan Fernandez or Valparaiso with our stock of provisions, and insisted on standing for the sea-track of Australian liners between the Horn and Sydney."

This explanation was received in dead silence. Wylie fidgeted, and his eye wandered round the room.

General Rolleston applied his compasses to the chart. "I find that the Proserpine was not one thousand miles from Easter Island. Why did you not make for that land?"

"We had no charts, sir," said Wylie to the merchant, "and I 'm no navigator."

"I see no land laid down hereaway, northeast of the spot where the ship went down."

"No," replied Wylie, "that 's what the men said when they made me 'bout ship."

"Then why did you lead the way northeast at all?"

"I 'm no navigator," answered the man, sullenly.

He then suddenly stammered out, "Ask my men what *we* went through. Why, sir (to Wardlaw), I can hardly believe that I am alive, and sit here talking to you about this cursed business. And nobody offers me a drop of anything."

Wardlaw poured him out a tumbler of wine. His brown hand trembled a little, and he gulped the wine down like water.

General Rolleston gave Mr. Wardlaw a look, and Wylie was dismissed. He slouched down the street all in a cold perspiration; but still clinging to his three thousand pounds, though small was now his hope of ever seeing it.

When he was gone General Rolleston paced that large and gloomy room in silence. Wardlaw eyed him with the greatest interest, but avoided speaking to him. At last he stopped short, and stood erect, as veterans halt, and pointed down at the chart.

"I 'll start at once for that spot," said he. "I 'll go in the next ship bound to Valparaiso, there I 'll charter a small vessel, and ransack those waters for some trace of my poor lost girl."

"Can you think of no better way than that?" said old Wardlaw, gently, and with a slight tone of reproach.

"No, — not at this moment. O yes, by the by, the Greyhound and Dreadnought are going out to survey the islands of the Pacific. I have interest enough to get a berth in the Greyhound."

"What! go in a Government ship! under the orders of a man, under the orders of another man, under the orders of a Board. Why, if you heard our poor girl was alive upon a rock, the Dreadnought would be sure to run up a bunch of red-tape to the fore that moment to recall the Greyhound, and the Greyhound would go back. No," said he, rising suddenly, and confronting the General, and with the color mounting for once in his sallow face, "You sail in no bottom but one freighted by Wardlaw and Son, and the captain shall be under no orders but yours. We have bought the steam sloop Springbok, seven hundred tons. I 'll victual her for a year, man her well, and you shall go out in her in less than a week. I give you my hand on that."

They grasped hands.

But this sudden warmth and tenderness coming from a man habitually cold, overpowered the stout General. "What, sir," he faltered; "your own son lies in danger, yet your heart goes so with me — such goodness — it is too much for me."

"No, no," faltered the merchant, affected in his turn; "it is nothing. Your poor girl was coming home in that cursed ship to marry my son. Yes, he lies ill for love of her; God help him and me too; but you most of all. Don't, General; don't! We have got work to do; we must be brave, sir; brave I say, and compose ourselves. Ah, my friend, you and I are of one age; and this is a heavy blow for us: and we are friends no more; it has made us brothers: she was to be my child as well as yours; well now she *is* my child, and our hearts they bleed together." At this, the truth must be told, the two stout old men embraced one another like two women, and cried together a little.

But that was soon over with such men as these. They sat together and plunged into the details of the expedition, and they talked themselves into hope.

In a week the Springbok steamed down the Channel on an errand inspired by love not reason; to cross one mighty ocean, and grope for a lost daughter in another.

CHAPTER XIX.

We return to the cutter, and her living freight.

After an anxious, but brief consultation, it was agreed that their best chance was to traverse as many miles of water as possible, while the wind was fair; by this means they would increase their small chance of being picked up, and also of falling in with land, and would, at all events, sail into a lovely climate, where intense cold was unknown, and gales of wind uncommon.

Mr. Hazel advised them to choose a skipper, and give him absolute power, especially over the provisions. They assented to this. He then recommended Cooper for that post. But they had not fathomed the sterling virtues of that taciturn seaman; so they offered the command to Welch, instead.

"Me put myself over Sam Cooper!" said he; "not likely."

Then their choice fell upon Michael Morgan. The other sailors' names were Prince, Fenner, and Mackintosh.

Mr. Hazel urged Morgan to put the crew and passengers on short allowance at once, viz. two biscuits a day, and four table-spoonsful of water: but Morgan was a common sailor; he could not see clearly very far ahead; and, moreover, his own appetite counteracted this advice; he dealt out a pound of biscuit and an ounce of ham to each person, night and morning, and a pint of water in course of the day.

Mr. Hazel declined his share of the ham, and begged Miss Rolleston so earnestly, not to touch it, that she yielded a silent compliance.

On the fourth day the sailors were all in good spirits, though the provisions were now very low. They even sang, and spun yarns. This was partly owing to the beauty of the weather.

On the fifth day Morgan announced that he could only serve out one biscuit per day: and this sudden decline caused some dissatisfaction and alarm.

Next day, the water ran so low, that only a teaspoonful was served out night and morning.

There were murmurs and forebodings.

In all heavy trials and extremities some man or other reveals great qualities, that were latent in him, ay, hidden from himself. And this general observation was verified on the present occasion, as it had been in the Indian mutiny, and many other crises. Hazel came out.

He encouraged the men, out of his multifarious stores of learning. He related at length stories of wrecks and sufferings at sea; which, though they had long been in print, were most of them new to these poor fellows. He told them, among the rest, what the men of the Bona Dea, waterlogged at sea, had suffered, — twelve days without any food but a rat and a kitten, — yet had all survived. He gave them some details of the Wager, the Grosvenor, the Corbin, the Medusa; but, above all, a most minute account of the Bounty, and Bligh's wonderful voyage in an open boat, short of provisions. He moralized on this, and showed his fellow-sufferers it was discipline and self-denial from the first, that had enabled those hungry spectres to survive, and to traverse two thousand eight hundred miles of water, in those very seas; and that in spite of hunger, thirst, disease, and rough weather.

By these means he diverted their minds in some degree from their own calamity, and taught them the lesson they most needed.

The poor fellows listened with more interest than you could have thought possible under the pressure of bodily distress. And Helen Rolleston's hazel eye dwelled on the narrator with unceasing wonder.

Yes, learning and fortitude, strengthened by those great examples learning furnishes, maintained a superiority, even in the middle of the Pacific; and not the rough sailors only, but the lady, who had rejected and scorned his love, hung upon the brave student's words: she was compelled to look up, with wonder, to the man she had hated and despised in her hours of ease.

On the sixth day the provisions failed entirely. Not a crust of bread: not a drop of water.

At 4 P. M. several flying-fish, driven into the air by the dolphins and cat-fish, fell into the sea again near the boat, and one struck the sail sharply, and fell into the boat. It was divided, and devoured raw, in a moment.

The next morning the wind fell, and, by noon, the ocean became like glass.

The horrors of a storm have been often painted; but who has described, or can describe, the horrors of a calm, to a boat-load of hungry, thirsty creatures, whose only chances of salvation or relief are wind and rain?

The beautiful, remorseless sky was one vault of purple, with a great flaming jewel in the centre, whose vertical rays struck, and parched, and scorched the living sufferers; and blistered and baked the boat itself, so that it hurt their hot hands to touch it: the beautiful, remorseless ocean was one sheet of glass, that glared in their blood-shot eyes, and reflected the intolerable heat of heaven upon these poor wretches, who were gnawed to death with hunger; and their raging thirst was fiercer still.

Towards afternoon of the eighth day, Mackintosh dipped a vessel in the sea, with the manifest intention of drinking the salt water.

"Stop him!" cried Hazel, in great agitation; and the others seized him, and overpowered him: he cursed them with such horrible curses, that Miss Rolleston put her fingers in her ears, and shuddered from head to foot. Even this was new to her, to hear foul language.

A calm voice rose in the midst, and said: "Let us pray."

There was a dead silence, and Mr. Hazel kneeled down and prayed loud and fervently; and, while he prayed, the furious cries subsided for a while, and deep groans only were heard. He prayed for food, for rain, for wind, for Patience.

The men were not so far gone but they could just manage to say "Amen."

He rose from his knees, and gathered the pale faces of the men together in one glance; and saw that intense expression of agony which physical pain can mould with men's features: and then he strained his eyes over the brassy horizon; but no cloud, no veil of vapor was visible.

"Water, water everywhere, but not a drop to drink."

"We must be mad," he cried, "to die of thirst, with all this water round us."

His invention being stimulated by this idea, and his own dire need, he eagerly scanned everything in the boat, and his eyes soon lighted on two objects disconnected in themselves, but it struck him he could use them in combination. These were a common glass bottle, and Miss Rolleston's life-preserving jacket, that served her for a couch. He drew this garment over his knees, and considered it attentively; then untwisted the brass nozzle through which the jacket was inflated, and so left a tube, some nine inches in length, hanging down from the neck of the garment.

He now applied his breath to the tube, and the jacket swelling rapidly proved that the whole receptacle was air-tight.

He then allowed the air to escape. Next, he took the bottle and filled it with water from the sea; then he inserted, with some difficulty, and great care, the neck of the bottle into the orifice of the tube: this done, he detached the wire of the brass nozzle, and whipped the tube firmly round the neck of the bottle.

"Now, light a fire," he cried; "no matter what it costs."

The fore thwart was chopped up, and a fire soon spluttered and sparkled, for ten eager hands were feeding it: the bottle was then suspended over it, and, in due course, the salt-water boiled and threw off vapor, and the belly of the jacket began to heave and stir. Hazel then threw cold water upon the outside, to keep it cool, and, while the men eagerly watched the bubbling bottle and swelling bag, his spirits rose, and he took occasion to explain that what was now going on under their eyes was, after all, only one of the great processes of Nature, done upon a small scale. "The clouds," said he, "are but vapors drawn from the sea, by the heat of the sun: these clouds are composed of fresh water, and so the steam we are now raising from salt-water will be fresh. We can't make whiskey, or brew beer, lads; but, thank Heaven, we can brew water; and it is worth all other liquors ten times told."

A wild "Hurrah!" greeted these words.

But every novel experiment seems doomed to fail, or meet with some disaster. The water in the bottle had been reduced too low, by vaporism, and the bottle burst suddenly, with a loud report. That report was followed by a piteous wail.

Hazel turned pale at this fatal blow: but, recovering himself, he said, "That is unfortunate; but it was a good servant while it lasted: give me the baler; and, Miss Rolleston, can you lend me a thimble?"

The tube of the life preserver was held over the baler, and out trickled a small quantity of pure water, two thimblesful apiece. Even that, as it passed over their swelling tongues and parched swallows, was a heavenly relief: but, alas, the supply was then exhausted.

Next day hunger seemed uppermost, and the men gnawed and chewed their tobacco-pouches: and two caps, that had been dressed with the hair on, were divided for food.

None was given to Mr. Hazel or Miss Rolleston; and this, to do the poor creatures justice, was the first instance of injustice or partiality the sailors had shown.

The lady, though tormented with hunger, was more magnanimous; she offered to divide the contents of her little medicine chest; and the globules were all devoured in a moment.

And now their tortures were aggravated by the sight of abundance. They drifted over coral rocks, at a considerable depth, but the water was so exquisitely clear that they saw five fathoms down. They discerned small fish drifting over the bottom; they looked like a driving cloud, so vast was their number; and every now and then there was a scurry among them, and porpoises and dog-fish broke in and feasted on them. All this they saw, yet could not catch one of those billions for their lives. Thus they were tantalized as well as starved.

The next day was like the last, with this difference, that the sufferers could no longer endure their torments in silence.

The lady moaned constantly: the sailors groaned, lamented, and cursed.

The sun baked and blistered, and the water glared.

The sails being useless, the sailors rigged them as an awning, and salt-water was constantly thrown over them.

Mr. Hazel took a baler and drenched his own clothes and Miss Rolleston's upon their bodies. This relieved the hell of thirst in some degree: but the sailors could not be persuaded to practise it.

In the afternoon Hazel took Miss Rolleston's Bible from her wasted hands, and read aloud the forty-second Psalm.

When he had done, one of the sailors asked him to pass the Bible forward. He did so; and in half an hour the leaves were returned him; the vellum binding had been cut off, divided and eaten.

He looked piteously at the leaves, and after a while, fell upon his knees, and prayed silently.

He rose, and, with Miss Rolleston's consent, offered the men the leaves as well. "It is the Bread of Life for men's souls, not their bodies," said he. "But God is merciful; I think he will forgive you; for your need is bitter."

Cooper replied that the binding was man's, but the pages were God's; and, either for this or another more obvious reason, the leaves were declined for food.

All that afternoon Hazel was making a sort of rough spoon out of a fragment of wood.

The night that followed was darker than usual, and, about midnight, a hand was laid on Helen Rolleston's shoulder, and a voice whispered, "Hush! say nothing. I have got something for you."

At the same time, something sweet and deliciously fragrant, was put to her lips; she opened her mouth, and received a spoonful of marmalade. Never did marmalade taste like that before. It dissolved itself like Ambrosia over her palate, and even relieved her parched throat in some slight degree by the saliva it excited.

Nature could not be resisted; her body took whatever he gave. But her high mind rebelled.

"O, how base I am," said she, and wept.

"Why, it is your own," said he, soothingly; "I took it out of your cabin expressly for you."

"At least, oblige me by eating some yourself, sir," said Helen, "or (with a sudden burst) I will die ere I touch another morsel."

"I feel the threat, Miss Rolleston; but I do not need it, for I am very, very hungry. But no; if *I* take any, I must divide it all with *them*. But if you will help me unrip the jacket, I will suck the inside — after you."

Helen gazed at him, and wondered at the man, and at the strange love which had so bitterly offended her, when she was surrounded by comforts; but now it extorted her respect.

They unripped the jacket, and found some moisture left. They sucked it, and it was a wonderful, an incredible relief to their parched gullets.

The next day was a fearful one. Not a cloud in the sky to give hope of rain; the air so light, it only just moved them along; and the sea glared, and the sun beat on the poor wretches, now tortured into madness with hunger and thirst.

The body of man, in this dire extremity, can suffer internal agony as acute as any that can be inflicted on its surface by the knife; and the cries, the screams, the groans, the prayers, the curses, intermingled, that issued from the boat, were not to be distinguished from the cries of men horribly wounded in battle, or writhing under some terrible operation in hospitals.

O, it was terrible and piteous to see and hear the boat-load of ghastly victims, with hollow cheeks, and wild-beast eyes, go groaning, cursing, and shrieking loud, upon that fair glassy sea, below that purple vault and glorious sun.

Towards afternoon, the sailors got together, forward, and left Hazel and Miss Rolleston alone in the stern. This gave him an opportunity of speaking to her confidentially. He took advantage of it, and said, "Miss Rolleston, I wish to consult you. Am I justified in secreting the marmalade any longer? There is nearly a spoonful apiece."

"No," said Helen, "divide it amongst them all. O, if I had only a woman beside me, to pray with, and cry with, and die with: for die we must."

"I am not so sure of that," said Hazel, faintly, but with a cool fortitude all his own. "Experience proves that the human body can subsist a prodigious time on very little food: and saturating the clothes with water is, I know, the best way to allay thirst. And women, thank Heaven, last longer than men, under privations."

"I shall not last long, sir," said Helen. "Look at their eyes."

"What do you mean?"

"I mean that those men there are going to kill me."

CHAPTER XX.

HAZEL thought her reason was going; and, instead of looking at the men's eyes, it was hers he examined. But no; the sweet cheek was white, the eyes had a fearful hollow all round them, but, out of that cave, the light hazel eye, preternaturally large, but calm as ever, looked out, full of fortitude, resignation, and reason.

"Don't look at *me*," said she, quietly; "but take an opportunity and look at *them*. They mean to kill me."

Hazel looked furtively round; and, being enlightened in part by the woman's intelligence, he observed that some of the men were actually glaring at himself and Helen Rolleston, in a dreadful way. There was a remarkable change in their eyes since he looked last. The pupils seemed diminished, the whites enlarged; and, in a word, the characteristics of humanity had, somehow, died out of those bloodshot orbs, and the animal alone shone in them now; the wild beast, driven desperate by hunger.

What he saw, coupled with Helen's positive interpretation of it, was truly sickening.

These men were six, and he but one. They had all clasp-knives; and he had only an old penknife that would be sure to double up, or break off, if a blow were dealt with it.

He asked himself, in utter terror, what on earth he should do.

The first thing seemed to be to join the men, and learn their minds: it might also be as well to prevent this secret conference from going further.

He went forward boldly, though sick at heart, and said, "Well, my lads, what is it?"

The men were silent directly, and looked sullenly down, avoiding his eye; yet not ashamed.

In a situation so terrible, the senses are sharpened; and Hazel dissected, in his mind, this sinister look, and saw that Morgan, Prince, and Mackintosh were hostile to him.

But Welch and Cooper he hoped were still friendly.

"Sir," said Fenner, civilly but doggedly, "we are come to this now, that one must die, for the others to live: and the greater part of us are for casting lots all round, and let every man, and every woman too, take their chance. That is fair, Sam, is n't it?"

"It is fair," said Cooper, with a terrible doggedness. "But it is hard," he added.

"Harder that seven should die for one," said Mackintosh. "No, no; one must die for the seven."

Hazel represented, with all the force language possesses, that what they meditated was a crime, the fatal result of which was known by experience.

But they heard in ominous silence.

Hazel went back to Helen Rolleston, and sat down right before her.

"Well!" said she, with supernatural calmness.

"You were mistaken," said he.

"Then why have you placed yourself between them and me. No, no; their eyes have told me they have singled me out. But what does it matter? We poor creatures are all to die; and that one is the happiest that dies first, and dies unstained by such a crime. *I heard every word you said, sir.*"

Hazel cast a piteous look on her, and, finding he could no longer deceive her as to their danger, and being weakened by famine, fell to trembling and crying.

Helen Rolleston looked at him with calm and gentle pity. For a moment, the patient fortitude of a woman made her a brave man's superior.

Night came, and, for the first time, Hazel claimed two portions of the rum; one for himself and one for Miss Rolleston.

He then returned aft, and took the helm. He loosened it, so as to be ready to unship it in a moment, and use it as a weapon.

The men huddled together forward; and it was easy to see that the boat was now divided into two hostile camps.

Hazel sat quaking, with his hand on the helm, fearing an attack every moment.

Both he and Helen listened acutely, and, about three o'clock in the morning, a new incident occurred, of a terrible nature.

Mackintosh was heard to say, "Serve out the rum, no allowance," and the demand was instantly complied with by Morgan.

Then Hazel touched Miss Rolleston on the shoulder, and insisted on her taking half what was left of the marmalade, and he took the other half. The time was gone by for economy; what they wanted now was strength, in case the wild beasts, maddened by drink as well as hunger, should attack them.

Already the liquor had begun to tell, and wild hallos and yells, and even fragments of ghastly songs, mingled with the groans of misery, in the doomed boat.

At sunrise there was a great swell upon the water, and sharp gusts at intervals; and on the horizon, to windward, might be observed a black spot in the sky, no bigger than a fly. But none saw that; Hazel's eye never left the raving wretches in the forepart of the boat; Cooper and Welch sat in gloomy despair amidships; and the others were huddled together forward, encouraging each other to a desperate act.

It was about eight o'clock in the morning Helen Rolleston awoke from a brief doze, and said, "Mr. Hazel, I have had a strange dream. I dreamed there was food, and plenty of it, on the outside of this boat."

While these strange words were yet in her mouth, three of the sailors suddenly rose up with their knives drawn, and eyes full of murder, and staggered aft as fast as their enfeebled bodies could.

Hazel uttered a loud cry, "Welch! Cooper! will

you see us butchered?" and, unshipping the helm, rose to his feet.

Cooper put out his arm to stop Mackintosh, but was too late. He did stop Morgan, however, and said, "Come, none of that; no foul play!"

Irritated by this unexpected resistance, and maddened by drink, Morgan turned on Cooper and stabbed him; he sank down with a groan; on this Welch gave Morgan a fearful gash, dividing his jugular, and was stabbed, in return, by Prince, but not severely: these two grappled and rolled over one another, stabbing and cursing at the bottom of the boat; meantime, Mackintosh was received by Hazel with a point blank thrust in the face from the helm, that staggered him, though a very powerful man, and drove him backwards against the mast; but, in delivering this thrust, Hazel's foot slipped, and he fell with great violence on his head and arm; Mackintosh recovered himself, and sprang upon the stern thwart with his knife up and gleaming over Helen Rolleston. Hazel writhed round where he lay, and struck him desperately on the knee with the helm. The poor woman knew only how to suffer; she cowered a little, and put up two feeble hands.

The knife descended.

But not upon that cowering figure.

CHAPTER XXI.

A PURPLE rippling line upon the water had for some little time been coming down upon them with great rapidity; but, bent on bloody work, they had not observed it. The boat heeled over under the sudden gust; but the ruffian had already lost his footing under Hazel's blow, and the boom striking him almost at the same moment, he went clean over the gunwale into the sea; he struck it with his knife first.

All their lives were now gone if Cooper, who had already recovered his feet, had not immediately cut the sheet with his knife; there was no time to slack it; and even as it was, the lower part of the sail was drenched, and the boat full of water. "Ship the helm!" he roared.

The boat righted directly the sheet was cut, the wet sail flapped furiously, and the boat having way on her yielded to the helm and wriggled slowly away before the whistling wind.

Mackintosh rose a few yards astern, and swam after the boat, with great glaring eyes; the loose sail was not drawing, but the wind moved the boat onward. However, Mackintosh gained slowly, and Hazel held up an oar like a spear, and shouted to him that he must promise solemnly to forego all violence, or he should never come on board alive.

Mackintosh opened his mouth to reply; but, at the same moment, his eyes suddenly dilated in a fearful way, and he went under water, with a gurgling cry. Yet, not like one drowning, but with a jerk.

The next moment there was a great bubbling of the water, as if displaced by some large creatures struggling below, and then the surface was stained with blood.

And, lest there should be any doubt as to the wretched man's fate, the huge back fin of a monstrous shark came soon after, gliding round and round the rolling boat, awaiting the next victim.

Now, while the water was yet stained with his life-blood, who, hurrying to kill, had met with a violent death, the unwounded sailor, Fenner, excited by the fracas, broke forth into singing, and so completed the horror of a wild and awful scene: for still while he shouted, laughed, and sang, the shark swam calmly round and round, and the boat crept on, her white sail bespattered with blood, — which was not so before, — and in her bottom lay one man dead as a stone; and two poor wretches, Prince and Welch, their short-lived feud composed forever, sat openly sucking their bleeding wounds, to quench, for a moment, their intolerable thirst.

O, little do we, who never pass a single day without bite or sup, know the animal man, in these dire extremities.

CHAPTER XXII.

AT last Cooper ordered Fenner to hold his jaw, and come aft, and help sail the boat.

But the man, being now stark mad, took no notice of the order. His madness grew on him, and took a turn by no means uncommon in these cases. He saw before him sumptuous feasts, and streams of fresh water flowing. These he began to describe with great volubility and rapture, smacking his lips, and exulting: and so he went on tantalizing them till noon.

Meantime, Cooper asked Mr. Hazel if he could sail the boat.

"I can steer," said he, "but that is all. My right arm is benumbed."

The silvery voice of Helen Rolleston then uttered brave and welcome words. "I will do whatever you tell me, Mr. Cooper."

"Long life to you, miss!" said the wounded seaman. He then directed her how to reef the sail, and splice the sheet which he had been obliged to cut; and, in a word, to sail the boat; which she did with some little assistance from Hazel.

And so they all depended upon her, whom some of them had been for killing: and the blood-stained boat glided before the wind.

At two P.M. Fenner jumped suddenly up, and, looking at the sea with rapture, cried out, "Aha! my boys, here 's a beautiful green meadow; and there 's a sweet brook with bulrushes: green, green, green! Let 's have a roll among the daisies." And, in a moment, ere any of his stiff and wounded shipmates could put out a hand, he threw himself on his back upon the water, and sunk forever, with inexpressible rapture on his corpse-like face.

A feeble groan was the only tribute those who remained behind could afford him.

At three P.M. Mr. Hazel happened to look over the weather-side of the boat, as she heeled to leeward under a smart breeze, and he saw a shell or two fastened to her side, about eleven inches above keel. He looked again, and gave a loud hurrah. "Barnacles! barnacles!" he cried. "I see them sticking."

He leaned over, and, with some difficulty, detached one, and held it up.

It was not a barnacle, but a curious oblong shell-fish, open at one end.

At sight of this, the wounded forgot their wounds, and leaned over the boat's side, detaching the shell-fish with their knives. They broke them with the handles of their knives, and devoured the fish. They were as thick as a man's finger, and about an inch long, and as sweet as a nut. It seems that in the long calm these shell-fish had fastened on the boat. More than a hundred of them were taken off her weather-side, and evenly divided.

Miss Rolleston, at Hazel's earnest request, ate only six, and these very slowly, and laid the rest by. But the sailors could not restrain themselves; and Prince, in particular, gorged himself so fiercely that he turned purple in the face, and began to breathe very hard.

That black speck on the horizon, had grown by noon to a beetle, and by three o'clock to something more like an elephant, and it now diffused itself into a huge black cloud, that gradually overspread the heavens; and at last, about half an hour before sunset, came a peculiar chill, and then, in due course, a drop or two fell upon the parched wretches. They sat, less like animals than like plants, all stretching towards their preserver.

Their eyes were turned up to the clouds, so were their open mouths, and their arms and hands held up towards it.

The drops increased in number, and praise went up to heaven in return.

Patter, patter, patter; down came a shower, a rain, — a heavy, steady rain.

With cries of joy, they put out every vessel to catch it; they lowered the sail, and, putting ballast in the centre, bellied it into a great vessel to catch it. They used all their spare canvas to catch it. They filled the water-cask with it; they filled the keg that had held the fatal spirit; and all the time they were sucking the wet canvas, and their own clothes, and their very hands and garments on which the life-giving drops kept falling.

Then they set their little sail again, and prayed for land to Him who had sent them wind and rain.

CHAPTER XXIII.

The breeze declined at sunset; but it rained at intervals during the night; and by the morning they were somewhat chilled.

Death had visited them again during the night. Prince was discovered dead and cold; his wounds were mere scratches, and there seems to be no doubt that he died by gorging himself with more food than his enfeebled system could possibly digest.

Thus dismally began a day of comparative bodily comfort, but mental distress, especially to Miss Rolleston and Mr. Hazel.

Now that this lady and gentleman were no longer goaded to madness by physical suffering, their higher sensibilities resumed their natural force, and the miserable contents of the blood-stained boat shocked them terribly. Two corpses and two wounded men.

Mr. Hazel, however, soon came to one resolution, and that was to read the funeral service over the dead, and then commit them to the deep. He declared this intention, and Cooper, who, though wounded, and apparently sinking, was still skipper of the boat, acquiesced readily.

Mr. Hazel then took the dead men's knives and their money out of their pockets, and read the burial-service over them; they were then committed to the deep. This sad ceremony performed, he addressed a few words to the survivors.

"My friends, and brothers in affliction, we ought not to hope too much from Divine mercy for ourselves; or we should come soon to forget Divine justice. But we are not forbidden to hope for others. Those, who are now gone, were guilty of a terrible crime; but then they were tempted more than their flesh could bear; and they received their punishment here on earth: we may therefore hope they will escape punishment hereafter. And it is for us to profit by their fate, and bow to Heaven's will: even when they drew their knives, food in plenty was within their reach, and the signs of wind were on the sea, and of rain in the sky. Let us be more patient than they were, and place our trust — What is that upon the water to leeward? A piece of wood floating?"

Welch stood up and looked. "Can't make it out. Steer alongside it, miss, if you please." And he crept forward.

Presently he became excited, and directed those in the stern how to steer the boat close to the object without going over it. He begged them all to be silent. He leaned over the boat side as they neared it. He clutched it suddenly with both hands and flung it into the boat with a shout of triumph; but sank exhausted by the effort.

It was a young turtle; and being asleep on the water, or inexperienced, had allowed them to capture it.

This was indeed a godsend: twelve pounds of succulent meat. It was instantly divided, and Mr. Hazel contrived, with some difficulty, to boil a portion of it. He enjoyed it greatly; but Miss Rolleston showed a curious and violent antipathy to it, scarcely credible under the circumstances. Not so the sailors. They devoured it raw, what they could get at all. Cooper could only get down a mouthful or two: he had received his death-wound, and was manifestly sinking.

He revived, however, from time to time, and spoke cheerfully, whenever he spoke at all. Welch informed him of every incident that took place, however minute. Then he would nod, or utter a syllable or two.

On being told that they were passing through seaweed, he expressed a wish to see some of it, and when he had examined it, he said to Hazel, "Keep up your heart, sir; you are not a hundred miles from land." He added gently, after a pause, "but I am bound for another port."

About five in the afternoon, Welch came aft, with the tears in his eyes, to say that Sam was just going to slip his cable, and had something to say to them.

They went to him directly, and Hazel took his hand, and exhorted him to forgive all his enemies.

"Ha'n't a got none," was the reply.

Hazel then, after a few words of religious exhortation and comfort, asked him if he could do anything for him.

"Ay," said Cooper, solemnly. "Got pen and ink aboard, any of ye?"

"I have a pencil," said Helen, earnestly; then tearfully, "O dear! it is to make his will." She opened her prayer-book which had two blank leaves under each cover.

The dying man saw them, and rose into that remarkable energy, which sometimes precedes the departure of the soul.

"Write!" said he, in his deep, full tones.

"I, Samuel Cooper, able seaman, am going to slip my cable, and sail into the presence of my Maker."

He waited till this was written.

"And so I speak the truth."

"The ship Proserpine was destroyed wilful."

"The men had more allowance than they signed for."

"The mate was always plying the captain with liquor."

"Two days before ever the ship leaked, the mate got the long-boat ready."

"When the Proserpine sank, we was on her port quarter, aboard the cutter, was me and my messmate Tom Welch."

"We saw two auger holes in her stern, about two inches diameter."

"Them two holes was made from within, for the splinters showed outside."

"She was a good ship, and met with no stress of weather to speak of, on that voyage."

"Joe Wylie scuttled her and destroyed her people."

"D—n his eyes!"

Mr. Hazel was shocked at this finale: but he knew what sailors are, and how little meaning there is in their set phrases. However, as a clergyman, he could not allow these to be Cooper's last words; so he said earnestly, "Yes, but my poor fellow, you said you forgave all your enemies. We all need forgiveness, you know."

"That is true, sir."

"And you forgive this Wylie, do you not?"

"O Lord, yes," said Cooper, faintly. "I forgive the lubber; d—n him!"

Having said these words with some difficulty, he became lethargic, and so remained for two hours. Indeed he spoke but once more, and that was to Welch; though they were all about him then. "Messmate," said he, in a voice that was now faint and broken, "you and I must sail together on this new voyage. I'm going out of port first; but" (in a whisper of inconceivable tenderness and simple cunning) "I'll lie to outside the harbor till you come out, my boy." Then he paused a moment. Then he added, softly, "For I love you, Tom."

These sweet words were the last of that rugged, silent sailor, who never threw a word away, and whose rough breast enclosed a friendship as of the ancient world, tender, true, and everlasting; that sweetened his life and ennobled his death. As he deserved mourners, so he had true ones. His last words went home to the afflicted hearts that heard them, and the lady and gentleman, whose lives he had saved at cost of his own, wept aloud over their departed friend. But his messmate's eye was dry. When all was over, he just turned to the mourners, and said, gravely, "Thank ye, sir; thank ye kindly, ma'am." And then he covered the body decently with the spare canvas, and lay quietly down, with his own head pillowed upon those loved remains.

Towards afternoon, seals were observed sporting on the waters; but no attempt was made to capture them. Indeed, Miss Rolleston had quite enough to do to sail the boat with Mr. Hazel's assistance.

The night passed, and the morning brought nothing new; except that they fell in with sea-weed in such quantities, the boat could hardly get through it.

Mr. Hazel examined this sea-weed carefully, and brought several kinds upon deck. Amongst the varieties, was one like thin green strips of spinach, very tender and succulent. His botanical researches included sea-weed, and he recognized this as one of the edible rock-weeds.

There was very little of it comparatively, but he took great pains, and, in two hours' time, had gathered as much as might fill a good slop-basin.

He washed it in fresh water, and then asked Miss Rolleston for a pocket handkerchief. This he tied so as to make a bag, and contrived to boil it with the few chips of fuel that remained on board.

After he had boiled it ten minutes, there was no more fuel, except a bowl or two, and the boat-hook, one pair of oars, and the midship and stern thwarts.

He tasted it, and found it glutinous and delicious; he gave Miss Rolleston some, and then fed Welch with the rest. He, poor fellow, enjoyed this sea spinach greatly; he could no longer swallow meat.

While Hazel was feeding him, a flight of ducks passed over their heads, high in the air.

Welch pointed up at them.

"Ah!" said Helen, "if we had but their wings!"

Presently a bird was seen coming in the same direction, but flying very low; it wabbled along towards them very slowly, and at last, to their great surprise, came flapping and tried to settle on the gunwale of the boat. Welch, with that instinct of slaughter which belongs to men, struck the boat-hook into the bird's back and it was soon despatched. It proved to be one of that very flock of ducks that had passed over their heads, and a crab was found fastened to its leg. It is supposed that the bird, to break its long flight, had rested on some reef, and, perhaps, been too busy fishing; and caught this Tartar.

Hazel pounced upon it. "Heaven has sent this for you, because you cannot eat turtle." But the next moment he blushed and recovered his reason. "See," said he, referring to her own words, "this poor bird had wings, yet death overtook her."

He sacrificed a bowl for fuel, and boiled the duck and the crab in one pot, and Miss Rolleston ate demurely but plentifully of both. Of the crab's shell he made a little drinking-vessel for Miss Rolleston.

Cooper remained without funeral rites all this time; the reason was that Welch lay with his head pillowed upon his dead friend, and Hazel had not the heart to disturb him.

But it was the survivors' duty to commit him to the deep, and so Hazel sat down by Welch, and asked him kindly whether he would not wish the services of the Church to be read over his departed friend.

"In course, sir," said Welch. But the next moment he took Hazel's meaning, and said hurriedly, "No, no; I can't let Sam be buried in the sea. Ye see, sir, Sam and I, we are used to one another, and I can't abide to part with him, alive or dead."

"Ah!" said Hazel, "the best friends must part when death takes one."

"Ay, ay, when t'other lives. But, Lord bless you, sir! I sha'n't be long astarn of my messmate here; can't you see that?"

"Heaven forbid!" said Hazel, surprised and alarmed. "Why you are not wounded mortally, as Cooper was. Have a good heart, man, and we three will all see old England yet."

"Well, sir," said Welch, coolly, "I 'll tell ye: me and my shipmate, Prince, was a cutting at one another with our knives a smart time, (and I do properly wonder, when I think of that day's work, for I liked the man well enough, but rum atop of starvation plays hell with seafaring men), well sir, as I was a-saying, he let more blood out of me than I could afford to lose under the circumstances. And, ye see, I can't make fresh blood, because my throat is so swelled by the drought, I can't swallow much meat, so I 'm safe to lose the number of my mess; and, another thing, my heart is n't altogether set towards living. Sam, here, he give me an order; what, did n't ye hear him? 'I 'll lie to outside the bar,' says he, 'till you come out.' He expects me to come out in his wake. Don't ye, Sam, — that was?" and he laid his hand gently on the remains. "Now, sir, I shall ax the lady and you a favor. I want to lie alongside Sam. But if you bury him in the sea, and me ashore, why d—n my eyes if I sha'n't be a thousand years or so before I can find my own messmate. Etarnity is a 'nation big place, I 'm told, a hundred times as big as both oceans. No, sir; you 'll make land, by Sam's reckoning, to-morrow, or next day, wind and tide permitting. I 'll take care of Sam's hull till then, and we 'll lie together till the angel blows that there trumpet; and then we 'll go aloft together, and, as soon as ever we have made our scrape to our betters, we 'll both speak a good word for you and the lady, a very pretty lady she is, and a good-hearted, and the best plucked one I ever did see in any distressed craft; now don't ye cry, miss, don't ye cry, your trouble is pretty near over; *he* said you was not a hundred miles from land: I don't know how he knew that, he was always a better seaman than I be; but say it he did, and that is enough, for he was a man as never told a lie, nor wasted a word."

Welch could utter no more just then; for the glands of his throat were swollen, and he spoke with considerable difficulty.

What could Hazel reply? The judgment is sometimes ashamed to contradict the heart with cold reasons.

He only said, with a sigh, that he saw no signs of land, and believed they had gone on a wrong course, and were in the heart of the Pacific.

Welch made no answer, but a look of good-natured contempt. The idea of this parson contradicting Sam Cooper!

The sun broke, and revealed the illimitable ocean; themselves a tiny speck on it.

Mr. Hazel whispered Miss Rolleston that Cooper *must* be buried to-day.

At ten P. M. they passed through more sea-weed; but this time they had to eat the sea-spinach raw, and there was very little of it.

At noon, the sea was green in places.

Welch told them this was a sign they were nearing land.

At four P. M. a bird, about the size and color of a woodpecker, settled on the boat's mast.

Their glittering eyes fastened on it; and Welch said, "Come, there 's a supper for you as can eat it."

"No, poor thing!" said Helen Rolleston.

"You are right," said Hazel, with a certain effort of self-restraint. "Let our sufferings make us gentle, not savage: that poor bird is lost like us upon this ocean. It is a land-bird."

"How do you know?"

"Water-birds have webbed feet, — to swim with."

The bird, having rested, flew to the northwest.

Helen, by one of those inspired impulses her sex have, altered the boat's course directly, and followed the bird.

Half an hour before sunset, Helen Rolleston, whose vision was very keen, said she saw something at the verge of the horizon, like a hair standing upright.

Hazel looked, but could not see anything.

In ten minutes more, Helen Rolleston pointed it out again; and then Hazel did see a vertical line, more like a ship's mast, than anything else one could expect to see there.

Their eyes were now strained to make it out, and, as the boat advanced, it became more and more palpable, though it was hard to say exactly what it was.

Five minutes before the sun set, the air being clearer than ever, it stood out clean against the sky. A tree, — a lofty, solitary tree; with a tall stem, like a column, and branches only at the top.

A palm-tree — in the middle of the Pacific.

CHAPTER XXIV.

AND but for the land-bird which rested on their mast, and for their own mercy in sparing it, they would have passed to the eastward, and never seen that giant palm-tree in mid-ocean.

"O, let us put out all our sails, and fly to it!" cried Helen.

Welch smiled and said, "No, miss, ye must n't. Lord love ye; what! run on to a land ye don't know, happy go lucky, in the dark, like that? Lay her head for the tree, and welcome, but you must lower the mainsel, and treble-reef the foresel; and so creep on a couple of knots an hour, and, by day-break, you 'll find the island close under your lee. Then you can look out for a safe landing-place."

"The island, Mr. Welch!" said Helen. "There is no island, or I should have seen it."

"O, the island was hull down. Why, you don't think as palm-trees grow in the water? You do as I say, or you 'll get wrecked on some thundering reef or other."

Upon this Mr. Hazel and Miss Rolleston set to work, and, with considerable difficulty lowered the mainsail, and treble-reefed the foresail.

"That is right," said Welch. "To-morrow, you 'll land in safety, and bury my messmate and me."

"O no!" cried Helen Rolleston. "We must bury him, but we mean to cure you."

They obeyed Welch's instructions, and so crept on all night; and, so well had this able seaman calculated distance and rate of sailing, that, when the sun rose, sure enough there was an island under their lee, distant about a league, though it looked much less. But the palm-tree was more than twice that distance. Owing to wind and current they had made lee-way all night, and that tree stood on the most westerly point of the island.

Hazel and Miss Rolleston stood up and hurrahed for joy; then fell on their knees in silent gratitude. Welch only smiled.

But the breeze had freshened, and, though there were no great waves at sea, yet breakers, formidable to such a craft as theirs, were seen foaming over long disjointed reefs ahead, that grinned black and dangerous here and there.

They then consulted Welch, and he told them

they must tack directly, and make a circuit of the island; he had to show them how to tack; and, the sea rising, they got thoroughly wetted, and Miss Rolleston rather frightened; for here was a peril they had wonderfully escaped hitherto.

However, before eleven o'clock, they had stood out to sea, and coasted the whole south side of the island: they then put the boat before the wind, and soon ran past the east coast, which was very narrow, — in fact, a sort of bluff-head, — and got on the north side of the island. Here the water was comparatively smooth, and the air warm and balmy. They ranged along the coast at about a mile's distance, looking out for a good landing.

Here was no longer an unbroken line of cliffs, but an undulating coast, with bulging rocks, and lines of reef. After a mile or two of that the coast ran out seaward, and they passed close to a most extraordinary phenomenon of vegetation. Great tangled woods crowned the shore and the landward slopes, and their grand foliage seemed to flow over into the sea: for here was a broad rocky flat, intersected with a thousand little channels of the sea; and the thousand little islets so formed, were crowded, covered, and hidden with luxuriant vegetation. Huge succulent leaves of the richest hue hung over the water, and some of the most adventurous showed, by the crystals that sparkled on their green surface, that the waves had actually been kissing them at high tide. This ceased, and they passed under a cliff, wooded nearly to the point.

This cliff was broad and irregular, and in one of its cavities a cascade of pure fresh water came sparkling, leaping and tumbling down to the foot of the rock. There it had formed a great basin of water, cool, deep, transparent, which trickled over on to a tongue of pink sand, and went in two crystal gutters to the sea.

Great and keen was the rapture this sight caused our poor parched voyagers; and eager their desire to land at once, if possible, and plunge their burning lips, and swelling throats, and fevered hands into that heavenly liquid; but the next moment they were diverted from that purpose by the scene that burst on them.

This wooded cliff, with its wonderful cascade, was the very gate of paradise. They passed it, and in one moment were in a bay, — a sudden bay, wonderfully deep for its extent, and sheltered on three sides. Broad sands with rainbow tints, all sparkling, and dotted with birds, some white as snow, some gorgeous. A peaceful sea of exquisite blue kissing these lovely sands with myriad dimples; and, from the land side, soft emerald slopes, embroidered with silver threads of water, came to the very edge of the sands; so that, from all those glorious hues, that flecked the prismatic and sparkling sands, the eye of the voyagers passed at once to the vivid, yet sweet and soothing, green of Nature; and over this paradise, the breeze they could no longer feel, wafted spicy but delicate odors from unseen trees.

Even Welch raised himself in the boat, and sniffed the heavenly air, and smiled at the heavenly spot. "Here 's a blessed haven!" said he. "Down sail, and row her ashore."

CHAPTER XXV.

They rowed more than a mile, so deep was the glorious bay; and then their oars struck the ground. But Hazel with the boat-hook propelled the boat gently over the pellucid water, that now seemed too shallow to float a canoe; and at last looked like the mere varnish of that picture, the prismatic sands below; yet still the little craft glided over it, till it gently grazed the soft sand, and was stationary. So placidly ended that terrible voyage.

Mr. Hazel and Miss Rolleston were on shore in a moment, and it was all they could do not to fall upon the land and kiss it.

Never had the sea disgorged upon that fairy isle such ghastly spectres. They looked, not like people about to die, but that had died, and been buried, and just come out of their graves to land on that blissful shore. *We* should have started back with horror; but the birds of that virgin isle merely stepped out of their way, and did not fly.

They had landed in paradise.

Even Welch yielded to that universal longing men have to embrace the land after perils at sea, and was putting his leg slowly over the gunwale, when Hazel came back to his assistance. He got ashore, but was contented to sit down with his eyes on the dimpled sea and the boat, waiting quietly till the tide should float his friend to his feet again.

The sea-birds walked quietly about him, and minded him not.

Miss Rolleston ascended a green slope very slowly, for her limbs were cramped, and was lost to view.

Hazel now went up the beach, and took a more minute survey of the neighborhood.

The west side of the bay was varied. Half of it presented the soft character that marked the bay in general; but a portion of it was rocky, though streaked with vegetation, and this part was intersected by narrow clefts, into which, in some rare tempests and high tides combined, tongues of the sea had entered, licking the sides of the gullies smooth; and these occasional visits were marked by the sand, and broken shells, and other *débris* the tempestuous and encroaching sea had left behind.

The true high-water mark was several feet lower than these *débris*, and was clearly marked. On the land above the cliffs he found a tangled jungle of tropical shrubs, into which he did not penetrate, but skirted it, and walking eastward, came out upon a delicious down or grassy slope, that faced the centre of the bay. It was a gentleman's lawn of a thousand acres, with an extremely gentle slope from the centre of the island down to the sea.

A river flowing from some distant source ran eastward through this down, but at its verge, and almost encircled it. Hazel traversed the lawn until this river, taking a sudden turn towards the sea, intercepted him at a spot which he immediately fixed on as Helen Rolleston's future residence.

Four short, thick, umbrageous trees stood close to the stream on this side, and on the eastern side was a grove of gigantic palm-trees, at whose very ankles the river ran. Indeed, it had undermined one of these palm-trees, and that giant at this moment lay all across the stream, leaving a gap through which Hazel's eye could pierce to a great depth among those grand columns; for they stood wide apart, and there was not a vestige of brushwood, jungle, or even grass, below their enormous crowns. He christened the place St. Helen's on the spot.

He now dipped his baler into the stream and found it pure and tolerably cool.

He followed the bend of the stream; it evaded the slope and took him by its own milder descent to the sands: over these it flowed smooth as glass into the sea.

Hazel ran to Welch to tell him all he had discovered, and to give him his first water from the island.

He found a roan-colored pigeon, with a purplish neck, perched on the sick man's foot. The bird shone like a rainbow, and cocked a saucy eye at Hazel, and flew up into the air a few yards, but it soon appeared that fear had little to do with this movement; for, after an airy circle or two, he fanned Hazel's cheek with his fast-flapping wings, and lighted on the very edge of the baler, and was for sipping.

"O, look here, Welch!" cried Hazel, in an ecstasy of delight.

"Ay, sir," said he. "Poor things, they han't a found us out yet."

The talking puzzled the bird, if it did not alarm him, and he flew up to the nearest tree, and, perching there, inspected these new and noisy bipeds at his leisure.

Hazel now laid his hand on Welch's shoulder and reminded him gently they had a sad duty to perform, which could not be postponed.

"Right you are, sir," said Welch, "and very kind of you to let me have my way with him. Poor Sam!"

"I have found a place," said Hazel, in a low voice. "We can take the boat close to it. But where is Miss Rolleston?"

"O, she is not far off; she was here just now, and brought me this here little cocoa-nut, and patted me on the back, she did, then off again on a cruise. Bless her little heart!"

Hazel and Welch then got into the boat, and pushed off without much difficulty, and punted across the bay to one of those clefts we have indicated. It was now nearly high water, and they moored the boat close under the cleft Hazel had selected.

Then they both got out and went up to the extremity of the cleft, and there, with the axe and with pieces of wood, they scraped out a resting-place for Cooper. This was light work; for it was all stones, shells, fragments of coral, and dried sea-weed, lying loosely together. But now came a hard task in which Welch could not assist. Hazel unshipped a thwart, and laid the body on it: then by a great effort staggered with the burden up to the grave and deposited it. He was exhausted by the exertion, and had to sit down panting for some time. As soon as he was recovered, he told Welch to stand at the head of the grave, and he stood at the foot, bareheaded, and then, from memory, he repeated the service of our church, hardly missing or displacing a word.

This was no tame recital; the scene, the circumstances, the very absence of the book, made it tender and solemn. And then Welch repeated those beautiful words after Hazel, and Hazel let him. And how did he repeat them? In such a hearty loving tone, as became one who was about to follow, and all this but a short leave-taking. So uttered, for the living as well as the dead, those immortal words had a strange significance and beauty.

And presently a tender, silvery voice came down to mingle with the deep and solemn tones of the male mourners. It was Helen Rolleston. She had watched most of their movements unseen herself, and now, standing at the edge of the ravine, and looking down on them, uttered a soft but thrilling amen to every prayer. When it was over, and the men prepared to fill in the grave, she spoke to Welch in an undertone, and begged leave to pay her tribute first; and with this, she detached her apron, and held it out to them. Hazel easily climbed up to her, and found her apron was full of sweet-smelling bark and aromatic leaves, whose fragrance filled the air.

"I want you to strew these over his poor remains," she said. "O, not common earth! He saved our lives. And his last words were, 'I love you, Tom.' O dear, O dear, O dear!" And with that she gave him the apron, and turned her head away to hide her tears.

Hazel blessed her for the thought, which, indeed, none but a lady would have had; and Welch and he, with the tears in their eyes, strewed the spicy leaves first; and soon a ridge of shingle neatly bound with sea-weed marked the sailor's grave.

Hazel's next anxiety, and that a pressing one, was to provide shelter for the delicate girl and the sick man, whom circumstances had placed under his care. He told Miss Rolleston Welch and he were going to cross the bay again, and would she be good enough to meet them at the bend of the river where she would find four trees? She nodded her head and took that road accordingly. Hazel rowed eastward across the bay, and it being now high water, he got the boat into the river itself near the edge of the shore, and, as this river had worn a channel, he contrived with the boat-hook to propel the boat up the stream, to an angle in the bank within forty yards of the four trees. He could get no farther, the stream being now not only shallow, but blocked here and there with great and rough fragments of stone. Hazel pushed the boat into the angle out of the current, and moored her fast. He and Welch then got ashore, and Miss Rolleston was standing at the four trees. He went to her and said enthusiastically, "This is to be your house. Is it not a beautiful site?"

"Yes, it is a beautiful site, but — forgive me — I really don't see the house," was her reply.

"But you see the framework."

Helen looked all about, and then said, ruefully, "I suppose I am blind, sir, or else you are dreaming, for I see nothing at all."

"Why here 's a roof ready made, and the frame of a wall. We have only to wattle a screen between these four uprights."

"Only to wattle a screen! But I don't know what wattling a screen is. Who does?"

"Why you get some of the canes that grow a little farther up the river, and a certain long wiry grass I have marked down, and then you fix and weave till you make a screen from tree to tree; this could be patched with wet clay; I know where there is plenty of that. Meantime see what is done to our hands. The crown of this great palm-tree lies at the southern aperture of your house, and blocks it entirely up: that will keep off the only cold wind, the south wind, from you to-night. Then look at these long, spiky leaves interlaced over your head. (These trees are screw-pines.) There is a roof ready made. You must have another roof underneath that, but it will do for a day or two."

"But you will wattle the screen directly," said Helen. "Begin at once, please. I am anxious to see a screen wattled."

"Well," said Welch, who had joined them, "landsmen are queer folk, the best of 'em. Why, miss, it would take him a week to screen you with rushes and reeds, and them sort of weeds; and I'd do it in half an hour, if I was the Tom Welch I used to be. Why, there 's spare canvas enough in the boat to go between these four trees breast high, and then there 's the foresel besides; the mainsel is all you and me shall want, sir."

"O, excuse me," said Miss Rolleston, "I will not be sheltered at the expense of my friends."

"Welch, you are a trump," said Hazel, and ran off for the spare canvas. He brought it, and the carpenter's basket of tools. They went to work, and Miss Rolleston insisted on taking part in it. Finding her so disposed, Hazel said that they had better divide their labors since the time was short. Accordingly he took the axe and chopped off a great many scales of the palm-tree and lighted a great fire between the trees, while the other two worked on the canvas.

"This is to dry the soil as well as cook our provisions," said he; "and now I must go and find food. Is there anything you fancy?" He turned his head from the fire he was lighting and addressed this question both to Welch and Miss Rolleston.

Miss Rolleston stared at this question, then smiled, and, in the true spirit of a lady, said, "I think I should like a good large cocoa-nut, if you can find one." She felt sure there was no other eatable thing in the whole island.

"I wants a cabbage," said Welch, in a loud voice.

"O, Mr. Welch, we are not at home," said Miss Rolleston, blushing at the preposterous demand.

"No, miss, in Capericorn. Whereby we shan't have to pay nothing for this here cabbage. I 'll tell ye, miss: when a sailor comes ashore he always goes in for green vegetables, for why, he has eaten so much junk and biscuit, nature sings out for greens. Me and my shipmates was paid off at Portsmouth last year, and six of us agreed to dine together and each order his dish. Blest if six boiled legs of mutton did not come up smoking hot; three was with cabbage, and three with turmots. Mine was with turmots. But then I don't ask, so nigh the Line: don't ye go to think, because I 'm sick, and the lady and you is so kind to me, and to him that is a-waiting outside them there shoals for me, as I 'm onreasonable; turmots I wish you both and plenty of 'em, when some whaler gets driven out of her course and picks you up, and carries you into northern latitudes where turmots grow; but cabbage is my right, cabbage is my due, being paid off in a manner; for the ship is foundered and I 'm ashore: cabbage I ask for, as a seaman that has done his duty, and a man that won't live to eat many more of 'em; and" (losing his temper), "if you are the man I take you for, you 'll run and fetch me a cabbage fresh from the tree" (recovering his temper). "I know I did n't ought to ax a parson to shin up a tree for me: but, Lord bless you, there ain't no sarcy little boys a-looking on, and here 's a poor fellow mostly dying for it."

Miss Rolleston looked at Mr. Hazel with alarm in every feature; and whispered, "Cabbage from the tree. Is he wandering?"

Hazel smiled. "No," said he. "He has picked up a fable of these seas, that there is a tree which grows cabbages."

Welch heard him and said, with due warmth, "Of course there is a tree on all these islands, that grows cabbages; that was known a hundred years before you was born, and shipmates of mine have eaten them."

"Excuse me, what those old Admirals and Buccaneers, that set the legend afloat, were so absurd as to call a cabbage, and your shipmates may have eaten for one, is nothing on earth but the last year's growth of the palm-tree."

"Palm-tree be —" said Welch; and thereupon ensued a hot argument, which Helen's good sense cut short.

"Mr. Hazel," said she, "can you by any possi bility get our poor friend the *thing* he wants?"

"O, *that* is quite within the bounds of possibility," said Hazel, dryly.

"Well, then, suppose you begin by getting him the *thing*. Then I will boil the *thing*, and he will eat the *thing*; and after all that, it will be time to argue about the *name* we shall give to *the thing*."

The good sense of this struck Mr. Hazel forcibly. He started off at once, armed with the axe, and a net bag Welch had made since he became unfit for heavy labor: he called back to them as he went, to put the pots on.

Welch and Miss Rolleston complied; and then the sailor showed the lady how to sew sailor-wise, driving the large needle with the palm of the hand, guarded by a piece of leather. They had nailed two breadths of canvas to the trees on the north and west sides, and run the breadths rapidly together; and the water was boiling and bubbling in the balers, when Miss Rolleston uttered a scream, for Hazel came running over the prostrate palm-tree as if it was a proper bridge, and lighted in the midst of them.

"Lot one," said he, cheerfully, and produced from his net some limes, two cocoa-nuts, and a land-turtle; from this last esculent Miss Rolleston withdrew with undisguised horror, and it was in vain he assured her it was a great delicacy.

"No matter: it is a reptile. O, please send it away."

"The Queen of the Island reprieves you," said he, and put down the terrapin, which went off very leisurely for a reprieved reptile.

Then Hazel produced a fine bream, which he had found struggling in a rock-pool, the tide having turned, and three sea cray-fish, bigger than any lobster. He chopped their heads off outside, and threw their tails into the pots; he stuck a piece of pointed wood through the bream, and gave it to Welch to toast; but Welch waved it aside.

"I see no cabbage," said he, grimly.

"O, I forgot: but that is soon found," said Hazel. "Here, give me the fish, and you take the saw, and examine the head of this palm-tree, which lies at Miss Rolleston's door. Saw away the succulent part of last year's growth, and bring it here."

Welch got up slowly.

"I 'll go with you, Mr. Welch," said Miss Rolleston.

She will not be alone with me for a moment, if she can help it, thought Hazel, and sat moody by the fire. But he shook off his sadness, and forced on a cheerful look the moment they came back. They brought with them a vegetable very like the heart of a cabbage, only longer and whiter.

"There," said Welch, "what d' ye call that?"

"The last year's growth of the palm," said Hazel, calmly.

This vegetable was cut in two and put into the pots.

"There, take the toasting-fork again," said Hazel to Welch, and drew out from his net three huge scallop-shells. "Soup-plates," said he, and washed them in the running stream: then put them before the fire to dry.

While the fish and vegetable were cooking, he went and cut off some of the leafy, pinnated branches of the palm-tree, and fastened them horizontally above the strips of canvas. Each palm-branch traversed a whole side of the bower. This closed the northern and western sides.

On the southern side, the prostrate palm-tree, on striking the ground, had so crushed its boughs and leaves together, as to make a thick wall of foliage.

Then he took to making forks; and primitive ones they were. He selected a bough the size of a thick walking-stick; sawed it off the tree; sawed a piece six inches long off it, peeled that, split it in four, and, with his knife, gave each piece three points, by merely tapering off and serrating one end; and so he made a fork a minute. Then he brought all the rugs and things from the boat, and, the ground being now thoroughly dried by the fire, placed them for seats; gave each person a large leaf for a plate, besides a scallop-shell; and served out supper. It was eaten with rare appetite; the palm-tree vegetable in particular was delicious, tasting between a cabbage and a cocoa-nut.

When they had supped, Hazel removed the plates and went to the boat. He returned, dragging the foremast and foresail, which were small, and called Welch out. They agreed to rig the mainsail tarpaulin-wise and sleep in the boat. Accordingly they made themselves very busy screening the east side of Miss Rolleston's new abode with the foresail, and fastened a loop and drove a nail into the tree, and looped the sail to it, then suddenly bade her good night in cheerful tones, and were gone in a moment, leaving her to her repose as they imagined. Hazel, in particular, having used all his ingenuity to secure her personal comfort, was now too bent on showing her the most delicate respect and forbearance to think of anything else. But, justly counting on the delicacy, he had forgotten the timidity, of her sex, and her first night in the island was a terribly trying one.

Thrice she opened her mouth to call Welch and Hazel back, but could not. Yet, when their footsteps were out of hearing, she would have given the world to have them between her and the perils with which she felt herself surrounded.

Tigers; Snakes; Scorpions; Savages! what would become of her during the long night?

She sat and cowered before the hot embers. She listened to what seemed the angry roar of the sea. What with the stillness of the night and her sharpened senses she heard it all round the island. She seemed environed with peril, and yet surrounded by desolation. No one at hand to save her in time from a wild beast. No one anywhere near except a sick sailor, and one she would almost rather die than call singly to her aid, for he had once told her he loved her.

"O papa! O Arthur!" she cried, "are you praying for your poor Helen?" Then she wept and prayed; and half nerved herself to bear the worst. Finally, her vague fears completely overmastered her. Then she had recourse to a stratagem that belongs to her sex, — she hid herself from the danger, and the danger from her: she covered herself face and all, and so lay trembling, and longing for the day.

At the first streak of dawn she fled from her place of torture, and after plunging her face and hands in the river, which did her a world of good, she went off, and entered the jungle, and searched it closely, so far as she could penetrate it. Soon she heard "Miss Rolleston" called in anxious tones. But she tossed her little head, and revenged herself for her night of agony by not replying.

However, Nature took her in hand; imperious hunger drew her back to her late place of torture; and there she found a fire, and Hazel cooking cray-fish. She ate the cray-fish heartily, and drank cocoa-nut milk out of half a cocoa-nut, which the ingenious Hazel had already sawn, polished, and mounted for her.

After that, Hazel's whole day was occupied in stripping a tree that stood on the high western promontory of the bay, and building up the materials of a bonfire a few yards from it, that if any whaler should stray that way, they might not be at a loss for means to attract her attention.

Welch was very ill all day, and Miss Rolleston nursed him. He got about towards evening, and Miss Rolleston asked him, rather timidly, if he could put her up a bell-rope.

"Why, yes, miss," said Welch, "that is easy enough; but I don't see no bell."

O, she did not want a bell, — she only wanted a bell-rope.

Hazel came up during this conversation, and she then gave her reason.

"Because, then, if Mr. Welch is ill in the night, and wants me, I could come to him. Or —" finding herself getting near the real reason she stopped short.

"Or what?" inquired Hazel, eagerly.

She replied to Welch. "When tigers and Things come to me, I can let you know, Mr. Welch, if you have any curiosity about the result of their visit."

"Tigers!" said Hazel, in answer to this side slap; "there are no tigers here; no large animals of prey exist in the Pacific."

"What makes you think that?"

"It is notorious: naturalists are agreed."

"But I am not. I heard noises all night. And little I expected that anything of me would be left this morning, except, *perhaps*, my back hair. Mr. Welch, you are clever at rigging things, — that is what you call it, — and so please rig me a bell-rope, then I shall not be eaten alive without creating some *little* disturbance."

"I'll do it, miss," said Welch, "this very night."

Hazel said nothing, but pondered. Accordingly, that very evening a piece of stout twine, with a stone at the end of it, hung down from the roof of Helen's house; and this twine clove the air, until it reached a ring upon the mainmast of the cutter; thence it descended, and was to be made fast to something or somebody. The young lady inquired no further. The very sight of this bell-rope was a great comfort to her; it reunited her to civilized life.

That night she lay down, and quaked considerably less. Yet she woke several times; and an hour before daylight she heard distinctly a noise that made her flesh creep. It was like the snoring of some great animals. This horrible sound was faint and distant; but she heard it between the roll of the waves, and that showed it was not the sea roaring; she hid herself in her rugs, and cowered till daybreak. A score of times she was minded to pull her bell-rope; but always a womanly feeling, strong as her love of life, withheld her. "Time to pull that bell-rope when the danger was present or imminent," she thought to herself. "The Thing will come smelling about before it attacks me, and then I will pull the bell"; and so she passed an hour of agony.

Next morning, at daybreak, Hazel met her just issuing from her hut, and pointing to his net told her he was going to forage; and would she be good enough to make the fire and have boiling water ready: he was sorry to trouble her; but poor Welch was worse this morning. Miss Rolleston cut short his excuses. "Pray do not take me for a child; of course I will light the fire, and boil the water. Only I have no lucifer matches."

"Here are two," said he. "I carry the box, wrapped in oil-skin: for if anything happen to *them*, Heaven help us."

He crossed the prostrate palm-tree, and dived into the wood. It was a large beautiful wood, and except at the western edge, the trees were all of the palm-tree genus, but contained several species, including the cocoa-nut tree. The turf ran under these trees for about forty yards and then died gradually away under the same thick shade which destroyed all other vegetation in this wood, and made it so easy to see and travel.

He gathered a few cocoa-nuts that had burst out of their ripe pods and fallen to the ground; and ran on till he reached a belt of trees and shrubs, that bounded the palm forest. Here his progress was no longer easy: but he found trees covered with a small fruit resembling quinces in every particular, of look, taste, and smell, and that made him persevere, since it was most important to learn the useful products of the island. Presently he burst through some brushwood into a swampy bottom surrounded by low trees, and instantly a dozen large birds of the Osprey kind rose flapping into the air like windmills rising. He was quite startled by the whirring and flapping, and not a little amazed at the appearance of the place. Here was a very charnel-house; so thick lay the shells, skeletons, and loose bones of fish. Here too he found three terrapin killed but not eaten: and also some fish, more or less pecked. "Aha! my worthy executioners, much obliged," said he: "you have saved me that job": and into the bag went the terrapin, and two plump fish, but slightly mutilated. Before he had gone many yards, back came the sailing wings, and the birds settled again before his eyes. The rest of the low wood was but thin, and he soon emerged upon the open country: but it was most unpromising; and fitter for geese than men: a vast sedgy swamp with water in the middle, thin fringes of great fern-trees, and here and there a disconsolate tree like a weeping-willow, and at the end of this lake and swamp, which altogether formed a triangle, was a barren hill without a blade of vegetation on it, and a sort of jagged summit, volcanic! Hazel did not at all like the look of.

Somewhat dismayed at finding so large a slice of the island worthless, he returned through the wood, guiding himself due west by his pocket-compass, and so got down to the shore, where he found scallops and cray-fish in incredible abundance. Literally, he had only to go into the water and gather them. But "enough" is as good as "a feast." He ran to the pots with his miscellaneous bag, and was not received according to his deserts. Miss Rolleston told him, a little severely, the water had been boiling a long time. Then he produced his provender, by way of excuse.

"Tortoises again!" said she, and shuddered visibly.

But the quinces and cocoa-nuts were graciously received. Welch, however, cried out for cabbage.

"What am I to do?" said Hazel. "For every such cabbage, a king must die."

"Goodness me!"

"A monarch of the grove."

"O, a King Log. Why, then down with them all, of course; sooner than dear Mr. Welch shall go without his cabbage."

He cast a look of admiration on her, which she avoided, and very soon his axe was heard ringing in the wood hard by. Then came a loud crash. Then another. Hazel came running with the cabbage, and a cocoa-pod. "There," said he, "and there are a hundred more about. Whilst you cook that for Welch, I will store them." Accordingly he returned to the wood with his net, and soon came back with five pods in it, each as big as a large pumpkin.

He chucked these one at a time across the river, and then went for more. It took him all the afternoon to get all the pods across the river. He was obliged to sit down and rest.

But a suggestion of Helen's soon set him to work again.

"You were kind enough to say you would store these for me. Could you not store them so as to wall out those terrible beasts with them."

"What terrible beasts?"

"That roar so all night, and don't eat us, only because they have not found out we are here yet. But they will."

"I deny their existence," said Hazel. "But I'll wall them out all the same," said he.

"Pray do," said Helen. "Wall them out first, and disprove them afterwards; I shall be better able to believe they don't exist, when they are well walled out — much."

Hazel went to work, and with her assistance laid cocoa-pods two wide and three deep, outside the northern and western side of her leafy bower, and he promised to complete the walls by the same means in two days more.

They all then supped together, and, to oblige him, she ate a little of the terrapin, and when they parted for the night, she thanked him, and said, with a deep blush, "You have been a good friend to me — of late."

He colored high, and his eyes sparkled with delight; and she noticed, and almost wished she had kept her gratitude to herself.

That night, what with her bell-rope and her little bit of a wall, she was somewhat less timorous, and went to sleep early.

But even in sleep she was watchful, and she was awakened by a slight sound in the neighborhood of the boat.

She lay watching, but did not stir.

Presently she heard a footstep.

With a stifled cry she bounded up, and her first impulse was to rush out of the tent. But she conquered this, and gliding to the south side of her bower, she peered through the palm-leaves, and the first thing she saw, was the figure of a man standing between her and the boat.

She drew her breath hard. The outline of the man was somewhat indistinct. But it was not a savage: the man was clothed; and his stature betrayed him.

He stood still for some time. "He is listening to see if I am awake," said Helen, to herself.

The figure moved towards her bower.

Then all in a moment she became another woman. She did not rely on her bell-rope; she felt it was fast to nothing that could help her. She looked round for no weapon; she trusted to herself. She drew herself hastily up, and folded her arms; her bosom panted, but her cheek never paled. Her modesty was alarmed; her blood was up, and life or death were nothing to her.

The footsteps came nearer; they stopped at her door; they went north; they came back south. They kept her in this high-wrought attitude for half an hour. Then they retired softly; and when they were gone, she gave way, and fell on her knees, and began to cry hysterically. Then she got calmer, and then she wondered and puzzled herself; but she slept no more that night.

In the morning she found that the fire was lighted on a sort of shelf close to the boat. Mr. Hazel had cut the shelf and lighted the fire there for Welch's sake, who had complained of cold in the night.

Whilst Hazel was gone for the cray-fish, Welch asked Helen to go for her prayer-book. She brought it directly, and turned the leaves to find the prayers for the sick. But she was soon undeceived as to his intention.

"Sam had it wrote down how the Proserpine was foundered, and I should like to lie alongside my messmate on that there paper, as well as in t' other place" (meaning the grave). "Begin as Sam did, that this is my last word."

"O, I hope not. O, Mr. Welch, pray do not leave me!"

"Well, well then, never mind that; but just put down as I heard Sam; and his dying words, that the parson took down, were the truth."

"I have written that."

"And that the two holes was on her port-side, and seven foot from her starn-post; and *I* say them very augers that is in our cutter made them holes. Set down that."

"It is down."

"Then I'll put my mark under it; and you are my witness."

Helen, anxious to please him in everything, showed him where to put his mark. He did so; and she signed her name as his witness.

"And now, Mr. Welch," said she, "do not you fret about the loss of the ship; you should rather think how good Providence has been to us in saving us three out of so many that sailed in that poor ship. That Wylie was a wicked man; but he is drowned, or starved, no doubt, and there is an end of him. You are alive, and we are all three to see Old England again. But to live, you must eat; and so now do pray make a good breakfast to-day. Tell me what you can fancy. A cabbage?"

"What, you own it is a cabbage?"

"Of course I do," said Helen, coaxing. "You must excuse Mr. Hazel; these learned men are so crotchety in some things, and go by books; but you and I go by our senses, and to us a cabbage is a cabbage, grow where it will. Will you have one?"

"No, miss, not this morning. What I wants this morning very bad, indeed, it is, — I wants a drink made of the sweet-smelling leaves, like as you strewed over my messmate, — the Lord in heaven bless you for it."

"O, Mr. Welch, that is a curious fancy; but you shall not ask me twice for anything; the jungle is full of them, and I'll fetch you some in five minutes. So you must boil the water."

She scudded away to the jungle, and soon returned with some aromatic leaves. Whilst they were infusing, Hazel came up, and on being informed of Welch's fancy, made no opposition; but, on the contrary, said that such men had sometimes very happy inspirations. He tasted it, however, and said the smell was the best part of it in his opinion. He then put it aside to cool for the sick man's use.

They ate their usual breakfast, and then Welch sipped his spice tea, as he called it. Morning and afternoon he drank copious draughts of it, and seemed to get suddenly better, and told them not to hang about him any longer; but go to their work: he was all right now.

To humor him they went off in different directions; Hazel with his axe to level cocoa-nut trees: and Helen to search for fruits in the jungle.

She came back in about an hour, very proud of some pods she had found with nutmegs inside them. She ran to Welch. He was not in the boat. She saw his waistcoat, however, folded and lying on the thwart: so she knew he could not be far off, and concluded he was in her bower. But he was not there; and she called to Mr. Hazel. He came to the side of the river laden with cocoa-nuts.

"Is he with you?" said Helen.

"Who? Welch? no."

"Well, then, he is not here. O dear! something is the matter."

Hazel came across directly. And they both began to run anxiously to every part whence they could command a view to any distance.

They could not see him anywhere, and met, with blank faces, at the bower.

Then Helen made a discovery.

This very day, while hanging about the place, Hazel had torn up from the edge of the river an old trunk, whose roots had been loosened by the water washing away the earth that held them, and this stump he had set up in her bower for a table, after sawing the roots down into legs. Well, on the smooth part of this table, lay a little pile of money, a ring with a large pearl in it, and two gold earrings, Helen had often noticed in Welch's ears.

She pointed at these and turned pale. Then suddenly waving her hand to Hazel to follow her, she darted out of the bower, and, in a moment, she was at the boat.

There she found, beside his waistcoat, his knife, and a little pile of money, placed carefully on the thwart; and, underneath it, his jacket rolled up, and his shoes and sailor's cap, all put neatly and in order.

Hazel found her looking at them. He began to have vague misgivings. "What does this mean?" he said, faintly.

"'What does it mean!'" cried Helen, in agony. "Don't you see? A Legacy! The poor thing has divided his little all. O, my heart! What has become of him? Then, with one of those inspirations her sex have, she cried, "Ah! Cooper's grave!"

Hazel, though not so quick as she was, caught her meaning at a word, and flew down the slope to the sea-shore. The tide was out: a long irregular track of footsteps indented the sand. He stopped a moment and looked at them. They pointed towards that cleft where the grave was. He followed them all across the sand. They entered the cleft, and did not return. Full of heavy foreboding he rushed into the cleft.

Yes; his arms hanging on each side of the grave, and his cheek laid gently on it, there lay Tom Welch, with a loving smile on his dead face. Only a man; yet faithful as a dog.

Hazel went back slowly, and crying. Of all men living, he could best appreciate Fidelity, and mourn its fate.

But, as he drew near Helen, he dried his eyes; for it was his duty to comfort her.

She had at first endeavored to follow him; but after a few steps her knees smote together, and she was fain to sit down on the grassy slope that overlooked the sea.

The sun was setting huge and red over that vast and peaceful sea.

She put her hands to her head, and, sick at heart, looked heavily at that glorious and peaceful sight. Hazel came up to her. She looked at his face, and that look was enough for her. She rocked herself gently to and fro.

"Yes," said he in a broken voice: "He was there, — quite dead."

He sat gently down by her side, and looked at that setting sun and illimitable ocean and his heart felt deadly sad. "He is gone, — and we are alone, — on this island."

The man said this in one sense only: but the woman heard it in more than one.

Alone!

She glanced timidly round at him, and, without rising, edged a little away from him, and wept in silence.

CHAPTER XXVI.

After a long silence, Hazel asked her in a low voice if she could be there in half an hour. She said yes, in the same tone, but without turning her head. On reaching the graves, she found that Hazel had spared her a sad sight; nothing remained but to perform the service. When it was over she went slowly away in deep distress on more accounts than one. In due course Hazel came to her bower, but she was not there. Then he lighted the fire, and prepared everything for supper; and he was so busy, and her foot so light, he did not hear her come. But, by and by, lifting his head, he saw her looking wistfully at him, as if she would read his soul in his minutest actions. He started and brightened all over with pleasure at the sudden sight of her, and said eagerly, "Your supper is quite ready."

"Thank you, sir," said she, sadly and coldly (she had noted that expression of joy), "I have no appetite; do not wait for me." And soon after strolled away again.

Hazel was dumbfoundered. There was no mistaking her manner; it was chilly and reserved all of a sudden. It wounded him; but he behaved like a man; what! I keep her out of her own house, do I? said he to himself. He started up, took a fish out of the pot, wrapped it in a leaf, and stalked off to his boat. Then he ate a little of the fish, threw the rest away, and went down upon the sands, and paced them in a sad and bitter mood.

But the night calmed him, and some hours of tranquil thought brought him fortitude, patience, and a clearer understanding. He went to his boat, elevated by generous and delicate resolutions. Now worthy resolves are tranquillizing, and he slept profoundly.

Not so she, whose sudden but very natural change of demeanor had hurt him. When she returned and found he was gone for the night, she began to be alarmed at having offended him.

For this and other reasons she passed the night in sore perplexity, and did not sleep till morning; and so she overslept her usual time. However, when she was up, she determined to find her own breakfast; she felt it would not do to be too dependent, and on a person of uncertain humor; such for the moment she chose to pretend to herself was Hazel. Accordingly she went down to the sea to look for crayfish. She found abundance. There they lay in the water; you had but to stoop and pick them up.

But alas! they were black, lively, viperish; she went with no great relish for the task to take one up; it wriggled maliciously: she dropped it, and at that very moment, by a curious coincidence, remembered she was sick and tired of crayfish; she would breakfast on fruits. She crossed the sand, took off her shoes, and paddled through the river, and, having put on her shoes again, was about to walk up through some rank grass to the big wood, when she heard a voice behind her, and it was Mr. Hazel. She bit her lip (it was broad daylight now), and prepared quietly to discourage this excessive assiduity. He came up to her panting a little, and taking off his hat, said, with marked respect, "I beg your pardon, Miss Rolleston, but I know you hate reptiles; now there are a few snakes in that long grass; not poisonous ones."

"Snakes!" cried Helen; "let me get home: there, — I 'll go without my breakfast."

"Oh, I hope not," said Hazel, ruefully; "why, I have been rather fortunate this morning, and it is all ready."

"That is a different thing," said Helen, graciously; "you must not have your trouble for nothing, I suppose."

Directly after breakfast, Hazel took his axe and some rope from the boat, and went off in a great hurry to the jungle. In half an hour or so he returned, dragging a large conical shrub, armed with spikes for leaves, incredibly dense and prickly.

"There," said he, "there 's a vegetable porcupine for you. This is your best defence against that roaring Bugbear."

"That little tree!" said Helen; "the tiger would soon jump over that."

"Ay, but not over this and sixty more; a wall of stilettos. Don't touch it, please."

He worked very hard all day, and brought twelve of these prickly trees to the bower by sunset. He was very dissatisfied with his day's work; seemed quite mortified.

"This comes of beginning at the wrong end," he said; "I went to work like a fool. I should have begun by making a cart."

"But you can't do that," said Helen, soothingly; "no gentleman can make a cart."

"O, surely anybody can make a cart, by a little thinking," said he.

"I wish," said Helen, listlessly, "you would think of something for *me* to do; I begin to be ashamed of not helping."

"Hum! you can plait?"

"Yes, as far as seven strands."

"Then you need never be unemployed. We want ropes, and shall want large mats for the rainy weather."

He went to the place where he had warned her of the snakes, and cut a great bundle of long silky grass, surprisingly tough, yet neither harsh nor juicy; he brought it her, and said he should be very glad of a hundred yards of light cord, three ply and five ply.

She was charmed with the grass, and the very next morning she came to breakfast with it nicely prepared, and a good deal of cord made and hanging round her neck. She found some preparations for carpenters' work lying about.

"Is that great log for the cart?" said she.

"Yes! it is a section of a sago-tree."

"What, our sago?"

"The basis. See, in the centre it is all soft pith." He got from the boat one of the augers that had scuttled the Proserpine, and soon turned the pith out. "They pound that pith in water, and run it through linen; then set the water in the sun to evaporate. The sediment is the sago of commerce, and sad insipid stuff it is."

"O, please don't call anything names one has eaten in England," said Helen, sorrowfully.

After a hasty meal, she and Mr. Hazel worked for a wager. Her taper fingers went like the wind, and though she watched him, and asked questions, she never stopped plaiting. Mr. Hazel was no carpenter, he was merely Brains spurred by Necessity. He went to work and sawed off four short discs of the sago-log.

"Now what are those, pray?" asked Helen.

"The wheels: primeval wheels. And here are the linchpins, made of hard wood; I wattled them at odd times."

He then produced two young lime-trees he had rooted up that morning, and sawed them into poles in a minute. Then he bore two holes in each pole, about four inches from either extremity, and fitted his linchpins; then he drew out his linchpins, passed each pole first through one disc, and then through another, and fastened his linchpins. Then he ran to the boat, and came back with the stern and midship thwarts. He drilled with his centre-bit three rows of holes in these, two inches from the edge: and now Helen's work came in; her grass rope bound the thwarts tight to the horizontal poles leaving the discs room to play easily between the thwarts and the linchpins; but there was an open space thirteen inches broad between the thwarts; this space Hazel herring-boned over with some of Helen's rope drawn as tight as possible. The cart was now made. Time occupied in its production, three hours and forty minutes.

The coachmaker was very hot: and Helen asked him timidly whether he had not better rest and eat. "No time for that," said he. "The day is not half long enough for what I have to do." He drank copiously from the stream; put the carpenter's basket into the cart: got the tow-rope from the boat and fastened it to the cart in this shape Λ, putting himself in the centre. So now the coachmaker was the horse, and off they went, rattling and creaking, to the jungle.

Helen turned her stool and watched this pageant enter the jungle. She plaited on, but not so merrily. Hazel's companionship and bustling way somehow kept her spirits up.

But, whenever she was left alone, she gazed on the blank ocean, and her heart died within her. At last she strolled pensively towards the jungle, plaiting busily as she went, and hanging the rope round her neck as fast as she made it.

At the edge of the jungle she found Hazel in a difficulty. He had cut down a wagon-load of prickly trees and wanted to get all this mass of *noli me tangere* on to that wretched little cart, but had not rope enough to keep it together: she gave him plenty of new line, and partly by fastening a small rope to the big rope, and so making the big rope a receptacle, partly by artful tying, they dragged home an incredible load. To be sure some of it draggled half along the ground: and came after, like a peacock's tail.

He made six trips, and then the sun was low; so he began to build. He raised a rampart of these prickly trees, a rampart three feet wide and eight feet high; but it only went round two sides and a half of the bower. So, then, he said he had failed again; and lay down worn out by fatigue.

Helen Rolleston, though dejected herself, could not help pitying him for his exhaustion in her service, and for his bleeding hands: she undertook the cooking, and urged him kindly to eat of every dish; and, when he rose to go, she thanked him with as much feeling as modesty for the great pains he had taken to lessen those fears of hers, which she saw he did not share.

These kind words more than repaid him. He went to his little den in a glow of spirits; and the next morning went off in a violent hurry, and, for once, seemed glad to get away from her.

"Poor Mr. Hazel," said she, softly, and watched him out of sight. Then she got her plait, and went to the high point where he had barked a tree; and looked far and wide for a sail. The air was wonderfully clear; the whole ocean seemed in sight: but all was blank.

A great awe fell upon her, and sickness of heart; and then first she began to fear she was out of the known world, and might die on that island; or never be found by the present generation: and this sickening fear lurked in her from that hour and led to consequences that will be related shortly.

She did not return for a long while, and, when she did, she found Hazel had completed her fortifications. He invited her to explore the western part of the island, but she declined.

"Thank you," said she; "not to-day; there is something to be done at home. I have been comparing my abode with yours, and the contrast makes me uncomfortable, if it does n't you. Oblige me by building yourself a house."

"What, in an afternoon?"

"Why not? you made a cart in a forenoon. How can I tell your limits? you are quite out of my poor little depth. Well, at all events, you must roof the boat, or something. Come, be good for once, and think a little of yourself. There, I 'll sit by and — what shall I do whilst you are working to oblige me?"

"Make a fishing net of cocoa-nut fibre, four feet deep. Here 's plenty of material all prepared."

"Why, Mr. Hazel, you must work in your sleep."

"No; but of course I am not idle when I am alone; and luckily I have made a spade out of hard wood at odd hours, or all the afternoon would go in making that."

"A spade! You are going to dig a hole in the ground and call it a house. That will not do for me."

"You will see," said Hazel.

The boat lay in a little triangular creek; the surrounding earth was alluvial clay; a sort of black cheesy mould, stiff, but kindly to work with the spade. Hazel cut and chiselled it out at a grand rate, and throwing it to the sides, raised, by degrees, two mud banks, one on each side the boat; and at last he dug so deep that he was enabled to draw the boat another yard inland.

As Helen sat by netting and forcing a smile now and then, though sad at heart, he was on his mettle, and the mud walls he raised in four hours were really wonderful. He squared their inner sides with the spade. When he had done, the boat lay in a hollow, the walls of which, half natural, half artificial, were five feet above her gunwale, and, of course, eight feet above her bottom, in which Hazel used to lie at night. He then made another little wall at the boat's stern, and laid palm-branches over all, and a few huge banana-leaves from the jungle; got a dozen large stones out of the river, tied four yards-lengths of Helen's grass-rope from stone to stone, and so passing the ropes over the roof, confined it, otherwise a sudden gust of wind might lift it.

"There," said he; "am I not as well off as you? — I, a great tough man. Abominable waste of time, I call it."

"Hum!" said Helen, doubtfully, "all this is very clever; but I doubt whether it will keep out much rain."

"More than yours will," said Hazel, "and that is a very serious thing. I am afraid you little know how serious. But, to-morrow, if you please, I will examine our resources, and lay our whole situation before you, and ask your advice. As to your Bugbear, let him roar his heart out, his reign is over. Will you not come and see your wooden walls?"

He then took Helen and showed her the tremendous nature of her fortification, and assured her that no beast of prey could face it, nor even smell at it with impunity. And, as to the door, here the defence was double and treble; but attached to four grass cords; two passed into the abode round each of the screw pine-trees at the east side, and were kept in their places by pegs driven into the trees.

"When you are up," said Hazel, "you pull these four cords steadily, and your four guards will draw back right and left, with all their bayonets, and you can come out."

Helen was very much pleased with this arrangement, and did not disguise her gratitude. She slept in peace and comfort that night. Hazel, too, profited by the mud walls and leafy roof she had compelled him to rear; for this night was colder, as it happened, than any preceding night since they came ashore. In the morning, Hazel saw a green turtle on the shore, which was unusual at that time of year. He ran and turned her, with some difficulty; then brought down his cart, cut off her head with a blow, and, in due course, dragged her up the slope. She weighed two hundred pounds. He showed Miss Rolleston the enormous shell, gave her a lecture on turtles, and especially on the four species known to South Sea navigators, — the trunk turtle, the logger-head, the green turtle, and the hawksbill, from which last, and not from any tortoise, he assured her came the tortoise-shell of commerce.

"And now," said he, "will you not give up, or suspend, your Reptile theory, and eat a little green turtle, the king of them all?"

"I think I must after all that," said she; and rather relished it.

That morning he kept his word, and laid their case before her.

He said: "We are here on an island that has probably been seen, and disregarded, by a few whalers, but is not known to navigators nor down on any chart. There is a wide range of vegetation, proving a delightful climate on the whole, and one particularly suited to you, whose lungs are delicate. But then, comparing the beds of the rivers with the banks, a tremendous fall of rain is indicated. The rainy months (in these latitudes) are at hand, and if these rains catch us in our present condition, it will be a calamity. You have walls, but no roof to keep it out. I tremble when I think of it. This is my main anxiety. My next is about our sustenance during the rains: we have no stores under cover; no fuel; no provisions, but a few cocoa-nuts. We use two lucifer matches a day; and what is to become of us at that rate? In theory, fire can be got by rubbing two pieces of wood together; Selkirk is said to have so obtained it from pimento wood on Juan Fernandez; but, in fact, I believe, the art is confined to savages. I never met a civilized man who could do it, and I have questioned scores of voyagers. As for my weapons, they consist of a boat-hook and an axe; no gun, no harpoon, no bow, no lance. My tools are a blunt saw, a blunter axe, a wooden spade, two great augers, that I believe had a hand in bringing us here, but have not been any use to us since, a centre-bit, two planes, a hammer, a pair of pincers, two brad-awls, three gimlets, two scrapers, a plumb-lead and line, a large pair of scissors, and you have a small pair, two gauges, a screw-driver, five claspknives, a few screws and nails of various sizes, two small barrels, two bags, two tin bowls, two wooden bowls, and the shell of this turtle, and that is a very good soup tureen, only we have no meat to make soup with."

"Well, sir," said Miss Rolleston, resignedly, "we can but kneel down and die."

"That would be cutting the gordian knot, indeed," said Hazel. "What, die to shirk a few difficulties? No. I propose an amendment to that. After the words kneel down, insert the words, 'and get up again, trusting in that merciful Providence which has saved us so far, but expects us to exert ourselves too.'"

"It is good and pious advice," said Helen, "and let us follow it this moment."

"Now, said Hazel, "I have three propositions to lay before you. 1st, That I hereby give up walking and take to running; time is so precious. 2d, That we both work by night as well as day. 3d, That we each tell the other our principal wants, so that there may be four eyes on the lookout, as we go, instead of two."

"I consent," said Helen; "Pray what are your wants?"

"Iron, oil, salt, tar, a bellows, a pickaxe, planks, thread, nets, light matting for roofs, bricks, chimney-pots, jars, glass, animal food, some variety of vegetable food, and so on. I'll write down the entire list for you."

"You will be puzzled to do that without ink or paper."

"Not in the least. I shall engrave it in *alto relievo*, make the words with pebbles on the turf just above high-water mark. Now tell me *your* wants."

"Well, I want — Impossibilities."

"Enumerate them."

"What is the use?"

"It is the method we have agreed upon."

"O, very well, then. I want — a sponge."

"Good. What next?"

"I have broken my comb."

"Good."

"I'm glad you think so. I want, — O, Mr. Hazel, what *is* the use? — well, I should like a mattress to lie on."

"Hair or wool?"

"I don't care which. And it is a shame to ask you for either."

"Go on."

"I want a looking-glass."

"Great Heaven! What for?"

"O, never mind: I want one; and some more towels, and some soap, and a few hair-pins; and some elastic bands; and some pen, ink, and paper, to write my feelings down in this island for nobody ever to see."

When she began Hazel looked bright, but the list was like a wasp, its sting lay in its tail. However, he put a good face on it. "I 'll try and get you all those things: only give me time. Do you know I am writing a dictionary on a novel method."

"That means on the sand."

"No; the work is suspended for the present. But two of the definitions in it are, — DIFFICULTIES, — things to be subdued; IMPOSSIBILITIES, — things to be trampled on."

"Well, subdue mine. Trample on — a sponge for me."

"That is just what I was going to do," said he; opened a claspknife and jumped coolly into the river.

Helen screamed faintly, but after all the water was only up to his knees.

He soon cut a large sponge off a piece of slimy rock, and held it up to her. "There," said he, "why, there are a score of them at your very door, and you never saw them?"

"O, excuse me, I did see them, and shuddered; I thought they were reptiles; dormant, and biding their time."

When he was out of the river again, she thought a little, and asked him whether *old* iron would be of any use to him.

"O, certainly," said he; "what do you know of any?"

"I think I saw some one day. I 'll go and look for it."

She took the way of the shore; and he got his cart and spade, and went post-haste to his clay-pit.

He made a quantity of bricks, and brought them home, and put them to dry in the sun. He also cut great pieces of the turtle, and wrapped them in fresh banana-leaves, and enclosed them in clay. He then tried to make a large narrow-necked vessel, and failed utterly; so he made the clay into a great rude platter like a shallow milk-pan. Then he peeled the sago-log, off which he had cut his wheels, and rubbed it with turtle-fat, and using it as a form, produced two clay cylinders. These he set in the sun, with bricks round them to keep them from falling. Leaving all these to dry and set before he baked them, he went off to the marsh for fern-leaves. The soil being so damp the trees were covered with a brownish-red substance, scarce distinguishable from wool. This he had counted on. But he also found in the same neighborhood a long cypress-haired moss that seemed to him very promising. He made several trips, and raised quite a stack of fern-leaves. By this time the sun had operated on his thinner pottery; so he laid down six of his large thick tiles, and lighted a fire on them with dry banana-leaves, and cocoa-nut, etc., and such light combustibles, until he had heated and hardened the clay; then he put the ashes on one side, and swept the clay clean; then he put the fire on again, and made it hotter and hotter till the clay began to redden.

While he was thus occupied, Miss Rolleston came from the jungle radiant, carrying vegetable treasures in her apron. First she produced some golden apples with reddish leaves.

"There," said she; "and they smell delicious"

Hazel eyed them keenly.

"You have not eaten any of them?"

"What! by myself?" said Helen.

"Thank Heaven!" said Hazel, turning pale. "These are the manchanilla, the poison apple of the Pacific."

"Poison!" said Helen, alarmed in her turn.

"Well, I don't *know* that they are poison; but travellers give them a very bad name. The birds never peck them; and I have read that even the leaves falling into still water have killed the fish. You will not eat anything here till you have shown it me, will you?" said he, imploringly.

"No, no," said Helen; and sat down with her hand to her heart a minute. "And I was so pleased when I found them," she said; "they reminded me of home. I wonder whether these are poison, too?" and she opened her apron wide, and showed him some long yellow pods, with red specks, something like a very large banana.

"Ah, that is a very different affair," said Hazel, delighted; "these are plantains, and the greatest find we have made yet. The fruit is meat, the wood is thread, and the leaf is shelter and clothes. The fruit is good raw, and better baked, as you shall see, and, I believe this is the first time the dinner and the dish were both baked together."

He cleared the now heated hearth, put the meat and fruit on it, then placed his great platter over it, and heaped fire round the platter, and light combustibles over it. Whilst this was going on, Helen took him to her bower, and showed him three rusty iron hoops, and a piece of rotten wood with a rusty nail, and the marks where others had been. "There," said she; "that is all I could find."

"Why, it is a treasure," cried he; "you will see. I have found something, too."

He then showed her the vegetable wool and vegetable hair he had collected, and told her where they grew. She owned they were wonderful imitations, and would do as well as the real things; and ere they had done comparing notes, the platter and the dinner under it were both baked. Hazel removed the platter or milk-pan, and served the dinner in it.

If Hazel was inventive, Helen was skilful and quick at any kind of woman's work; and the following is the result of three weeks' work under his direction. She had made as follows: —

1. Thick mattress, stuffed with the vegetable hair and wool described above. The mattress was only two feet six inches wide; for Helen found that she never turned in bed now. She slept as she had never slept before. This mattress was made with plantain-leaves, sewed together with the thread furnished by the tree itself, and doubled at the edges.

2. A long shallow net four feet deep, — cocoa-fibre.

3. A great quantity of stout grass-rope, and light but close matting for the roof, and some cocoa-nut matting for the ground, and to go under the mattress. But Hazel instructed by her had learned to plait, — rather clumsily, — and he had a hand in the matting.

Hazel in the mean time heightened his own mud banks in the centre, and set up brick fireplaces with hearth and chimney, one on each side; and now did all the cooking; for he found the smoke from wood made Miss Rolleston cough. He also made a number of pigeon-holes in his mud walls and lined them with clay. One of these he dried with fire, and made a pottery door to it, and there kept the lucifer-box. He made a vast number of bricks, but did nothing with them. After several failures he made two large pots, and two great pans, that would all four bear fire under them, and in the pans he boiled sea-water till it all evaporated and left him a sediment of salt. This was a great addition to their food, and he managed also to put by a little. But it was a slow process.

He made a huge pair of bellows, with a little assistance from Miss Rolleston; the spout was a sago stick, with the pith driven out, and the substitute for leather was the skin of a huge eel he found stranded at the east point.

Having got his bellows and fixed them to a post he drove into the ground, he took for his anvil a huge flint stone, and a smaller one for hammer; heated his old iron to a white heat, and hammered it with a world of trouble into straight lengths; and at last with a portion of it produced a long saw without teeth, but one side sharper than the other. This by repeated experiments of heating and immersing in water, he at last annealed; and when he wanted to saw, he blew his embers to a white heat (he kept the fire alive now night and day); heated his original saw red-hot, and soon sawed through the oleaginous woods of that island. If he wanted to cut down a tree in the jungle, he put the bellows and a pot of embers on his cart with other fuel, and came and lighted the fire under the tree and soon had it down. He made his pickaxe in half an hour, but with his eyes rather than his hands. He found a young tree growing on the rock, or at least on soil so shallow that the root was half above ground and at right angles to the stem. He got this tree up, shortened the stem, shaped the root, shod the point with some of his late old iron; and with this primitive tool, and a thick stake baked at the point, he opened the ground to receive twelve stout uprights, and he drove them with a tremendous mallet made upon what might be called the compendious or Hazelian method; it was a section of a hard tree with a thick shoot growing out of it, which shoot, being shortened, served for the handle. By these arts he at last saw a goal to his labors. Animal food, oil, pitch, ink, paper, were still wanting; but fish were abundant, and plantains and cocoa-nuts stored. Above all, Helen's hut was now weather-tight. Stout horizontal bars were let into the trees, and, being bound to the uprights, they mutually supported each other; smaller horizontal bars at intervals kept the prickly ramparts from being driven in by a sudden gust. The canvas walls were removed, and the nails stored in a pigeon-hole, and a stout network substituted, to which huge plantain-leaves were cunningly fastened with plantain-thread. The roof was double: first that extraordinary mass of spiked leaves which the four trees threw out, then several feet under that the huge piece of matting the pair had made. This was strengthened by double strips of canvas at the edges and in the centre, and by single strips in other parts. A great many cords and strings made of that wonderful grass was sewn to the canvas-strengthened edges, and so it was fastened to the trees, and fastened to the horizontal bars.

When this work drew close to its completion, Hazel could not disguise his satisfaction.

But he very soon had the mortification of seeing that she for whom it was all done did not share his complacency.

A change took place in her; she often let her work fall, and brooded. She spoke sometimes sharply to Mr. Hazel, and sometimes with strained civility. She wandered away from him, and from his labors for her comfort, and passed hours at Telegraph Point, eying the illimitable ocean. She was a Riddle. All sweetness at times, but at others irritable, moody, and scarce mistress of herself. Hazel was sorry and perplexed, and often expressed a fear she was ill. The answer was always in the negative. He did not press her, but worked on for her, hoping the mood would pass. And so it would no doubt, if the cause had not remained.

Matters were still in this uncomfortable and mysterious state when Hazel put his finishing stroke to her abode.

He was in high spirits that evening: for he had made a discovery; he had at last found time for a walk, and followed the river to its source, a very remarkable lake in a hilly basin. Near this was a pond, the water of which he had tasted and found it highly bituminous; and making further researches, he had found at the bottom of a rocky ravine a very wonderful thing, a dark resinous fluid bubbling up in quite a fountain, which, however, fell down again as it rose, and hardly any overflowed. It was like thin pitch.

Of course, in another hour he was back there with a great pot, and half filled it. It was not like water: it did not bubble so high, when some had been taken: so he just took what he could get. Pursuing his researches a little farther he found a range of rocks with snowy summits apparently; but the snow was the guano of centuries. He got to the western extremity of the island, saw another deep bay or rather branch of the sea, and on the other side of it a tongue of high land running out to sea: on that promontory stood a gigantic palm-tree. He recognized that with a certain thrill, but was in a great hurry to get home with his pot of pitch; for it was in truth a very remarkable discovery, though not without a parallel. He could not wait till morning, so with embers and cocoa-nut he made a fire in the bower, and melted his pitch which had become nearly solid, and proceeded to smear the inside of the matting in places, to make it thoroughly water-tight.

Helen treated the discovery at first with mortifying indifference: but he hoped she would appreciate Nature's bounty more when she saw the practical use of this extraordinary production. He endeavored to lead her to that view. She shook her head, sorrowfully. He persisted. She met him with silence. He thought this peevish, and ungrateful to Heaven; we have all different measures of the wonderful; and to him a fountain of pitch was a thing to admire greatly and thank God for: he said as much.

To Helen it was nasty stuff, and who cares where it came from. She conveyed as much by a shrug of the shoulders, and then gave a sigh that told her mind was far away.

He was a little mortified, and showed it.

One word led to another, and at last what had been long fermenting came out.

"Mr. Hazel," said she, "you and I are at cross purposes. You mean to live here. I do not."

Hazel left off working and looked greatly perplexed, the attack was so sudden in its form, though it had been a long time threatening. He found nothing to say, and she was impatient now to speak her mind, so she replied to his look.

"You are making yourself at home here. You are contented. Contented? You are happy in this horrible prison."

"And why not?" said Hazel. But he looked rather guilty. "Here are no traitors; no murderers. The animals are my friends, and the one human being I see makes me better to look at her."

"Mr. Hazel, I am in a state of mind, that romantic nonsense jars on me. Be honest with me, and talk to me like a man. I say that you beam all over with happiness and content, and that you — now answer me one question; why have you never lighted the bonfire on Telegraph Point?"

"Indeed I don't know," said he, submissively. "I have been so occupied."

"You have: and how? Not in trying to deliver us both from this dreadful situation, but to reconcile me to it. Yes sir, under pretence (that is a harsh word, but I can't help it) of keeping out the rain. Your rain is a Bugbear: it never rains, it never will rain. You are killing yourself almost to make me comfortable in this place. Comfortable?" She began to tremble all over with excitement long restrained. "And do you really suppose you can make me live on like this, by building me a nice hut. Do you think I am all body and no soul, that shelter and warmth and enough to eat can keep my heart from breaking, and my cheeks from blushing night and day. When I wake in the morning I find myself blushing to my fingers' ends." Then she walked away from him. Then she walked back. "O, my dear father, why did I ever leave you!" "Keep me here? make me live months and years on this island. Have you sisters? Have you a mother? Ask yourself, is it likely? No; if you will not help me, and they don't love me enough to come and find me and take me home, I'll go to another home without your help or any man's." Then she rose suddenly to her feet. "I'll tie my clothes tight round me, and fling myself down from that point on to the sharp rocks below. I'll find a way from this place to Heaven, if there's no way from it to those I love on earth."

Then she sank down and rocked herself and sobbed hard.

The strong passion of this hitherto gentle creature quite frightened her unhappy friend, who knew more of books than women. He longed to soothe her and comfort her; but what could he say. He cried out in despair, "My God, can I do nothing for her?"

She turned on him like lightning, "You can do anything: everything. You can restore us both to our friends. You can save my life, my reason. For that will go first, I think. What *had* I done? what had I *ever* done since I was born, to be so brought down? Was ever an English lady —? And then I have such an irritation on my skin, all over me. I sometimes wish the tiger would come and tear me all to pieces; yes, all to pieces." And with that her white teeth clicked together convulsively. "Do!" said she, darting back to the point as swiftly as she had rushed away from it. "Why, put down that nasty stuff; and leave off inventing fifty little trumpery things for me, and do one great thing instead. O, do not fritter that great mind of yours away in painting and patching my prison; but bring it all to bear on getting me *out* of my prison. Call sea and land to our rescue. Let them know a poor girl is here in unheard-of, unfathomable misery: here, in the middle of this awful ocean."

Hazel sighed deeply. "No ships seem to pass within sight of us," he muttered.

"What does that matter to *you?* You are not a common man; you are an inventor. Rouse all the powers of your mind. There must be some way. Think for me. THINK! THINK! or my blood will be on your head."

Hazel turned pale and put his head in his hands, and tried to think.

She leaned towards him with great flashing eyes of purest hazel.

The problem dropped from his lips a syllable at a time. "To diffuse — intelligence — a hundred leagues from a fixed point — an island?"

She leaned towards him with flashing expectant eyes.

But he groaned, and said; "That seems impossible."

"Then trample on it," said she, bringing his own words against him; for she used to remember all he said to her in the day, and ponder it at night. "Trample on it, subdue it, or never speak to me again. Ah, I am an ungrateful wretch to speak so harshly to you. It is my misery, not me. Good, kind, Mr. Hazel, O pray, pray, pray bring all the powers of that great mind to bear on this one thing, and save a poor girl, to whom you have been so kind, so considerate, so noble, so delicate, so forbearing; now save me from despair."

Hysterical sobs cut her short here, and Hazel, whose loving heart she had almost torn out of his body, could only falter out in a broken voice, that he would obey her. "I'll work no more for you at present," said he, "sweet as it has been. I will think instead. I will go this moment beneath the stars and think all night."

The young woman was now leaning her head languidly back against one of the trees, weak as water after her passion. He cast a look of ineffable love and pity on her, and withdrew slowly to think beneath the tranquil stars.

Love has set men hard tasks in his time. Whether this was a light one, our reader shall decide.

TO DIFFUSE INTELLIGENCE FROM A FIXED ISLAND OVER A HUNDRED LEAGUES OF OCEAN

CHAPTER XXVII.

THE perplexity into which Hazel was thrown by the outburst of his companion, rendered him unable to reduce her demand at once to an intelligible form. For some moments he seriously employed his mind on the problem until it assumed this shape.

Firstly: I do not know where this island is, having no means of ascertaining either its latitude or longitude.

Secondly: If I had such a description of its locality, how might the news be conveyed beyond the limits of the place?

As the wildness of Helen's demand broke upon his mind, he smiled sadly, and sat down upon the bank of the little river, near his boat-house, and buried his head in his hands. A deep groan burst from him, and the tears at last came through his fingers, as in despair he thought how vain must be any effort to content or to conciliate her. Impatient with his own weakness he started to his feet, when a hand was laid gently upon his arm. She stood beside him.

"Mr. Hazel," she said, hurriedly, — her voice was husky, — "do not mind what I have said. I am unreasonable; and I am sure I ought to feel obliged to you for all the — "

Hazel turned his face towards her, and the moon glistened on the tears that still flowed down his cheeks. He tried to check the utterance of her apology; but, ere he could master his voice, the girl's cold and constrained features seemed to melt. She turned away, wrung her hands, and with a sharp quivering cry, she broke forth, —

"O sir! O Mr. Hazel! do forgive me. I am not ungrateful, indeed, indeed, I am not; but I am mad with despair. Judge me with compassion. At this moment, those who are very very dear to me are awaiting my arrival in London; and when they learn the loss of the Proserpine, how great will be their misery! Well, that misery is added to mine. Then my poor papa: he will never know how much he loved me until this news reaches him. And to think that I am dead to them, yet living! living here helplessly, helplessly. Dear, dear, Arthur, how you will suffer for my sake. O papa, papa! shall I never see you again?" and she wept bitterly.

"I am helpless either to aid or to console you, Miss Rolleston. By the act of a Divine Providence you were cast upon this desolate shore, and by the same Will I was appointed to serve and to provide for your welfare. I pray God that He will give me health and strength to assist you. Good night."

She looked timidly at him for a moment, then slowly regained her hut. He had spoken coldly, and with dignity. She felt humbled, the more so, that he had only bowed his acknowledgment to her apology.

For more than an hour she watched him, as he paced up and down between the boat-house and the shore; then he advanced a little towards her shelter, and she shrank into her bed, after gently closing the door. In a few moments she crept again to peep forth, and to see if he were still there, but he had disappeared.

The following morning Helen was surprised to see the boat riding at anchor in the surf, and Hazel busily engaged on her trim. He was soon on shore, and by her side.

"I am afraid I must leave you for a day, Miss Rolleston," he said. "I wish to make a circuit of the island; indeed, I ought to have done so many days ago."

"Is such an expedition necessary? Surely you have had enough of the sea."

"It is very necessary. You have urged me to undertake this enterprise. You see, it is the first step towards announcing to all passing vessels our presence in this place. I have commenced operations already. See on yonder bluff, which I have called Telegraph Point, I have mounted the boat's ensign, and now it floats from the top of the tree beside the bonfire. I carried it there at sunrise. Do you see that pole I have shipped on board the boat? that is intended as a signal, which shall be exhibited on your great palm-tree. The flag will then stand for a signal on the northern coast, and the palm-tree, thus accoutred, will serve for a similar purpose on the western extremity of the island. As I pass along the southern and eastern shores, I propose to select spots where some mark can be erected, such as may be visible to ships at sea."

"But will they remark such signals?"

"Be assured they will, if they come within sight of the place."

Hazel knew that there was little chance of such an event; but it was something not to be neglected. He also explained that it was necessary he should arrive at a knowledge of the island, the character of its shores; and from the sea he could rapidly obtain a plan of the place, ascertain what small rivers there might be, and, indeed, see much of its interior; for he judged it to be not more than ten miles in length, and scarce three in width.

Helen felt rather disappointed that no trace of the emotion he displayed on the previous night remained in his manner, or in the expression of his face. She bowed her permission to him rather haughtily, and sat down to breakfast on some baked yams, and some rough oysters, which he had raked up from the bay while bathing that morning. The young man had regained an elasticity of bearing, an independence of tone, to which she was not at all accustomed; his manners were always soft and deferential; but his expression was more firm, and she felt that the reins had been gently removed from her possession, and there was a will to guide her which she was bound to acknowledge and obey.

She did not argue in this wise, for it is not human to reason and to feel at the same moment. She felt then instinctively that the man was quietly asserting his superiority, and the child pouted.

Hazel went about his work briskly; the boat was soon laden with every requisite. Helen watched these preparations askance, vexed with the expedition which she had urged him to make. Then she fell to reflecting on the change that seemed to have taken place in her character; she, who was once so womanly, so firm, so reasonable, — why had she become so petulant, childish, and capricious?

The sail was set, and all ready to run the cutter into the surf of the rising tide, when, taking a sudden resolution, as it were, Helen came rapidly down, and said, "I will go with you, if you please," half in command and half in doubt. Hazel looked a little surprised, but very pleased; and then she added, "I hope I shall not be in your way."

He assured her, on the contrary, that she might be of great assistance to him; and now with doubled alacrity, he ran out the little vessel and leaped into the prow as she danced over the waves. He taught her how to bring the boat's head round with the help of an oar, and when all was snug, left her at the helm. On reaching the mouth of the bay, if it could so be called, he made her remark that it was closed by reefs, except to the north and to the west. The wind being southerly, he had decided to pass to the west, and so they opened the sea about half a mile from the shore.

For about three miles they perceived it consisted of a line of bluffs, cleft at intervals by small narrow bays, the precipitous sides of which were lined with dense foliage. Into these fissures the sea entered with a mournful sound, that died away as it crept up the yellow sands with which these nooks were carpeted. An exclamation from Helen attracted his attention to the horizon on the northwest, where a long line of breakers glittered in the sun. A reef or low sandy bay appeared to exist in that direction, about fifteen miles away, and something more than a mile in length. As they proceeded, he marked

EXPLORING THE ISLAND.—See page 64.

roughly on the side of his tin baler, with the point of a pin borrowed from Helen, the form of the coast line.

An hour and a half brought them to the northwestern extremity of the island. As they cleared the shelter of the land, the southerly breeze coming with some force across the open sea caught the cutter, and she lay over in a way to inspire Helen with alarm; she was about to let go the tiller, when Hazel seized it, accidentally enclosing her hand under the grasp of his own, as he pressed the tiller hard to port.

"Steady, please; don't relinquish your hold; it is all right, — no fear," he cried, as he kept his eye on their sail.

He held this course for a mile or more, and then judging with a long tack he could weather the southerly side of the island, he put the boat about. He took occasion to explain to Helen how this operation was necessary, and she learned the alphabet of navigation. The western end of their little land now lay before them; it was about three miles in breadth. For two miles the bluff coast line continued unbroken; then a deep bay, a mile in width and two miles in depth, was made by a long tongue of sand projecting westerly; on its extremity grew the gigantic palm, well recognized as Helen's landmark. Hazel stood up in the boat to reconnoitre the coast. He perceived the sandy shore was dotted with multitudes of dark objects. Erelong, these objects were seen to be in motion, and, pointing them out to Helen, with a smile, he said, —

"Beware, Miss Rolleston, yonder are your bugbears, — and in some force, too. Those dark masses, moving upon the hillocks of sand, or rolling on the surf, are sea-lions, — the *phoca leonina*, or lion-seal."

Helen strained her eyes to distinguish the forms, but only descried the dingy objects. While thus engaged, she allowed the cutter to fall off a little, and, ere Hazel had resumed his hold upon the tiller, they were fairly in the bay; the great palm-tree on their starboard-bow.

"You seem determined to make the acquaintance of your nightmares," he remarked; "you perceive that we are embayed."

Her consternation amused him; she saw that if they held their present course, the cutter would take the beach about a mile ahead, where these animals were densely crowded.

At this moment, something dark bulged up close beside her in the sea, and the rounded back of a monster rolled over and disappeared. Hazel let drop the sail, for they were now fairly in the smooth water of the bay, and close to the sandy spit, the gigantic stem of the palm-tree was on their quarter, about half a mile off.

He took to the oars, and rowed slowly towards the shore. A small seal rose behind the boat and followed them, playing with the blade, its gambols resembling that of a kitten. He pointed out to Helen the mild expression of the creature's face, and assured her that all this tribe were harmless animals, and susceptible of domestication. The cub swam up to the boat quite fearlessly, and he touched its head gently; he encouraged her to do the like, but she shrank from its contact. They were now close ashore, and Hazel, throwing out his anchor in two feet of water, prepared to land the beam of wood he had brought to decorate the palm-tree as a signal.

The huge stick was soon heaved overboard, and he leaped after it. He towed it to the nearest landing to the tree, and dragged it high up on shore. Scarcely had he disposed it conveniently, intending to return in a day or two, with the means of affixing it in a prominent and remarkable manner, in the form of a spar across the trunk of the palm, when a cry from Helen recalled him. A large number of the sea-lions were coasting quietly down the surf towards the boat; indeed, a dozen of them had made their appearance around it.

Hazel shouted to her not to fear, and desiring that her alarm should not spread to the swarm, he passed back quietly but rapidly. When he reached the water, three or four of the animals were already floundering between him and the boat. He waded slowly towards one of them, and stood beside it. The man and the creature looked quietly at each other, and then the seal rolled over, with a snuffling, self-satisfied air, winking its soft eyes with immense complacency.

Helen, in her alarm, could not resist a smile at this conclusion of so terrible a demonstration; for, with all their gentle expression, the tusks of the brute looked formidable. But, when she saw Hazel pushing them aside, and patting a very small cub on the back, she recovered her courage completely.

Then he took to his oars again; and, aided by the tide, which was now on the ebb, he rowed round the southwestern extremity of the island. He found the water here, as he anticipated, very shallow.

It was midday when they were fairly on the southern coast; and now, sailing with the wind aft, the cutter ran through the water at racing speed. Fearing that some reefs or rocky formations might exist in their course, he reduced sail, and kept away from the shore, about a mile. At this distance he was better able to see inland, and mark down the accidence of its formation.

The southern coast was uniform, and Helen said it resembled the cliffs of the Kentish or Sussex coast of England, only the English white was here replaced by the pale volcanic gray. By one o'clock they came abreast the very spot where they had first made land; and, as they judged, due south of their residence. Had they landed here, a walk of three miles across the centre of the island would have brought them home.

For about a similar distance the coast exhibited monotonous cliffs unbroken even by a rill. It was plain that the water-shed of the island was all northward. They now approached the eastern end, where rose the circular mountain of which mention has been already made. This eminence had evidently at one time been detached from the rest of the land to which it was now joined by a neck of swamp about a mile and a half in breadth, and two miles in length.

Hazel proposed to reconnoitre this part of the shore nearly, and ran the boat close in to land. The reeds or canes with which this bog was densely clothed, grew in a dark spongy soil. Here and there this waste was dotted with ragged trees which he recognized as the cypress: from its gaunt branches hung a black, funeral kind of weeper, a kind of moss, resembling iron gray horsehair both in texture and uses, though not so long in the staple.

This parasite, Hazel explained to Helen, was very common in such marshy ground, and was the death-flag hung out by Nature to warn man that malaria and fever were the invisible and inalienable inhabitants of that fatal neighborhood.

Looking narrowly along the low shore for some good landing, where under shelter of a tree they might repose for an hour, and spread their midday repast, they discovered an opening in the reeds, a kind of lagoon or bayou, extending into the morass between the highlands of the island and the circular mountain, but close under the base of the latter. This inlet he proposed to explore, and accordingly the sail was taken down and the cutter was poled into the narrow creek. The water here was so shallow that the keel slid over the quicksand into which the oar sank freely. The creek soon became narrow, the water deeper, and of a blacker color, and the banks more densely covered with canes. These grew to the height of ten and twelve feet, and as close as wheat in a thick crop. The air felt dank and heavy, and hummed with myriads of insects. The black water became so deep and the bottom so sticky that Hazel took to the oars again. The creek narrowed as they proceeded, until it proved scarcely wide enough to admit of his working the boat. The height of the reeds hindered the view on either side. Suddenly, however, and after proceeding very slowly through the bends of the canal, they decreased in height and density, and they emerged into an open space of about five acres in extent, a kind of oasis in this reedy desert, created by a mossy mound which arose amidst the morass, and afforded firm footing, of which a grove of trees and innumerable shrubs availed themselves. Helen uttered an exclamation of delight as this island of foliage in a sea of reeds met her eyes, that had been famished with the arid monotony of the brake.

They soon landed.

Helen insisted on the preparations for their meal being left to her, and having selected a sheltered spot she was soon busy with their frugal food. Hazel surveyed the spot, and selecting a red cedar, was soon seated forty feet above her head; making a topographical survey of the neighborhood. He found that the bayou by which they had entered continued its course to the northern shore, thus cutting off the mountain or easterly end, and forming of it a separate island. He saw that a quarter of a mile farther on the bayou or canal parted, forming two streams, of which that to the left seemed the main channel. This he determined to follow. Turning to the west, that is towards their home, he saw at a distance of two miles a crest of hills broken into cliffs, which defined the limit of the mainland. The sea had at one time occupied the site where the morass now stood. These cliffs formed a range, extending from north to south: their precipitous sides clothed here and there with trees, marked where the descent was broken by platforms. Between him and this range the morass extended. Hazel took note of three places where the descent from these hills into the marsh could, he believed, most readily be made.

On the eastern side, and close above him arose the peculiar mountain. Its form was that of a truncated cone, and its sides densely covered with trees of some size.

The voice of Helen called him from his perch, and he descended quickly, leaping into a mass of brushwood growing at the foot of his tree. Helen stood a few yards from him, in admiration, before a large shrub.

"Look, Mr. Hazel, what a singular production," said the girl, as she stooped to examine the plant. It bore a number of red flowers, each growing out of a fruit like a prickly pear. These flowers were in various stages; some were just opening like tulips others, more advanced, had expanded like umbrellas, and quite overlapped the fruit, keeping it from sun and dew; others had served their turn in that way, and been withered by the sun's rays. But, wherever this was the case, the fruit had also burst open and displayed or discharged its contents, and those contents looked like seeds; but on narrower inspection proved to be little insects with pink transparent wings, and bodies of incredibly vivid crimson.

Hazel examined the fruit and flowers very carefully, and stood rapt, transfixed.

"It must be! — and it is!" said he, at last. "Well, I'm glad I've not died without seeing it."

"What is it?" said she.

"One of the most valuable productions of the earth. It is cochineal. This is the Tunal-tree."

"O! indeed," said Helen, indifferently: "cochineal is used for a dye; but as it is not probable we shall require to dye anything, the discovery seems to me more curious than useful."

"You wanted some ink. This pigment, mixed with lime-juice, will form a beautiful red ink. Will you lend me your handkerchief and permit me to try if I have forgotten the method by which these little insects are obtained." He asked her to hold her handkerchief under a bough of the Tunal-tree, where the fruit was ripe. He then shook the bough. Some insects fell at once into the cloth. A great number rose and buzzed a little in the sun not a yard from where they were born; but the sun dried their blood so promptly that they soon fell dead in the handkerchief. Those that the sun so killed went through three phases of color before their eyes. They fell down black or nearly. They whitened on the cloth: and after that came gradually to their final color, a flaming crimson. The insect thus treated, appeared the most vivid of all.

They soon secured about half a tea-cup full; they were rolled up and put away, then they sat down and made a very hearty meal, for it was now past two o'clock. They re-entered the boat, and passing once more into the morass they found the channel of the bayou as it approached the northern shore less difficult of navigation. The bottom became sandy and hard, and the presence of trees in the swamp proved that spots of *terra firma* were more frequent. But the water shallowed, and as they opened the shore, he saw with great vexation that the tide in receding had left the bar at the mouth of the canal visible in some parts. He pushed on, however, until the boat grounded. This was a sad affair. There lay the sea not fifty yards ahead. Hazel leaped out, and examined and forded the channel, which at this place was about two hundred feet wide. He found a narrow passage near the eastern side, and to this he towed the boat. Then he begged Miss Rolleston to land, and relieved the boat of the mast, sail, and oars. Thus lightened, he dragged her into the passage: but the time occupied in these preparations had been also occupied by Nature, — the tide had receded, and the cutter stuck immovably in the water-way, about six fathoms short of deeper water.

"What is to be done now?" inquired Helen, when Hazel returned to her side, panting, but cheerful.

"We must await the rising of the tide. I fear we are imprisoned here for three hours at least."

There was no help for it. Helen made light of the misfortune. The spot where they had landed was enclosed between the two issues of the lagoon. They walked along the shore to the more easterly, and the narrower canal, and, on arriving, Hazel found to his great annoyance that there was ample water to have floated the cutter had he selected that, the least promising road. He suggested a return by the road they came, and, passing into the other canal, by that to reach the sea. They hurried back, but found by this time the tide had left the cutter high and dry on the sand. So they had no choice but to wait.

Having three hours to spare, Hazel asked Miss Rolleston's permission to ascend the mountain. She assented to remain near the boat while he was engaged in this expedition. The ascent was too rugged and steep for her powers, and the seashore and adjacent groves would find her ample amusement during his absence. She accompanied him to the bank of the smaller lagoon, which he forded, and waving an adieu to her he plunged into the dense wood with which the sides of the mountain were clothed.

She waited some time, and then she heard his voice shouting to her from the heights above. The mountain-top was about three quarters of a mile from where she stood, but seemed much nearer. She turned back towards the boat, walking slowly, but paused as a faint and distant cry again reached her ear. It was not repeated, and then she entered the grove.

The ground beneath her feet was soft with velvety moss, and the dark foliage of the trees rendered the air cool and deliciously fragrant. After wandering for some time, she regained the edge of the grove near the boat, and selecting a spot at the foot of an aged cypress, she sat down with her back against its trunk. Then she took out Arthur's letter, and began to read those impassioned sentences: as she read she sighed deeply, as earnestly she found herself pitying Arthur's condition more than she regretted her own. She fell into reverie, and from reverie into a drowsy languor. How long she remained in this state she could not remember, but a slight rustle overhead recalled her senses. Believing it to be a bird moving in the branches she was resigning herself again to rest when she became sensible of a strange emotion, a conviction that something was watching her with a fixed gaze. She cast her eyes around, but saw nothing. She looked upwards. From the tree immediately above her lap depended a snake, its tail coiled around a dead branch. The reptile hung straight, its eyes fixed like two rubies upon Helen's, as very slowly it let itself down by its uncoiling tail. Now its head was on a level with hers; in another moment it must drop into her lap.

She was paralyzed.

CHAPTER XXVIII.

After toiling up a rugged and steep ascent, encumbered with blocks of gray stone, of which the island seemed to be formed, forcing his way over fallen trees and through the tangled undergrowth of a species of wild vine, which abounded on the mountain-side, Hazel stopped to breathe and peer around, as well as the dense foliage permitted. He was up to his waist in scrub, and the stiff leaves of the bayonet plant rendered caution necessary in walking. At moments, through the dense foliage, he caught a glisten of the sea. The sun was in the north behind him, and by this alone he guided his road due southerly and upward. Once only he found a small cleared space about an acre in extent, and here it was he uttered the cry Helen heard. He waited a few moments in the hope to hear her voice in reply, but it did not reach him. Again he plunged upward, and now the ascent became at times so arduous that more than once he almost resolved to relinquish, or, at least, to defer his task; but a moment's rest recalled him to himself, and he was one not easily baffled by difficulty or labor, so he toiled on until he judged the summit ought to have been reached. After pausing to take breath and counsel, he fancied that he had borne too much to the left, the ground to his right appeared to rise more than the path that he was pursuing, which had become level, and he concluded, that, instead of ascending, he was circling the mountain-top. He turned aside, therefore, and after ten minutes' hard climbing he was pushing through a thick and high scrub, when the earth seemed to give way beneath him, and he fell — into an abyss.

He was engulfed. He fell from bush to bush — down — down — scratch — rip — plump! until he lodged in a prickly bush more winded than hurt. Out of this he crawled, only to discover himself thus landed in a great and perfectly circular plain of about thirty acres in extent, or about 350 yards in diameter. In the centre was a lake, also circular, the broad belt of shore around this lake was covered with rich grass, level as a bowling-green, and all this again was surrounded by a nearly perpendicular cliff, down which indeed he had fallen: this cliff was thickly clothed with shrubs and trees.

Hazel recognized the crater of an extinct volcano.

On examining the lake he found the waters impregnated with volcanic products. Its bottom was formed of asphaltum. Having made a circuit of the shores, he perceived on the westerly side — that next the island — a break in the cliff; and on a narrow examination he discovered an outlet. It appeared to him that the lake at one time had emptied its waters through this ancient water-course. The descent here was not only gradual, but the old river-bed was tolerably free from obstructions, especially of the vegetable kind.

He made his way rapidly downwards, and in half an hour reached marshy ground. The cane-brake now lay before him. On his left he saw the sea on the south, about a third of a mile. He knew that to the right must be the sea on the north, about half a mile or so. He bent his way thither. The edge of the swamp was very clear, and though somewhat spongy, afforded good walking unimpeded As he approached the spot where he judged the boat to be, the underwood thickened, the trees again interlaced their arms, and he had to struggle through the foliage. At length he struck the smaller lagoon, and, as he was not certain whether it was fordable, he followed its course to the shore, where he had previously crossed. In a few moments he reached the boat, and was pleased to find her afloat. The rising tide had even moved her a few feet back into the canal.

Hazel shouted to apprise Miss Rolleston of his return, and then proceeded to restore the mast to its place, and replace the rigging and the oars. This occupied some little time. He felt surprised that she had not appeared. He shouted again. No reply.

CHAPTER XXIX.

Hazel advanced hurriedly into the grove, which he hunted thoroughly, but without effect. He satisfied himself that she could not have quitted the spot, since the marsh enclosed it on one side, the canals on the second and third, the sea on the fourth. He returned to the boat more surprised than anxious. He waited a while, and again shouted her name,—stopped,—listened,—no answer.

Yet surely Helen could not have been more than a hundred yards from where he stood. His heart beat with a strange sense of apprehension. He heard nothing but the rustling of the foliage and the sop of the waves on the shore, as the tide crept up the shingle. As his eyes roved in every direction, he caught sight of something white near the foot of a withered cypress-tree, not fifty yards from where he stood. He approached the bushes in which the tree was partially concealed on that side, and quickly recognized a portion of Helen's dress. He ran towards her,—burst through the underwood, and gained the enclosure. She was sitting there, asleep, as he conjectured, her back leaning against the trunk. He contemplated her thus for one moment, and then he advanced, about to awaken her; but was struck speechless. Her face was ashy pale, her eyes open and widely distended; her bosom heaved slowly. Hazel approached rapidly, and called to her.

Her eyes never moved, not a limb stirred. She sat glaring forward. On her lap was coiled a snake,—gray, mottled with muddy green.

Hazel looked round and selected a branch of the dead tree, about three feet in length. Armed with this, he advanced slowly to the reptile. It was very quiet, thanks to the warmth of her lap. He pointed the stick at it; the vermin lifted its head, and its tail began to quiver; then it darted at the stick, throwing itself its entire length. Hazel retreated, the snake coiled again, and again darted. By repeating this process four or five times, he enticed the creature away; and then availing himself of a moment before it could recoil, he struck it a smart blow on the neck.

When Hazel turned to Miss Rolleston, he found her still fixed in the attitude into which terror had transfixed her. The poor girl had remained motionless for an hour, under the terrible fascination of the reptile, comatized. He spoke to her, but a quick spasmodic action of her throat and a quivering of her hands, alone responded. The sight of her suffering agonized him beyond expression, but he took her hands,—he pressed them, for they were icy cold,—he called piteously on her name. But she seemed incapable of effort. Then stooping he raised her tenderly in his arms, and carried her to the boat, where he laid her still unresisting and incapable.

With trembling limbs and weak hands, he launched the cutter; and they were once more afloat and bound homeward.

He dipped the baler into the fresh water he had brought with him for their daily supply, and dashed it on her forehead. This he repeated until he perceived her breathing became less painful and more rapid. Then he raised her a little, and her head rested upon his arm. When they reached the entrance of the bay he was obliged to pass it, for the wind being still southernly, he could not enter by the north gate, but came round and ran in by the western passage, the same by which they had left the same morning.

Hazel bent over Helen, and whispered tenderly that they were at home. She answered by a sob. In half an hour, the keel grated on the sand, near the boat-house. Then he asked her if she were strong enough to reach her hut. She raised her head, but she felt dizzy; he helped her to land; all power had forsaken her limbs; her head sank on his shoulder, and his arm, wound round her lithe figure, alone prevented her falling helplessly at his feet. Again he raised her in his arms and bore her to the hut. Here he laid her down on her bed, and stood for a moment beside her, unable to restrain his tears.

CHAPTER XXX.

It was a wretched and anxious night for Hazel. He watched the hut, without the courage to approach it. That one moment of weakness which occurred to him on board the Proserpine when he had allowed Helen to perceive the nature of his feelings towards her, had rendered all his actions open to suspicion. He dared not exhibit towards her any sympathy,—he might not extend to her the most ordinary civility. If she fell ill, if fever supervened! how could he nurse her, attend upon her? His touch must have a significance, he knew that; for, as he bore her insensible form, he embraced rather than carried the precious burden. Could he look upon her in her suffering without betraying his forbidden love? And then would not his attentions afflict more than console?

Chewing the cud of such bitter thoughts, he passed the night, without noticing the change which was taking place over the island. The sun rose; and this awakened him from his reverie, which had replaced sleep; he looked around, and then became sensible of the warnings in the air.

The sea-birds flew about vaguely and absurdly, and seemed sporting in currents of wind; yet there was but little wind down below. Presently clouds came flying over the sky, and blacker masses gathered on the horizon. The sea changed color.

Hazel knew the weather was breaking. The wet season was at hand,—the moment when fever, if such an invisible inhabitant there was on that island, would visit them. In a few hours the rain would be upon them, and he reproached himself with want of care in the construction of the hut. For some hours he hovered around it, before he ventured to approach the door, and call to Helen. He thought he heard her voice faintly, and he entered. She lay there as he had placed her. He knelt beside her, and was appalled at the change in her appearance.

The poor girl's system had received a shock for which it was unprepared. Her severe sufferings at sea had, strange to say, reduced her in appearance less than could have been believed; for her physical endurance proved greater than that of the strong men around her. But the food which the island supplied was not suited to restore her strength, and the nervous shock to which she had been subjected was followed by complete prostration.

Hazel took her unresisting hand, which he would have given a world to press. He felt her pulse; it was weak, but slow. Her cheeks were hollow, her eyes sunken; her hand dropped helplessly when he released it.

Leaving the hut quietly, but hastily, he descended the hill to the rivulet, which he crossed. About half a mile above the boat-house the stream forked, one of its branches coming from the west, the other from the east. Between this latter branch and Terrapin Wood, was a stony hill; to this spot Hazel went, and fell to gathering a handful of poppies. When he had obtained a sufficient quantity he returned to the boat-house, made a small fire of chips, and filling his tin baler with water, he set down the poppies to boil. When the liquor was cool, he measured out a portion and drank it. In about twenty minutes his temples began to throb, a sensation which was rapidly followed by nausea.

It was midday before he recovered from the effects of his experiment sufficiently to take food. Then he waited for two hours, and felt much restored. He stole to the hut and looked in. Helen lay there as he had left her. He stooped over her: her eyes were half-closed, and she turned them slowly upon him; her lips moved a little, — that was all. He felt her pulse again; it was still weaker, and slower. He rose and went away, and regaining the boat-house, he measured out a portion of the poppy liquor, one third of the dose he had previously taken, and drank it. No headache or nausea succeeded; he felt his pulse; it became quick and violent, while a sense of numbness overcame him, and he slept. It was but for a few minutes. He awoke with a throbbing brow, and some sickness; but with a sense of delight at the heart, for he had found an opiate, and prescribed its quantity.

He drained the liquor away from the poppy leaves, and carried it to the hut. Measuring with great care a small quantity, he lifted the girl's head and placed it to her lips. She drank it mechanically. Then he watched beside her, until her breathing and her pulse changed in character. She slept. He turned aside then, and buried his face in his hands and prayed fervently for her life, — prayed as we pray for the daily bread of the heart. He prayed and waited.

CHAPTER XXXI.

The next morning, when Helen awoke, she was very weak; her head ached, but she was herself. Hazel had made a broth for her from the fleshy part of a turtle; this greatly revived her, and by midday, she was able to sit up. Having seen that her wants were within her reach, he left her; but in a few moments, she heard him busily engaged on the roof of her hut.

On his return, he explained to her his fears that the structure was scarcely as weather-proof as he desired; and he anticipated hourly the commencement of the rainy season. Helen smiled and pointed to the sky, which here was clear and bright. But Hazel shook his head doubtingly. The wet season would commence probably with an atmospheric convulsion, and then settle down to uninterrupted rain. Helen refused obstinately to believe in more rain than they had experienced on board the boat, — a genial shower.

"You will see," replied Hazel. "If you do not change your views within the next three days, then call me a false prophet."

The following day passed, and Helen recovered more strength, but still was too weak to walk; but she employed herself, at Hazel's request, in making a rope of cocoa-nut fibre, some forty yards long. This he required to fish up the spar to a sufficient height on the great palm-tree, and bind it firmly in its place. While she worked nimbly, he employed himself in gathering a store of such things as they would require during the coming wintry season. She watched him with a smile, but he persevered. So that day passed. The next morning the rope was finished. Helen was not so well, and was about to help herself to the poppy liquor, when Hazel happily stopped her hand in time; he showed her the exact dose necessary, and explained minutely the effects of a larger draught. Then he shouldered the rope, and set out for Palm-tree Point.

He was absent about six hours, of which Helen slept four. And for two, which seemed very long, she ruminated. What was she thinking of that made her smile and weep at the same moment? and she looked so impatiently towards the door.

He entered at last, very fatigued. It was eleven miles to the Point and back. While eating his frugal supper, he gave her a detail of his day's adventures. Strange to say, he had not seen a single seal on the sands. He described how he had tied one end of her rope to the middle of the spar, and with the other between his teeth, he climbed the great palm. For more than an hour he toiled; he gained its top, passed the rope over one of its branches, and hauled up the spar to about eighty feet above the ground; then descending with the other end, he wound the rope spirally round and round the tree, thus binding to its trunk the first twenty feet by which the spar hung from the branch.

She listened very carelessly, he thought, and betrayed little interest in this enterprise which had cost him so much labor and fatigue.

When he had concluded, she was silent a while, and then, looking up quickly, said, to his great surprise, —

"I think I may increase the dose of your medicine there. You are mistaken in its power. I am sure I can take four times what you gave me."

"Indeed you are mistaken," he answered, quickly. "I gave you the extreme measure you can take with safety."

"How do you know that? you can only guess at its effects. At any rate, I shall try it."

Hazel hesitated, and then confessed that he had made a little experiment on himself before risking its effects upon her.

Helen looked up at him as he said this so simply and quietly. Her great eyes filled with an angelic light. Was it admiration? Was it thankfulness? Her bosom heaved, and her lips quivered. It was but a moment, and she felt glad that Hazel had turned away from her and saw nothing.

A long silence followed this little episode, when she was aroused from her reverie.

Patter — pat — pat — patter.

She looked up.

Pat — patter — patter.

Their eyes met. It was the rain. Hazel only smiled a little, and then ran down to his boat-house, to see that all was right there, and then returned with a large bundle of chips, with which he made a fire, for the sky had darkened overhead. Gusts of wind ran along the water; it had become suddenly chilly. They had almost forgotten the feel of wet weather.

Ere the fire had kindled, the rain came down in torrents, and the matted roof being resonant, they heard it strike here and there above their heads.

Helen sat down on her little stool and reflected.

In that hut were two persons. One had foretold this, and feared it, and provided against it. The other had said petulantly it was a bugbear.

And now the rain was pattering, and the Prophet was on his knees making her as comfortable as he could in spite of all, and was not the man to remind her he had foretold it.

She pondered his character while she watched his movements. He put down his embers, then he took a cocoa-pod out from the wall, cut it in slices with his knife, and made a fine clear fire; then he ran out again, in spite of Helen's remonstrance, and brought a dozen large scales of the palm-tree. It was all the more cheering for the dismal scene without and the pattering of the rain on the resounding roof.

But thanks to Hazel's precaution, the hut proved weather-tight; of which fact having satisfied himself, he bade her good night. He was at the door when her voice recalled him.

"Mr. Hazel, I cannot rest this night without asking your pardon for all the unkind things I may have done and said; without thanking you humbly for your great forbearance and your — respect for the unhap — I mean the unfortunate girl thus cast upon your mercy."

She held out her hand; he took it between his own, and faintly expressed his gratitude for her kindness; and so she sent him away brimful of happiness.

The rain was descending in torrents. She heard it, but he did not feel it; for she had spread her angel's wings over his existence, and he regained his sheltered boat-house he knew not how.

CHAPTER XXXII.

The next day was Sunday. Hazel had kept a calendar of the week, and every seventh day was laid aside with jealousy, to be devoted to such simple religious exercises as he could invent. The rain still continued, with less violence indeed, but without an hour's intermission. After breakfast he read to her the exodus of the Israelites, and their sufferings during that desert life. He compared those hardships with their own troubles, and pointed out to her how their condition presented many things to be thankful for. The island was fruitful, the climate healthy. They might have been cast away on a sandy key or reef, where they would have perished slowly and miserably of hunger and exposure. Then they were spared to each other. Had she been alone there, she could not have provided for herself; had he been cast away a solitary man, the island would have been to him an intolerable prison.

In all these reflections Hazel was very guarded that no expression should escape him to arouse her apprehension. He was so careful of this, that she observed his caution and watched his restraint. And Helen was thinking more of this than of the holy subject on which he was discoursing. The disguise he threw over his heart was penetrable to the girl's eye. She saw his love in every careful word, and employed herself in detecting it under his rigid manner. Secure in her own position, she could examine his from the loopholes of her soul, and take a pleasure in witnessing the suppressed happiness she could bestow with a word. She did not wonder at her power. The best of women have the natural vanity to take for granted the sway they assume over the existence which submits to them.

A week passed thus, and Hazel blessed the rain that drove them to this sociability. He had prepared the bladder of a young seal which had drifted ashore dead. This membrane dried in the sun formed a piece of excellent parchment, and he desired to draw upon it a map of the island. To accomplish this, the first thing was to obtain a good red ink from the cochineal, which is crimson. He did according to his means. He got one of the tin vessels, and filed it till he had obtained a consider able quantity of the metal. This he subjected for forty hours to the action of lime-juice. He then added the cochineal, and mixed till he obtained a fine scarlet. In using it he added a small quantity of a hard and pure gum, — he had found gum abounded in the island. His pen was made from an osprey's feather, hundreds of which were strewn about the cliffs, and some of these he had already secured and dried.

Placing his tin baler before him, on which he had scratched his notes, he drew a map of the island.

"What shall we call it?" said he.

Helen paused, and then replied, "Call it 'God-send' Island."

"So I will," he said, and wrote it down.

Then they named the places they had seen. The reef Helen had discovered off the northwest coast they called "White Water Island," because of the breakers. Then came "Seal Bay," Palm-tree Point," "Mount Lookout" (this was the hill due south of where they lived). They called the canebrake "Wild Duck Swamp," and the spot where they lunched "Cochineal Clearing." The mountain was named "Mount Cavity."

"But what shall we call the capital of the kingdom — this hut?" said Miss Rolleston, as she leaned over him and pointed to the spot.

"Saint Helen's," said Hazel, looking up; and he wrote it down ere she could object.

Then there was a little awkward pause, while he was busily occupied in filling up some topographical details. She turned it off gayly.

"What are those caterpillars that you have drawn there, sprawling over my kingdom?" she asked.

"Caterpillars! you are complimentary, Miss Rolleston. Those are mountains."

"O, indeed; and those lines you are now drawing are rivers, I presume."

"Yes; let us call this branch of our solitary estuary, which runs westward, the River Lee, and this, to the east, the River Medway. Is such your majesty's pleasure?"

"*La Reine le veut*," replied Helen, smiling. "But, Master Geographer, it seems to me, that you are putting in mountains and rivers which you have never explored: how do you know that these turns and twists in the stream exist as you represent them? and those spurs, which look so real, have you not added them only to disguise the caterpillar character of your range of hills!"

Hazel laughed as he confessed to drawing on his fancy for some little details. But pleaded that all geographers, when they drew maps, were licensed to fill in a few such touches, where discovery had failed to supply particulars.

Helen had always believed religiously in maps, and was amused when she reflected on her former credulity.

CHAPTER XXXIII.

Helen's strength was coming back to her but slowly; she complained of great lassitude and want of appetite. But the following day having cleared up, the sun shone out with great power and brilhancy. She gladly welcomed the return of the fine weather, but Hazel shook his head; ten days' rain was not their portion, — the bad weather would return, and complete the month or six weeks' winter to which Nature was entitled. The next evening the appearance of the sky confirmed his opinion. The sun set like a crimson shield; gory, and double its usual size. It entered into a thick bank of dark violet cloud that lay on the horizon, and seemed to split the vapor into rays, but of a dusky kind; immediately above this crimson, the clouds were of a brilliant gold, but higher they were the color of rubies, and went gradually off to gray.

But, as the orb dipped to the horizon a solid pile of unearthly clouds came up from the southeast; their bodies were singularly and unnaturally black, and mottled with copper color, and hemmed with a fiery yellow: and these infernal clouds towered up their heads, pressing forward as if they all strove for precedency; it was like Milton's fiends attacking the sky. The rate at which they climbed was wonderful. The sun set and the moon rose full, and showed those angry masses surging upwards and jostling each other as they flew.

Yet below it was dead calm.

Having admired the sublimity of the scene, and seen the full moon rise, but speedily lose her light in a brassy halo, they entered the hut, which was now the head-quarters, and they supped together there.

While they were eating their little meal the tops of the trees were heard to sigh, so still was everything else. None the less did those strange clouds fly northward, eighty miles an hour. After supper Helen sat busy over the fire, where some gum, collected by Hazel, resembling India-rubber, was boiling; she was preparing to cover a pair of poor Welch's shoes, inside and out, with a coat of this material, which Hazel believed to be waterproof. She sat in such a position that he could watch her. It was a happy evening. She seemed content. She had got over her fear of him; they were good comrades if they were nothing more. It was happiness to him to be by her side even on those terms. He thought of it all as he looked at her. How distant she had seemed once to him; what an unapproachable goddess. Yet there she was by his side in a hut he had made for her.

He could not help sipping the soft intoxicating draught her mere presence offered him. But by and by he felt his heart was dissolving within him, and he was trifling with danger. He must not look on her too long, seated by the fire like a wife. The much-enduring man rose, and turned his back upon the sight he loved so dearly: he went out at the open door intending to close it and bid her good night. But he did not do so, just then; for his attention as an observer of nature was arrested by the unusual conduct of certain animals. Gannets and other sea-birds were running about the opposite wood and craning their necks in a strange way. He had never seen one enter that wood before.

Seals and sea-lions were surrounding the slope, and crawling about, and now and then plunging into the river, which they crossed with infinite difficulty, for it was running very high and strong. The trees also sighed louder than ever. Hazel turned back to tell Miss Rolleston something extraordinary was going on. She sat in sight from the river, and as he came towards the hut, he saw her sitting by the fire reading.

He stopped short. Her work lay at her feet: she had taken out a letter, and she was reading it by the fire.

As she read it her face was a puzzle. But Hazel saw the act alone; and a dart of ice seemed to go through and through him.

This, then, was her true source of consolation. He thought it was so before. He had even reason to think so. But never seeing any palpable proofs, he had almost been happy. He turned sick with jealous misery, and stood there rooted and frozen.

Then came a fierce impulse to shut the sight out that caused this pain.

He almost flung her portcullis to, and made his hands bleed. But a bleeding heart does not feel scratches.

"Good night," said he, hoarsely.

"Good night," said she, kindly.

And why should she not read his letter? She was his affianced bride, bound to him by honor as well as inclination. This was the reflection to which, after a sore battle with his loving heart, the much-enduring man had to come at last; and he had come to it, and was getting back his peace of mind, though not his late complacency, and about to seek repose in sleep, when suddenly a clap of wind came down like thunder, and thrashed the island and everything in it.

Everything animate and inanimate seemed to cry out as the blow passed.

Another soon followed, and another, — intermittent gusts at present, but of such severity that not one came without making its mark.

Birds were driven away like paper; the sea-lions whimpered, and crouched into corners, and huddled together, and held each other, whining.

Hazel saw but one thing; the frail edifice he had built for the creature he adored. He looked out of his boat, and fixed his horror-stricken eyes on it; he saw it waving to and fro, yet still firm. But he could not stay there. If not in danger she must be terrified. He must go and support her. He left his shelter, and ran towards her hut. With a whoop and a scream another blast tore through the wood, and caught him. He fell, dug his hands into the soil, and clutched the earth. While he was in that position, he heard a sharp crack; he looked up in dismay, and saw that one of Helen's trees had broken like a carrot, and the head was on the ground leaping about; while a succession of horrible sounds of crashing, and rending, and tearing, showed the frail hut was giving way on every side; racked and riven, and torn to pieces. Hazel, though a stout man, uttered cries of terror death would never have drawn from him; and, with a desperate headlong rush, he got to the place where the bower had been; but now it was a prostrate skeleton, with the mat roof flapping like a loose sail above it, and Helen below.

As he reached the hut, the wind got hold of the last of the four shrubs, that did duty for a door, and tore it from the cord that held it, and whirled it into the air; it went past Hazel's face like a bird flying.

Though staggered himself by the same blow of wind, he clutched the tree and got into the hut.

He found her directly. She was kneeling beneath the mat that a few minutes ago had been her roof. He extricated her in a moment, uttering inarticulate cries of pity and fear.

"Don't be frightened," said she. "I am not hurt."

But he felt her quiver from head to foot. He

wrapped her in all her rugs, and, thinking of nothing but her safety, lifted her in his strong arms to take her to his own place, which was safe from wind at least.

But this was no light work. To go there erect was impossible.

Holding tight by the tree, he got her to the lee of the tent and waited for a lull. He went rapidly down the hill, but ere he reached the river, a gust came careering over the sea. A sturdy young tree was near him. He placed her against it, and wound his arms round her and its trunk. The blast came: the tree bent down almost to the ground, then whirled round, recovered, shivered; but he held firmly. It passed. Again he lifted her, and bore her to the boat-house. As he went, the wind almost choked her, and her long hair lashed his face like a whip. But he got her in, and then sat panting and crouching, but safe. They were none too soon; the tempest increased in violence, and became more continuous. No clouds, but a ghastly glare all over the sky. No rebellious waves, but a sea hissing and foaming under its master's lash. The river ran roaring and foaming by, and made the boat heave even in its little creek. The wind, though it could no longer shake them, went screaming terribly close over their heads, — no longer like air in motion, but, solid and keen, it seemed the Almighty's scythe mowing down Nature; and soon it became, like turbid water, blackened with the leaves, branches, and fragments of all kinds it whirled along with it. The trees fell crashing on all sides, and the remains passed over their heads into the sea.

Helen behaved admirably. Speech was impossible, but she thanked him without it, — eloquently; she nestled her little hand into Hazel's, and, to Hazel that night, with all its awful sights and sounds, was a blissful one. She had been in danger, but now was safe by his side. She had pressed his hand to thank him, and now she was cowering a little towards him in a way that claimed him as her protector. Her glorious hair blew over him and seemed to net him: and now and then, as they heard some crash nearer and more awful than another, she clutched him quickly though lightly; for, in danger, her sex love to feel a friend; it is not enough to see him near: and once, when a great dusky form of a sea-lion came crawling over the mound, and whimpering, peeped into the boat-house, she even fled to his shoulder with both hands for a moment, and was there, light as a feather, till the creature had passed on. And his soul was full of peace, and a great tranquillity overcame it. He heard nothing of the wrack, knew nothing of the danger.

O mighty Love! The tempest might blow, and fill the air and earth with ruin, so that it spared her. The wind was kind, and gentle the night, which brought that hair round his face, and that head so near his shoulder, and gave him the holy joy of protecting under his wing the soft creature he adored.

CHAPTER XXXIV.

On the morning that followed this memorable night, our personages seemed to change characters. Hazel sat down before the relics of the hut — three or four strings dangling, and a piece of network waving — and eyed them with shame, regret, and humiliation. He was so absorbed in his self-reproaches that he did not hear a light footstep, and Helen Rolleston stood near him a moment or two, and watched the play of his countenance with a very inquisitive and kindly light in her own eyes.

"Never mind," said she, soothingly.

Hazel started at the music.

"Never mind your house being blown to atoms, and mine has stood?" said he, half reproachfully.

"You took too much pains with mine."

"I will take a great deal more with the next."

"I hope not. But I want you to come and look at the havoc. It is terrible; and yet so grand." And thus she drew him away from the sight that caused his pain.

They entered the wood by a path Hazel had cut from the seashore, and viewed the devastation in Terrapin Wood. Prostrate trees lay across one another in astonishing numbers, and in the strangest positions; and their glorious plumes swept the earth. "Come," said she, "it is a bad thing for the poor trees, but not for us. See, the place is strewed with treasures. Here is a tree full of fans all ready made. And what is that? A horse's tail growing on a cocoa-tree! and a long one too! that will make ropes for you, and thread for me. Ah, and here is a cabbage. Poor Mr. Welch! Well, for one thing, you need never saw nor climb any more. See the advantages of a hurricane."

From the wood she took him to the shore, and there they found many birds lying dead; and Hazel picked up several that he had read of as good to eat. For certain signs had convinced him his fair and delicate companion was carnivora, and must be nourished accordingly. Seeing him so employed, she asked him archly whether he was beginning to see the comforts of a hurricane. "Not yet," said he; "the account is far from even."

"Then come to where the rock was blown down." She led the way gayly across the sands to a point where an overhanging crag had fallen, with two trees, and a quantity of earth and plants that grew above it. But, when they got nearer, she became suddenly grave, and stood still. The mass had fallen upon a sheltered place, where seals were hiding from the wind, and had buried several; for two or three limbs were sticking out, of victims overwhelmed in the ruin; and a magnificent sea-lion lay clear of the smaller rubbish, but quite dead. The cause was not far to seek: a ton of hard rock had struck him, and then ploughed up the sand in a deep furrow, and now rested within a yard or two of the animal, whose back it had broken. Hazel went up to the creature and looked at it: then he came to Helen; she was standing aloof. "Poor bugbear," said he. "Come away: it is an ugly sight for you."

"O yes," said Helen. Then, as they returned, "Does not that reconcile you to the loss of a hut? We are not blown away nor crushed."

"That is true," said Hazel; "but suppose your health should suffer from the exposure to such fearful weather. So unlucky! so cruel! just as you were beginning to get stronger."

"I am all the better for it. Shall I tell you? excitement is a good thing; not too often, of course; but now and then; and when we are in the humor for it, it is meat and drink, and medicine to us."

"What! to a delicate young lady?"

"Ay, 'to a delicate young lady.' Last night has done me a world of good. It has shaken me out of myself. I am in better health and spirits. Of course I am very sorry the hut is blown down, — because you took so much trouble to build it: but on my own account, I really don't care a straw. Find me some corner to nestle in at night, and all day I mean to be about, and busy as a bee, helping you, and — Breakfast! breakfast! O, how hungry I am." And this spirited girl led the way to the boat with a briskness and a vigor that charmed and astonished him.

Souvent femme varie.

This gracious behavior did not blind Hazel to the serious character of the situation, and all breakfast-time he was thinking and thinking, and often kept a morsel in his mouth, and forgot to eat it for several seconds, he was so anxious and puzzled. At last, he said, "I know a large hollow tree with apertures. If I were to close them all but one, and keep that for the door? No: trees have betrayed me; I'll never trust another tree with you. Stay; I know — I know — a cavern. He uttered the verb rather loudly, but the substantive with a sudden feebleness of intonation that was amusing. His timidity was superfluous; if he had said he knew "a bank whereon the wild thyme grows," the suggestion would have been well received that morning.

"A cavern!" cried Helen. "It has always been the dream of my life to live in a cavern."

Hazel brightened up. But the next moment he clouded again. "But I forgot. It will not do: there is a spring running right through it; it comes down nearly perpendicular, through a channel it has bored, or enlarged; and splashes on the floor."

"How convenient!" said Helen; "now I shall have a bath in my room, instead of having to go miles for it. By the by, now you have invented the shower-bath, please discover Soap. Not that one really wants any in this island; for there is no dust, and the very air seems purifying. But who can shake off the prejudices of early education?"

Hazel said, "Now I'll laugh as much as you like, when once this care is off my mind."

He ran off to the cavern, and found it spacious and safe; but the spring was falling in great force, and the roof of the cave glistening with moisture. It looked a hopeless case. But if Necessity is the mother of Invention, surely Love is the father. He mounted to the rock above, and found the spot where the spring suddenly descended into the earth with the loudest gurgle he had ever heard; a gurgle of defiance. Nothing was to be done there. But he traced it upwards a little way, and found a place where it ran beside a deep decline. "Aha, my friend!" said he. He got his spade, and with some hours' hard work dug it a fresh channel, and carried it away entirely from its course. He returned to the cavern. Water was dripping very fast; but, on looking up, he could see the light of day twinkling at the top of the spiral watercourse he had robbed of its supply. Then he conceived a truly original idea: why not turn his empty watercourse into a chimney, and so give to one element what he had taken from another? He had no time to execute this just then, for the tide was coming in, and he could not afford to lose any one of those dead animals. So he left the funnel to drip, that being a process he had no means of expediting, and moored the sea-lion to the very rock that had killed him, and was proceeding to dig out the seals, when a voice he never could hear without a thrill, summoned him to dinner.

It was a plentiful repast, and included roast pintado and cabbage-palm. Helen Rolleston informed him during dinner that he would no longer be allowed to monopolize the labor attendant upon their condition.

"No," said she, "you are always working for me, and I shall work for you. Cooking and washing are a woman's work, not a man's; and so are plaiting and netting."

This healthy resolution once formed was adhered to with a constancy that belonged to the girl's character. The roof of the ruined hut came ashore in the bay that evening, and was fastened over the boat. Hazel lighted a bonfire in the cavern, and had the satisfaction of seeing some of the smoke issue above. But he would not let Miss Rolleston occupy it yet. He shifted her things to the boat, and slept in the cave himself. However, he lost no time in laying down a great hearth, and built a fireplace and chimney in the cave. The chimney went up to the hole in the arch of the cave; then came the stone funnel, stolen from Nature; and above, on the upper surface of the cliff, came the chimney-pot. Thus, the chimney acted like a German stove: it stood in the centre, and soon made the cavern very dry and warm, and a fine retreat during the rains. When it was ready for occupation, Helen said she would sail to it: she would not go by land; that was too tame for her. Hazel had only to comply with her humor, and at high water they got into the boat, and went down the river into the sea with a rush that made Helen wince. He soon rowed her across the bay to a point distant not more than fifty yards from the cavern, and installed her. But he never returned to the river; it was an inconvenient place to make excursions from; and, besides, all his work was now either in or about the cavern; and that convenient hurricane, as Helen called it, not only made him a builder again; it also made him a currier, a soap-boiler, and a salter. So they drew the boat just above high-water mark in a sheltered nook, and he set up his arsenal ashore.

In this situation, day glided by after day, and week after week, in vigorous occupations, brightened by social intercourse, and in some degree by the beauty and the friendship of the animals. Of all this industry we can only afford a brief summary. Hazel fixed two uprights at each side of the cavern's mouth, and connected each pair by a beam; a netting laid on these, and covered with gigantic leaves from the prostrate palms, made a sufficient roof in this sheltered spot. On this terrace they could sit even in the rain, and view the sea. Helen cooked in the cave, but served dinner up on this beautiful terrace. So now she had a But and a Ben, as the Scotch say. He got a hogshead of oil from the sea-lion; and so the cave was always lighted now, and that was a great comfort, and gave them more hours of in-door employment and conversation. The poor bugbear really brightened their existence. Of the same oil, boiled down and mixed with wood-ashes, he made soap, to Helen's great delight. The hide of this animal was so thick he could do nothing with it but cut off pieces to make the soles of shoes if required. But the seals were miscellaneous treasures; he contrived with guano and aromatics to curry their skins; of their bladders he made vile parchment, and of their entrails gut, catgut, and twine, beyond compare. He salted two cubs, and laid up the rest in store, by enclosing large pieces in clay. When these were to be used, the clay was just put into hot embers for some hours, then broken, and the meat eaten with all its juices preserved.

Helen cooked and washed, and manufactured salt; and collected quite a store of wild cotton, though it grew very sparingly, and it cost her hours to find a few pods. But in hunting for it she found other things, — health for one. After sunset she was generally employed a couple of hours on matters which occupy the fair in every situation of life. She made herself a sealskin jacket and pork-pie hat. She made Mr. Hazel a man's cap of seal-skin with a point. But her great work was with the cotton, which will be described hereafter.

However, for two hours after sunset, no more (they rose at peep of day), her physician allowed her to sit and work; which she did, and often smiled, while he sat by and discoursed to her of all the things he had read, and surprised himself by the strength and activity of his memory. He attributed it partly to the air of the island. Nor were his fingers idle even at night. He had tools to sharpen for the morrow, glass to make and polish out of a laminated crystal he had found. And then the hurricane had blown away, amongst many properties, his map; so he had to make another with similar materials. He completed the map in due course, and gave it to Helen. It was open to the same strictures she had passed on the other. Hazel was no chartographer. Yet this time she had nothing but praise for it. How was that?

To the reader it is now presented, not as a specimen of chartographic art, but as a little curiosity in its way, being a *fac-simile* of the map John Hazel drew for Helen Rolleston, with such out-of-the-way materials as that out-of-the-way island afforded. Above all, it will enable the reader to follow our personages in their little excursions past and future, and also to trace the course of a mysterious event we have to record.

Relieved of other immediate cares, Hazel's mind had time to dwell upon the problem Helen had set him; and one fine day a conviction struck him that he had taken a narrow and puerile view of it, and that, after all, there must be in the nature of things some way to attract ships from a distance. Possessed with this thought, he went up to Telegraph Point, abstracted his mind from all external objects, and fixed it on this idea, — but came down as he went. He descended by some steps he had cut zigzag for Helen's use, and as he put his foot on the fifth step, — whoo — whirr — whizz — came nine ducks, cooling his head, they whizzed so close; and made right for the lagoons.

"Hum!" thought Hazel; "I never see you ducks fly in any other direction but that."

This speculation rankled in him all night, and he told Helen he should reconnoitre at daybreak, but should not take her, as there might be snakes. He made the boat ready at daybreak, and certain gannets, pintadoes, boobies, and noddies, and divers with eyes in their heads like fiery jewels — birds whose greedy maws he had often gratified — chose to fancy he must be going a fishing, and were on the alert, and rather troublesome. However, he got adrift, and ran out through North Gate, with a light westerly breeze, followed by a whole fleet of birds. These were joined in due course by another of his satellites, a young seal he called Tommy, also fond of fishing.

The feathered convoy soon tailed off; but Tommy stuck to him for about eight miles. He ran that distance to have a nearer look at a small island which lay due north of Telegraph Point. He satisfied himself it was little more than a very long, large reef, the neighborhood of which ought to be avoided by ships of burden, and resolving to set some beacon or other on it erelong, he christened it White Water Island, on account of the surf: he came about and headed for the East Bluff.

Then Tommy gave him up in disgust; perhaps thought his conduct vacillating. Animals all despise that.

He soon landed almost under the volcano, and moored his boat not far from a cliff peaked with guano. Exercising due caution this time, he got up to the lagoons, and found a great many ducks swimming about. He approached little parties to examine their varieties. They all swam out of his way; some of them even flew a few yards, and then settled. Not one would let him come within forty yards. This convinced Hazel the ducks were not natives of the island, but strangers, who were not much afraid, because they had never been molested on this particular island; but still distrusted man.

While he pondered thus, there was a great noise of wings, and about a dozen ducks flew over his head on the rise, and passed westward still rising till they got into the high currents, and away upon the wings of the wind for distant lands.

The grand rush of their wings and the off-hand way in which they spurned, abandoned, and disappeared from, an island that held him tight, made Hazel feel very small. His thoughts took the form of Satire. "Lords of the creation, are we? We sink in water; in air we tumble; on earth we stumble."

These pleasing reflections did not prevent his taking their exact line of flight, and barking a tree to mark it. He was about to leave the place, when he heard a splashing not far from him, and there was a duck jumping about on the water in a strange way. Hazel thought a snake had got hold of her and ran to her assistance. He took her out of the water and soon found what was the matter; her bill was open and a fish's tail was sticking out. Hazel inserted his finger and dragged out a small fish which had erected the spines on its back so opportunely as nearly to kill its destroyer. The duck recovered enough to quack in a feeble and dubious manner. Hazel kept her for Helen, because she was a plain brown duck. With some little reluctance he slightly shortened one wing, and stowed away his captive in the hold of the boat.

He happened to have a great stock of pitch in the boat, so he employed a few hours in writing upon the guano rocks. On one he wrote in huge letters: —

AN ENGLISH LADY WRECKED. HERE.

HASTE TO HER RESCUE.

On another he wrote in smaller letters: —

BEWARE THE REEFS ON THE NORTH SIDE.

LIE OFF FOR SIGNALS.

Then he came home and beached the boat, and brought Helen his captive.

"Why, it is an English duck!" she cried, and was enraptured.

By this visit to the lagoons, Hazel gathered that this island was a half-way house for migrating birds, especially ducks; and he inferred that the line those vagrants had taken was the shortest way from this island to the nearest land. This was worth knowing, and set his brain working. He begged Helen to watch for the return of the turtle-doves

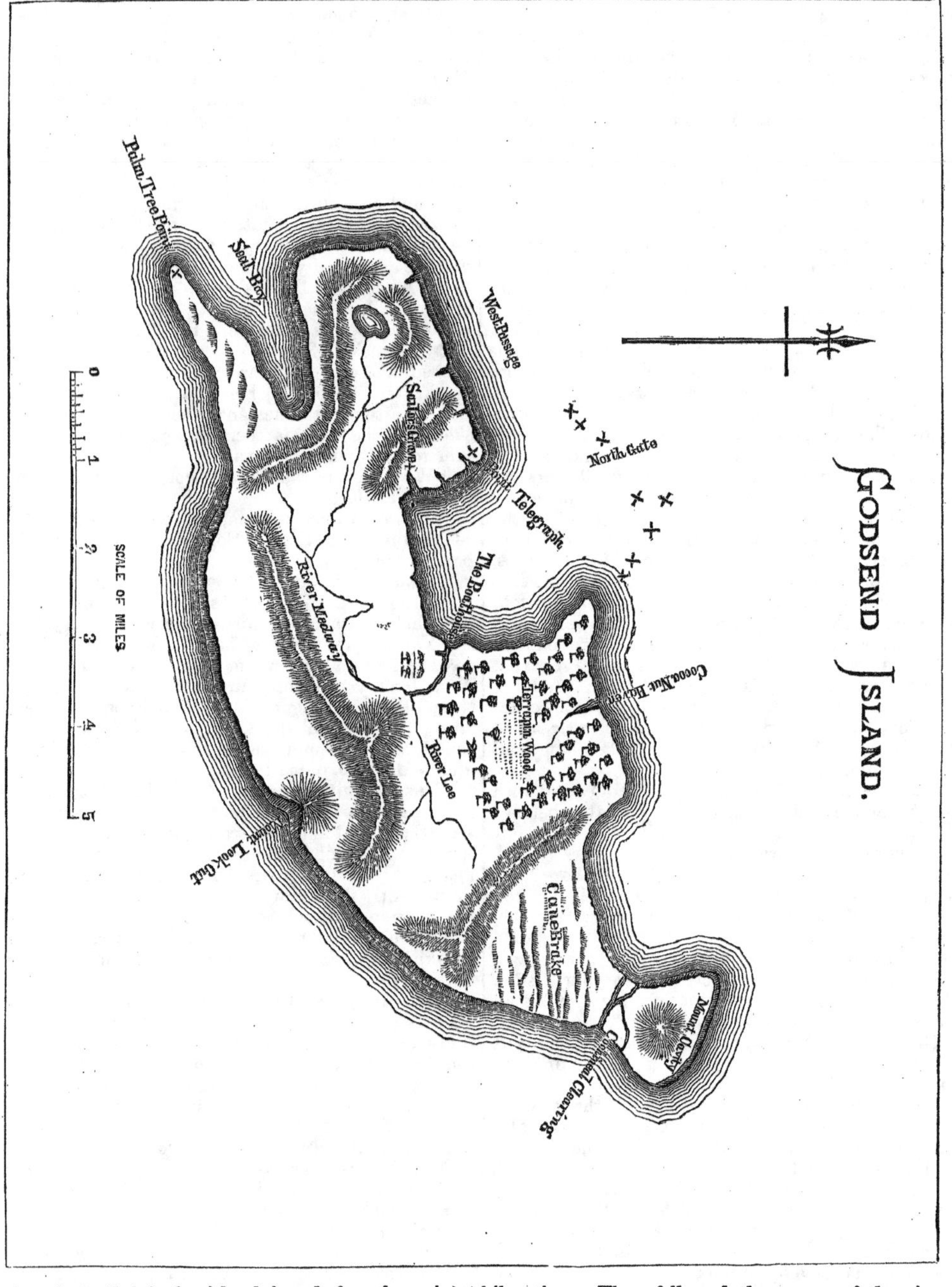

(they had all left the island just *before* the rain) and learn, if possible, from what point of the compass they arrived.

The next expedition was undertaken to please Helen; she wished to examine the beautiful creeks and caves on the north side, which they had seen from a distance when they sailed round the island.

They started on foot one delightful day, and walked briskly, for the air, though balmy, was exhilarating. They followed the course of the river till they came to the lake that fed it, and was fed itself by hundreds of little natural gutters down which the hills discharged the rains. This was new to Helen, though not to Hazel: she produced the map, and told the lake slyly that it was incorrect, a little too big. She took some of the water in her hand, sprinkled the lake with it, and called it Hazelmere. They bore a little to the right and proceeded till they found a creek shaped like a wedge, at whose broad end shone an arch of foliage studded with flowers, and the sparkling blue water peeped behind. This was tempting, but the descent was rather hazardous at first; great square blocks of rock, one below another, and these rude steps were coated with mosses of rich hue, but wet and slippery; Hazel began to be alarmed for his companion. However, after one or two difficulties, the fissure opened wider to the sun, and they descended from the slimy rocks into a sloping hotbed of exotic flowers, and those huge succulent leaves that are the glory of the tropics. The ground was carpeted a yard deep with their luxuriance, and others more aspiring, climbed the warm sides of the diverging cliffs, just as creepers go up a wall, lining every crevice as they rose. In this blessed spot, warmed, yet not scorched, by the tropical sun, and fed with trickling waters, was seen what marvels "boon Nature" can do. Here our vegetable dwarfs were giants, and our flowers were trees. One lovely giantess of the jasmine tribe, but with flowers shaped like a marigold, and scented like a tuberose, had a stem as thick as a poplar, and carried its thousand buds and amber-colored flowers up eighty feet of broken rock, and planted on every ledge suckers, that flowered again, and filled the air with perfume. Another tree about half as high was covered with a cascade of snow-white tulips, each as big as a small flower-pot, and scented like honeysuckle. An aloe, ten feet high, blossomed in a corner, unheeded among loftier beauties. And at the very mouth of the fissure a huge banana leaned across, and flung out its vast leaves, that seemed translucent gold against the sun; under it shone a monstrous cactus in all her pink and crimson glory, and through the maze of color streamed the deep blue of the peaceful ocean, laughing, and catching sunbeams.

Helen leaned against the cliff and quivered with delight, and that deep sense of flowers that belongs to your true woman.

Hazel feared she was ill.

"Ill?" said she. "Who *could* be ill here? It is heaven upon earth. O, you dears! O, you loves! And they all seemed growing on the sea, and floating in the sun."

"And it is only one of a dozen such," said Hazel. "If you would like to inspect them at your leisure, I'll just run to Palm-tree Point; for my signal is all askew. I saw that as we came along."

Helen assented readily, and he ran off; but left her the provisions. She was not to wait dinner for him.

Helen examined two or three of the flowery fissures, and found fresh beauties in each, and also some English leaves, that gave her pleasure of another kind; and, after she had revelled in the flowers, she examined the shore, and soon discovered that the rocks, which abounded here, (though there were also large patches of clear sand,) were nearly all pure coral, in great variety. Red coral was abundant; and even the pink coral, to which fashion was just then giving a fictitious value, was there by the ton. This interested her, and so did some beautiful shells that lay sparkling. The time passed swiftly; and she was still busy in her researches, when suddenly it darkened a little, and, looking back, she saw a white vapor stealing over the cliff, and curling down.

Upon this, she thought it prudent to return to the place where Hazel had left her; the more so as it was near sunset.

The vapor descended and spread, and covered sea and land. Then the sun set: and it was darkness visible. Coming from the south, the sea-fret caught Hazel sooner and in a less favorable situation. Returning from the palm-tree, he had taken the shortest cut through a small jungle, and been so impeded by the scrub, that, when he got clear, the fog was upon him. Between that and the river, he lost his way several times, and did not hit the river till near midnight. He followed the river to the lake, and coasted the lake, and then groped his way towards the creek. But, after a while, every step he took was fraught with danger; and the night was far advanced when he at last hit off the creek, as he thought. He halloed; but there was no reply; halloed again, and to his joy, her voice replied; but at a distance. He had come to the wrong creek. She was farther westward. He groped his way westward, and came to another creek. He halloed to her, and she answered him. But to attempt the descent would have been mere suicide. She felt that herself, and almost ordered him to stay where he was.

"Why, we can talk all the same," said she; "and it is not for long."

It was a curious position, and one typical of the relation between them. So near together, yet the barrier so strong.

"I am afraid you must be very cold," said he.

"O no; I have my seal-skin jacket on; and it is so sheltered here. I wish you were as well off."

"You are not afraid to be alone down there?"

"I am not alone when your voice is near me. Now don't you fidget yourself, dear friend. I like these little excitements. I have told you so before. Listen: how calm and silent it all is; the place; the night! The mind seems to fill with great ideas, and to feel its immortality."

She spoke with solemnity, and he heard in silence.

Indeed it was a reverend time and place: the sea, whose loud and penetrating tongue had, in some former age, created the gully where they both sat apart, had of late years receded, and kissed the sands gently that calm night: so gently, that its long, low murmur seemed but the echo of tranquillity.

The voices of that pair sounded supernatural, one speaking up, and the other down, the speakers quite invisible.

"Mr. Hazel," said Helen, in a low, earnest voice; "they say that Night gives wisdom even to the wise; think now, and tell me your true thoughts. Has the foot of man ever trod upon this island before?"

There was a silence due to a question so grave, and put with solemnity, at a solemn time, in a solemn place.

At last Hazel's thoughtful voice came down. "The world is very, very, very old. So old, that the words, 'Ancient History' are a falsehood, and Moses wrote but as yesterday. And man is a very old animal upon this old, old planet; and has been everywhere. I cannot doubt he has been here."

Her voice went up. "But have you seen any signs?"

His voice came down. "I have not looked for them. The bones and the weapons of primeval man are all below earth's surface at this time of day."

There was a dead silence. Then Helen's voice went up again. "But in modern times? Has no man landed here from far-off places, since ships were built?"

The voice came sadly down. "I do not know."

The voice went up. "But think!"

The voice came down. "What calamity can be new in a world so old as this? Everything we can do, and suffer, others of our race have done, and suffered."

The voice went up. "Hush! there's something moving on the sand."

CHAPTER XXXV.

HAZEL waited and listened. So did Helen, and her breath came fast; for in the stilly night she heard light but mysterious sounds. Something was moving on the sand very slowly and softly, but nearer and nearer. Her heart began to leap. She put out her hand instinctively to clutch Mr. Hazel; but he was too far off. She had the presence of mind and the self-denial to disguise her fears; for she knew he would come headlong to her assistance.

She said in a quivering whisper, "I'm not frightened; only v—very c—curious."

And now she became conscious that not only one but several things were creeping about.

Presently the creeping ceased, and was followed by a louder and more mysterious noise. In that silent night it sounded like raking and digging. Three or four mysterious visitants seemed to be making graves.

This was too much; especially coming as it did after talk about the primeval dead. Her desire to scream was so strong, and she was so afraid Hazel would break his neck, if she relieved her mind in that way, that she actually took her handkerchief and bit it hard.

But this situation was cut short by a beneficent luminary. The sun rose with a magnificent bound, — it was his way in that latitude, — and everything unpleasant winced that moment; the fog shivered in its turn, and appeared to open in furrows as great javelins of golden light shot through it from the swiftly rising orb. Soon, those golden darts increased to streams of potable fire, that burst the fog and illumined the wet sands: and Helen burst out laughing like chanticleer, for this first break of day revealed the sextons that had scared her, — three ponderous turtles, crawling, slow and clumsy, back to sea. Hazel joined her, and they soon found what these evil spirits of the island had been at, poor wretches. They had each buried a dozen eggs in the sand: one dozen of which were very soon set boiling. At first, indeed, Helen objected that they had no shells, but Hazel told her she might as well complain of a rose without a thorn. He assured her turtles' eggs were a known delicacy, and very superior to birds' eggs; and so she found them; they were eaten with the keenest relish.

"And now," said Helen, "for my discoveries. First, here are my English leaves, only bigger. I found them on a large tree."

"English leaves!" cried Hazel, with rapture. "Why it is the caoutchouc!"

"O dear," said Helen, disappointed; "I took it for the India-rubber tree."

"It is the India-rubber tree; and I have been hunting for it all over the island in vain, and using wretchedly inferior gums for want of it."

"I'm so glad," said Helen. "And now I have something else to show you: something that curdled my blood; but I dare say I was very foolish." She then took him half across the sand and pointed out to him a number of stones dotted over the sand in a sort of oval. These stones, streaked with sea grass, and encrusted with small shells, were not at equal distances, but yet, allowing for gaps, they formed a decided figure. Their outline resembled a great fish, wanting the tail.

"Can this be chance?" asked Helen; "O, if it should be what I fear, and that is — Savages!"

Hazel considered it attentively a long time. "Too far at sea for living savages," said he. "And yet it cannot be chance. What on earth is it? It looks Druidical. But how can that be? The island was smaller when these were placed here than it is now." He went nearer and examined one of the stones; then he scraped away the sand from its base, and found it was not shaped like a stone, but more like a whale's rib. He became excited; went on his knees, and tore the sand up with his hands. Then he rose up agitated, and traced the outline again. "Great Heaven!" said he, "why it is a ship."

"A ship!"

"Ay," said he, standing in the middle of it; "here, beneath our feet, lies man; with his work, and his treasures. This carcass has been here for many a long year; not so very long neither; she is too big for the 16th century, and yet she must have been sunk when the island was smaller. I take it to be a Spanish or Portuguese ship: probably one of those treasure-ships our commodores, and chartered pirates, and the American buccaneers, used to chase about these seas. Here lie her bones, and the bones of her crew. Your question was soon answered. All that we can say has been said; can do has been done; can suffer has been suffered."

They were silent, and the sunk ship's bones moved them strangely. In their deep isolation from the human race, even the presence of the dead brought humanity somehow nearer to them.

They walked thoughtfully away, and made across the sands for Telegraph Point.

Before they got home, Helen suggested that perhaps, if he were to dig in the ship, he might find something useful.

He shook his head. "Impossible! The iron has all melted away like sugar long before this. Nothing can have survived but gold and silver, and they are not worth picking up, much less digging for; my time is too precious. No, you have found two buried treasures to-day, — turtles' eggs, and a ship, freighted, as I think, with what men call the precious metals. Well, the eggs are gold, and the gold is a drug, — there it will lie for me."

Both discoveries bore fruits. The ship: Hazel made a vow that never again should any poor ship lay her ribs on this island for want of warning. He buoyed the reefs. He ran out to White Water Island, and wrote an earnest warning on the black reef, and, this time, he wrote with white on black. He wrote a similar warning, with black on white, at the western extremity of Godsend Island.

The eggs: Hazel watched for the turtles at daybreak; turned one now and then; and fed Helen on the meat or its eggs, morn, noon, and night.

For some time she had been advancing in health and strength. But, when the rains declined considerably, and she was all day in the air, she got the full benefit of the wonderful climate, and her health, appetite, and muscular vigor became truly astonishing; especially under what Hazel called the turtle cure; though, indeed, she was cured before. She ate three good meals a day, and needed them; for she was up with the sun, and her hands and feet never idle till he set.

Four months on the island had done this. But four months had not shown those straining eyes the white speck on the horizon; the sail, so looked and longed for.

Hazel often walked the island by himself; not to explore, for he knew the place well by this time, but he went his rounds to see that all his signals were in working order.

He went to Mount Look-out one day with this view. It was about an hour before noon. Long before he got to the mountain he had scanned the horizon carefully, as a matter of course; but not a speck. So, when he got there, he did not look seaward, but just saw that his flagstaff was all right and was about to turn away and go home, when he happened to glance at the water; and there, underneath him, he saw — a ship; standing towards the island.

CHAPTER XXXVI.

He started, and rubbed his eyes, and looked again. It was no delusion. Things never did come as they are expected to come. There was still no doubtful speck on the horizon; but within eight miles of the island — and in this lovely air that looked nearly close — was a ship, under canvas. She bore S.E. from Mount Look-out, and S.S.E. from the East Bluff of the island, towards which her course was apparently directed. She had a fair wind, but was not going fast; being heavily laden, and under no press of sail. A keen thrill went through him; and his mind was a whirl. He ran home with the great news.

But, even as he ran, a cold sickly feeling crawled over him.

"That ship parts her and me."

He resisted the feeling as a thing too monstrous and selfish, and resisted it so fiercely, that, when he got to the slopes and saw Helen busy at her work, he waved his hat and hurrahed again and again, and seemed almost mad with triumph.

Helen stood transfixed, she had never seen him in such a state.

"Good news!" he cried; "great news! A ship in sight! You are rescued!"

Her heart leaped into her mouth.

"A ship!" she screamed. "Where? Where?"

He came up to her, panting.

"Close under the island. Hid by the bluff; but you will see her in half an hour. God be praised! Get everything ready to go. Hurrah! This is our last day on the island."

The words were brave, and loud, and boisterous, but the face was pale and drawn, and Helen saw it, and though she bustled and got ready to leave, the tears were in her eyes. But the event was too great to be resisted. A wild excitement grew on them both. They ran about like persons crazed, and took things up, and laid them down again, scarcely knowing what they were doing. But presently they were sobered a little, for the ship did not appear. They ran across the sands, where they could see the Bluff; she ought to have passed that half an hour ago.

Hazel thought she must have anchored.

Helen looked at him steadily.

"Dear friend," said she, "are you sure there is a ship at all? Are you not under a delusion? This island fills the mind with fancies. One day I though I saw a ship sailing in the sky. Ah!" She uttered a faint scream, for, while she was speaking, the bowsprit and jib of a vessel glided past the Bluff so closely, they seemed to scrape it, and a ship emerged grandly, and glided along the cliff.

"Are they mad," cried Hazel, "to hug the shore like that? Ah! they have seen my warning."

And it appeared so, for the ship just then came up in the wind several points, and left the Bluff dead astern.

She sailed a little way on that course, and then paid off again, and seemed inclined to range along the coast. But presently she was up in the wind again, and made a greater offing. She was sailed in a strange, vacillating way; but Hazel ascribed this to her people's fear of the reefs he had indicated to all comers. The better to watch her manœuvres, and signal her, if necessary, they both went up to Telegraph Point. They could not go out to her, being low water. Seen from this height, the working of this vessel was unaccountable. She was to and off the wind as often as if she was drunk herself, or commanded by a drunken skipper. However, she was kept well clear of the home reefs, and made a good offing, and so at last she opened the bay heading N.W., and distant four miles, or thereabouts. Now was the time to drop her anchor. So Hazel worked the telegraph to draw her attention, and waved his hat and hand to her. But the ship sailed on. She yawed immensely, but she kept her course; and, when she had gone a mile or two more, the sickening truth forced itself at last upon those eager watchers. She had decided not to touch at the island. In vain their joyful signals. In vain the telegraph. In vain that cry for help upon the eastern cliff: it had saved her but not pleaded for them. The monsters saw them on the height, — their hope, their joy, — saw and abandoned them.

They looked at one another with dilating eyes, to read in a human face whether such a deed as this could really be done by man upon his fellow. Then they uttered wild cries to the receding vessel.

Vain, vain, all was in vain.

Then they sat down stupefied, but still glaring at the ship, and each at the same moment held out a hand to the other, and they sat hand in hand; all the world to each other just then, for there was the world in sight abandoning them in cold blood.

"Be calm, dear friend," said Helen, patiently. "O my poor father!" And her other hand threw her apron over her head, and then came a burst of anguish that no words could utter.

At this Hazel started to his feet in fury.

"Now may the God that made sea and land judge between those miscreants there and you!"

"Be patient," said Helen, sobbing. "O be patient."

"No! I will not be patient," roared Hazel

"ST. HELEN'S."—See page 68.

"Judge thou her cause, O God; each of these tears against a reptile's soul."

And so he stood glaring, and his hair blowing wildly to the breeze; while she sighed patiently at his knee.

Presently he began to watch the vessel with a grim and bitter eye. Anon he burst out suddenly, "Aha! that is right. Well steered. Don't cry, sweet one; our cause is heard. Are they blind? Are they drunk? Are they sick? I see nobody on deck! Perhaps I have been too — God forgive me, the ship's ashore!"

CHAPTER XXXVII.

HELEN looked up; and there was the ship fast, and on her side. She was on the White Water Reef. Not upon the black rocks themselves, but on a part of them that was under water.

Hazel ran down to the beach; and there Helen found him greatly agitated. All his anger was gone; he had but one thought now, — to go out to her assistance. But it still wanted an hour to high water, and it was blowing smartly, and there was nearly always a surf upon that reef. What if the vessel should break up, and lives be lost?

He paced the sands like a wild beast in its cage, in an agony of pity, remorse, and burning impatience. His feelings became intolerable; he set his back to the boat, and with herculean strength forced it down a little way to meet the tide. He got logs and put them down for rollers. He strove, he strained, he struggled, till his face and hands were purple. And at last he met the flowing tide, and in a moment, jumped into the boat, and pushed off. Helen begged with sparkling eyes to be allowed to accompany him.

"What, to a ship smitten with scurvy or Heaven knows what? Certainly not. Besides, you would be wet through; it is blowing rather fresh, and I shall carry on. Pray for the poor souls I go to help; and for me, who have sinned in my anger."

He hoisted his sail, and ran out.

Helen stood on the bank, and watched him with tender admiration. How good and brave he was! And he could go into a passion too, when she was wronged, or when he thought she was. Well! she admired him none the less for that. She watched him at first with admiration, but soon with anxiety; for he had no sooner passed North Gate, than the cutter having both sails set, though reefed, lay down very much and her hull kept disappearing. Helen felt anxious, and would have been downright frightened, but for her confidence in his prowess.

By and by only her staggering sails were visible; and the sun set ere she reached the creek. The wind declined with the sun, and Helen made two great fires, and prepared food for the sufferers; for she made sure Hazel would bring them off in a few hours more. She promised herself the happiness of relieving the distressed. But to her infinite surprise she found herself almost regretting that the island was likely to be peopled with strangers. No matter, she should sit up for them all night, and be very kind to them, poor things; though they had not been very kind to her.

About midnight, the wind shifted to the northwest, and blew hard.

Helen ran down to the shore, and looked seaward. This was a fair wind for Hazel's return; and she began to expect him every hour. But no; he delayed unaccountably.

And the worst of it was, it began to blow a gale; and this wind sent the sea rolling into the bay in a manner that alarmed her seriously.

The night wore on; no signs of the boat; and now there was a heavy gale outside, and a great sea rolling in, brown and foaming.

Day broke, and showed the sea for a mile or two; the rest was hidden by driving rain.

Helen kneeled on the shore and prayed for him.

Dire misgivings oppressed her. And soon these were heightened to terror; for the sea began to disgorge things of a kind that had never come ashore before. A great ship's mast came tossing: huge as it was, the waves handled it like a toy. Then came a barrel; then a broken spar. These were but the forerunners of more fearful havoc.

The sea became strewed and literally blackened with fragments; part wreck, part cargo of a broken vessel.

But what was all this compared with the horror that followed?

A black object caught her eye; driven in upon the crest of a wave.

She looked, with her hair flying straight back, and her eyes almost starting from her head.

It was a boat, bottom up; driven on, and tossed like a cork.

It came nearer, nearer, nearer.

She dashed into the water with a wild scream, but a wave beat her backward on the sand, and, as she rose, an enormous roller lifted the boat upright into the air, and breaking, dashed it keel uppermost on the beach at her side — empty!

CHAPTER XXXVIII.

HELEN uttered a shriek of agony, and her knees smote together, and she would have swooned on the spot but for the wind and the spray that beat against her.

To the fearful stun succeeded the wildest distress. She ran to and fro like some wild animal bereaved; she kept wringing her hands and uttering cries of pity and despair, and went back to the boat a hundred times; it held her by a spell.

It was long before she could think connectedly, and, even then, it was not of herself, nor of her lonely state, but only, Why did not she die with him? Why did she not die instead of him?

He had been all the world to her; and now she knew it. O, what a friend, what a champion, what a lover these cruel waves had destroyed?

The morning broke, and still she hovered and hovered about the fatal boat, with great horror-stricken eyes, and hair flying to the breeze; and not a tear. If she could only have smoothed his last moments, have spoken one word into his dying ear! But no! Her poor hero had died in going to save others; died thinking her as cold as the waters that had destroyed him.

Dead or alive he was all the world to her now. She went, wailing piteously, and imploring the waves to give her at least his dead body to speak to, and mourn over. But the sea denied her even that dismal consolation.

The next tide brought in a few more fragments of the wreck, but no corpse floated ashore.

Then at last, as the waves once more retired, leaving, this time, only petty fragments of wreck on the beach, she lifted up her voice, and almost wept her heart out of her body.

Such tears as these are seldom without effect on the mind: and Helen now began to rebel, though faintly, against despair. She had been quite crushed, at first, under the material evidence, — the boat driven empty by the very wind and waves that had done the cruel deed. But the heart is averse to believe calamity and especially bereavement; and very ingenious in arguing against that bitterest of all woes. So she now sat down and brooded, and her mind fastened with pathetic ingenuity on every circumstance that could bear a favorable construction. The mast had not been broken; how, then, had it been lost? The body had not come ashore. He had had time to get to the wreck before the gale from the north came on at all; and why should a fair wind, though powerful, upset the boat? On these slender things she began to build a superstructure of hope; but soon her heart interrupted the reasoning. "What would *he* do in my place? would he sit guessing while hope had a hair to hang by?" That thought struck her like a spur: and in a moment she bounded into action, erect, her lips fixed, and her eye on fire, though her cheek was very pale. She went swiftly to Hazel's store, and searched it; there she found the jib-sail, a boat-hook, some rope, and one little oar, that Hazel was making for her, and had not quite completed. The sight of this, his last work, overpowered her again; and she sat down and took it on her knees, and kissed it, and cried over it. And these tears weakened her for a time. She felt it, and had the resolution to leave the oar behind. A single oar was of no use to row with. She rigged the boat-hook as a mast; and fastened the sail to it; and, with this poor equipment, she actually resolved to put out to sea.

The wind still blew smartly, and there was no blue sky visible.

And now she remembered she had eaten nothing; that would not do. Her strength might fail her. She made ready a meal, and ate it almost fiercely, and by a pure effort of resolution; as she was doing all the rest.

By this time, it was nearly high-tide. She watched the water creeping up. Will it float the boat? It rises over the keel; two inches, three inches. Five inches water! Now she pushes with all her strength. No; the boat has water in it she had forgotten to bale out. She strained every nerve, but could not move it. She stopped to take breath, and husband her strength. But, when she renewed her efforts, the five inches were four, and she had the misery of seeing the water crawl away by degrees, and leave the boat high and dry.

She sighed, heart-broken, a while; then went home and prayed.

When she had prayed a long time for strength and wisdom, she lay down for an hour, and tried to sleep, but failed. Then she prepared for a more serious struggle with the many difficulties she had to encounter. Now she thanked God more than ever for the health and rare strength she had acquired in this island: without them she could have done nothing now. She got a clay platter, and baled the vessel nearly dry. She left a little water for ballast. She fortified herself with food, and put provisions and water on board the boat. In imitation of Hazel, she went and got two round logs, and as soon as the tide crawled up to four inches, she lifted the bow a little, and got a roller under. Then she went to the boat's stern, set her teeth, and pushed with a rush of excitement that gave her almost a man's strength.

The stubborn boat seemed elastic, and all but moved. Then instinct taught her where her true strength lay. She got to the stern of the boat, and setting the small of her back under the projecting gunwale, she gathered herself together and gave a superb heave, that moved the boat a foot. She followed it up, and heaved again with like effect. Then, with a cry of joy, she ran and put down another roller forward. The boat was now on two rollers: one more magnificent heave with all her zeal, and strength, and youth, and the boat glided forward. She turned and rushed at it as it went, and the water deepening, and a gust catching the sail, it went out to sea, and she had only just time to throw herself across the gunwale, panting. She was afloat. The wind was S.W., and before she knew where she was, the boat headed towards the home reefs, and slipped through the water pretty fast considering how small a sail she carried. She ran to the helm. Alas! the rudder was broken off above the water-line. The helm was a mockery, and the boat running for the reefs. She slacked the sheet and the boat lost her way, and began to drift with the tide, which luckily had not yet turned. It carried her in shore.

Helen cast her eyes around for an expedient, and she unshipped one of the transoms, and by trailing over the side, and alternately slacking and hauling the sheet, she contrived to make the boat crawl like a winged bird through the western passage. After that it soon got becalmed under the cliff, and drifted into two feet water.

Instantly she tied a rope to the mast, got out into the water, and took the rope ashore. She tied it round a heavy barrel she found there, and set the barrel up, and heaped stones round it and on it, which, unfortunately, was a long job, though she worked with feverish haste; then she went round the point, sometimes wet and sometimes dry, for the little oar she had left behind, because it broke her heart to look at. Away with such weakness now! With that oar, his last work, she might steer if she could not row. She got it. She came back to the boat to recommence her voyage.

She found the boat all safe but in six inches of water, and the tide going out. So ended her voyage; four hundred yards at most, and then to wait another twelve hours for the tide.

It was too cruel: and every hour so precious; for, even if Hazel was alive, he would die of cold and hunger ere she could get to him. She cried like any woman.

She persisted like a man.

She made several trips, and put away things in the boat that could possibly be of use, — abundant provision, and a keg of water; Hazel's wooden spade to paddle or steer with; his basket of tools, &c. Then she snatched some sleep; but it was broken by sad and terrible dreams: then she waited in an agony of impatience for high-water.

We are not always the best judges of what is good for us. Probably these delays saved her own life. She went out at last under far more favorable circumstances, — a light westerly breeze, and no reefs to pass through. She was, however, severely incommoded with a ground-swell.

At first she steered with the spade as well as she could; but she found this was not sufficient. The current ran westerly, and she was drifting out of her course. Then she remembered Hazel's lessons, and made shift to fasten the spade to the helm, and then lashed the helm. Even this did not quite do; so she took her little oar, kissed it, cried over it a little, and then pulled manfully with it so as to keep the true course. It was a muggy day, neither wet nor dry. White Water Island was not in sight from Godsend Island; but as soon as she lost the latter, the former became visible, — an ugly grinning reef, with an eternal surf on the south and western sides.

Often she left off rowing, and turned to look at it. It was all black and blank, except the white and fatal surf.

When she was about four miles from the nearest part of the reef, there was a rush and bubble in the water, and a great shark came after the boat. Helen screamed, and turned very cold. She dreaded the monster not for what he could do now; but for what he might have done. He seemed to know the boat, he swam so vigilantly behind it. Was he there when the boat upset with Hazel in it? Was it in his greedy maw the remains of her best friend must be sought. Her lips opened, but no sound. She shuddered and hid her face at this awful thought.

The shark followed steadily.

She got to the reef, but did not hit it off as she intended. She ran under its lee, lowered the little sail, and steered the boat into a nick where the shark could hardly follow her.

But he moved to and fro like a sentinel, while she landed in trepidation and secured the boat to the branches of a white coral rock.

She found the place much larger than it looked from Telegraph Point. It was an archipelago of coral reef incrusted here and there with shells. She could not see all over it, where she was, so she made for what seemed the highest part, a bleak, seaweedy mound, with some sandy hillocks about it. She went up to this, and looked eagerly all round.

Not a soul.

She called as loud as her sinking heart would let her.

Not a sound.

She felt very sick, and sat down upon the mound.

When she had yielded a while to the weakness of her sex, she got up, and was her father's daughter again. She set to work to examine every foot of the reef.

It was no easy task. The rocks were rugged and sharp in places, slippery in others; often she had to go about, and once she fell and hurt her pretty hands and made them bleed; she never looked at them, nor heeded, but got up and sighed at the interruption: then patiently persisted. It took her two hours to examine thus, in detail, one half the island: but at last she discovered something. She saw at the eastern side of the reef a wooden figure of a woman, and, making her way to it, found the figure-head, and a piece of the bow, of the ship, with a sail on it, and a yard on that. This fragment was wedged into an angle of the reef, and the seaward edge of it shattered in a way that struck terror to Helen, for it showed her how omnipotent the sea had been. On the reef itself she found a cask with its head stove in, also a little keg and two wooden chests or cases. But what was all this to her?

She sat down again, for her knees failed her. Presently there was a sort of moan near her, and a seal splashed into the water and dived out of her sight. She put her hands on her heart, and bowed her head down, utterly desolate. She sat thus for a long time indeed, until she was interrupted by a most unexpected visitor.

Something came sniffing up to her and put a cold nose to her hand. She started violently and both her hands were in the air in a moment.

It was a dog, a pointer. He whimpered and tried to gambol, but could not manage it; he was too weak. However, he contrived to let her see with the wagging of his tail, and a certain contemporaneous twist of his emaciated body, that she was welcome. But, having performed this ceremony, he trotted feebly away, leaving her very much startled, and not knowing what to think; indeed, this incident set her trembling all over.

A dog saved from the wreck! Then why not a man? And why not that life? O, thought she, would God save that creature, and not pity my poor angel and me?

She got up animated with hope, and recommenced her researches. She now kept at the outward edge of the island, and so went all round till she reached her boat again. The shark was swimming to and fro, waiting for her with horrible pertinacity. She tried to eat a mouthful, but, though she was faint, she could not eat. She drank a mouthful of water, and then went to search the very small portion that remained of the reef, and to take the poor dog home with her, because he she had lost was so good to animals. Only his example is left me, she said; and with that came another burst of sorrow. But she got up and did the rest of her work, crying as she went. After some severe travelling she got near the northeast limit, and in a sort of gully she saw the dog, quietly seated high on his tail. She called him; but he never moved. So, then, she went to him, and, when she got near him, she saw why he would not come. He was watching. Close by him lay the form of a man nearly covered with seaweed. The feet were visible, and so was the face, the latter deadly pale. It was he. In a moment she was by him, and leaning over him with both hands quivering. Was he dead? No; his eyes were closed; he was fast asleep.

Her hands flew to his face to feel him alive, and then grasped both his hands and drew them up towards her panting bosom: and the tears of joy streamed from her eyes, as she sobbed and murmured over him, she knew not what. At that he awoke and stared at her. He uttered a loud ejaculation of joy and wonder, then taking it all in, burst into tears himself and fell to kissing her hands and blessing her. The poor soul had almost given himself up for lost. And to be saved, all in a moment, and by her!

They could neither of them speak, but only mingled tears of joy and gratitude.

Hazel recovered himself first; and rising somewhat stiffly, lent her his arm. Her father's spirit went out of her in the moment of victory, and she was all woman, — sweet, loving, clinging woman. She got hold of his hand as well as his arm, and clutched it so tight, her little grasp seemed velvet and steel.

"Let me feel you," said she: "but no words! no words!"

He supported his preserver tenderly to the boat, then, hoisting the sail, he fetched the east side in two tacks, shipped the sail and yard, and also the cask, keg, and boxes. He then put a great quantity of loose oysters on board, each as large as a plate. She looked at him with amazement.

"What," said she, when he had quite loaded the boat, "only just out of the jaws of death, and yet you can trouble your head about oysters and things."

"Wait till you see what I shall do with them," said he. "These are pearl oysters. I gathered them for *you*, when I had little hope I should ever see you again to give them you."

This was an unlucky speech. The act, that seemed so small and natural a thing to him, the woman's heart measured more correctly. Something rose in her throat; she tried to laugh instead of crying, and so she did both, and went into a violent fit of hysterics that showed how thoroughly her nature had been stirred to its depths. She quite frightened Hazel; and, indeed, the strength of an excited woman's weakness is sometimes alarming to manly natures.

He did all he could to soothe her; without much success. As soon as she was better he set sail, thinking home was the best place for her. She leant back exhausted, and, after a while, seemed to be asleep. We don't believe she was, but Hazel did; and sat, cold and aching in body, but warm at heart, worshipping her with all his eyes.

At last they got ashore; and he sat by her fire and told her all, while she cooked his supper and warmed clothes at the fire for him.

"The ship," said he, "was a Dutch vessel, bound from Batavia to Callao, that had probably gone on her beam ends, for she was full of water. Her crew had abandoned her; I think they underrated the buoyancy of the ship and cargo. They left the poor dog on board. Her helm was lashed a-weather a couple of turns, but why that was done, I cannot tell for the life of me. I boarded her; unshipped my mast, and moored the boat to the ship; fed the poor dog; rummaged in the hold, and contrived to hoist up a small cask of salted beef, and a keg of rum, and some cases of grain and seeds. I managed to slide these on to the reef by means of the mast and oar lashed together. But a roller ground the wreck farther on to the reef, and the sudden snap broke the rope, as I suppose, and the boat went to sea. I never knew the misfortune till I saw her adrift. I could have got over that by making a raft; but the gale from the north brought such a sea on us. I saw she must break up, so I got ashore how I could. Ah, I little thought to see your face again, still less that I should owe my life to you."

"Spare me," said Helen, faintly.

"What, must not I thank you even for my life?"

"No. *The account is far from even yet.*"

"You are no arithmetician to say so. What astonishes me most is, that you have never once scolded me for all the trouble and anxiety —"

"I am too happy to see you sitting there, to scold you. But, still I do ask you, to leave the sea alone, after this. The treacherous monster! O, think what you and I have suffered on it."

She seemed quite worn out. He saw that, and retired for the night, casting one more wistful glance on her. But at that moment she was afraid to look at him. Her heart was welling over with tenderness for the dear friend whose life she had saved.

Next morning Hazel rose at daybreak as usual, but found himself stiff in the joints, and with a pain in his back. The mat that hung at the opening of Helen's cave was not removed as usual. She was on her bed with a violent headache.

Hazel fed Ponto, and corrected him. He was at present a civilized dog; so he made a weak rush at the boobies and noddies directly.

He also smelt Tommy inquisitively, to learn was he an eatable. Tommy somehow divined the end of this sinister curiosity, and showed his teeth.

Then Hazel got a rope, and tied one end round his own waist, and one round Ponto's neck, and at every outbreak of civilization, jerked him sharply on to his back. The effect of this discipline was rapid; Ponto soon found that he must not make war on the inhabitants of the island. He was a docile animal, and, in a very short time, consented to make one of "the happy family," as Hazel called the miscellaneous crew that beset him.

Helen and Hazel did not meet till past noon; and, when they did meet, it was plain she had been thinking a great deal, for her greeting was so shy and restrained as to appear cold and distant to Hazel. He thought to himself, I was too happy yesterday, and she too kind. Of course it could not last.

This change in her seemed to grow rather than diminish. She carried it so far as to go and almost hide during the working hours. She made off to the jungle, and spent an unreasonable time there. She professed to be collecting cotton, and it must be admitted she brought a good deal home with her. But Hazel could not accept cotton as the only motive for this sudden separation.

He lost the light of her face till the evening. Then matters took another turn: she was too polite. Ceremony and courtesy appeared to be gradually encroaching upon tender friendship and familiarity: yet, now and then, her soft hazel eyes seemed to turn on him in silence, and say, forgive me all this. Then at those sweet looks, love and forgiveness poured out of his eyes. And then hers sought the ground. And this was generally followed by a certain mixture of stiffness, timidity, and formality, too subtle to describe.

The much-enduring man began to lose patience.

"This is caprice," said he. "Cruel caprice."

Our female readers will probably take a deeper view of it than that. Whatever it was, another change was at hand. Since he was so exposed to the weather on the reef, Hazel had never been free from pain; but he had done his best to work it off. He had collected all the valuables from the wreck, made a new mast, set up a rude capstan to draw the boat ashore, and cut a little dock for her at low water, and clayed it in the full heat of the sun; and, having accomplished this drudgery, he got at last to his labor of love; he opened a quantity of pearl oysters, fed Tommy and the duck with them, and began the great work of lining the cavern with them The said cavern was somewhat shell-shaped, and his idea was to make it out of a gloomy cavern into a vast shell, lined entirely, roof and sides, with glorious, sweet, prismatic, mother-of-pearl, fresh from ocean. Well, one morning, while Helen was in the jungle, he made a cement of guano, sand, clay, and water, nipped some shells to a shape with the pincers, and cemented them neatly, like Mosaic almost; but in the middle of his work he was cut down by the disorder he had combated so stoutly. He fairly gave in, and sat down groaning with pain. And in this state Helen found him.

"O, what is the matter?" said she.

He told her the truth and said he had violent pains

on the back and head. She did not say much, but she turned pale. She bustled and lighted a great fire, and made him lie down by it. She propped his head up; she set water on to boil for him, and would not let him move for anything; and all the time her features were brimful of the liveliest concern. He could not help thinking how much better it was to be ill and in pain, and have her so kind, than to be well, and see her cold and distant. Towards evening he got better, or rather he mistook an intermission for cure, and retired to his boat; but she made him take her rug with him; and, when he was gone, she could not sleep for anxiety; and it cut her to the heart to think how poorly he was lodged compared with her.

Of all the changes fate could bring, this she had never dreamed of, that she should be so robust, and he should be sick and in pain.

She passed an uneasy, restless night, and long before morning she awoke for the sixth or seventh time, and she awoke with a misgiving in her mind, and some sound ringing in her ears. She listened and heard nothing; but in a few moments it began again.

It was Hazel talking, — talking in a manner so fast, so strange, so loud, that it made her blood run cold. It was the voice of Hazel, but not his mind.

She drew near, and, to her dismay, found him fever-stricken, and pouring out words with little sequence. She came close to him and tried to soothe him, but he answered her quite at random, and went on flinging out the strangest things in stranger order. She trembled and waited for a lull, hoping then to soothe him with soft words and tones of tender pity.

"*Dens and caves!*" he roared, answering an imaginary detractor. "Well, never mind, love shall make that hole in the rock a palace for a queen; for *a* queen? For *the* queen." Here he suddenly changed characters and fancied he was interpreting the discourse of another. "He means the Queen of the Fairies," said he, patronizingly: then, resuming his own character with loud defiance, "I say her chamber shall outshine the glories of the Alhambra, as far as the lilies outshone the artificial glories of King Solomon. O mighty Nature, let others rely on the painter, the gold-beater, the carver of marble, come you and help me adorn the temple of my beloved. Amen."

(The poor soul thought, by the sound of his own words, it must be a prayer he had uttered.)

And now Helen, with streaming eyes, tried to put in a word, but he stopped her with a wild hush! and went off into a series of mysterious whisperings. "Make no noise, please, or we shall frighten her. There — that is her window — no noise, please! I've watched and waited four hours, just to see her sweet, darling shadow on the blinds, and shall I lose it for your small talk? all paradoxes and platitudes! excuse my plain speaking — hush! here it comes, — her shadow — hush — how my heart beats. It is gone. So now" (speaking out), "Good night, base world! Do you hear? you company of liars, thieves, and traitors, called the world, go and sleep if you can. I *shall* sleep: because my conscience is clear. *False accusations!* Who can help them? They are the act of others. Read of Job, and Paul, and Joan of Arc. No, no, no, no; I did n't say read 'em *out* with those stentorian lungs. I must be allowed a *little* sleep, a man that wastes the midnight oil, yet brushes the early dew. Good night."

He turned round and slept for several hours as he supposed; but in reality he was silent for just three seconds. "Well," said he, "and is a gardener a man to be looked down upon by upstarts? When Adam delved and Eve span, where was then the gentleman? Why, where the spade was. Yet I went through the Herald's College and not one of our mushroom aristocracy ('bloated' I object to; they don't eat half as much as their footmen) had a spade for a crest. There 's nothing ancient west of the Caspian. Well, all the better. For there 's no fool like an old fool. A spade 's a spade for a that, an a that, an a that, an a that, — an a that, — an a that. Hallo! Stop that man; he 's gone off on his cork leg, of a that, on a that, — and it is my wish to be quiet. Allow me respectfully to observe," said he striking off suddenly into an air of vast politeness, "that man requires change. I 've done a jolly good day's work with the spade for this old Buffer, and now the intellect claims its turn. The mind retires above the noisy world to its Acropolis, and there discusses the great problem of the day; the Insular Enigma. To be or not to be, that is the question, I believe. No it is not. That is fully discussed elsewhere. Hum! To diffuse — intelligence — from a fixed island — over one hundred leagues of water.

"It 's a stinger. But I can't complain. I had read Lempriere, and Smith and Bryant, and mythology in general: yet I must go and fall in love with the Sphinx. Men are so vain. Vanity whispered she will set you a light one; why is a cobbler like a king, for instance. She is in love with you, ye fool, if you are with her. The harder the riddle the higher the compliment the Sphinx pays you. That is the way all sensible men look at it. She is not the Sphinx: she is an angel, and I call her my Lady Caprice. *Hate her for being Caprice?* You incorrigible muddle head. Why, I love Caprice for being her shadow. Poor, impotent love that can't solve a problem. The only one she ever set me. I 've gone about it like a fool. What is the use putting up little bits of telegraphs on the island? I 'll make a kite a hundred feet high, get five miles of rope ready against the next hurricane; and then I 'll rub it with phosphorus and fly it. But what can I fasten it to? No tree would hold it. Dunce! To the island itself, of course. And now go to Stantle, Magg, Melton, and Copestake for one thousand yards of silk, — *Money! Money! Money!* Well, give them a mortgage on the island, and a draft on the galleon. Now stop the pitch-fountain, and bore a hole near it; fill fifty balloons with gas, inscribe them with the latitude and longitude, fly them, and bring all the world about our ears. The problem is solved. It is solved, and I am destroyed. She leaves me; she thinks no more of me. Her heart is in England."

Then he muttered for a long time unintelligibly; and Helen ventured near, and actually laid her hand on his brow to soothe him. But suddenly his muttering ceased, and he seemed to be puzzling hard over something.

The result came out in a clear articulate sentence, that made Helen recoil, and holding by the mast, cast an indescribable look of wonder and dismay on the speaker.

The words that so staggered her were these, to the letter.

"She says she hates reptiles. Yet she marries Arthur Wardlaw."

CHAPTER XXXIX.

The very name of Arthur Wardlaw startled Helen, and made her realize how completely her thoughts had been occupied with another.

But add to that the strange and bitter epigram! Or was it a mere fortuitous concourse of words?

She was startled, amazed, confounded, puzzled. And, ere she could recover her composure, Hazel was back to his problem again: but no longer with the same energy.

He said in a faint and sleepy voice: "'He maketh the winds His messengers, and flames of fire His ministers.' Ah! if I could do that! Well, why not? I can do anything she bids me, —

Græculus esuriens cœlum jusseris ibit."

And soon after this doughty declaration he dozed off, and forgot all his trouble for a while.

The sun rose, and still he slept, and Helen watched him with undisguised tenderness in her face; undisguised now that he could not see it.

Erelong she had companions in her care. Ponto came out of his den, and sniffed about the boat; and then began to scratch it, and whimper for his friend. Tommy swam out of the sea, came to the boat, discovered, Heaven knows how, that his friend was there, and, in the way of noises, did everything but speak. The sea-birds followed and fluttered here and there in an erratic way, with now and then a peck at each other. All animated nature seemed to be uneasy at this eclipse of their Hazel.

At last Tommy raised himself quite perpendicular, in a vain endeavor to look into the boat, and invented a whine in the minor key, which tells on dogs: it set Ponto off in a moment; he sat upon his tail, and delivered a long and most deplorable howl.

"Everything loves him," thought Helen.

With Ponto's music Hazel awoke, and found her watching him, with tears in her eyes; he said softly: "Miss Rolleston! There is nothing the matter, I hope. Why am I not up getting things for your breakfast?"

"Dear friend," said she, "why you are not doing things for me and forgetting yourself, is because you have been very ill. And I am your nurse. Now tell me what I shall get you. Is there nothing you could fancy?"

No; he had no appetite; she was not to trouble about him. And then he tried to get up; but that gave him such a pain in his loins, he was fain to lie down again. So then he felt that he had got rheumatic fever. He told her so; but seeing her sweet anxious face, begged her not to be alarmed, — he knew what to take for it. Would she be kind enough to go to his arsenal and fetch some specimens of bark she would find there, and also the keg of rum.

She flew at the word, and soon made him an infusion of the barks in boiling water; to which the rum was added.

His sweet nurse administered this from time to time. The barks used were of the cassia-tree, and a wild citron-tree. Cinchona did not exist in this island, unfortunately. Perhaps there was no soil for it at a sufficient elevation above the sea.

Nevertheless with these inferior barks they held the fever in check. But the pain was obstinate, and cost Helen many a sigh; for if she came softly, she could often hear him moan; and the moment he heard her foot, he set-to and whistled, for a blind; with what success may be imagined. She would have bought those pains, or a portion of them; ay, and paid a heavy price for them.

But pain, like everything, intermits, and in those blessed intervals his mind was more active than ever, and ran a great deal upon what he called the Problem.

But she, who had set it him, gave him little encouragement now to puzzle over it.

The following may serve as a specimen of their conversation on that head.

"The air of this island," said he, "gives one a sort of vague sense of mental power. It leads to no result in my case: still, it is an agreeable sensation to have it floating across my mind that some day I shall solve the Great Problem. Ah! if I was only an inventor!"

"And so you are."

"No, no," said Hazel, disclaiming as earnestly as some people claim; "I do things that look like acts of invention, but they are acts of memory. I could show you plates and engravings of all the things I have seemed to invent. A man who studies books instead of skimming them, can cut a dash in a desert island, until the fatal word goes forth, — invent; and then you find him out."

"I am sure I wish I had never said the fatal word. You will never get well if you puzzle your brain over impossibilities."

"Impossibilities! But is not that begging the question? The measure of impossibilities is lost in the present age. I propose a test. Let us go back a century, and suppose that three problems were laid before the men of that day, and they were asked to decide which is the most impossible: 1st, to diffuse intelligence from a fixed island over a hundred leagues of water: 2d, to make the sun take in thirty seconds likenesses more exact than any portrait-painter ever took, — likenesses that can be sold for a shilling at fifty per cent profit: 3d, for New York and London to exchange words by wire so much faster than the earth can turn, that London shall tell New York at ten on Monday morning what was the price of consols at two o'clock Monday afternoon."

"That is a story," said Helen, with a look of angelic reproach.

"I accept that reply," said Hazel. "As for me, I have got a smattering of so many subjects, all full of incredible truths, that my faith in the impossibility of anything is gone. Ah! if James Watt was only here instead of John Hazel, — James Watt from the Abbey with a head as big as a pumpkin, — he would not have gone groping about the island, writing on rocks, and erecting signals. No; he would have had some grand and bold idea worthy of the proposition."

"Well, so I think," said Helen, archly; "that great man with a great head would have begun by making a kite a hundred yards high."

"Would he? Well, he was quite capable of it."

"Yes; and rubbed it with phosphorus, and flown it the first tempest, and made the string fast to — the island itself."

"Well, that is an idea," said Hazel, staring; "rather hyperbolical, I fear. But after all, it is an idea."

"Or else," continued Helen, "he would weave a thousand yards of some light fabric, and make balloons; then he would stop the pitch-fountain, bore a hole in the rock near it, and so get the gas, fill the balloons, inscribe them with our sad story and our latitude and longitude, and send them flying all over the ocean, — there!"

Hazel was amazed.

"I resign my functions to you," said he. "What imagination! What invention!"

"O dear no," said Helen, slyly; "acts of memory sometimes pass for invention, you know. Shall I tell you? when first you fell ill, you were rather light-headed, and uttered the strangest things. They would have made me laugh heartily, only I could n't, — for crying. And you said that about kites and balloons, every word."

"Did I? then I have most brains when I have least reason, that 's all."

"Ay," said Helen, "and other strange things, — very strange and bitter things. One I should like to ask you about, what on earth you could mean by it; but perhaps you meant nothing after all."

"I 'll soon tell you," said Hazel; but he took the precaution to add, "Provided I know what it means myself."

She looked at him steadily, and was on the point of seeking the explanation so boldly offered; but her own courage failed her. She colored and hesitated.

"I shall wait," said she, "till you are quite, quite well. That will be soon, I hope; only you must be good, and obey my prescriptions. Cultivate patience; it is a wholesome plant; bow the pride of that intellect which you see a fever can lay low in an hour: aspire no more beyond the powers of man. Here we shall stay unless Providence sends us a ship. I have ceased to repine: and don't you begin. Dismiss that problem altogether; see how hot it has made your poor brow. Be good now, and dismiss it; or else do as I do, — fold it up, put it quietly away in a corner of your mind, and, when you least expect, it will pop out solved."

[O, comfortable doctrine! But how about Jamie Watt's headaches? And why are the signs of hard thoughts so much stronger in his brow and face than in Shakespeare's? Mercy on us, there is another problem.]

Hazel smiled, well-pleased, and leaned back, soothed, silenced, subdued, by her soft voice, and the exquisite touch of her velvet hand on his hot brow; for, woman-like, she laid her hand like down on that burning brow to aid her words in soothing it. Nor did it occur to him just then that this admonition delivered with a kind maternal hand, maternal voice, came from the same young lady who had flown at him like a wild cat with this very problem in her mouth. She mesmerized him, problem and all; he subsided into a complacent languor, and at last went to sleep, thinking only of her. But the topic had entered his mind too deeply to be finally dismissed. It returned next day, though in a different form. You must know that Hazel, as he lay on his back in the boat, had often, in a half-drowsy way, watched the effect of the sun upon the boat's mast: it now stood, a bare pole, and at certain hours acted like the needle of a dial, by casting a shadow on the sands. Above all, he could see pretty well by means of this pole and its shadow when the sun attained its greatest elevation. He now asked Miss Rolleston to assist him in making this observation exactly.

She obeyed his instructions, and the moment the shadow reached its highest angle, and showed the minutest symptom of declension, she said, "Now," and Hazel called out in a loud voice: —

"Noon!"

"And forty-nine minutes past eight at Sydney," said Helen, holding out her chronometer; for she had been sharp enough to get it ready of her own accord.

Hazel looked at her and at the watch with amazement and incredulity.

"What?" said he. "Impossible. You can't have kept Sydney time all this while."

"And pray why not?" said Helen. "Have you forgotten that once somebody praised me for keeping Sydney time; it helped you, somehow or other, to know where we were."

"And so it will now," cried Hazel, exultingly. "But no! it is impossible. We have gone through scenes that — you can't have wound that watch up without missing a day."

"Indeed but I have," said Helen. "Not wind my watch up! Why, if I was dying I should wind my watch up. See, it requires no key; a touch or two of the fingers and it is done. O, I am remarkably constant in all my habits; and this is an old friend I never neglect. Do you remember that terrible night in the boat, when neither of us expected to see the morning, — O, how good and brave you were! — well, I remember winding it up that night. I kissed it, and bade it good by; but I never dreamed of not winding it up, because I was going to be killed. What! am I not to be praised again, as I was on board ship? Stingy! can't afford to praise one twice for the same thing."

"Praised!" cried Hazel, excitedly; "worshipped, you mean. Why, we have got the longitude by means of your chronometer. It is wonderful! It is providential! It is the finger of Heaven! Pen and ink, and let me work it out."

In his excitement he got up without assistance, and was soon busy calculating the longitude of Godsend Isle.

CHAPTER XL.

"THERE," said he. "Now the latitude I must guess at by certain combinations. In the first place the slight variation in the length of the days. Then I must try and make a rough calculation of the sun's parallax. And then my botany will help me a little; spices furnish a clew; there are one or two that will not grow outside the tropic. It was the longitude that beat me, and now we have conquered it. Hurrah! Now I know what to diffuse, and in what direction; east, southeast; the ducks have shown me that much. So there 's the first step towards the impossible problem."

"Very well," said Helen; "and I am sure one step is enough for one day. I forbid you the topic for twelve hours at least. I detest it because it always makes your poor head so hot."

"What on earth does that matter?" said Hazel, impetuously, and almost crossly.

"Come, come, come, sir," said Helen, authoritatively; "it matters to me."

But when she saw that he could think of nothing else, and that opposition irritated him, she had the tact and good sense not to strain her authority, nor to irritate her subject.

Hazel spliced a long, fine-pointed stick to the mast-head, and set a plank painted white with guano at right angles to the base of the mast; and so whenever the sun attained his meridian altitude, went into a difficult and subtle calculation to arrive at the latitude, or as near it as he could without proper instruments; and he brooded and brooded over his discovery of the longitude, but unfortunately he could not advance. In some problems the first step once gained leads, or at least points to the next; but to know whereabouts they were, and to let others know it, were two difficulties heterogeneous and distinct.

Having thought and thought till his head was dizzy, at last he took Helen's advice and put it by for a while. He set himself to fit and number a quantity of pearl oyster shells, so that he might be able to place them at once, when he should be able to recommence his labor of love in the cavern.

One day Helen had left him so employed, and was busy cooking the dinner at her own place, but, mind you, with one eye on the dinner and another on her patient, when suddenly she heard him shouting very loud, and ran out to see what was the matter.

He was roaring like mad, and whirling his arms over his head like a demented windmill.

She ran to him.

"Eureka! Eureka!" he shouted, in furious excitement.

"O dear!" cried Helen; "never mind." She was all against her patient exciting himself.

But he was exalted beyond even her control. "Crown me with laurel," he cried; "I have solved the problem": and up went his arms.

"O, is that all?" said she, calmly.

"Get me two squares of my parchment," cried he; "and some of the finest gut."

"Will not after dinner do?"

"No; certainly not," said Hazel, in a voice of command. "I would n't wait a moment for all the flesh-pots of Egypt."

Then she went like the wind and fetched them.

"O, thank you! thank you! Now I want, — let me see, — ah, there 's an old rusty hoop that was washed ashore, on one of that ship's casks. I put it carefully away; how the unlikeliest things come in useful soon or late!"

She went for the hoop, but not so rapidly, for here it was that the first faint doubt of his sanity came in. However, she brought it, and he thanked her.

"And now," said he, "while I prepare the intelligence, will you be so kind as to fetch me the rushes."

"The what?" said Helen, in growing dismay.

"The rushes! I 'll tell you where to find some."

Helen thought the best thing was to temporize. Perhaps he would be better after eating some wholesome food. "I 'll fetch them directly after dinner," said she. "But it will be spoiled if I leave it for long; and I do so want it to be nice for you to-day."

"Dinner?" cried Hazel. "What do I care for dinner now. I am solving my problem. I'd rather go without dinner for years than interrupt a great idea. Pray let dinner take its chance, and obey me for once."

"For once!" said Helen, and turned her mild hazel eyes on him with such a look of gentle reproach.

"Forgive me! But don't take me for a child, asking you for a toy; I 'm a poor crippled inventor, who sees daylight at last. O, I am on fire; and, if you want me not to go into a fever, why, get me my rushes."

"Where shall I find them?" said Helen, catching fire at him.

"Go to where your old hut stood, and follow the river about a furlong: you will find a bed of high rushes: cut me a good bundle, cut them below the water, choose the stoutest. Here is a pair of shears I found in the ship."

She took the shears and went swiftly across the sands and up the slope. He watched her with an admiring eye; and well he might, for it was the very poetry of motion. Hazel in his hours of health had almost given up walking; he ran from point to point, without fatigue or shortness of breath. Helen, equally pressed for time, did not run; but she went almost as fast. By rising with the dawn, by three meals a day of animal food, by constant work, and heavenly air, she was in a condition women rarely attain to. She was *trained.* Ten miles was no more to her than ten yards. And, when she was in a hurry, she got over the ground by a grand but feminine motion not easy to describe. It was a series of smooth undulations, not vulgar strides, but swift rushes, in which the loins seemed to propel the whole body, and the feet scarcely to touch the ground: it was the vigor and freedom of a savage, with the grace of a lady.

And so it was she swept across the sands and up the slope,

Et vera incessu patuit Dea.

While she was gone, Hazel cut two little squares of seals' bladder, one larger than the other. On the smaller he wrote: "An English lady wrecked on an island. Longitude , S., latitude between the and parallels. Haste to her rescue." Then he folded this small, and enclosed it in the larger slip, which he made into a little bag, and tied the neck extremely tight with fine gut, leaving a long piece of the gut free.

And now Helen came gliding back, as she went, and brought him a large bundle of rushes.

Then he asked her to help him fasten these rushes round the iron hoop.

"It must not be done too regularly," said he; "but so as to look as much like a little bed of rushes as possible."

Helen was puzzled still, but interested. So she set to work, and, between them, they fastened rushes all round the hoop, although it was a large one.

But, when it was done, Hazel said they were too bare.

"Then we will fasten another row," said Helen, good-humoredly. And, without more ado, she was off to the river again.

When she came back, she found him up, and he said the great excitement had cured him, — such power has the brain over the body. This convinced her he had really hit upon some great idea. And when she had made him eat his dinner by her fire, she asked him to tell her all about it.

But, by a natural reaction, the glorious and glowing excitement of mind, that had battled his very rheumatic pains, was now followed by doubt and dejection.

"Don't ask me yet," he sighed. "Theory is one thing; practice is another. We count without our antagonists. I forgot they will set their wits against mine: and they are many, I am but one. And I have been so often defeated. And, do you know, I have observed that whenever I say beforehand now I am going to do something clever, I am always defeated. Pride really goes before destruction, and vanity before a fall."

The female mind, rejecting all else, went like a

needle's point at one thing in this explanation.

"Our antagonists?" said Helen, looking sadly puzzled. "Why, what antagonists have we?"

"The messengers," said Hazel, with a groan. "The aërial messengers."

That did the business. Helen dropped the subject with almost ludicrous haste; and, after a few commonplace observations, made a nice comfortable dose of grog and bark for him. This she administered as an independent transaction, and not at all by way of comment on his antagonists, the aërial messengers.

It operated unkindly for her purpose: it did him so much good, that he lifted up his dejected head, and his eyes sparkled again, and he set to work, and, by sunset, prepared two more bags of bladder with inscriptions inside, and long tails of fine gut hanging. He then set to work, and, with fingers far less adroit than hers, fastened another set of rushes round the hoop. He set them less evenly, and some of them not quite perpendicular; and, while he was fumbling over this, and examining the effect with paternal glances, Helen's hazel eye dwelt on him with furtive pity; for, to her, this girdle of rushes was now an instrument, that bore an ugly likeness to the sceptre of straw, with which vanity run to seed sways imaginary kingdoms in Bedlam or Bicetre.

And yet he was better. He walked about the cavern and conversed charmingly; he was dictionary, essayist, *raconteur*, anything she liked; and, as she prudently avoided and ignored the one fatal topic, it was a delightful evening: her fingers were as busy as his tongue: and, when he retired, she presented him with the fruits of a fortnight's work, a glorious wrapper made of fleecy cotton enclosed in a plaited web of flexible and silky grasses. He thanked her, and blessed her, and retired for the night.

About midnight she awoke and felt uneasy: so she did what since his illness she had done a score of times without his knowledge, she stole from her lair to watch him.

She found him wrapped in her present, which gave her great pleasure; and sleeping like an infant, which gave her joy. She eyed him eloquently for a long time; and then very timidly put out her hand, and, in her quality of nurse, laid it lighter than down upon his brow.

The brow was cool, and a very slight moisture on it showed the fever was going or gone.

She folded her arms and stood looking at him; and she thought of all they two had done and suffered together. Her eyes absorbed him, devoured him. The time flew by unheeded. It was so sweet to be able to set her face free from its restraint, and let all its sunshine beam on him: and even when she retired at last, those light hazel eyes, that could flash fire at times, but were all dove-like now, hung and lingered on him as if they could never look at him enough.

Half an hour before daybreak she was awakened by the dog howling piteously. She felt a little uneasy at that: not much. However she got up, and issued from her cavern, just as the sun showed his red eye above the horizon. She went towards the boat as a matter of course. She found Ponto tied to the helm: the boat was empty, and Hazel nowhere to be seen.

She uttered a scream of dismay.

The dog howled and whined louder than ever.

CHAPTER XLI.

WARDLAW senior was not what you would call a tender-hearted man: but he was thoroughly moved by General Rolleston's distress, and by his fortitude. The gallant old man! Landing in England one week, and going back to the Pacific the next! Like goes with like; and Wardlaw senior, energetic and resolute himself, though he felt for his son, stricken down by grief, gave his heart to the more valiant distress of his contemporary. He manned and victualled the Springbok for a long voyage, ordered her to Plymouth, and took his friend down to her by train.

They went out to her in a boat. She was a screw steamer, that could sail nine knots an hour without burning a coal. As she came down the Channel, the General's trouble got to be well known on board her, and, when he came out of the harbor, the sailors by an honest, hearty impulse, that did them credit, waited for no orders, but manned the yards to receive him with the respect due to his services, and his sacred calamity.

On getting on board, he saluted the captain and the ship's company with sad dignity, and retired to his cabin with Mr. Wardlaw. There the old merchant forced on him by way of loan seven hundred pounds, chiefly in gold and silver, telling him there was nothing like money, go where you will. He then gave him a number of notices he had printed, and a paper of advice and instructions: it was written in his own large, clear, formal hand.

General Rolleston tried to falter out his thanks. John Wardlaw interrupted him.

"Next to you I am her father; am I not?"

"You have proved it."

"Well, then. However, if you do find her, as I pray to God you may, I claim the second kiss, mind that: not for myself, though; for my poor Arthur, that lies on a sick-bed for her."

General Rolleston assented to that in a broken voice. He could hardly speak.

And so they parted: and that sad parent went out to the Pacific.

To him it was indeed a sad and gloomy voyage; and the hope with which he went on board oozed gradually away as the ship traversed the vast tracks of ocean. One immensity of water to be passed before that other immensity could be reached, on whose vast, uniform, surface the search was to be made.

To abridge this gloomy and monotonous part of our tale, suffice it to say that he endured two months of water and infinity ere the vessel, fast as she was, reached Valparaiso. Their progress, however, had been more than once interrupted to carry out Wardlaw's instructions. The poor General himself had but one idea; to go and search the Pacific with his own eyes; but Wardlaw, more experienced, directed him to overhaul every whaler and coasting vessel he could, and deliver printed notices; telling the sad story, and offering a reward for any positive information, good or bad, that should be brought in to his agent at Valparaiso. Acting on these instructions they had overhauled two or three coasting vessels as they steamed up from the Horn. They now placarded the port of Valparaiso, and put the notices on board all vessels bound westward; and the captain of the Springbok spoke to the skippers in the port. But they all shook their heads, and could hardly be got to give their minds seriously to the inquiry when they heard in what water the cutter was last seen, and on what course.

One old skipper said, "Look on Juan Fernandez, and then at the bottom of the Pacific; but the sooner you look *there* the less time you will lose."

From Valparaiso they ran to Juan Fernandez, which indeed seemed the likeliest place; if she was alive.

When the larger island of that group, the island dear alike to you who read, and to us who write, this tale, came in sight, the father's heart began to beat higher.

The ship anchored and took in coal, which was furnished at a wickedly high price by Mr. Joshua Fullalove, who had virtually purchased the island from Chili, having got it on lease for longer than the earth itself is to last, we hear.

And now Rolleston found the value of Wardlaw's loan; it enabled him to prosecute his search through the whole group of islands; and he did hear at last of three persons, who had been wrecked on Masa Fuero; one of them a female. He followed this up and at last discovered the parties. He found them to be Spaniards, and the woman smoking a pipe.

After this bitter disappointment he went back to the ship, and she was to weigh her anchor next morning.

But while General Rolleston was at Masa Fuero, a small coasting vessel had come in, and brought a strange report at second-hand, that in some degree unsettled Captain Moreland's mind; and, being hotly discussed on the forecastle, set the ship's company in a ferment.

CHAPTER XLII.

Hazel had risen an hour before dawn for reasons well known to himself. He put on his worst clothes, and a leathern belt, his little bags round his neck, and took his bundle of rushes in his hand. He also provided himself with some pieces of raw fish and fresh oyster; and, thus equipped, went up through Terrapin Wood, and got to the neighborhood of the lagoons before daybreak.

There was a heavy steam on the water, and nothing else to be seen. He put the hoop over his head, and walked into the water, not without an internal shudder, it looked so cold.

But instead of that, it was very warm, unaccountably warm. He walked in up to his middle, and tied his iron hoop to his belt, so as to prevent it sinking too deep. This done, he waited motionless, and seemed a little bed of rushes. The sun rose, and the steam gradually cleared away, and Hazel, peering through a hole or two he had made expressly in his bed of rushes, saw several ducks floating about, and one in particular, all purple, without a speck but his amber eye. He contrived to detach a piece of fish, that soon floated to the surface near him. But no duck moved towards it. He tried another, and another; then a mallard he had not observed swam up from behind him, and was soon busy pecking at it within a yard of him. His heart beat; he glided slowly and cautiously forward till the bird was close to the rushes.

Hazel stretched out his hand with the utmost care, caught hold of the bird's feet, and dragged him sharply under the water, and brought him up within the circle of the rushes. He quacked and struggled. Hazel soused him under directly, and so quenched the sound; then he glided slowly to the bank, so slowly that the rushes merely seemed to drift ashore. This he did not to create suspicion, and so spoil the next attempt. As he glided, he gave his duck air every now and then, and soon got on *terra firma*. By this time he had taught the duck not to quack, or he would get soused and held under. He now took the long gut-end and tied it tight round the bird's leg, and so fastened the bag to him. Even while he was effecting this, a posse of ducks rose at the west end of the marsh, and took their flight from the island. As they passed, Hazel threw his captive up in the air; and such was the force of example, aided, perhaps, by the fright the captive had received, that Hazel's bird instantly joined these travellers, rose with them into the high currents, and away, bearing the news eastward upon the wings of the wind. Then Hazel returned to the pool, and twice more he was so fortunate as to secure a bird, and launch him into space.

So hard is it to measure the wit of man, and to define his resources. The problem was solved; the aërial messengers were on the wing, diffusing over hundreds of leagues of water the intelligence that an English lady had been wrecked on an unknown island, in longitude 103 deg. 30 min., and between the 32d and 25th parallels of south latitude; and calling good men and ships to her rescue for the love of God.

CHAPTER XLIII.

And now for the strange report that landed at Juan Fernandez while General Rolleston was searching Masa Fuero.

The coaster who brought it ashore had been in company at Valparaiso, with a whaler from Nantucket, who told him he had fallen in with a Dutch whaler out at sea, and distressed for water: he had supplied the said Dutchman, who had thanked him, and given him a runlet of Hollands, and had told him in conversation that he had seen land and a river reflected on the sky, in waters where no land was marked in the chart; namely, somewhere between Juan Fernandez and Norfolk Island; and that, believing this to be the reflection of a part of some island near at hand, and his water being low, though not at that time run out, he had gone considerably out of his course in hopes of finding this watered island, but could see nothing of it. Nevertheless, as his grandfather, who had been sixty years at sea, and logged many wonderful things, had told him the sky had been known to reflect both ships and land at a great distance, he fully believed there was an island somewhere in that longitude, not down on any chart: an island wooded and watered.

This tale soon boarded the Springbok, and was hotly discussed on the forecastle. It came to Captain Moreland's ears, and he examined the skipper of the coasting-smack. But this examination elicited nothing new, inasmuch as the skipper had the tale only at third hand. Captain Moreland, however, communicated it to General Rolleston on his arrival, and asked him whether he thought it worth while to deviate from their instructions upon information of such a character. Rolleston shook his head. "An island reflected in the sky!"

"No, sir: a portion of an island containing a river."

"It is clearly a fable," said Rolleston, with a sigh.

"What is a fable, General?"

"That the sky can reflect terrestrial objects."

"O, there I can't go with you. The phenomenon is rare, but it is well established. I never saw it myself, but I have come across those that have. Suppose we catechise the forecastle. Hy! Fok'-sel!"

"Sir!"

"Send a man aft: the oldest seaman aboard."

"Ay, ay, sir."

There was some little delay: and then a sailor of about sixty slouched aft, made a sea scrape, and, removing his cap entirely, awaited the captain's commands.

"My man," said the captain, "I want you to answer a question. Do you believe land and ships have ever been seen in the sky, reflected?"

"A many good seamen holds to that, sir," said the sailor, cautiously.

"Is it the general opinion of seamen before the mast? Come, tell us. Jack 's as good as his master in these matters."

"Could n't say for boys and lubbers, sir. But I never met a full-grown seaman as denied that there. Sartainly few has seen it: but all of 'em has seen them as has seen it; ships, and land, too; but mostly ships. Hows'ever, I had a messmate once as was sailing past a rock they call Ailsa Craig, and saw a regiment of soldiers marching in the sky. Logged it, did the mate; and them soldiers was a marching between two towns in Ireland at that very time."

"There, you see, General," said Captain Moreland.

"But this is all second-hand," said General Rolleston, with a sigh; "and I have learned how everything gets distorted in passing from one to another."

"Ah," said the captain, "we can't help that; the thing is rare. I never saw it for one; and I suppose you never *saw* a phenomenon of the kind, Isaac?"

"Ha'n't I!" said Isaac, grimly. Then, with sudden, and not very reasonable, heat, "D—— my eyes and limbs if I ha'n't seen the Peak o' Teneriffe in the sky topsy-turvy, and as plain as I see that there cloud there" (pointing upwards).

"Come," said Moreland; "now we are getting to it. Tell us all about that."

"Well, sir," said the seaman, "I don't care to larn them as laughs at everything they ha'n't seen in maybe a dozen voyages at most; but you know me, and I knows you; though you command the ship, and I work before the mast. Now I axes you, sir, should you say Isaac Aiken was the man to take a sugar-loaf, or a cocked hat, for the Peak o' Teneriffe?

"As likely as I am myself, Isaac."

"No commander can say fairer nor that," said Isaac, with dignity. "Well, then, your honor, I'll tell ye the truth, and no lie: We was bound for Teneriffe with a fair wind, though not so much of it as we wanted, by reason she was a good sea-boat, but broad in the bows. The Peak hove in sight in the sky, and all the glasses was at her. She lay a point or two on our weather-quarter like, full two hours, and then she just melted away like a lump o' sugar. We kept on our course a day and a half, and, at last, we sighted the real Peak, and anchored off the port; whereby, when we saw Teneriffe Peak in the sky to winnard, she lay a hundred leagues to looard, s' help me God!"

"That is wonderful," said General Rolleston.

"That will do, Isaac," said the captain. "Mr. Butt, double his grog for a week, for having seen more than I have."

The captain and General Rolleston had a long discussion; but the result was, they determined to go to Easter Island first, for General Rolleston was a soldier, and had learned to obey as well as command. He saw no sufficient ground for deviating from Wardlaw's positive instructions.

This decision soon became known throughout the ship; and she was to weigh anchor at 11 A.M. next day, by high water.

At eight next morning, Captain Moreland and General Rolleston being on deck, one of the ship's boys, a regular pet, with rosy cheeks and black eyes, comes up to the gentlemen, takes off his cap, and, panting audibly at his own audacity, shoves a paper into General Rolleston's hand, and scuds away for his life.

"This won't do," said the captain, sternly.

The high-bred soldier handed the paper to him unopened.

The captain opened it, looked a little vexed, but more amused, and handed it back to the General.

It was a ROUND ROBIN.

Round Robins are not ingratiating as a rule. But this one came from some rough but honest fellows, who had already shown that kindliness and tact may reside in a coarse envelope. The sailors of the Springbok, when they first boarded her in the Thames, looked on themselves as men bound on an empty cruise; and nothing but the pay, which was five shillings per month above the average, reconciled them to it; for a sailor does not like going to sea for nothing, any more than a true sportsman likes to ride to hounds that are hunting a red herring trailed.

But the sight of the General had touched them afar off. His gray hair and pale face, seen as he rowed out of Plymouth Harbor, had sent them to the yards by a gallant impulse; and all through the voyage the game had been to put on an air of alacrity and hope, whenever they passed the General or came under his eye.

If hypocrisy is always a crime, this was a very criminal ship; for the men, and even the boys, were hypocrites, who, feeling quite sure that the daughter was dead at sea months ago, did, nevertheless, make up their faces to encourage the father into thinking she was alive, and he was going to find her. But people who pursue this game too long, and keep up the hopes of another, get infected at last themselves; and the crew of the Springbok arrived at Valparaiso infected with a little hope. Then came the Dutchman's tale, and the discussion, which ended adversely to their views; and this elicited the circular we have now the honor to lay before our readers.

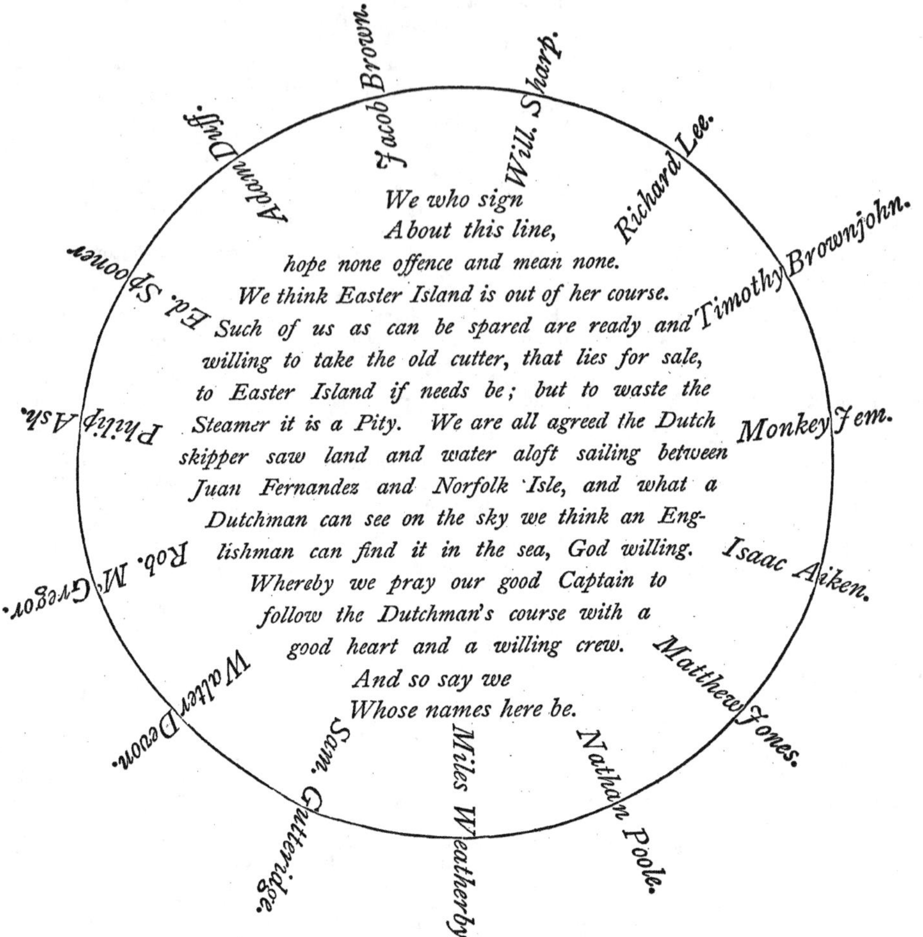

General Rolleston and Captain Moreland returned to the cabin and discussed this document. They came on deck again, and the men were piped aft. General Rolleston touched his cap, and with the Round Robin in his hand, addressed them thus: —

"My men, I thank you for taking my trouble to heart as you do. But it would be a bad return to send any of you to Easter Island in that cutter: for she is not seaworthy: so the captain tells me. I will not consent to throw away your lives in trying to save a life that is dear to me: but, as to the Dutchman's story, about an unknown island, our captain seems to think that is possible; and you tell us you are of the same opinion. Well, then, I give up my own judgment, and yield to yours. Yes, we will go westward with a good heart (he sighed), and a willing crew."

The men cheered. The boatswain piped; the anchor was heaved, and the Springbok went out on a course that bade fair to carry her within a hundred miles of Godsend Island.

She ran fast. On the second day, some ducks passed over her head, one of which was observed to have something attached to its leg.

She passed within sixty miles of Mount Look-out; but never saw Godsend Island: and so pursued her way to the Society Islands; sent out her boats; made every inquiry around about the islands, but with no success; and, at last, after losing a couple of months there, brought the heart-sick father back on much the same course, but rather more northerly.

CHAPTER XLIV.

Hazel returned homewards in a glow of triumph, and for once felt disposed to brag to Helen of his victory, — a victory by which she was to profit; not he.

They met in the wood; for she had tracked him by his footsteps. She seemed pale and disturbed, and speedily interrupted his exclamations of triumph by one of delight, which was soon, however, followed by one of distress.

"O, look at you!" she said. "You have been in the water: it is wicked; wicked."

"But I have solved the problem. I caught three ducks one after the other, and tied the intelligence to their legs: they are at this moment careering over the ocean, with our story and our longitude, and a guess at our latitude. Crown me with bays."

"With foolscap, more likely," said Helen: "only just getting well of rheumatic fever, and to go and stand in water up to the middle."

"Why, you don't listen to me!" cried Hazel, in amazement. "I tell you I have solved the problem."

"It is you that don't listen to common sense," retorted Helen. "If you go and make yourself ill, all the problems in the world will not compensate me. And I must say I think it was not very kind of you to run off so without warning: why give me hours of anxiety for want of a word? But there, it is useless to argue with a boy: yes, sir, a boy. The fact is, I have been too easy with you of late. One indulges sick children. But then they must not slip away and stand in the water, or there is an end of indulgence; and one is driven to severity. You must be ruled with a rod of iron. Go home this moment, sir, and change your clothes; and don't you presume to come into the presence of the nurse you have offended, till there's not a wet thread about you."

And so she ordered him off. The inventor in his moment of victory slunk away crestfallen to change his clothes.

So far Helen Rolleston was a type of her sex in its treatment of inventors. At breakfast she became a brilliant exception. The moment she saw Hazel seated by her fire in dry clothes she changed her key, and made him relate the whole business, and expressed the warmest admiration and sympathy.

"But," said she, "I do ask you not to repeat this exploit too often; now, don't do it again for a fortnight. The island will not run away. Ducks come and go every day, and your health is very, very precious."

He colored with pleasure, and made the promise at once. But, during this fortnight, events occurred. In the first place, he improved his invention. He remembered how a duck, over-weighted by a crab, which was fast to her leg, had come on board the boat. Memory dwelling on this, and invention digesting it, he resolved to weight his next batch of ducks; for he argued thus: "Probably our ducks go straight from this to the great American Continent. Then it may be long ere one of them falls into the hands of a man; and perhaps that man will not know English. But, if I could impede the flight of my ducks, they might alight on ships: and three ships out of four know English."

Accordingly, he now inserted stones of various sizes into the little bags. It was a matter of nice calculation: the problem was to weight the birds just so much that they might be able to fly three or four hundred miles, or about half as far as their unencumbered companions.

But in the midst of all this, a circumstance occurred that would have made a vain man, or indeed most men, fling the whole thing away. Helen and he came to a rupture. It began by her fault, and continued by his. She did not choose to know her own mind, and, in spite of secret warnings from her better judgment, she was driven by curiosity or by the unhappy restlessness to which her sex are peculiarly subject at odd times, to sound Hazel as to the meaning of a certain epigram that rankled in her. And she did it in the most feminine way, that is to say, in the least direct: whereas the safest way would have been to grasp the nettle, if she could not let it alone.

Said she one day, quietly, though with a deep blush: "Do you know Mr. Arthur Wardlaw?"

Hazel gave a shiver, and said "I do."

"Do you know anything about him?"

"I do."

"Nothing to his discredit, I am sure."

"If you are sure, why ask me? Do I ever mention his name?"

"Perhaps you do, sometimes, without intending it."

"You are mistaken: he is in your thoughts, no doubt; but not in mine."

"Ought I to forget people entirely, and what I owe them?"

"That is a question I decline to go into."

"How harshly you speak to me? Is that fair? You know my engagement, and that honor and duty draw me to England; yet I am happy here. You, who are so good and strong, might pity me at least; for I am torn this way and that:" and here the voice ceased, and the tears began to flow.

"I do pity you," said Hazel: "I must pity any one who is obliged to mention honor and duty in the same breath as Arthur Wardlaw."

At this time Helen drew back, offended bitterly. "*That* pity I reject and scorn," said she. "No, I plighted my faith with my eyes open, and to a worthy object. I never knew him blacken any person who was not there to speak for himself, and that is a very worthy trait, in my opinion. The absent are like children; they are helpless to defend themselves."

Hazel racked with jealousy, and irritated at this galling comparison, lost his temper for once, and said those who lay traps must not complain if others fall into them.

"Traps! Who lay them?"

"You did, Miss Rolleston. Did I ever condescend to mention that man's name since we have been on the island? It is you make me talk of him."

"Condescend?"

"That is the word. Nor will I ever deign to mention him again. If my love had touched your heart, I should have been obliged to mention him, for then I should have been bound to tell you a story in which he is mixed, my own miserable story, — my blood boils against the human race when I think of it. But no, I see I am nothing to you; and I will be silent."

"It is very cruel of you to say that," replied Helen, with tears in her eyes; "tell me your story, and you will see whether you are nothing to me."

"Not one word of it," said Hazel, slowly, "until you have forgotten that man exists."

"Oh! thank you, sir, this is plain speaking. I am to forget honor and plighted faith; and then you will trust me with your secrets, when I have shown myself unworthy to be trusted with anything. Keep your secrets, and I'll try and keep faith; ay, and I shall keep it, too, as long as there's life in my body."

"Can't you keep faith without torturing me, who love you?"

Helen's bosom began to heave at this, but she fought bravely. "Love me less, and respect me more," said she, panting; "you affront me, you frighten me. I looked on you as a brother, a dear brother. But now I am afraid of you — I am afraid —"

He was so injudicious as to interrupt her, instead of giving her time to contradict herself. "You have nothing to fear," said he; "keep this side of the island, and I'll live on the other, rather than hear the name of Arthur Wardlaw."

Helen's courage failed her at that spirited proposal, and she made no reply at all, but turned her back haughtily, and went away from him, only when she had got a little way her proud head drooped, and she went crying.

A coolness sprang up between them, and neither of them knew how to end it. Hazel saw no way to serve her now, except by flying weighted ducks; and he gave his mind so to this that one day he told her he had twenty-seven ducks in the air, all charged, and two thirds of them weighted. He thought that must please her now. To his surprise and annoyance, she received the intelligence coldly, and asked him whether it was not cruel to the birds.

Hazel colored with mortification at his great act of self-denial being so received.

He said, "I don't think my worst enemy can say I am wantonly cruel to God's creatures."

Helen threw in, deftly, "And I am not your worst enemy."

"But what other way is there to liberate you from this island, where you have nobody to speak to but me? Well, selfishness is the best course. Think only of others, and you are sure not to please them."

"If you want to please people, you must begin by understanding them," said the lady, not ill-naturedly.

"But if they don't understand themselves?"

"Then pity them; you can, for you are a man."

"What hurts me," said Hazel, "is that you really seem to think I fly these ducks for my pleasure. Why, if I had my wish, you and I should never leave this island, nor any other person set a foot on it. I am frank, you see."

"Rather too frank."

"What does it matter, since I do my duty all the same, and fly the ducks? But sometimes I do yearn for a word of praise for it; and that word never comes."

"It is a praiseworthy act," said Helen, but so icily that it is a wonder he ever flew another duck after that.

"No matter," said he, and his hand involuntarily sought his heart; "you read me a sharp but wholesome lesson, that we should do our duty for our duty's sake. And as I am quite sure it is my duty to liberate you and restore you to those you — I'll fly three ducks to-morrow morning instead of two."

"It is not done by my advice," said Helen. "You will certainly make yourself ill."

"O, that is all nonsense!" said Hazel.

"You are rude to me," said Helen, "and I am not aware that I deserve it."

"Rude, am I? Then I'll say no more," said Hazel, half humbly, half doggedly.

His parchment was exhausted, and he was driven to another expedient. He obtained alcohol by distillation from rum, and having found dragon's blood in its pure state, little ruby drops, made a deep red varnish that defied water; he got slips of bark, white inside, cut his inscription deep on the inner side, and filled the incised letters with this red varnish. He had forty-eight ducks in the air, and was rising before daybreak to catch another couple, when he was seized with a pain in the right hip and knee, and found he could hardly walk, so he gave in that morning, and kept about the premises. But he got worse, and he had hardly any use in his right side, from the waist downwards, and was in great pain.

As the day wore on, the pain and loss of power increased, and resisted all his remedies; there was no fever to speak of; but Nature was grimly revenging herself for many a gentler warning neglected. When he realized his condition, he was terribly cut up, and sat on the sand with his head in his hands for nearly two hours. But, after that period of despondency, he got up, took his boat-hook, and using it as a staff, hobbled to his arsenal, and set to work.

Amongst his materials was a young tree he had pulled up; the roots ran at right angles to the stem He just sawed off the ends of the roots, and then proceeded to shorten the stem.

But meantime, Helen, who had always a secret eye on him and his movements, had seen there was something wrong, and came timidly and asked what was the matter.

"Nothing," said he, doggedly.

"Then why did you sit so long on the sand? I never saw you like that."

"I was ruminating."

"What upon? Not that I have any right to ask."

"On the arrogance and folly of men; they attempt more than they can do, and despise the petty prudence and common-sense of women, and smart for it; as I am smarting now for being wiser than you."

"O!" said Helen; "why, what is the matter? and what is that you have made? It looks like — O dear!"

"It is a crutch," said Hazel, with forced calmness; "and I am a cripple."

Helen clasped her hands, and stood trembling.

Hazel lost his self-control for a moment, and cried out in a voice of agony, "A useless cripple. I wish I was dead and out of the way."

Then, ashamed of having given way before *her*, he seized his crutch, placed the crook under his arm, and turned sullenly away from her.

Four steps he took with his crutch.

She caught him with two movements of her supple and vigorous frame.

She just laid her left hand gently on his shoulder, and with her right she stole the crutch softly away, and let it fall upon the sand. She took his right hand, and put it to her lips like a subject paying homage to her sovereign; and then she put her strong arm under his shoulder, still holding his right hand in hers, and looked in his face. "No wooden crutches when I am by," said she, in a low voice, full of devotion.

He stood surprised, and his eyes began to fill.

"Come," said she, in a voice of music. And, thus aided, he went with her to her cavern. As they went, she asked him tenderly where the pain was.

"It *was* in my hip and knee," he said: "but now it is nowhere; for joy has come back to my heart.'

"And to mine too," said Helen; "except for this."

The quarrel dispersed like a cloud, under this calamity. There was no formal reconciliation; no discussion; and this was the wisest course: for the unhappy situation remained unchanged; and the friendliest discussion could only fan the embers of discord and misery gently, instead of fiercely.

The pair so strangely thrown together commenced a new chapter of their existence. It was not patient and nurse over again; Hazel, though very lame, had too much spirit left to accept that position. But still the sexes became in a measure reversed,—Helen the fisherman and forager, Hazel the cook and domestic.

He was as busy as ever, but in a narrow circle; he found pearl oysters near the sunk galleon, and, ere he had been lame many weeks, he had entirely lined the sides of the cavern with mother-of-pearl set in cement, and close as mosaic.

Every day he passed an hour in Paradise; for his living crutch made him take a little walk with her; her hand held his; her arm supported his shoulder; her sweet face was near his, full of tender solicitude; they seemed to be one; and spoke in whispers to each other, like thinking aloud. The causes of happiness were ever present; the causes of unhappiness were out of sight, and showed no signs of approach.

And of the two, Helen was the happiest. Before a creature so pure as this marries and has children, the great maternal instinct is still there, but feeds on what it can get, — first a doll, and then some helpless creature or other. Too often she wastes her heart's milk on something grown up, but as selfish as a child. Helen was more fortunate; her child was her hero, now so lame that he must lean on her to walk. The days passed by, and the island was fast becoming the world to those two, and as bright a world as ever shone on two mortal creatures.

It was a happy dream.

What a pity that dreams dissolve so soon! This had lasted for nearly two months, and Hazel was getting better, though still not well enough, or not fool enough, to dismiss his live crutch, when one afternoon Helen, who had been up on the heights, observed a dark cloud in the blue sky towards the west. There was not another cloud visible, and the air marvellously clear; time, about three quarters of an hour before sunset. She told Hazel about this solitary cloud, and asked him, with some anxiety, if it portended another storm. He told her to be under no alarm, — there were no tempests in that latitude except at the coming in and going out of the rains, — but he should like to go round the Point and look at her cloud.

She lent him her arm, and they went round the Point; and there they saw a cloud entirely different from anything they had ever seen since they were on the island. It was like an enormous dark ribbon stretched along the sky, at some little height above the horizon. Notwithstanding its prodigious length it got larger before their very eyes.

Hazel started.

Helen felt him start, and asked him, with some surprise, what was the matter.

"Cloud!" said he, "that is no cloud. That is smoke."

"Smoke!" echoed Helen, becoming agitated in her turn.

"Yes; the breeze is northerly, and carries the smoke nearer to us; it is the smoke of a steamboat."

CHAPTER XLV.

Both were greatly moved; and after one swift glance Helen stole at him, neither looked at the other. They spoke in flurried whispers.

"Can they see the island?"

"I don't know; it depends on how far the boat is to windward of her smoke."

"How shall we know?"

"If she sees the island, she will make for it that moment."

"Why? do ships never pass an unknown island?"

"Yes. But that steamer will not pass us."

"But why?"

At this question Hazel hung his head, and his lip quivered. He answered her at last. "Because she is looking for *you*."

Helen was struck dumb at this.

He gave his reasons. "Steamers never visit these waters. Love has brought that steamer out; love that will not go unrewarded. Arthur Wardlaw is on board that ship."

"Have they seen us yet?"

Hazel forced on a kind of dogged fortitude. He said, "When the smoke ceases to elongate, you will know they have changed their course, and they will change their course the moment the man at the masthead sees us."

"Oh! But how do you know they have a man at the masthead?"

"I know by myself. I should have a man at the masthead night and day."

And now the situation was beyond words. They both watched, and watched, to see the line of smoke cease.

It continued to increase, and spread eastward; and that proved the steamer was continuing her course.

The sun drew close to the horizon.

"They don't see us," said Helen, faintly.

"No," said Hazel; "not yet."

"And the sun is just setting. It is all over." She put her handkerchief to her eyes a moment, and then, after a sob or two, she said almost cheerfully, "Well, dear friend, we were happy till that smoke came to disturb us: let us try and be as happy now it is gone. Don't smile like that, it makes me shudder."

"Did I smile? It must have been at your simplicity in thinking we have seen the last of that steamer."

"And so we have."

"Not so. In three hours she will be at anchor in that bay."

"Why, what will bring her?"

"I shall bring her."

"You? How?"

"By lighting my bonfire."

CHAPTER XLVI.

Helen had forgotten all about the bonfire. She now asked whether he was sure those on board the steamer could see the bonfire. Then Hazel told her that it was now of prodigious size and height. Some six months before he was crippled he had added and added to it.

"That bonfire," said he, "will throw a ruddy glare over the heavens, that they can't help seeing on board the steamer. Then, as they are not on a course, but on a search, they will certainly run a few miles southward to see what it is. They will say it is either a beacon or a ship on fire; and, in either case, they will turn the boat's head this way. Well, before they have run southward half a dozen miles, their look-out will see the bonfire, and the island in its light. Let us get to the boat, my lucifers are there.

She lent him her arm to the boat, and stood by while he made his preparations. They were very simple. He took a pine torch and smeared it all over with pitch; then put his lucifer-box in his bosom, and took his crutch. His face was drawn pitiably, but his closed lips betrayed unshaken and unshakable resolution. He shouldered his crutch, and hobbled up as far as the cavern. Here Helen interposed.

"Don't you go toiling up the hill," said she. "Give me the lucifers and the torch, and let me light the beacon. I shall be there in half the time you will."

"Thank you! thank you!" said Hazel, eagerly, not to say violently.

He wanted it done; but it killed him to do it. He then gave her his instructions.

"It is as big as a haystack," said he, "and as dry as a chip; and there are eight bundles of straw placed expressly. Light the bundles to windward first, then the others; it will soon be all in a blaze."

"Meanwhile," said Helen, "you prepare our supper. I feel quite faint — for want of it."

Hazel assented.

"It is the last we shall —" he was going to say it was the last they would eat together; but his voice failed him, and he hobbled into the cavern, and tried to smother his emotion in work. He lighted the fire, and blew it into a flame with a palmetto-leaf, and then he sat down awhile, very sick at heart; then he got up and did the cooking, sighing all the time; and, just when he was beginning to wonder why Helen was so long lighting eight bundles of straw, she came in, looking pale.

"Is it all right?" said he.

"Go and look," said she. "No, let us have our supper first.

Neither had any appetite: they sat and kept casting strange looks at one another.

To divert this anyhow Hazel looked up at the roof, and said faintly, "If I had known, I would have made more haste, and set pearl *there* as well."

"What does that matter?" said Helen, looking down.

"Not much, indeed," replied he, sadly. "I am a fool to utter such childish regrets; and, more than that, I am a mean selfish cur to *have* a regret. Come, come, we can't eat; let us go round the Point and see the waves reddened by the beacon that gives you back to the world you were born to embellish."

Helen said she would go directly. And her languid reply contrasted strangely with his excitement. She played with her supper, and wasted time in a very unusual way, until he told her plump she was not really eating, and he could wait no longer, he must go and see how the beacon was burning.

"O, very well," said she; and they went down to the beach.

She took his crutch and gave it to him. This little thing cut him to the heart. It was the first time she had accompanied him so far as that without offering herself to be his crutch. He sighed deeply, as he put the crutch under his arm; but he was too proud to complain, only he laid it all on the approaching steamboat.

The subtle creature by his side heard the sigh, and smiled sadly at being misunderstood, — but what man could understand her? They hardly spoke till they reached the Point. The waves glittered in the moonlight: there was no red light on the water.

"Why, what is this?" said Hazel. "You can't have lighted the bonfire in eight places, as I told you."

She folded her arms and stood before him in an attitude of defiance; all but her melting eye.

"I have not lighted it at all," said she.

Hazel stood aghast. "What have I done?" he cried. "Duty, manhood, everything, demanded that I should light that beacon, and I trusted it to you."

Helen's attitude of defiance melted away: she began to cower, and hid her blushing face in her hands. Then she looked up imploringly. Then she uttered a wild and eloquent cry, and fled from him like the wind.

CHAPTER XLVII.

THAT cloud was really the smoke of the Springbok, which had mounted into air so thin that it could rise no higher. The boat herself was many miles to the northward, returning full of heavy hearts from a fruitless search. She came back in a higher parallel of latitude, intending afterwards to steer N.W. to Easter Island. The life was gone out of the ship; the father was deeply dejected, and the crew could no longer feign the hope they did not feel. Having pursued the above course to within four hundred miles of Juan Fernandez, General Rolleston begged the captain to make a bold deviation to the S.W., and then see if they could find nothing there before going to Easter Island.

Captain Moreland was very unwilling to go to the S.W., the more so as coal was getting short. However, he had not the heart to refuse General Rolleston anything. There was a northerly breeze. He had the fires put out, and, covering the ship with canvas, sailed three hundred miles S.W. But found nothing. Then he took in sail, got up steam again, and away for Easter Island. The ship ran so fast that she had got into latitude thirty-two by ten A.M. next morning.

At 10h. 15m. the dreary monotony of this cruise was broken by the man at the mast-head.

"On deck there!"

"Hullo!"

"The schooner on our weather-bow!"

"Well, what of her?"

"She has luffed."

"Well, what o' that?"

"She has altered her course."

"How many points?"

"She was sailing S.E., and now her head is N.E."

"That is curious."

General Rolleston, who had come and listened with a grain of hope, now sighed, and turned away.

The captain explained kindly that the man was quite right to draw his captain's attention to the fact of a trading-vessel altering her course. "There is a sea-grammar, General," said he; "and, when one seaman sees another violate it, he concludes there is some reason or other. Now, Jack, what d' ye make of her?"

"I can't make much of her: she don't seem to know her own mind, that is all. At ten o'clock she was bound for Valparaiso or the Island. But now she has come about and beating to windward."

"Bound for Easter Island?"

"I dunno."

"Keep your eye on her."

"Ay, ay, sir."

Captain Moreland told General Rolleston that very few ships went to Easter Island, which lies in a lovely climate, but is a miserable place; and he was telling the General that it is inhabited by savages of a low order, who half worship the relics of masonry left by their more civilized predecessors, when Jack hailed the deck again.

"Well," said the captain.

"I think she is bound for the Springbok."

The soldier received this conjecture with astonishment and incredulity, not to be wondered at. The steamboat headed N.W., right in the wind's eye. Sixteen miles off, at least, a ship was sailing N.E. So that the two courses might be represented thus:—

A B

And there hung in the air, like a black mark against the blue sky, a fellow, whose oracular voice came down and said B was endeavoring to intercept A.

Nevertheless, time confirmed the conjecture; the schooner, having made a short board to the N.E., came about, and made a long board due west, which was as near as she could lie to the wind. On this Captain Moreland laid the steamboat's head due north. This brought the vessels rapidly together.

When they were about two miles distant, the stranger slackened sail and hove to, hoisting stars and stripes at her mizzen. The union jack went up the shrouds of the Springbok directly, and she pursued her course, but gradually slackened her steam.

General Rolleston walked the deck in great agitation, and now indulged in wild hopes, which Captain Moreland thought it best to discourage at once.

"Ah, sir," he said; "don't you run into the other extreme, and imagine he has come on our business. It is at sea as it is ashore: if a man goes out of his course to speak to you, it is for his own sake, not yours. This Yankee has got men sick with scurvy, and is come for lime-juice. Or his water is out. Or—hallo, savages aboard."

It was too true. The schooner had a cargo of savages, male and female; the males were nearly naked, but the females, strange to say, were dressed to the throat in ample robes, with broad and flowing skirts, and had little coronets on their heads. As soon as the schooner hove to, the fiddle had struck up, and the savages were now dancing in parties of four; the men doing a sort of monkey hornpipe in quick pace, with their hands nearly touching the ground; the women, on the contrary, erect and queenly, swept about in slow rhythm, with most graceful and coquettish movements of the arms and hands, and bewitching smiles.

The steamboat came alongside, but at a certain distance, to avoid all chance of collision; and the crew clustered at the side and cheered the savages dancing. The poor General was forgotten at the merry sight.

Presently a negro in white cotton, with a face blacker than the savages, stepped forward and hoisted a board, on which was printed very large

ARE YOU

Having allowed this a moment to sink into the mind, he reversed the board, and showed these words, also printed large, THE SPRINGBOK?

There was a thrilling murmur on board; and, after a pause of surprise, the question was answered by a loud cheer and waving of hats.

The reply was perfectly understood; almost immediately a boat was lowered by some novel machinery, and pulled towards the steamer. There were two men in it: the skipper and the negro. The skipper came up the side of the Springbok. He was loosely dressed in some light drab-colored stuff and a huge straw hat; a man with a long Puritanical head, a nose inclined to be aquiline, a face bronzed by weather and heat, thin, resolute lips, and a square chin. But for a certain breadth between his keen gray eyes, which revealed more intellect than Cromwell's Ironsides were encumbered with, he might have passed for one of that hard-praying, harder-hitting fraternity.

He came on deck, just touched his hat, as if to brush away a fly, and, removing an enormous cigar from his mouth, said, "Wal, and so this is the Springbok. Spry little boat she is: how many knots can ye get out of her now? Not that I am curious."

"About twelve knots."

"And when the steam's off the bile, how many can you sail? Not that it is my business."

"Eight or nine. What *is* your business?"

"Hum! You have been over *some* water looking for that gal. Where do ye hail from last?"

"The Society Islands. Did you board me to hear me my catechism?"

"No, I am not one of your prying sort. Where are ye bound for now?"

"I am bound for Easter Island."

"Have you heard anything of the gal?"

"No."

"And when do ye expec' to go back to England as wise as ye came?"

"Never while the ship can swim," cried Moreland, angrily, to hide his despondency from this stranger. "And now it is my turn, I think. What schooner is this? by whom commanded, and whither bound?"

"The Julia Dodd; Joshua Fullalove; bound for Juan Fernandez with the raw material of civilization—look at the varmint skippin'—and a printing-press; an' that's the instrument of civilization, I ratther think."

"Well, sir; and why in Heaven's name did you change your course?"

"Wal, I reckon I changed it—to tell you a lie."

"To tell us a lie?"

"Ay; the darnedest etarnal lie that ever came out of a man's mouth. Fust, there's an unknown island somewheres about. That's a kinder flourish beforehand. On that island there's an English gal wrecked."

Exclamations burst forth on every side at this.

"And she is so tarnation 'cute, she is flying ducks all over creation with a writing tied to their legs, telling the tale, and setting down the longitude. There, if that is n't a buster, I hope I may never live to tell another."

"God bless you, sir," cried the General. "Where is the island?"

"What island?"

"The island where my child is wrecked."

"What, are you the gal's father?" said Joshua, with a sudden touch of feeling.

"I am, sir. Pray withhold nothing from me you know."

"Why, Cunnle," said the Yankee, soothingly; "don't I tell you it's a buster. However, the lie is none o' mine. It's that old cuss Skinflint set it afloat; he is always pisoning these peaceful waters."

Rolleston asked eagerly who Skinflint was, and where he could be found.

"Wal, he is a sorter sea Jack-of-all-trades, etarnally cruising about to buy gratis,—those he buys of call it stealing. Got a rotten old cutter, manned by his wife and family. They get coal out of me for fur, and sell the coal at double my price; they kill seals and dress the skins aboard; kill fish and salt 'em aboard. Ye know when that fam'ly is at sea by the smell that pervades the briny deep an' heralds their approach. Yesterday the air smelt awful: so I said to Vespasian here, I think that sea-skunk is out, for there's something a pisoning the cerulean waves an' succumambient air. We had n't sailed not fifty miles more before we run agin him. *Their clothes were drying all about the rigging.* Hails me, the varmint does. Vesp and I, we work the printing-press together, an' so order him to looward, not to taint our Otaheitans, that stink of ile at home, but I had 'em biled before I'd buy 'em, an' now they're vilets. 'Wal, now, Skinflint,' says I; 'I reckon you're come to bring me that harpoon o' mine you stole last time you was at my island?' 'I never saw your harpoon,' says he, 'I want to know, have you come across the Springbok?' 'Mebbe, I have,' says I; 'why do you ask?' 'Got news for her,' says he; 'and can't find her nowheres.' So then we set to and fenced a bit; and this old varmint, to put me off the truth, told me the buster. A month ago or more he was boarded—by a duck. And this yar duck had a writing tied to his leg, and this yar writing said an English gal was wrecked on an island, and put down the very longitude. 'Show me that duck,' says I, ironical. 'D' ye take us for fools?' says he; 'we ate the duck for supper.' 'That was like ye,' says I; 'if an angel brought your pardon down from heights celestial, you'd roast him, and sell his feathers for swan's-down; mebbe ye ate the writing? I know yar a hungry lot.' 'The writing is in my cabin,' says he. 'Show it me,' says I, 'an' mebbe I'll believe ye.' No, the cuss would only show it to the Springbok; 'there's a reward,' says he. 'What's the price of a soul aboard your cutter?' I asked him. 'Have you parted with yours, as you want to buy one?' says he. 'Not one as would carry me right slick away to everlasting blazes,' says I. So then we said good morning, and he bore away for Valparaiso. Presently I saw your smoke, and that you would never overhaul old Stinkamalee on that track; so I came about. Now I tell ye that old cuss knows where the gal is, and mebbe got her tied hand and fut in his cabin. An' I'm kinder sot on English gals; they put me in mind of butter and honey. Why, my schooner is named after one. So, now, Cunnle, clap on steam for Valparaiso, and you'll soon overhaul the old stink-pot: you may know him by the brown patch in his jib-sail, the ontidy varmint. Pull out your purse and bind him to drop lying about ducks and geese, and tell you the truth; he knows where your gal is, I swan. Wal, ye need n't smother me." For by this time he was the centre of a throng, all pushing and driving to catch his words.

Captain Moreland begged him to step down into his cabin, and there the General thanked him with great warmth and agitation for his humanity. "We will follow your advice at once," he said. "Is there anything I can offer you, without offence?"

"Wal," drawled the Yankee, "I guess not. Business an' sentiment won't mix no how. Business took me to the island, sentiment brought me here. I'll take a shake hand all round: and if y' have got live fowls to spare, I'll be obliged to you for a couple. Ye see I'm colonizing that darned island: an' sowing in with grain, an' Otaheitans, an' niggers, an' Irishmen, an' all the cream o' creation; an' I'd be glad of a couple o' Dorkins to crow the lazy varmint up."

This very moderate request was heartily complied with, and the acclamations and cheers of the crew followed this strange character to his schooner, at which his eye glistened and twinkled with quiet satisfaction, but he made it a point of honor not to move a muscle.

Before he could get under way, the Springbok took a circuit, and, passing within a hundred yards of him, fired a gun to leeward by way of compliment, set a cloud of canvas, and tore through the water at her highest speed. Outside the port of Valparaiso she fell in with Skinflint, and found him not quite so black as he was painted. The old fellow showed some parental feeling, produced the bag at once to General Rolleston, and assured him a wearied duck had come on board, and his wife had detached the writing.

They took in coal: and then ran westward once more, every heart beating high with confident hope.

CHAPTER XLVIII.

HELEN'S act was strange, and demands a word of explanation. If she had thought the steamboat was a strange vessel, she would have lighted the bonfire: if she had known her father was on board, she would have lighted it with joy. But Hazel, whose every word now was gospel, had said it was Arthur Wardlaw in that boat, searching for her.

Still, so strong is the impulse in all civilized beings to get back to civilization, that she went up that hill as honestly intending to light the bonfire as Hazel intended it to be lighted. But, as she went, her courage cooled, and her feet began to go slowly, as her mind ran swiftly forward to consequence upon consequence. To light that bonfire was to bring Arthur Wardlaw down upon herself and Hazel living alone and on intimate terms. Arthur would come and claim her to his face. Could she disallow his claim? Gratitude would now be on his side as well as good faith. What a shock to Arthur! What torture for Hazel! torture that he foresaw, or why the face of anguish, that dragged even now at her heart-strings? And then it could end only in one way; she and Hazel would leave the island in Arthur's ship. What a voyage for all three! She stood transfixed by shame; her whole body blushed at what she saw coming. Then once more Hazel's face rose before her; poor crippled Hazel! her hero and her patient. She sat down and sighed, and could no more light the fire than she could have put it out if another had lighted it.

She was a girl that could show you at times she

had a father as well as a mother: but that evening she was all woman.

They met no more that night.

In the morning his face was haggard, and showed a mental struggle; but hers placid and quietly beaming, for the very reason that she had made a great sacrifice. She was one of that sort.

And this difference between them was a foretaste.

His tender conscience pricked him sore. To see her sit beaming there, when, if he had done his own duty with his own hands, she would be on her way to England! Yet his remorse was dumb; for, if he gave it vent, then he must seem ungrateful to *her* for her sacrifice.

She saw his deep and silent compunction, approved it secretly; said nothing, but smiled, and beamed, and soothed. He could not resist this: and wild thrills of joy and hope passed through him, visions of unbroken bliss far from the world.

But this sweet delirium was followed by misgivings of another kind. And here she was at fault. What could they be?

It was the voice of conscience telling him that he was really winning her love, once inaccessible; and, if so, was bound to tell her his whole story, and let her judge between him and the world, before she made any more sacrifices for him. But it is hard to stop great happiness: harder to stop it and ruin it. Every night, as he lay alone, he said, "To-morrow I will tell her all, and make her the judge." But in the morning her bright face crushed his purpose by the fear of clouding it. His limbs got strong and his heart got weak: and they used to take walks, and her head came near his shoulder: and the path of duty began to be set thicker than ever with thorns; and the path of love with primroses. One day she made him sit to her for his portrait; and under cover of artistic enthusiasm, told him his beard was godlike, and nothing in the world could equal it for beauty. She never saw but one at all like it, poor Mr. Seaton's; but even that was very inferior to his: and then she dismissed the sitter: "Poor thing," said she, "you are pale and tired." And she began to use ornaments: took her bracelets out of her bag, and picked pearls out of her walls, and made a coronet, under which her eyes flashed at night with superlative beauty,—conscious beauty brightened by the sense of being admired and looked at by the eye she desired to please.

She revered him. He had improved her character, and she knew it, and often told him so. "Call me Hazelia," she said; "make me liker you, still."

One day, he came suddenly through the jungle, and found her reading her prayer-book.

He took it from her, not meaning to be rude, neither, but inquisitive.

It was open at the marriage-service, and her cheeks were dyed scarlet.

His heart panted. He was a clergyman; he could read that service over them both.

Would it be a marriage?

Not in England: but in some countries it would. Why not in this? This was not England.

He looked up. Her head was averted; she was downright distressed.

He was sorry to have made her blush: so he took her hand and kissed it tenderly, so tenderly that his heart seemed to go into his lips. She thrilled under it, and her white brow sank upon his shoulder.

The sky was a vault of purple with a flaming topaz in the centre; the sea, a heavenly blue; the warm air breathed heavenly odors; flaming macaws wheeled overhead; humming-birds, more gorgeous than any flower, buzzed round their heads, and amazed the eye with delight, then cooled it with the deep green of the jungle into which they dived.

It was a Paradise with the sun smiling down on it, and the ocean smiling up, and the air impregnated with love. Here they were both content now to spend the rest of their days—

"The world forgetting; by the world forgot"

CHAPTER XLIX.

The Springbok arrived in due course at longitude 103 deg. 31 min. but saw no island. This was dispiriting; but still Captain Moreland did not despair.

He asked General Rolleston to examine the writing carefully, and tell him was that Miss Rolleston's handwriting.

The General shook his head sorrowfully.

"No," said he; "it is nothing like my child's hand."

"Why, all the better," said Captain Moreland; "the lady has got somebody about her who knows a thing or two. The man that could catch wild ducks and turn 'em into postmen could hit on the longitude somehow; and he does n't pretend to be exact in the latitude."

Upon this he ran northward 400 miles; which took him three days; for they stopped at night.

No island.

He then ran south 500 miles; stopping at night.

No island.

Then he took the vessel zigzag.

Just before sunset, one lovely day, the man at the mast-head sang out:—

"On deck there!"

"Hullo!"

"Something in sight; on our weather-bow."

"What is it?"

"Looks like a mast. No. Don't know what it is."

"Point."

The sailor pointed with his finger.

Captain Moreland ordered the ship's course to be altered accordingly. By this time, General Rolleston was on deck. The ship ran two miles on the new course; and all this time the topman's glass was levelled, and the crew climbed about the rigging all eyes and ears.

At last the clear hail came down.

"I can make it out now, sir."

"What is it?"

"It is a palm-tree."

The captain jumped on a gun, and waved his hat grandly, and instantly the vessel rang with a lusty cheer; and, for once, sailors gabbled like washerwomen.

They ran till they saw the island in the moonlight, and the giant Palm, black, and sculptured out of the violet sky; then they set the lead going, and it warned them not to come too close. They anchored off the west coast.

At daybreak they moved slowly on, still sounding as they went; and, rounding the West Point, General Rolleston saw written on the guanoed rocks in large letters:—

AN ENGLISH LADY WRECKED HERE. HASTE TO HER RESCUE.

He and Moreland shook hands; and how their eyes glistened!

Presently there was a stranger inscription still upon the rocks, — a rough outline of the island on an enormous scale, showing the coast-line, the reefs, the shallow water, and the deep water.

"Ease her! Stop her!"

The captain studied this original chart with his glass, and crept slowly on for the west passage.

But, warned by the soundings marked on the rock, he did not attempt to go through the passage, but came to an anchor, and lowered his boat.

The sailors were all on the *qui vive* to land, but the captain, to their infinite surprise, told them only three persons would land that morning, — himself, his son, and General Rolleston.

The fact is, this honest captain had got a misgiving, founded on a general view of human nature. He expected to find the girl with two or three sailors, one of them united to her by some nautical ceremony, duly witnessed, but such as a *military* officer of distinction could hardly be expected to approve. He got into the boat in a curious state of delight, dashed with uncomfortable suspense; and they rowed gently for the west passage.

As for General Rolleston, now it was he needed all his fortitude. Suppose the lady was not Helen! After all, the chances were against her being there. Suppose she was dead and buried in that island! Suppose that fatal disease, with which she had sailed, had been accelerated by hardships, and Providence permitted him only to receive her last sigh. All these misgivings crowded on him the moment he drew so near the object, which had looked all brightness so long as it was unattainable. He sat, pale and brave, in the boat; but his doubts and fears were greater than his hope.

They rounded Telegraph Point, and in a moment Paradise Bay burst on them, and Hazel's boat within a hundred yards of them. It was half-tide. They beached the boat, and General Rolleston landed. Captain Moreland grasped his hand, and said, "Call us, if it is all right."

General Rolleston returned the pressure of that honest hand, and marched up the beach just as if he was going into action.

He came to the boat. It had an awning over the stern, and was clearly used as a sleeping-place. A series of wooden pipes standing on uprights led from this up to the cliff. The pipes were in fact mere sections of the sago-tree with the soft pith driven out. As this was manifestly a tube of communication, General Rolleston followed it until he came to a sort of veranda with a cave opening on it; he entered the cave, and was dazzled by its most unexpected beauty. He seemed to be in a gigantic nautilus. Roof and sides, and the very chimney, were one blaze of mother-of-pearl. But, after the first start, brighter to him was an old shawl he saw on a nail; for that showed it was a woman's abode. He tore down the old shawl, and carried it to the light. He recognized it as Helen's. Her rugs were in a corner; he rushed in, and felt them all over with trembling hands. They were still warm, though she had left her bed some time. He came out wild with joy, and shouted to Moreland, "She is alive! She is alive! She is alive!" Then fell on his knees and thanked God.

A cry came down to him from above: he looked up as he knelt, and there was a female figure dressed in white, stretching out its hands as if it would fly down to him. Its eyes gleamed; he knew them all that way off. He stretched out his hands as eloquently, and then he got up to meet her; but the stout soldier's limbs were stiffer than of old; and he got up so slowly, that, ere he could take a step, there came flying to him with little screams and inarticulate cries, no living skeleton, nor consumptive young lady, but a grand creature, tanned here and there, rosy as the morn, and full of lusty vigor; a body all health, strength, and beauty, a soul all love. She flung herself all over him in a moment, with cries of love unspeakable; and then it was "O my darling, my darling! O my own, own! Ha, ha, ha, ha! O, O, O, O! Is it you? is it? can it? Papa! Papa!" then little convulsive hands patting him, and feeling his beard and shoulders; then a sudden hail of violent kisses on his head, his eyes, his arms, his hands, his knees. Then a stout soldier, broken down by this, and sobbing for joy. "O my child! My flesh and blood! O, O, O!" Then all manhood melted away except paternity; and a father turned mother, and clinging, kissing, and rocking to and fro with his child, and both crying for joy as if their hearts would burst.

A sight for angels to look down at and rejoice. But what mortal pen could paint it?

CHAPTER L.

They gave a long time to pure joy before either of them cared to put questions or compare notes. But at last he asked her, "Who was on the island besides her?"

"O," said she, "only my guardian angel. Poor Mr. Welch died the first week we were here."

He parted the hair on her brow, and kissed it tenderly. "And who is your guardian angel?"

"Why, you are now, my own papa: and well you have proved it. To think of your being the one to come, at your age!"

"Well, never mind me. Who has taken such care of my child? — this the sick girl they frightened me about!"

"Indeed, papa, I *was* a dying girl. My very hand was wasted. Look at it now; brown as a berry, but so plump; you owe that to him: and, papa, I can walk twenty miles without fatigue: and so strong; I could take you up in my arms and carry, I know. But I am content to eat you." (A shower of kisses.) "I hope you will like him."

"My own Helen. Ah! I am a happy old man this day. What is his name?"

"Mr. Hazel. He is a clergyman. O papa, I hope you *will* like him, for he has saved my life more than once: and then he has been so generous, so delicate, so patient; for I used him very ill at first; and you will find my character as much improved as my health: and all owing to Mr. Hazel. He is a clergyman; and O, so good, so humble, so clever, so self-denying! Ah! how can I ever repay him?"

"Well, I shall be glad to see this paragon, and shake him by the hand. You may imagine what I feel to any one that is kind to my darling. An old gentleman? about my age?"

"O no, papa."

"Hum!"

"If he had been old I should not be here; for he has had to fight for me against cruel men with knives: and work like a horse. He built me a hut, and made me this cave, and almost killed himself in my service. Poor Mr. Hazel!"

"How old is he?"

"Dearest papa, I never asked him that: but I think he is four or five years older than me, and a hundred years better than I shall ever be, I am afraid. What is the matter, darling?"

"Nothing, child, nothing."

"Don't tell me. Can't I read your dear face?"

"Come, let me read yours. Look me in the face, now: full."

He took her by the shoulders, firmly, but not the least roughly, and looked straight into her hazel eyes. She blushed at this ordeal, — blushed scarlet; but her eyes, pure as Heaven, faced his fairly, though with a puzzled look.

He concluded this paternal inspection by kissing her on the brow. "I was an old fool," he muttered.

"What do you say, dear papa?"

"Nothing, nothing. Kiss me again. Well, love, you had better find this guardian angel of yours, that I may take him by the hand and give him a father's blessing, and make him some little return by carrying him home to England along with my darling."

"I'll call him, papa. Where can he be gone, I wonder."

She ran out to the terrace, and called, —

"Mr. Hazel! Mr. Hazel! I don't see him; but he can't be far off. Mr. Hazel!"

Then she came back, and made her father sit down: and she sat at his knee, beaming with delight.

"Ah, papa," said she, "it was you who loved me best in England. It was you that came to look for me."

"No," said he, "there are others there that love you as well in their way. Poor Wardlaw! on his sick-bed for you, cut down like a flower the moment he heard you were lost in the Proserpine. Ah, and I have broken faith."

"That is a story," said Helen; "you could n't."

"For a moment I mean; I promised the dear old man — he furnished the ship, the men, and the money, to find you. He says you are as much his daughter as mine."

"Well, but what did you promise him?" said Helen, blushing and interrupting hastily, for she could not bear the turn matters were taking.

"O, only to give you the second kiss from Arthur. Come, better late than never." She knelt before him, and put out her forehead instead of her lips. "There," said the General, "that kiss is from Arthur Wardlaw, your intended. Why, who the deuce is this?"

A young man was standing wonder-struck at the entrance, and had heard the General's last words; they went through him like a knife. General Rolleston stared at him.

Helen uttered an ejaculation of pleasure, and said, "This is my dear father, and he wants to thank you —"

"I don't understand this," said the General. "I thought you told me there was nobody on the island but you and your guardian angel. Did you count this poor fellow for nobody? Why, he did you a good turn once."

"O papa!" said Helen, reproachfully. "Why, this *is* my guardian angel. This is Mr. Hazel."

The General looked from one to another in amazement, then he said to Helen, "This your Mr. Hazel?"

"Yes, papa."

"Why, you don't mean to tell me you don't know this man?"

"Know him, papa! why, of course I know Mr. Hazel; know him and revere him, beyond all the world, except you."

The General lost patience. "Are you out of your senses?" said he; "this man here is no Hazel. Why, this is James Seaton — our gardener — a ticket-of-leave man."

CHAPTER LI.

At this fearful insult Helen drew back from her father with a cry of dismay, and then moved towards Hazel with her hands extended, as if to guard him from another blow, and at the same time deprecate his resentment. But then she saw his dejected attitude; and she stood confounded, looking from one to the other.

"I knew him in a moment by his beard," said the General, coolly.

"Ah!" cried Helen, and stood transfixed. She glared at Hazel and his beard with dilating eyes, and began to tremble.

Then she crept back to her father and held him tight; but still looked over her shoulder at Hazel with dilating eyes and paling cheek.

As for Hazel, his deportment all this time went far towards convicting him; he leaned against the side of the cave, and hung his head in silence: and his face was ashy pale. When General Rolleston saw his deep distress, and the sudden terror and repugnance the revelation seemed to create in his daughter's mind, he felt sorry he had gone so far, and said, "Well, well; it is not for me to judge you harshly; for you have laid me under a deep obligation: and, after all, I can see good reasons why you should conceal your name from other people. But you ought to have told my daughter the truth."

Helen interrupted him; or, rather, she seemed unconscious he was speaking. She had never for an instant taken her eye off the culprit: and now she spoke to him:

"Who, and what, are you, sir?"

"My name is Robert Penfold."

"Penfold! Seaton!" cried Helen. "Alias upon alias!" And she turned to her father in despair. Then to Hazel again. "Are you what papa says?"

"I am."

"O papa! papa!" cried Helen, "then there is no truth nor honesty in all the world!" And she turned her back on Robert Penfold, and cried and sobbed upon her father's breast.

O the amazement and anguish of that hour! The pure affection and reverence, that would have blest a worthy man, wasted on a convict! Her heart's best treasures flung on a dunghill! This is a woman's greatest loss on earth. And Helen sank, and sobbed under it.

General Rolleston, whose own heart was fortified, took a shallow view of the situation; and, moreover, Helen's face was hidden on his bosom; and what he saw was Hazel's manly and intelligent countenance pale, and dragged with agony and shame.

"Come, come," he said, gently, "don't cry about it; it is not your fault: and don't be too hard on the man. You told me he had saved your life."

"Would he had not!" said the sobbing girl.

"There, Seaton," said the General. "Now you

see the consequences of deceit: it wipes out the deepest obligations." He resumed, in a different tone, "But not with me. This is a woman: but I am a man, and know how a bad man could have abused the situation in which I found you two."

"Not worse than he has done," cried Helen.

"What do you tell me, girl!" said General Rolleston, beginning to tremble in his turn.

"What could he do worse than steal my esteem and veneration, and drag my heart's best feelings in the dirt? O, where — where can I ever look for a guide, instructor, and faithful friend, after this? He seemed all truth; and he is all a lie: the world is all a lie: would I could leave it this moment!"

"This is all romantic nonsense," said General Rolleston, beginning to be angry. "You are a little fool, and in your ignorance and innocence have no idea how well this young fellow has behaved on the whole. I tell you what; — in spite of this one fault, I should like to shake him by the hand. I will too; and then admonish him afterwards."

"You shall not. You shall not," cried Helen, seizing him almost violently by the arm. "You take him by the hand! A monster! How dare you steal into my esteem? How dare you be a miracle of goodness, self-denial, learning, and every virtue that a lady might worship and thank God for, when all the time you are a vile, convicted —"

"I'll thank you not to say that word," said Hazel, firmly.

"I'll call you what you are, if I choose," said Helen, defiantly. But for all that she did not do it. She said piteously, "What offence had I ever given you? What crime had I ever committed, that you must make me the victim of this diabolical deceit? O, sir, what powers of mind you have wasted to achieve this victory over a poor unoffending girl! What was your motive? What good could come of it to you? He won't speak to me. He is not even penitent. Sullen and obstinate! He shall be taken to England, and well punished for it. Papa, it is your duty."

"Helen," said the General, "you ladies are rather too fond of hitting a man when he is down. And you speak daggers, as the saying is; and then wish you had bitten your tongue off sooner. You are my child, but you are also a British subject; and, if you charge me on my duty to take this man to England and have him imprisoned, I must. But, before you go that length, you had better hear the whole story."

"Sir," said Robert Penfold, quietly, "I will go back to prison this minute, if she wishes it."

"How dare you interrupt papa," said Helen, haughtily, but with a great sob.

"Come, come," said the General, "be quiet, both of you, and let me say my say. (To Robert.) You had better turn your head away, for I am a straightforward man, and I'm going to show her you are not a villain, but a madman. This Robert Penfold wrote me a letter, imploring me to find him some honest employment, however menial. That looked well, and I made him my gardener. He was a capital gardener; but one fine day he caught sight of you. *You* are a very lovely girl, though you don't seem to know it; and *he* is a madman; and he fell in love with you." Helen uttered an ejaculation of great surprise. The General resumed: "He can only have seen you at a distance, or you would recognize him; but (really it is laughable) he saw you somehow, though you did not see him, and — Well, his insanity hurt himself, and did not hurt you. You remember how he suspected burglars, and watched night after night under your window. That was out of love for you. His insanity took the form of fidelity and humble devotion. He got a wound for his pains, poor fellow! and you made Arthur Wardlaw get him a clerk's place."

"Arthur Wardlaw!" cried Seaton. "Was it to him I owed it?" and he groaned aloud.

Said Helen, "He hates poor Arthur, his benefactor." Then to Penfold: "If you are that James Seaton, you received a letter from me."

"I did," said Penfold; and putting his hand in his bosom he drew out a letter and showed it her.

"Let me see it," said Helen.

"O no! don't take this from me too," said he, piteously.

General Rolleston continued. "The day you sailed he disappeared; and I am afraid not without some wild idea of being in the same ship with you. This was very reprehensible. Do you hear, young man? But what is the consequence? You get shipwrecked together, and the young madman takes such care of you that I find you well and hearty, and calling him your guardian angel. And — another thing to his credit — he has set his wits to work to restore you to the world. These ducks, one of which brings me here? Of course it was he who contrived that, not you. Young man, you must learn to look things in the face; this young lady is not of your sphere, to begin; and, in the next place, she is engaged to Mr. Arthur Wardlaw; and I am come out in his steamboat to take her to him. And as for you, Helen, take my advice; think what most convicts are compared to this one. Shut your eyes entirely to his folly, as I shall; and let you and I think only of his good deeds, and so make him all the return we can. You and I will go on board the steamboat directly; and, when we are there, we can tell Moreland there is somebody else on the island. He then turned to Penfold, and said: "My daughter and I will keep in the after-part of the vessel, and anybody that likes can leave the ship at Valparaiso. Helen, I know it is wrong; but what can I do? — I am so happy. You are alive and well: how can I punish or afflict a human creature to-day? and, above all, how can I crush this unhappy young man, without whom I should never have seen you again in this world? My daughter! my dear lost child!" and he held her at arm's length and gazed at her, and then drew her to his bosom, and for him Robert Penfold ceased to exist, except as a man that had saved his daughter.

"Papa," said Helen, after a long pause, "just make him tell why he could not trust to me. Why he passed himself off to me for a clergyman."

"I am a clergyman," said Robert Penfold.

"O!" said Helen, shocked to find him so hardened, as she thought. She lifted her hands to heaven, and the tears streamed from her eyes. "Well, sir," said she, faintly, "I see I cannot reach your conscience. One question more, and then I have done with you forever. Why in all these months that we have been alone, and that you have shown me the nature, I don't say of an honest man, but of an angel, — yes, papa, of an angel, — why could you not show me one humble virtue, sincerity? It belongs to a man. Why could you not say, 'I have committed one crime in my life, but repented forever; judge by this confession, and by what you have seen of me, whether I shall ever commit another. Take me as I am, and esteem me as a penitent and more worthy man; but I will not deceive you and pass for a paragon.' Why could you not say as much as this to me? If you loved me, why deceive me so cruelly?"

These words, uttered no longer harshly, but in a mournful, faint, despairing voice, produced an effect the speaker little expected. Robert Penfold made two attempts to speak, but though he opened his mouth, and his lips quivered, he could get no word out. He began to choke with emotion; and though he shed no tears, the convulsion that goes with weeping in weaker natures overpowered him in a way that was almost terrible.

"Confound it!" said General Rolleston, "this is monstrous of you, Helen; it is barbarous. You are not like your poor mother."

She was pale and trembling, and the tears flowing; but she showed her native obstinacy. She said, hoarsely, "Papa, you are blind. He *must* answer me. He knows he must!"

"I must," said Robert Penfold, gasping still. Then he manned himself by a mighty effort, and repeated with dignity, "I will." There was a pause while the young man still struggled for composure and self-command.

"Was I not often on the point of telling you my sad story? Then is it fair to say that I should never have told it you? But, O Miss Rolleston, you don't know what agony it may be to an unfortunate man to tell the truth. There are accusations so terrible, so *defiling*, that, when a man has proved them false, they still stick to him and soil him. Such an accusation I labor under, and a judge and a jury have branded me. If they had called me a murderer, I would have told you; but *that* is such a dirty crime. I feared the prejudices of the world. I dreaded to see your face alter to me. Yes, I trembled, and hesitated, and asked myself whether a man is bound to repeat a foul slander against himself, even when thirteen shallow men have said it, and made the lie law."

"There," said General Rolleston, "I thought how it would be, Helen; you have tormented him into defending himself, tooth and nail; so now we shall have the old story; he is innocent; I never knew a convict that was n't, if he found a fool to listen to him. I decline to hear another word. You need n't excuse yourself for changing your name; I excuse it, and that is enough. But the boat is waiting, and we can't stay to hear you justify a felony."

"I AM NOT A FELON. I AM A MARTYR."

CHAPTER LII.

ROBERT PENFOLD drew himself up to his full height, and uttered these strange words with a sad majesty that was very imposing. But General Rolleston, steeled by experience of convicts, their plausibility, and their histrionic powers, was staggered only for a moment. He deigned no reply; but told Helen Captain Moreland was waiting for her, and she had better go on board at once.

She stood like a statue.

"No, papa, I'll not turn my back on him till I know whether he is a felon or a martyr."

"My poor child, has he caught you at once with a clever phrase? A judge and a jury have settled that."

"They settled it as you would settle it, by refusing to hear me."

"Have I refused to hear you?" said Helen. "What do I care for steamboats and captains? If I stay here to all eternity, I'll know from your own lips and your own face whether you are a felon or a martyr. It is no phrase, papa. He *is* a felon or a martyr; and I am a most unfortunate girl, or else a base, disloyal one."

"Fiddle-dee," said General Rolleston, angrily. Then, looking at his watch: "I give you five minutes to humbug us in — if you can."

Robert Penfold sighed patiently. But from that moment he ignored General Rolleston, and looked to Helen only. And she fixed her eyes upon his face with a tenacity and an intensity of observation that surpassed anything he had ever seen in his life. It dazzled him; but it did not dismay him.

"Miss Rolleston," said he, "my history can be told in the time my prejudiced judge allows me. I am a clergyman, and a private tutor at Oxford. One of my pupils was — Arthur Wardlaw. I took an interest in him because my father, Michael Penfold, was in Wardlaw's employ. This Arthur Wardlaw had a talent for mimicry; he mimicked one of the college officers publicly and offensively, and was about to be expelled, and that would have ruined his immediate prospects; for his father is just, but stern. I fought hard for him, and, being myself popular with the authorities, I got him off. He was grateful, or seemed to be, and we became greater friends than ever. We confided in each other. He told me he was in debt in Oxford, and much alarmed lest it should reach his father's ears, and lose him the promised partnership. I told him I was desirous to buy a small living near Oxford, which was then vacant; but I had only saved £400, and the price was £1,000; I had no means of raising the balance. Then he said, 'Borrow £2,000 of my father; give me fourteen hundred of it, and take your own time to repay the £600. I shall be my father's partner in a month or two,' said he; 'you can pay us back by instalments.' I thought this very kind of him. I did not want the living for myself, but to give my dear father certain comforts and country air every week; he needed it: he was born in the country. Well, I came to London about this business; and a stranger called on me, and said he came from Mr. Arthur Wardlaw, who was not well enough to come himself. He produced a note of hand for £ 2,000, signed John Wardlaw, and made me indorse it, and told me where to get it cashed; he would come next day for Arthur Wardlaw's share of the money. Well, I suspected no ill; would you? I went and got the note discounted, and locked the money up. It was not my money: the greater part was Arthur Wardlaw's. That same evening a policeman called, and asked several questions, which of course I answered. He then got me out of the house on some pretence, and arrested me as a forger."

"Oh!" cried Helen.

"I forgot the clergyman; I was a gentleman, and a man, insulted, and I knocked the officer down directly. But his myrmidons overpowered me. I was tried at the Central Criminal Court on two charges. First, the Crown (as they call the attorney that draws the indictment) charged me with forging the note of hand; and then with not forging it, but passing it, well knowing that somebody else had forged it. Well, Undercliff, the Expert, swore positively that the forged note was not written by me; and the Crown, as they call it, was defeated on that charge; but being proved a liar in a court of justice did not abash my accuser; the second charge was pressed with equal confidence.

The note, you are to understand, was forged: that admits of no doubt; and I passed it; the question was whether I passed it knowing it to be forged. How was that to be determined? And here it was that my own familiar friend, in whom I trusted, destroyed me. Of course, as soon as I was put in prison, I wrote and sent to Arthur Wardlaw. Would you believe it? he would not come to me. He would not even write. Then, as the time drew near, I feared he was a traitor. I treated him like one. I told my solicitor to drag him into court as my witness, and *make* him tell the truth. The clerk went down accordingly, and found he kept his door always locked; but the clerk outwitted him, and served him with the subpœna in his bedroom, before he could crawl under the bed. But he baffled us at last; he never appeared in the witness-box; and, when my counsel asked the court to imprison him, his father swore he could not come: he was dying, and all out of sympathy with me. Fine sympathy! that closed the lips, and concealed the truth; one syllable of which would have saved his friend and benefactor from a calamity worse than death. Is the truth poison, that to tell it makes a sick man die? Is the truth hell, that a dying man refuses to speak it? How can a man die better than speaking the truth? How can he die worse than withholding it? I believe his sickness and his death were lies like himself. For want of one word from Arthur Wardlaw to explain that I had every reason to expect a note of hand from him, the jury condemned me. They were twelve honest but shallow men — invited to go inside another man's bosom and guess what was there. They guessed that I knew and understood a thing which to this hour I neither know nor understand, by God!"

He paused a moment, then resumed: —

"I believe they founded their conjecture on my knocking down the officer. There was a reason for you! Why, forgers and their confederates are reptiles, and have no fight in them. Experience proves this. But these twelve men did not go by experience; they guessed, like babies, and, after much hesitation, condemned me; but recommended me to mercy. Mercy! What mercy did I deserve? Either I was innocent, or hanging was too good for me. No; in their hearts they doubted my guilt; and their doubt took that timid form instead of acquitting me. I was amazed at the verdict, and asked leave to tell the judge why Arthur Wardlaw had defied the court, and absented himself as my witness. Had the judge listened for one minute, he would have seen I was innocent. But no. I was in England where the mouth of the accused is stopped, if he is fool enough to employ counsel. The judge stopped my mouth, as your father just now tried to stop it; and they branded me as a felon.

"Up to that moment my life was honorable and worthy. Since that moment I have never wronged a human creature. Men pass from virtue to vice, from vice to crime; this is the ladder a soul goes down; but you are invited to believe that I jumped from innocence into a filthy felony, and then jumped back again none the worse, and was a gardener that fought for his employer,' and a lover that controlled his passion. It is a lie, — a lie that ought not to take in a child. But prejudice degrades a man below the level of a child. I'll say no more; my patience is exhausted by wrongs and insults. I am as honest a man as ever breathed; and the place where we stand is mine, for I made it. Leave it and me this moment. Go to England, and leave me where the animals, more reasonable than you, have the sense to see my real character. I'll not sail in the same ship with any man, nor any woman either, who can look me in the face, and take me for a felon."

He swelled and towered with the just wrath of an honest man driven to bay; and his eye shot black lightning. He was sublime.

Helen cowered; but her spirited old father turned red, and said, haughtily, "We take you at your word, and leave you, you insolent vagabond! Follow me this instant, Helen!"

And he marched out of the cavern in a fury.

But, instead of following him, Helen stood stock-still, and cowered, and cowered till she seemed sinking forward to the ground, and she got hold of Robert Penfold's hand, and kissed it, and moaned over it.

"Martyr! Martyr!" she whispered, and still kissed his hand, like a slave offering her master pity, and asking pardon.

"Martyr! Martyr! Every word is true — true as my love."

In this attitude, and with these words on her lips, they were surprised by General Rolleston, who came back, astonished at his daughter not following him Judge of his amazement now.

"What does this mean?" he cried, turning pale with anger.

"It means that he has spoken the truth, and that I shall imitate him. He is my martyr, and my love. When others cast shame on you, then it is time for me to show my heart. James Seaton, I love you for your madness and your devotion to her whom you had only seen at a distance. Ah! that was love! John Hazel, I love you for all that has passed between us. What can any other man be to me? — or woman to you? But, most of all, I love *you*, Robert Penfold, — my hero and my martyr. When I am told to your face that you are a felon, then to your face I say you are my idol, my hero, and my martyr. Love! the word is too tame, too common. I worship you, I adore you! How beautiful you are when you are angry! How noble you are now you forgive me! for you do forgive me, Robert; you must, you shall. No; you will not send your Helen away from you for her one fault so soon repented! Show me you forgive me; show me you love me still, almost as much as I love you. He is crying. O my darling, my darling, my darling!" And she was round his neck in a moment, with tears and tender kisses, the first she had ever given him.

Ask yourself whether they were returned.

A groan, or rather, we might say, a snort of fury, interrupted the most blissful moment either of these young creatures had ever known. It came from General Rolleston, now white with wrath and horror.

"You villain!" he cried.

Helen threw herself upon him, and put her hand before his mouth.

"Not a word more, or I shall forget I am your daughter. No one is to blame but I. I love him. I made him love me. He has been trying hard not to love me so much. But I am a woman; and could not deny myself the glory and the joy of being loved better than woman was ever loved before. And so I am; I am. Kill me, if you like; insult me, if you will: but not a word against him, or I give him my hand, and we live and die together on this island. O papa! he has often saved that life you value so; and I have saved his. He is all the world to me. Have pity on your child. Have pity on him who carries my heart in his bosom."

She flung herself on her knees, and strained him tight, and implored him, with head thrown back, and little clutching hands, and eloquent eyes.

Ah! it is hard to resist the voice and look and clinging of a man's own flesh and blood. Children are so strong — upon their knees: their dear faces, bright copies of our own, are just the height of our hearts then.

The old man was staggered, was almost melted. "Give me a moment to think," said he, in a broken voice. "This blow takes my breath away."

Helen rose, and laid her head upon her father's shoulder, and still pleaded for her love by her soft touch and her tears that now flowed freely.

He turned to Penford with all the dignity of age and station. "Mr. Penford," said he, with grave politeness, "after what my daughter has said, I must treat you as a man of honor, or I must insult her. Well, then, I expect you to show me you are what she thinks you, and are not what a court of justice has proclaimed you. Sir, this young lady is engaged with her own free will to a gentleman who is universally esteemed, and has never been accused *to his face* of any unworthy act. Relying on her plighted word, the Wardlaws have fitted out a steamer and searched the Pacific, and found her. Can you, as a man of honor, advise her to stay here and compromise her own honor in every way? Ought she to break faith with her betrothed on account of vague accusations made behind his back?"

"It was only in self-defence I accused Mr. Arthur Wardlaw," said Robert Penfold.

General Rolleston resumed: —

"You said just now there are accusations which soil a man. If you were in my place, would you let your daughter marry a man of honor, who had unfortunately been found guilty of a felony?"

Robert groaned and hesitated, but he said "No."

"Then what is to be done? She must either keep her plighted word, or else break it. For whom? For a gentleman she esteems and loves, but cannot marry. A leper may be a saint; but I would rather bury my child than marry her to a leper. A convict may be a saint; but I'll kill her with my own hand sooner than she shall marry a convict: and in your heart and conscience you cannot blame me. Were you a father, you would do the same. What then remains for her and me but to keep faith? and what can you do better than leave her, and carry away her everlasting esteem and her father's gratitude? It is no use being good by halves, or bad by halves. You must either be a selfish villain, and urge her to abandon all shame, and live here on this island with you forever, or you must be a brave and honest man, and bow to a parting that is inevitable. Consider, sir; your eloquence and her pity have betrayed this young lady into a confession that separates you. Her enforced residence here with you has been innocent. It would be innocent no longer, now she has been so mad as to own she loves you. And I tell you frankly, if, after that confession, you insist on going on board the steamer with her, I must take you; humanity requires it; but, if I do, I shall hand you over to the law as a convict escaped before his time. Perhaps I ought to do so as it is; but that is not certain; I don't know to what country this island belongs. I may have no right to capture you in strange dominions; but an English ship is England, — and if you set foot on the Springbok you are lost. Now, then, you are a man of honor; you love my child truly, and not selfishly; — you have behaved nobly until to-day; go one step farther on the right road; call worldly honor and the God whose vows you have taken, sir, to your aid, and do your duty."

"O man, man!" cried Robert Penfold, "you ask more of me than flesh and blood can bear. What shall I say? What shall I do?"

Helen replied, calmly: "Take my hand, and let us die together, since we cannot live together with honor."

General Rolleston groaned. "For this, then, I have traversed one ocean, and searched another, and found my child. I am nothing to her — nothing. O, who would be a father!" He sat down oppressed with shame and grief, and bowed his stately head in manly but pathetic silence.

"O papa, papa!" cried Helen, "forgive your ungrateful child!" And she kneeled and sobbed, with her forehead on his knees.

Then Robert Penfold, in the midst of his own agony, found room in that great suffering heart of his for pity. He knelt down himself, and prayed for help in this bitter trial. He rose haggard with the struggle, but languid and resigned, like one whose death-warrant has been read.

"Sir," said he, "there is but one way. You must take her home; and I shall stay here."

"Leave you all alone on this island!" said Helen. "Never! If you stay here, I shall stay to comfort you."

"I decline that offer. I am beyond the reach of comfort."

"Think what you do, Robert," said Helen, with unnatural calmness. "If you have no pity on yourself, have pity on us. Would you rob me of the very life you have taken such pains to save? My poor father will carry nothing to England but my dead body. Long before we reach that country I loved so well, and now hate it for its stupidity and cruelty to you, my soul will have flown back to this island to watch over you, Robert. You bid me to abandon you to solitude and despair. Neither of you two love me half as much as I love you both."

General Rolleston sighed deeply. "If I thought that," said he, — then, in a faint voice, "my own courage fails me now. I look into my heart, and I see that my child's life is dearer to me than all the world. She was dying, they say. Suppose I send Moreland to the Continent for a clergyman, and marry you. Then you can live on this island forever. Only you must let me live here too; for I could never show my face again in England after acting so dishonorably. It will be a miserable end of a life passed in honor; but I suppose it will not be for long. Shame can kill as quickly as disappointed love."

"Robert, Robert!" cried Helen in agony.

The martyr saw that he was master of the situation, and must be either base or very noble, — there was no middle way. He leaned his head on his hands, and thought with all his might.

"Hush!" said Helen: "he is wiser than we are. Let him speak."

"If I thought you would pine and die upon the voyage, no power should part us. But you are not such a coward. If my life depended on yours, would you not live?"

"You know I would."

"When I was wrecked on White-water Island, you played the man. Not one woman in a thousand could have launched a boat, and sailed it with a boat-hook for a mast, and —"

Helen interrupted him. "It was nothing; I loved you. I love you better now."

"I believe it, and therefore I ask you to rise above your sex once more, and play the man for me. This time it is not my life you are to rescue, but that which is more precious still: my good name."

"Ah! that would be worth living for!" cried Helen.

"You will find it very hard to do; but not harder for a woman than to launch a boat, and sail her without a mast. See my father, Michael Penfold. See Undercliff, the expert. See the solicitor — the counsel. Sift the whole story; and, above all, find out why Arthur Wardlaw dared not enter the witness-box. Be obstinate as a man; be supple as a woman; and don't talk of dying when there is a friend to be rescued from dishonor by living and working."

"Die! while I can rescue you from death or dishonor! I will not be so base. Ah, Robert, Robert, how well you know me!"

"Yes, I do know you, Helen. I believe that great soul of yours will keep your body strong to do this brave work for him you love, and who loves you. And as for me, I am man enough to live for years upon this island, if you will only promise me two things."

"I promise, then."

"Never to die, and never to marry Arthur Wardlaw, until you have reversed that lying sentence which has blasted me. Lay your hand on your father's head, and promise me that."

Helen laid her hand upon her father's head, and said, "I pledge my honor not to die, if life is possible, and never to marry any man, until I have reversed that lying sentence which has blasted the angel I love."

"And I pledge myself to help her," said General Rolleston, warmly, "for now I *know* you are a man of honor. I have too often been deceived by eloquence to listen much to that. But now you have proved by your actions what you are. You pass a forged check, knowing it to be forged! I'd stake my salvation it's a lie. There's my hand. God comfort you! God reward you, my noble fellow!"

"I hope he will, sir," sobbed Robert Penfold. "You are her father; and you take my hand; perhaps that will be sweet to think of by and by; but no joy can enter my heart now; it is broken. Take her away at once, sir. Flesh is weak. My powers of endurance are exhausted."

General Rolleston acted promptly on this advice. He rolled up her rugs, and the things she had made, and Robert had the courage to take them down to the boat. Then he came back, and the General took her bag to the boat.

All this time the girl herself sat wringing her hands in anguish, and not a tear. It was beyond that now.

As he passed Robert, the General said, "Take leave of her alone. I will come for her in five minutes. You see how sure I feel you are a man of honor."

When Robert went in, she rose and tottered to him, and fell on his neck. She saw it was the death-bed of their love, and she kissed his eyes, and clung to him. They moaned over each other, and clung to each other, in mute despair.

The General came back, and he and Robert took Helen, shivering and fainting, to the boat. As the boat put off, she awoke from her stupor, and put out her hands to Robert with one piercing cry.

They were parted.

CHAPTER LIII.

In that curious compound the human heart, a respectable motive is sometimes connected with a criminal act. And it was so with Joseph Wylie: he had formed an attachment to Nancy Rouse, and her price was two thousand pounds.

This Nancy Rouse was a character. She was General Rolleston's servant for many years; her place was the kitchen: but she was a woman of such restless activity, and so wanting in the proper pride of a servant, that she would help a housemaid, or a lady's maid, or do anything almost, except be idle! to use her own words, she was one as could n't abide to sit mumchance. That fatal foe to domestic industry, the London Journal, fluttered in vain down her area, for she could not read. She supported a sick mother out of her wages, aided by a few presents of money and clothes from Helen Rolleston, who had a great regard for Nancy, and knew what a hard fight she had to keep a sick woman out of her twenty pounds a year.

In love, Nancy was unfortunate; her buxom looks and sterling virtues were balanced by a provoking sagacity, and an irritating habit of speaking her mind. She humbled her lovers' vanity, one after another, and they fled. Her heart smarted more than once.

Nancy was ambitious; and her first rise in life took place as follows: When the Rollestons went to Australia, she had a good cry at parting with Helen; but there was no help for it: she could not leave her mother. However, she told Helen she could not stomach any other service, and, since she must be parted, was resolved to better herself. This phrase is sometimes drolly applied by servants, because they throw Independence into the scale. In Nancy's case it meant setting up as a washerwoman. Helen opened her hazel eyes with astonishment at this, the first round in the ladder of Nancy's ambition; however, she gave her ten pounds, and thirty introductions, twenty-five of which missed fire, and with the odd five Nancy set up her tub in the suburbs, and by her industry, geniality, and frugality, got on tolerably well. In due course she rented a small house backed by a small green, and advertised for a gentleman lodger. She soon got one; and soon got rid of him. However, she was never long without one.

Nancy met Joseph Wylie in company: and, as sailors are brisk wooers, he soon became her acknowledged suitor, and made some inroad into her heart, though she kept on the defensive, warned by past experience.

Wylie's love-making had a droll feature about it; it was most of it carried on in the presence of three washerwomen, because Nancy had no time to spare from her work, and Wylie had no time to lose in his wooing, being on shore for a limited period. And this absence of superfluous delicacy on his part gave him an unfair advantage over the tallow-chandler's foreman, his only rival at present. Many a sly thrust, and many a hearty laugh, from his female auditors, greeted his amorous eloquence: but, for all that, they sided with him, and Nancy felt her importance, and brightened along with her mates at the sailor's approach, which was generally announced by a cheerful hail. He was good company, to use Nancy's own phrase, and she accepted him as a sweetheart on probation. But, when Mr. Wylie urged her to marry him, she demurred, and gave a string of reasons, all of which the sailor and his allies, the subordinate washerwomen, combated in full conclave.

Then she spoke out, "My lad, the wash-tub is a saddle as won't carry double. I 've seen poverty enough in my mother's house, it sha'n't come in at my door to drive love out o' window. Two comes together with just enough for two; next year instead of two they are three, and one of the three can't work and wants a servant extra, and by and by there is half a dozen, and the money coming in at the spigot and going out at the bung-hole."

One day, in the middle of his wooing, she laid down her iron, and said, "You come along with me. And I wonder how much work will be done whilst my back is turned, for you three gabbling and wondering whatever I 'm agoing to do with this here sailor."

She took Wylie a few yards down the street, and showed him a large house with most of the windows broken. "There," said she, "there 's a sight for a seafaring man. That 's in Chancery."

"Well, it 's better to be there than in H——," said Wylie, meaning to be sharper.

"Wait till you 've tried 'em both," said Nancy.

Then she took him to the back of the house, and showed him a large garden attached to it.

"Now, Joseph," said she, "I 've showed you a lodging-house and a drying-ground; and I 'm a cook and a clear-starcher, and I 'm wild to keep lodgers and do for 'em, washing and all. Then, if their foul linen goes out, they follows it: the same if they has their meat from the cook-shop. Four hundred pounds a year lies there a waiting for me. I 've been at them often to let me them premises: but they says no, we have got no horder from the court to let. Which the court would rather see 'em go to rack an' ruin for nothing, than let 'em to an honest woman as would pay the rent punctual, and make her penny out of 'em, and nobody none the worse. And to sell them, the price is two thousand pounds, and if I had it I 'd give it this minit: but where are the likes of you and me to get two thousand pounds? But the lawyer he says, 'Miss Rouse, from *you* one thousand down, and the rest on mortgige at £45 the year,' which it is dirt cheap, I say. So now, my man, when that house is mine, I 'm yours. I 'm putting by for it o' my side. If you means all you say, why not save a bit o' yours. Once I get that house and garden, you need n't go to sea no more: nor you sha'n't. If I am to be bothered with a man, let me know where to put my finger on him at all hours, and not lie shivering and shaking at every window as creaks, and him out at sea. And if you are too proud to drive the linen in a light cart, why I could pay a man." In short she told him plainly she would not marry till she was above the world; and the road to above the world was through that great battered house and seedy garden, in Chancery.

Now it may appear a strange coincidence that Nancy's price to Wylie was two thousand pounds, and Wylie's to Wardlaw was two thousand pounds: but the fact is it was a forced coincidence. Wylie, bargaining with Wardlaw, stood out for two thousand pounds, because that was the price of the house and garden and Nancy.

Now, when Wylie returned to England safe after his crime and his perils, he comforted himself with the reflection that Nancy would have her house and garden, and he should have Nancy.

But young Wardlaw lay on his sick-bed; his father was about to return to the office, and the gold disguised as copper was ordered up to the cellars in Fenchurch Street. There, in all probability, the contents would be examined erelong, the fraud exposed, and other unpleasant consequences might follow over and above the loss of the promised £2,000.

Wylie felt very disconsolate, and went down to Nancy Rouse depressed in spirits. To his surprise she received him with more affection than ever, and, reading his face in a moment, told him not to fret.

"It will be so in your way of life," said this homely comforter; "your sort comes home empty-handed one day, and money in both pockets the next. I 'm glad to see you home at all, for I 've been in care about you. You 're very welcome, Joe. If you are come home honest and sober, why, that is the next best thing to coming home rich."

Wylie hung his head and pondered these words; and well he might, for he had not come home either so sober or so honest as he went out, but quite as poor.

However, his elastic spirits soon revived in Nancy's sunshine, and he became more in love with her than ever.

But when, presuming upon her affection, he urged her to marry him and trust to Providence, she laughed in his face.

"Trust to himprovidence, you mean," said she; "no, no, Joseph. If you are unlucky, I must be lucky, before you and me can come together."

Then Wylie resolved to have his £2,000 at all risks. He had one great advantage over a landsman who has committed a crime. He could always go to sea and find employment, first in one ship, and then in another. Terra firma was not one of the necessaries of life to him.

He came to Wardlaw's office to feel his way, and talked guardedly to Michael Penfold about the loss of the Proserpine. His apparent object was to give information; his real object was to gather it. He learned that old Wardlaw was very much occupied with fitting out a steamer; that the forty chests of copper had actually come up from the Shannon and were under their feet at that moment, and that young Wardlaw was desperately ill and never came to the office. Michael had not at that time learned the true cause of young Wardlaw's illness. Yet Wylie detected that young Wardlaw's continued absence from the office gave Michael singular uneasiness. The old man fidgeted, and washed the air with his hands, and with simple cunning urged Wylie to go and see him about the Proserpine, and get him to the office, if it was only for an hour or two. "Tell him we are all at sixes and sevens, Mr. Wylie; all at sixes and sevens."

"Well," said Wylie, affecting a desire to oblige, "give me a line to him; for I 've been twice, and could never get in."

Michael wrote an earnest line to say that Wardlaw senior had been hitherto much occupied in fitting out the Springbok, but that he was going into the books next week. What was to be done?

The note was received; but Arthur declined to see the bearer. Then Wylie told the servant it was Joseph Wylie, on a matter of life and death. "Tell him I must stand at the stair-foot and hallo it out, if he won't hear it any other way."

This threat obtained his admission to Arthur Wardlaw. The sailor found him on a sofa, in a darkened room, pale and worn to a shadow.

"Mr. Wardlaw," said Wylie, firmly, "you mustn't think I don't feel for you; but, sir, we are gone too far to stop, you and me. There is two sides to this business; it is £150,000 for you, and £2,000 for me, or it is —" "What do I care for money now?" groaned Wardlaw. "Let it all go to the devil, who tempted me to destroy her I loved better than money, better than all the world." "Well, but hear me out," said Wylie. "I say it is £150,000 to you and £2,000 to me, or else it is twenty years' penal servitude to both on us."

"Penal servitude!" And the words roused the merchant from his lethargy like a shower-bath.

"You know that well enough," said Wylie. "Why, 't was a hanging matter a few years ago. Come, come, there are no two ways; you must be a man, or we are undone."

Fear prevailed in that timorous breast, which even love of money had failed to rouse. Wardlaw sat up, staring wildly, and asked Wylie what he was to do.

"First, let me ring for a bottle of that old brandy of yours."

The brandy was got. Wylie induced him to drink a wineglassful neat, and then to sit at the table and examine the sailors' declaration and the logs. "I'm no great scholard," said he. "I warn't a going to lay these before the underwriters till you had overhauled them. There, take another drop now, — 't will do you good, — while I draw up this thundering blind."

Thus encouraged and urged, the broken-hearted schemer languidly compared the seamen's declaration with the logs; and, even in his feeble state of mind and body, made an awkward discovery at once.

"Why, they don't correspond!" said he.

"What don't correspond?"

"Your men's statement and the ship's log. The men speak of one heavy gale after another, in January, and the pumps going; but the log says, 'A puff of wind from the N. E.' And here, again, the entry exposes your exaggeration; one branch of our evidence contradicts the other; this comes of trying to prove too much. You must say the log was lost, went down with the ship."

"How can I?" cried Wylie. "I have told too many I had got it safe at home."

"Why did you say that? What madness!"

"Why were you away from your office at such a time? How can I know everything and do everything? I counted on you for the headwork ashore. Can't ye think of any way to square the log to that part of our tale? might paste in a leaf or two, eh?"

"That would be discovered at once. You have committed an irremediable error. What broad strokes this Hudson makes. He must have written with the stump of a quill."

Wylie received this last observation with a look of contempt for the mind that could put so trivial a question in so great an emergency.

"Are you quite sure poor Hudson is dead?" asked Wardlaw, in a low voice.

"Dead! Don't I tell you I saw him die!" said Wylie, trembling all of a sudden.

He took a glass of brandy, and sent it flying down his throat.

"Leave the paper with me," said Arthur, languidly, "and tell Penfold I'll crawl to the office to-morrow. You can meet me there; I shall see nobody else."

Wylie called next day at the office, and was received by Penfold, who had now learned the cause of Arthur's grief, and ushered the visitor in to him with looks of benevolent concern. Arthur was seated like a lunatic, pale and motionless; on the table before him was a roast fowl and a salad, which he had forgotten to eat. His mind appeared to alternate between love and fraud; for, as soon as he saw Wylie he gave himself a sort of shake, and handed Wylie the log and the papers.

"Examine them; they agree better with each other now."

Wylie examined the log, and started with surprise and superstitious terror. "Why, Hiram's ghost has been here at work!" said he. "It is his very handwriting."

"Hush!" said Wardlaw; "not so loud. Will it do?"

"The writing will do first-rate; but any one can see this log has never been to sea."

Inspired by the other's ingenuity, he then, after a moment's reflection, emptied the salt-cellar into a plate, and poured a little water over it. He wetted the leaves of the log with this salt water, and dog's-eared the whole book.

Wardlaw sighed. "See what expedients we are driven to," said he. He then took a little soot from the chimney, and mixed it with salad oil. He applied some of this mixture to the parchment cover, rubbed it off, and by much manipulation gave it a certain mellow look, as if it had been used by working hands.

Wylie was armed with these materials, and furnished with money, to keep his sailors to their tale, in case of their being examined.

Arthur begged, in his present affliction, to be excused from going personally into the matter of the Proserpine; and said that Penfold had the ship's log, and the declaration of the survivors, which the insurers could inspect, previously to their being deposited at Lloyd's.

The whole thing wore an excellent face, and nobody found a peg to hang suspicion on so far.

After this preliminary, and the deposit of the papers, nothing was hurried; the merchant, absorbed in his grief, seemed to be forgetting to ask for his money. Wylie remonstrated; but Arthur convinced him they were still on too ticklish ground to show any hurry without exciting suspicion.

And so passed two weary months, during which Wylie fell out of Nancy Rouse's good graces, for idling about doing nothing.

"Be you a waiting for the plum to fall into your mouth, young man?" said she.

The demand was made on the underwriters, and Arthur contrived that it should come from his father. The firm was of excellent repute, and had paid hundreds of insurances, without a loss to the underwriters. The Proserpine had foundered at sea; several lives had been lost, and of the survivors, one had since died, owing to the hardships he had endured. All this betokened a genuine calamity. Nevertheless, one ray of suspicion rested on the case, at first. The captain of the Proserpine had lost a great many ships; and, on the first announcement, one or two were resolved to sift the matter on that ground alone. But when five eye-witnesses, suppressing all mention of the word "drink," declared that Captain Hudson had refused to leave the vessel, and described his going down with the ship, from an obstinate and too exalted sense of duty, every chink was closed; and, to cut the matter short, the insurance money was paid to the last shilling, and Benson, one of the small underwriters, ruined. Nancy Rouse, who worked for Mrs. Benson, lost eighteen shillings and sixpence, and was dreadfully put out about it.

Wylie heard her lamentations, and grinned; for now his £2,000 was as good as in his pocket, he thought. Great was his consternation when Arthur told him that every shilling of the money was forestalled, and that the entire profit of the transaction was yet to come, viz. by the sale of the gold dust.

"Then, sell it," said Wylie.

"I dare not. The affair must cool down before I can appear as a seller of gold; and even then I must dribble it out with great caution. Thank Heaven, it is no longer in those cellars."

"Where is it, then?"

"That is my secret. You will get your two thousand all in good time; and, if it makes you one tenth part as wretched as it has made me, you will thank me for all these delays."

At last Wylie lost all patience, and began to show his teeth; and then Arthur Wardlaw paid him his two thousand pounds in forty crisp notes.

He crammed them into a side pocket, and went down triumphant to Nancy Rouse. Through her parlor window he saw the benign countenance of Michael Penfold. He then remembered that Penfold had told him some time before that he was going to lodge with her, as soon as the present lodger should go.

This, however, rather interrupted Wylie's design of walking in and chucking the two thousand pounds into Nancy's lap. On the contrary, he shoved them deeper down in his pocket, and resolved to see the old gentleman to bed, and then produce his pelf, and fix the wedding-day with Nancy.

He came in, and found her crying, and Penfold making weak efforts to console her. The tea-things were on the table, and Nancy's cup half emptied.

Wylie came in, and said, "Why, what is the matter now?"

He said this mighty cheerfully, as one who carried the panacea for all ills in his pocket, and a medicine peculiarly suited to Nancy Rouse's constitution. But he had not quite fathomed her yet.

As soon as ever she saw him she wiped her eyes, and asked him, grimly, what he wanted there. Wylie stared at the reception; but replied stoutly, that it was pretty well known by this time what he wanted in that quarter.

"Well, then," said Nancy, "Want will be your master. Why did you never tell me Miss Helen was in that ship? my sweet, dear mistress as was, that I feel for like a mother. You left her to drown, and saved your own great useless carcass, and drowned she is, poor dear. Get out o' my sight, do."

"It was n't my fault, Nancy," said Wylie, earnestly. "I did n't know who she was, and I advised her to come with us; but she would go with that parson chap."

"What parson chap? What a liar you be! She is Wardlaw's sweetheart, and don't care for no parsons. If you did n't know you was to blame, why did n't you tell me a word of your own accord? You kep' dark. Do you call yourself a man, to leave my poor young lady to shift for herself? —"

"She had as good a chance to live as I had," said Wylie, sullenly.

"No, she had n't; you took care o' yourself. Well, since you are so fond of yourself, keep yourself *to* yourself, and don't come here no more. After this, I hate the sight on ye. You are like the black dog in my eyes, and always will be. Poor, dear Miss Helen! Ah, I cried when she left, — my mind misgave me; but little I thought she would perish in the salt seas, and all for want of a man in the ship. If you had gone out again after in the steamboat, — Mr. Penfold have told me all about it, — I'd believe you were n't so much to blame. But no; lolloping and looking about all day for months. There's my door, Joe Wylie; I can't cry comfortable before you, as had a hand in drowning of her. You and me is parted forever. I'll die as I am, or I'll marry a *man;* which you ain't one, nor nothing like one. Is he waiting for you to hold the door open, Mr. Penfold? or don't I speak plain enough? Them as I gave the sack to afore you did n't want so much telling."

"Well, I'm going," said Wylie, sullenly; then, with considerable feeling, "This is hard lines."

But Nancy was inexorable, and turned him out, with the £2,000 in his pocket.

He took the notes out of his pocket, and flung them furiously down in the dirt.

Then he did what everybody does under similar circumstances, — he picked them up again, and pocketed them, along with the other dirt they had gathered.

Next day he went down to the docks, and looked out for a ship; he soon got one, and signed as second mate. She was to sail in a fortnight.

But, before a week was out, the bank-notes had told so upon him, that he was no longer game to go to sea. But the captain he had signed with was a Tartar, and not to be trifled with. He consulted a knowing friend, and that friend advised him to disguise himself till the ship had sailed. Accordingly he rigged himself out with a long coat, and a beard, and spectacles, and hid his sea-slouch as well as he could, and changed his lodgings. Finding he succeeded so well, he thought he might as well have the pleasure of looking at Nancy Rouse, if he could not talk to her. So he actually had the hardihood to take the parlor next door; and by this means he heard her move about in her room, and caught a sight of her at work on her little green; and he was shrewd enough to observe she did not sing and whistle as she used to do. The dog chuckled at that.

His bank-notes worried him night and day. He was afraid to put them in a bank; afraid to take them about with him into his haunts; afraid to leave them at home; and out of this his perplexity arose some incidents worth relating in their proper order.

Arthur Wardlaw returned to business; but he was a changed man. All zest in the thing was gone. His fraud set him above the world; and that was now enough for him, in whom ambition was dead, and, indeed, nothing left alive in him but deep regrets.

He drew in the horns of speculation, and went on in the old safe routine; and to the restless activity that had jeopardized the firm succeeded a strange torpidity. He wore black for Helen, and sorrowed without hope. He felt he had offended

Heaven, and had met his punishment in Helen's death. Wardlaw senior retired to Elm Trees, and seldom saw his son. When they did meet, the old man sometimes whispered hope, but the whisper was faint, and unheeded.

One day Wardlaw senior came up express, to communicate to Arthur a letter from General Rolleston, written at Valparaiso. In this letter, General Rolleston deplored his unsuccessful search: but said he was going westward, upon the report of a Dutch whaler, who had seen an island reflected in the sky, while sailing between Juan Fernandez and Norfolk Isle.

Arthur only shook his head with a ghastly smile. "*She* is in heaven," said he, "and I shall never see her again, not here or hereafter."

Wardlaw senior was shocked at this speech; but he made no reply. He pitied his son too much to criticise the expressions into which his bitter grief betrayed him. He was old, and had seen the triumphs of time over all things human, sorrow included. These, however, as yet, had done nothing for Arthur Wardlaw. At the end of six months, his grief was as sombre and as deadly as the first week.

But one day, as this pale figure in deep mourning sat at his table, going listlessly and mechanically through the business of scraping money together for others to enjoy, whose hearts, unlike his, might not be in the grave, his father burst in upon him, with a telegram in his hand, and waved it over his head in triumph. "She is found! she is found!" he roared: "read that!" and thrust the telegram into his hands.

Those hands trembled, and the languid voice rose into shrieks of astonishment and delight, as Arthur read the words, "We have got her, alive and well: shall be at Charing Cross Hotel, 8 P.M."

CHAPTER LIV.

WHILST the boat was going to the Springbok, General Rolleston whispered to Captain Moreland; and what he said may be almost guessed from what occurred on board the steamer soon afterwards. Helen was carried trembling to the cabin, and the order was given to heave the anchor and get under way. A groan of disappointment ran through the ship; Captain Moreland expressed the General's regret to the men, and divided £200 upon the capstan; and the groan ended in a cheer.

As for Helen's condition, that was at first mistaken for ill health. She buried herself for two whole days in her cabin; and from that place faint moans were heard now and then. The sailors called her the sick lady.

Heaven knows what she went through in that forty-eight hours.

She came upon deck at last in a strange state of mind and body: restless, strung up, absorbed. The rare vigor she had acquired on the island came out now with a vengeance. She walked the deck with briskness, and a pertinacity that awakened admiration in the crew at first, but by and by superstitious awe. For, while the untiring feet went briskly to and fro over leagues and leagues of plank every day, the great hazel eyes were turned inwards, and the mind, absorbed with one idea, skimmed the men and things about her listlessly.

She had a mission to fulfil, and her whole nature was stringing itself up to do the work.

She walked so many miles a day, partly from excitement, partly with a deliberate resolve to cherish her health and strength; "I may want them both," said she, "to clear Robert Penfold." Thought and high purpose shone through her so, that after a while nobody dared trouble her much with commonplaces. To her father, she was always sweet and filial, but sadly cold compared with what she had always been hitherto. He was taking her body to England, but her heart stayed behind upon that island: he saw this, and said it.

"Forgive me," said she, coldly; and that was all her reply.

Sometimes she had violent passions of weeping; and then he would endeavor to console her; but in vain. They ran their course, and were succeeded by the bodily activity and concentration of purpose they had interrupted for a little while.

At last, after a rapid voyage, they drew near the English coast; and then General Rolleston, who had hitherto spared her feelings, and been most indulgent and considerate, felt it was high time to come to an understanding with her as to the course they should both pursue.

"Now, Helen," said he, "about the Wardlaws!"

Helen gave a slight shudder. But she said, after a slight hesitation, "Let me know your wishes."

"O, mine are, not to be too ungrateful to the father, and not to deceive the son."

"I will not be ungrateful to the father, nor deceive the son," said Helen, firmly.

The General kissed her on the brow, and called her his brave girl. "But," said he, "on the other hand, it must not be published that you have been for eight months on an island alone with a convict. Anything sooner than that. You know the malice of your own sex; if one woman gets hold of that, you will be an outcast from society."

Helen blushed and trembled. "Nobody need be told that but Arthur; and I am sure he loves me well enough not to injure me with the world."

"But he would be justified in declining your hand, after such a revelation."

"Quite. And I hope he will decline it when he knows I love another, however hopelessly."

"You are going to tell Arthur Wardlaw all that?"

"I am."

"Then all I can say is, you are not like other women."

"I have been brought up by a man."

"If I was Arthur Wardlaw, it would be the last word you should ever speak to me."

"If you were Arthur Wardlaw, I should be on that dear island now."

"Well, suppose his love should be greater than his spirit, and —"

"If he does not go back when he hears of my hopeless love, I don't see how I can. I shall marry him: and try with all my soul to love him. I'll open every door in London to Robert Penfold; except one; my husband's. And that door, while I live, he shall never enter. O my heart; my heart!" She burst out sobbing desperately: and her father laid her head upon his bosom, and sighed deeply, and asked himself how all this would end.

Before they landed, her fortitude seemed to return; and of her own accord she begged her father to telegraph to the Wardlaws.

"Would you not like a day to compose yourself, and prepare for this trying interview?" said he.

"I should: but it is mere weakness. And I must cure myself of weakness, or I shall never clear Robert Penfold. And then, papa, I think of you. If old Mr. Wardlaw heard you had been a day in town, you might suffer in his good opinion. We shall be in London at seven. Ask them at eight. That will be one hour's respite. God help me, and strengthen poor Arthur to bear the blow I bring him!"

Long before eight o'clock that day, Arthur Wardlaw had passed from a state of sombre misery and remorse to one of joy, exultation, and unmixed happiness. He no longer regretted his crime, nor the loss of the Proserpine: Helen was alive and well, and attributed not her danger, but only her preservation, to the Wardlaws.

Wardlaw senior kept his carriage in town, and precisely at eight o'clock they drove up to the door of the hotel.

They followed the servant with bounding hearts, and rushed into the room where the General and Helen stood ready to receive them. Old Wardlaw went to the General with both hands out, and so the General met him, and between these two it was almost an embrace. Arthur ran to Helen with cries of joy and admiration, and kissed her hands again and again, and shed such genuine tears of joy over them that she trembled all over, and was obliged to sit down. He kneeled at her feet, and still imprisoned one hand, and mumbled it, while she turned her head away and held her other hand before her face to hide its real expression, which was a mixture of pity and repugnance. But as her face was hidden, and her eloquent body quivered, and her hand was not withdrawn, it seemed a sweet picture of feminine affection to those who had not the key.

At last she was relieved from a most embarrassing situation by old Wardlaw; he cried out on this monopoly, and Helen instantly darted out of her chair, and went to him, and put up her cheek to him, which he kissed; and then she thanked him warmly for his courage in not despairing of her life, and his goodness in sending out a ship for her.

Now, the fact is, she could not feel grateful; but she knew she ought to be grateful, and she was ashamed to show no feeling at all in return for so much; so she was eloquent, and the old gentleman was naturally very much pleased at first; but he caught an expression of pain on Arthur's face, and then he stopped her. "My dear," said he, "you ought to thank Arthur, not me; it is his love for you which was the cause of my zeal. If you owe me anything, pay it to him, for he deserves it best. He nearly died for you, my sweet girl. No, no, you must n't hang your head for that, neither. What a fool I am to revive old sorrows! Here we are, the happiest four in England." Then he whispered to her, "Be kind to poor Arthur, that is all I ask. His very life depends on you."

Helen obeyed this order, and went slowly back to Arthur; she sat, cold as ice, on the sofa beside him, and he made love to her. She scarcely heard what he said; she was asking herself how she could end this intolerable interview, and escape her father's looks, who knew the real state of her heart.

At last she rose, and went and whispered to him: "My courage has failed me. Have pity on me, and get me away. It is the old man; he kills me."

General Rolleston took the hint, and acted with more tact than one would have given him credit for. He got up and rang the bell for tea; then he said to Helen, "You don't drink tea now, and I see you are excited more than is good for you. You had better go to bed."

"Yes, papa," said Helen.

She took her candle, and as she passed young Wardlaw, she told him, in a low voice, she would be glad to speak to him alone to-morrow.

"At what hour?" said he, eagerly.

"When you like. At one."

And so she retired, leaving him in ecstasies. This was the first downright assignation she had ever made with him.

They met at one o'clock; he radiant as the sun, and a rose in his button-hole; she sad and sombre, and with her very skin twitching at the thought of the explanation she had to go through.

He began with amorous commonplaces; she stopped him, gravely. "Arthur," said she, "you and I are alone now, and I have a confession to make. Unfortunately, I must cause you pain — terrible pain. O! my heart flinches at the wound I am going to give you; but it is my fate either to wound you or to deceive you."

During this preamble, Arthur sat amazed, rather than alarmed. He did not interrupt her, though she paused, and would gladly have been interrupted, since an interruption is an assistance in perplexities.

"Arthur, we suffered great hardships on the boat, and you would have lost me but for one person. He saved my life again and again; I saved his upon the island. My constancy was subject to trials — O, such trials! So great an example of every manly virtue forever before my eyes! My gratitude and my pity eternally pleading! England and you seemed gone forever. Make excuses for me if you can. Arthur — I — I have formed an attachment."

In making this strange avowal she hung her head and blushed, and the tears ran down her cheeks. But we suspect they ran for *him*, and not for Arthur.

Arthur turned deadly sick at this tremendous blow, dealt with so soft a hand. At last he gasped out, "If you marry him, you will bury me."

"No, Arthur," said Helen, gently; "I could not marry him, even if you were to permit me. When you know more, you will see that, of us three unhappy ones, you are the least unhappy. But, since this is so, am I wrong to tell you the truth, and leave you to decide whether our engagement ought to continue? Of course, what I have owned to you releases you."

"Releases me! but it does not unbind my heart from yours," cried Arthur, in despair.

Then his hysterical nature came out, and he was so near fainting away that Helen sprinkled water on his temples, and applied eau-de-cologne to his nostrils, and murmured, "Poor, poor Arthur! O, was I born only to afflict those I esteem?"

He saw her with the tears of pity in her eyes, and he caught her hand, and said, "You were always the soul of honor; keep faith with me, and I will cure you of that unhappy attachment."

"What! Do you hold me to my engagement after what I have told you?"

"Cruel Helen! you know I have not the power to hold you."

"I am not cruel; and you have the power. But, O, think! For your own sake, not mine."

"I have thought; and this attachment to a man you cannot marry is a mere misfortune, — yours as well as mine. Give me your esteem until your love comes back, and let our engagement continue."

"It was for you to decide," said Helen, coldly, "and you have decided. There is one condition I must ask you to submit to."

"I submit to it."

"What, before you hear it?"

"Helen, you don't know what a year of misery I have endured, ever since the report came of your death. My happiness is cruelly dashed now, but still it is great happiness by comparison. Make your conditions. You are my queen, as well as my love and my life."

Helen hesitated. It shocked her delicacy to lower the man she had consented to marry.

"O Helen," said Arthur, "anything but secrets between you and me. Go on as you have begun, and let me know the worst at once."

"Can you be very generous, Arthur? — generous to him who has caused you so much pain?"

"I 'll try," said Arthur, with a groan.

"I would not marry him, unless you gave me up: for I am your betrothed, and you are true to me. I *could* not marry him, even if I were not pledged to you; but it so happens, I can do him one great service without injustice to you; and this service I have vowed to do before I marry. I shall keep that vow, as I keep faith with you. He has been driven from society by a foul slander; that slander I am to sift and confute. It will be long and difficult; but I shall do it; and you could help me if you chose. But that I will not be so cruel as to ask."

Arthur bit his lip with jealous rage; but he was naturally cunning, and his cunning showed him there was at present but one road to Helen's heart. He quelled his torture as well as he could, and resolved to take that road. He reflected a moment, and then he said, —

"If you succeed in that, will you marry me next day?"

"I will, upon my honor."

"Then I will help you."

"Arthur, think what you say. Women have loved as unselfishly as this; but no man, that ever I heard of."

"No man ever did love a woman as I love you. Yes, I would rather help you, though with a sore heart, than hold aloof from you. What have we to do together?"

"Did I not tell you? — to clear his character of a foul stigma, and restore him to England, and to the world which he is so fitted to adorn."

"Yes, yes," said Arthur; "but who is it? Why do I ask, though? He must be a stranger to me."

"No stranger at all," said Helen; "but one who is almost as unjust to you as the world has been to him"; then, fixing her eyes full on him, she said, "Arthur, it is your old friend and tutor, Robert Penfold."

CHAPTER LV.

Arthur Wardlaw was thunderstruck; and, for some time, sat stupidly staring at her. And to this blank gaze succeeded a look of abject terror, which seemed to her strange, and beyond the occasion. But this was not all; for, after glaring at her with scared eyes and ashy cheeks a moment or two, he got up and literally staggered out of the room without a word.

He had been taken by surprise, and, for once, all his arts had failed him.

Helen, whose eyes had never left his face, and had followed his retiring figure, was frightened at the weight of the blow she had struck; and strange thoughts and conjectures filled her mind. Hitherto, she had felt sure Robert Penfold was under a delusion as to Arthur Wardlaw, and that his suspicions were as unjust as they certainly were vague. Yet, now, at the name of Robert Penfold, Arthur turned pale, and fled like a guilty thing. This was a coincidence that confirmed her good opinion of Robert Penfold, and gave her ugly thoughts of Arthur. Still, she was one very slow to condemn a friend, and too generous and candid to condemn on suspicion; so she resolved as far as possible to suspend her unfavorable judgment of Arthur, until she should have asked him why this great emotion, and heard his reply.

Moreover, she was no female detective, but a pure creature bent on clearing innocence. The object of her life was, not to discover the faults of Arthur Wardlaw, or any other person, but to clear Robert Penfold of a crime. Yet Arthur's strange behavior was a great shock to her; for here, at the very outset, he had somehow made her feel she must hope for no assistance from *him*. She sighed at this check, and asked herself to whom she should apply first for aid. Robert had told her to see his counsel, his solicitor, his father, and Mr. Undercliff, an expert, and to sift the whole matter.

Not knowing exactly where to begin, she thought she would, after all, wait a day or two to give Arthur time to recover himself, and decide calmly whether he would co-operate with her or not.

In this trying interval, she set up a diary, — for the first time in her life; for she was no egotist: and she noted down what we have just related, only in a very condensed form, and wrote at the margin: *Mysterious.*

Arthur never came near her for two whole days. This looked grave. On the third day she said to General Rolleston:—

"Papa, *you* will help me in the good cause, — will you not?"

He replied that he would do what he could, but feared that would be little.

"Will you take me down to Elm-trees, this morning?"

"With all my heart."

He took her down to Elm-trees. On the way she said: "Papa, you must let me get a word with Mr. Wardlaw alone."

"O, certainly. But, of course, you will not say a word to hurt his feelings."

"O papa!"

"Excuse me: but, when a person of your age is absorbed with one idea, she sometimes forgets that other people have any feelings at all."

Helen kissed him meekly, and said that was too true; and she would be upon her guard.

To General Rolleston's surprise, his daughter no sooner saw old Wardlaw than she went — or seemed to go — into high spirits, and was infinitely agreeable.

But at last, she got him all to herself, and then she turned suddenly grave, and said: —

"Mr. Wardlaw, I want to ask you a question. It is something about Robert Penfold."

Wardlaw shook his head. "That is a painful subject, my dear. But what do you wish to know about that unhappy young man?"

"Can you tell me the name of the counsel who defended him at the trial?"

HELEN ROLLESTON AND ARTHUR WARDLAW.—See page 108.

"No, indeed, I cannot."

"But perhaps you can tell me where I could learn that."

"His father is in our office still; no doubt he could tell you."

Now, for obvious reasons, Helen did not like to go to the office; so she asked faintly if there was nobody else who could tell her.

"I suppose the solicitor could."

"But I don't know who was the solicitor," said Helen, with a sigh.

"Hum!" said the merchant. "Try the bill-broker. I'll give you his address"; and he wrote it down for her.

Helen did not like to be too importunate, and she could not bear to let Wardlaw senior know she loved anybody better than his son; and yet some explanation was necessary: so she told him, as calmly as she could, that her father and herself were both well acquainted with Robert Penfold, and knew many things to his credit.

"I am glad to hear that," said Wardlaw; "and I can believe it. He bore an excellent character here, till, in an evil hour, a strong temptation came, and he fell."

"What! You think he was guilty?"

"I do. Arthur, I believe, has his doubts still. But he is naturally prejudiced in his friend's favor: and, besides, he was not at the trial; I was."

"Thank you, Mr. Wardlaw," said Helen, coldly; and, within five minutes, she was on her way home.

"Arthur prejudiced in Robert Penfold's favor!" That puzzled her extremely.

She put down the whole conversation while her memory was fresh. She added this comment: "What darkness I am groping in!"

Next day she went to the bill-broker, and told him Mr. Wardlaw senior had referred her to him for certain information. Wardlaw's name was evidently a passport. Mr. Adams said obsequiously, "Anything in the world I can do, madam."

"It is about Mr. Robert Penfold. I wish to know the name of the counsel he had at his trial."

"Robert Penfold! What, the forger?"

"He was accused of that crime," said Helen, turning red.

"Accused, madam! He was convicted. I ought to know; for it was my partner he tried the game on. But I was too sharp for him. I had him arrested before he had time to melt the notes; indicted him, and sent him across the herring pond, in spite of his parson's coat, the rascal!"

Helen drew back, as if a serpent had stung her.

"It was you who had him transported!" cried she, turning her eyes on him with horror.

"Of course it was me," said Mr. Adams, firing up; "and I did the country good service. I look upon a forger as worse than a murderer. What is the matter? You are ill."

The poor girl was half fainting at the sight of the man who had destroyed her Robert, and owned it.

"No, no," she cried, hastily; "let me get away — let me get away from here, — you cruel, cruel man!"

She tottered to the door, and got to her carriage, she scarcely knew how, without the information she went for.

The bill-broker was no fool; he saw now how the land lay; he followed her down the stairs, and tried to stammer excuses.

"Charing Cross Hotel," said she faintly, and hid her face against the cushion to avoid the sight of him.

When she got home, she cried bitterly at her feminine weakness and her incapacity; and she entered this pitiable failure in her journal with a severity our male readers will hardly, we think, be disposed to imitate; and she added, by way of comment: "Is this how I carry out my poor Robert's precept: Be obstinate as a man; be supple as a woman?"

That night she consulted her father on this difficulty, so slight to any but an inexperienced girl. He told her there must be a report of the trial in the newspapers, and the report would probably mention the counsel; she had better consult a file.

Then the thing was where to find a file. After one or two failures, the British Museum was suggested. She went thither, and could not get in to read without certain formalities. While these were being complied with, she was at a stand-still.

That same evening came a line from Arthur Wardlaw: —

"DEAREST HELEN, — I hear from Mr. Adams that you desire to know the name of the counsel who defended Robert Penfold. It was Mr. Tollemache. He has chambers in Lincoln's Inn.

"Ever devotedly yours,

"ARTHUR WARDLAW."

Helen was touched with this letter, and put it away indorsed with a few words of gratitude and esteem; and copied it into her diary, and remarked, "This is one more warning not to judge hastily. Arthur's agitation was probably only great emotion at the sudden mention of one whose innocence he believes, and whose sad fate distresses him." She wrote back and thanked him sweetly, and in terms that encouraged a visit. Next day she went to Mr. Tollemache. A seedy man followed her at a distance. Mr. Tollemache was not at his chambers, nor expected till four o'clock. He was in court. She left her card, and wrote on it in pencil that she would call at four.

She went at ten minutes after four. Mr. Tollemache declined through his clerk to see her if she was a client; he could only be approached by her solicitor. She felt inclined to go away and cry; but this time she remembered she was to be obstinate as a man and supple as a woman. She wrote on a card: "I am not a client of Mr. Tollemache, but a lady deeply interested in obtaining some information, which Mr. Tollemache can with perfect propriety give me. I trust to his courtesy as a gentleman not to refuse me a short interview."

"Admit the lady," said a sharp little voice.

She was ushered in, and found Mr. Tollemache standing before the fire.

"Now, madam, what can I do for you?"

"Some years ago you defended Mr. Robert Penfold; he was accused of forgery."

"O, was he? I think I remember something about it. A banker's clerk, — was n't he?"

"O no, sir. A clergyman."

"A clergyman? I remember it perfectly. He was convicted."

"Do you think he was guilty, sir?"

"There was a strong case against him."

"I wish to sift that case."

"Indeed. And you want to go through the papers."

"What papers, sir?"

"The brief for the defence."

"Yes," said Helen, boldly, "would you trust me with that, sir. O, if you knew how deeply I am interested!" The tears were in her lovely eyes.

"The brief has gone back to the solicitor, of course. I dare say he will let you read it upon a proper representation."

"Thank you, sir. Will you tell me who is the solicitor, and where he lives?"

"O, I can't remember who was the solicitor. That is the very first thing you ought to have ascertained. It was no use coming to me."

"Forgive me for troubling you, sir," said Helen, with a deep sigh.

"Not at all, madam; I am only sorry I cannot be of more service. But do let me advise you to employ your solicitor to make these preliminary inquiries. Happy to consult with him, and re-open the matter, should he discover any fresh evidence." He bowed her out, and sat down to a brief while she was yet in sight.

She turned away heart-sick. The advice she had received was good; but she shrank from baring her heart to her father's solicitor.

She sat disconsolate awhile, then ordered another cab, and drove to Wardlaw's office. It was late, and Arthur was gone home; so, indeed, was everybody, except one young subordinate, who was putting up the shutters. "Sir," said she, "can you tell me where old Mr. Penfold lives?"

"Somewhere in the subbubs, miss."

"Yes, sir; but where?"

"I think it is out Pimlico way."

"Could you not give me the street? I would beg you to accept a present if you could."

This sharpened the young gentleman's wits; he went in, and groped here and there till he found the address, and gave it her: No. 3, Fairfield Cottages, Primrose Lane, Pimlico. She gave him a sovereign, to his infinite surprise and delight, and told the cabman to drive to the hotel.

The next moment the man, who had followed her, was chatting familiarly with the subordinate, and helping him put up the shutters.

"I say, Dick," said the youngster, "Penfolds is up in the market; a duchess was here just now, and gave me a sov. to tell her where he lived. Wait a moment till I spit on it for luck."

The agent, however, did not wait to witness that interesting ceremony. He went back to his hansom round the corner, and drove at once to Arthur Wardlaw's house with the information.

Helen noted down Michael Penfold's address in her diary, and would have gone to him that evening, but she was to dine *tête-à-tête* with her father.

Next day she went down to 3 Fairfield Cottages at half past four. On the way her heart palpitated, for this was a very important interview. Here at least she might hope to find some clew, by following out which she would sooner or later establish Robert's innocence. But then came a fearful thought: "Why had not his father done this already, if it was possible to do it? His father must love him. His father must have heard his own story, and tested it in every way. Yet his father remained the servant of a firm, the senior partner of which had told her to her face Robert was guilty."

It was a strange and terrible enigma. Yet she clung to the belief that some new light would come to her from Michael Penfold. Then came bashful fears. "How should she account to Mr. Penfold for the interest she took in his son, she who was affianced to Mr. Penfold's employer." She arrived at 3 Fairfield Cottages with her cheeks burning, and repeating to herself: "Now is the time to be supple as a woman but obstinate as a man."

She sent the cabman in to inquire for Mr. Penfold; a sharp girl of about thirteen came out to her, and told her Mr. Penfold was not at home.

"Can you tell me when he will be at home?"

"No, miss. He have gone to Scotland. A telegraphum came from Wardlaws' last night, as he was to go to Scotland first thing this morning; and he went at six o'clock."

"O, dear! How unfortunate!"

"Who shall I say called, miss?"

"Thank you, I will write. What time did the telegram come?"

"Between five and six last evening, miss."

She returned to the hotel. Fate seemed to be against her. Baffled at the very threshold! At the hotel she found Arthur Wardlaw's card, and a beautiful bouquet.

She sat down directly, and wrote to him affectionately, and asked him in the postscript if he could send her a report of the trial. She received a reply directly, that he had inquired in the office, for one of the clerks had reports of it; but this clerk was unfortunately out, and had locked up his desk.

Helen sighed. Her feet seemed to be clogged at every step in this inquiry.

Next morning however, a large envelope came for her, and a Mr. Hand wrote to her thus:—

"MADAM,

"Having been requested by Mr. Arthur Wardlaw to send you my extracts of a trial, the Queen *v.* Penfold, I herewith forward the same, and would feel obliged by your returning them at your convenience.

"Your obedient servant,
"JAMES HAND."

Helen took the enclosed extracts to her bedroom, and there read them both over many times.

In both these reports the case for the Crown was neat, clear, cogent, straightforward, and supported by evidence. The defence was chiefly argument of counsel to prove the improbability of a clergyman and a man of good character passing a forged note. One of the reports stated that Mr. Arthur Wardlaw, a son of the principal witness, had taken the accusation so much to heart that he was now dangerously ill at Oxford. The other report did not contain this, but, on the other hand, it stated that the prisoner, after conviction, had endeavored to lay the blame on Mr. Arthur Wardlaw, but that the judge had stopped him, and said he could only aggravate his offence by endeavoring to cast a slur upon the Wardlaws, who had both shown a manifest desire to shield him, but were powerless for want of evidence.

In both reports the summing up of the judge was moderate in expression, but leaned against the prisoner on every point, and corrected the sophistical reasoning of his counsel very sensibly. Both reports said an expert was called for the prisoner, whose ingenuity made the court smile, but did not counterbalance the evidence. Helen sat cold as ice with the extracts in her hand.

Not that her sublime faith was shaken, but that poor Robert appeared to have been so calmly and fairly dealt with by everybody. Even Mr. Hennessy, the counsel for the Crown, had opened the case with humane regret, and confined himself to facts, and said nobody would be more pleased than he would, if this evidence could be contradicted, or explained in a manner consistent with the prisoner's innocence.

What a stone she had undertaken to roll — up what a hill!

What was to be her next step? Go to the Museum, which was now open to her, and read more reports? She shrank from that.

"The newspapers are all against him," said she; "and I don't want to be told he is guilty, when I know he is innocent."

She now re-examined the extracts with a view to names, and found the only names mentioned were those of the counsel. The expert's name was not given in either. However, she knew that from Robert. She resolved to speak to Mr. Hennessy first, and try and get at the defendant's solicitor through him.

She found him out by the Law Directory, and called at a few minutes past four.

Hennessy was almost the opposite to Tollemache. He was about the size of a gentleman's wardrobe; and, like most enormous men, good-natured. He received her, saw with his practised eye that she was no common person, and, after a slight hesitation on professional grounds, heard her request. He sent for his note-book, found the case in one moment, remastered it in another, and told her the solicitor for the Crown in that case was Freshfield.

"Now," said he, "you want to know who was the defendant's solicitor? Jenkins, a stamped envelope. Write your name and address on that."

While she was doing it, he scratched a line to Mr. Freshfield, asking him to send the required information to the enclosed address.

She thanked Mr. Hennessy with the tears in her eyes.

"I dare not ask you whether you think him guilty," she said.

Hennessy shook his head with an air of good-natured rebuke.

"You must not cross-examine counsel," said he: "but, if it will be any comfort to you, I'll say this much, there was just a shadow of doubt, and Tollemache certainly let a chance slip. If I had defended your friend, I would have insisted on a postponement of the trial until this Arthur Wardlaw" (looking at his note-book) "could be examined, either in court or otherwise, if he was really dying. Is he dead, do you know?"

"No."

"I thought not. Sick witnesses are often at death's door; but I never knew one pass the threshold. Ha! ha! The trial ought to have been postponed till he got well. If a judge refused me a postponement in such a case, I would make him so odious to the jury, that the prisoner would get a verdict in spite of his teeth."

"Then, you think he was badly defended?"

"No; that is saying a great deal more than I would justify. But there are counsel who trust too much to their powers of reasoning, and underrate a chink in the evidence *pro* or *con*. Practice, and a few back-falls, cure them of that."

Mr. Hennessy uttered this general observation with a certain change of tone, which showed he thought he had said as much or more than his visitor had any right to expect from him; and she therefore left him, repeating her thanks. She went home, pondering on every word he had said, and entered it all in her journal, with the remark, "How strange! the first doubt of Robert's guilt comes to me from the lawyer who caused him to be found guilty. He calls it the shadow of a doubt."

That very evening, Mr. Freshfield had the courtesy to send her by messenger the name and address of the solicitor who had defended Robert Penfold, Lovejoy and James, Lincoln's Inn Fields. She called on them, and sent in her card. She was kept waiting a long time in the outer office, and felt ashamed, and sick at heart, seated among young clerks. At last she was admitted, and told Mr. Lovejoy she and her father, General Rolleston, were much interested in a late client of his, Mr. Robert Penfold; and would he be kind enough to let her see the brief for the defence?

"Are you a relation of the Penfolds, madam?"

"No, sir," said Helen, blushing.

"Humph!" said Lovejoy.

He touched a hand-bell. A clerk appeared.

"Ask Mr. Upton to come to me."

Mr. Upton, the managing clerk, came in due course, and Mr. Lovejoy asked him: —

"Who instructed us in the Queen *v.* Penfold?"

"It was Mr. Michael Penfold, sir."

Mr. Lovejoy then told Helen that she must just get a line from Mr. Michael Penfold, and then the papers should be submitted to her.

"Yes; but, sir," said Helen, "Mr. Penfold is in Scotland."

"Well, but you can write to him."

"No; I don't know in what part of Scotland he is."

"Then you are not very intimate with him?"

"No, sir; my acquaintance is with Mr. Robert Penfold."

"Have you a line from *him*?"

"I have no *written* authority from him; but will you not take my word that I act by his desire?"

"My dear madam," said the lawyer, "we go by rule. There are certain forms to be observed in these things. I am sure your own good sense will tell you it would be cruel and improper of me to submit those papers without an order from Robert or Michael Penfold. Pray consider this as a delay, not a refusal."

"Yes, sir," said Helen; "but I meet with nothing but delays, and my heart is breaking under them."

The solicitor looked sorry, but would not act irregularly. She went home sighing, and condemned to wait the return of Michael Penfold.

The cab-door was opened for her by a seedy man she fancied she had seen before.

Baffled thus, and crippled in every movement she made, however slight, in favor of Robert Penfold, she was seduced on the other hand into all the innocent pleasures of the town. Her adventure had transpired somehow or other, and all General Rolleston's acquaintances hunted him up; and both father and daughter were courted by people of ton as lions. A shipwrecked beauty is not offered to society every day. Even her own sex raved about her, and about the chain of beautiful pearls she had picked up somehow on her desolate island. She always wore them; they linked her to that sacred purpose she seemed to be forgetting. Her father drew her with him into the vortex, hiding from her that he embarked in it principally for her sake, and she went down the current with him out of filial duty. Thus unfathomable difficulties thrust her back from her up-hill task: and the world, with soft but powerful hand, drew her away to it. Arthur brought her a choice bouquet, or sent her a choice bouquet, every evening, but otherwise did not intrude much upon her; and though she was sure he would assist her, if she asked him, gratitude and delicacy forbade her to call him again to her assistance. She preferred to await the return of Michael Penfold. She had written to him at the office to tell him she had news of his son, and begged him to give her instant notice of his return from Scotland.

Day after day passed, and he did not write to her. She began to chafe, and then to pine. Her father saw, and came to a conclusion that her marriage with Arthur ought to be hastened. He resolved to act quietly but firmly towards that end.

CHAPTER LVI.

Up to this time Helen's sex, and its attributes, had been a great disadvantage to her. She had been stopped on the very threshold of her inquiry by petty difficulties, which a man would have soon surmounted. But one fine day the scale gave a little turn, and she made a little discovery, thanks to her sex. Women, whether it is that they are born to be followed, or are accustomed to be followed, seem to have eyes in the backs of their heads, and instinct to divine when somebody is after them. This inexperienced girl, who had missed seeing many things our readers have seen, observed in merely passing her window a seedy man in the courtyard of the hotel. Would you believe it, she instantly recognized the man who had opened her cab-door for her in Lincoln's Inn Fields. Quick as lightning it passed through her mind, "Why do I see the same figure in Lincoln's Inn Fields, and at Charing Cross." At various intervals she passed the window; and twice she saw the man again. She pondered, and determined to try a little experiment. Robert Penfold, it may be remembered, had mentioned an expert as one of the persons she was to see. She had looked for his name in the Directory; but experts were not down in the book. Another fatality! But at last she had found Undercliff, a lithographer, and she fancied that must be the same person. She did not hope to learn much from him; the newspapers said his evidence had caused a smile. She had a distinct object in visiting him, the nature of which will appear. She ordered a cab, and dressed herself. She came down, and entered the cab; but, instead of telling the man where to drive, she gave him a slip of paper, containing the address of the lithographer. "Drive there," said she, a little mysteriously. The cabman winked, suspecting an intrigue, and went off to the place. There she learned Mr. Undercliff had moved to Frith Street, Soho, number not known. She told the cabman to drive slowly up and down the street, but could not find the name. At last she observed some lithographs in a window. She let the cabman go all down the street, then stopped him, and paid him off. She had no sooner done this than she walked very briskly back, and entered the little shop, and inquired for Mr. Undercliff. He was out, and not expected back for an hour. "I will wait," said Helen; and she sat down with her head upon her white hand. A seedy man passed the window rapidly with a busy air; and, if his eye shot a glance into the shop, it was so slight and careless nobody could suspect he was a spy, and had done his work effectually as he flashed by. In that moment the young lady, through the chink of her fingers, which she had opened for that purpose, not only recognized the man, but noticed his face, his hat, his waistcoat, his dirty linen, and the pin in his neck-tie.

"Ah!" said she, and flushed to the brow.

She lifted up her head and became conscious of a formidable old woman, who was standing behind the counter at a side door, eying her with the severest scrutiny. This old woman was tall and thin, and had a fine face, the lower part of which was feminine enough; but the forehead and brows were alarming. Though her hair was silvery, the brows were black and shaggy, and the forehead was divided by a vertical furrow into two temples. Under those shaggy eyebrows shone dark-gray eyes, that passed for black with most people; and those eyes were fixed on Helen, reading her. Helen's light-hazel eyes returned their gaze. She blushed, and, still looking, said, "Pray, madam, can I see Mr. Undercliff?"

"My son is out for the day, miss," said the old lady, civilly.

"O, dear! how unfortunate I am!" said Helen with a sigh.

"He comes back to-night. You can see him to-morrow at ten o'clock. A question of handwriting?"

"Not exactly," said Helen; "but he was witness in favor of a person, I know was innocent."

"But he was found guilty," said the other with cool keenness.

"Yes, madam: and he has no friend to clear him but me: a poor weak girl, baffled and defeated which-ever way I turn." She began to cry.

The old woman looked at her crying with that steady composure which marks her sex on these occasions; and, when she was better, said quietly "You are not so weak as you think." She added, after a while, "If you wish to retain my son, you had better leave a fee."

"With pleasure, madam. What is the fee?"

"One guinea. Of course, there is a separate charge for any work he may do for you."

"That is but reasonable, madam." And with this she paid the fee, and rose to go.

"Shall I send any one home with you?"

"No, thank you," said Helen. "Why?"

"Because you are followed, and because you are not used to be followed."

"Why, how did you find that out?"

"By your face, when a man passed the window,—a shabby-genteel fellow; he was employed by some gentleman, no doubt. Such faces as yours will be followed in London. If you feel uneasy, miss, I will put on my bonnet, and see you home."

Helen was surprised at this act of substantial civility from the Gorgon. "O, thank you, Mrs. Undercliff," said she. "No, I am not the least afraid. Let them follow me, I am doing nothing that I am ashamed of. Indeed, I am glad I am thought worth the trouble of following. It shows me I am not so thoroughly contemptible. Good-by, and many thanks. Ten o'clock to-morrow."

And she walked home without looking once behind her till the Hotel was in sight; then she stopped at a shop-window, and in a moment her swift eye embraced the whole landscape. But the shabby-genteel man was nowhere in sight

---

CHAPTER LVII.

When Joseph Wylie disappeared from the scene, Nancy Rouse made a discovery, which very often follows the dismissal of a suitor,—that she was considerably more attached to him than she had thought. The house became dull, the subordinate washerwomen languid: their taciturnity irritated and depressed Nancy by turns.

In the midst of this, Michael Penfold discovered that Helen had come back safe. He came into her parlor, beaming with satisfaction, and told her of the good news. It gave her immense delight at first. But, when she had got used to her joy on that score, she began to think she had used Joe Wylie very ill. Now that Helen was saved, she could no longer realize that Wylie was so very much to blame.

She even persuaded herself that his disappearance was the act of a justly offended man: and, as he belonged to a class, of whose good sense she had a poor opinion, she was tormented with fears that he would do some desperate act, — drown himself, or go to sea; or, worst of all, marry some trollop. She became very anxious and unhappy. Before this misfortune she used to go about singing the first verse of a song, and whistling the next, like any ploughboy; an eccentric performance, but it made the house gay. Now both song and whistle were suspended! and, instead, it was all hard work and hard crying; turn about.

She attached herself to Michael Penfold because he had known trouble, and was sympathetic: and these two opened their hearts to one another, and formed a friendship that was very honest and touching.

The scene of their conversation and mutual consolation was Nancy's parlor; a little mite of a room she had partitioned off from her business. "For," said she, "a lady I'll be, — after my work is done, — if it is only in a cupboard." The room had a remarkably large fireplace, which had originally warmed the whole floor, but now was used as a ventilator only. The gas would have been stifling without it. As for lighting a fire in it, that was out of the question.

On a certain evening, soon after Mr. Penfold's return from Scotland, the pair sat over their tea, and the conversation fell on the missing sweetheart. Michael had been thinking it over, and was full of encouragement. He said: —

"Miss Rouse, something tells me that, if poor Mr. Wylie could only know your heart, he would turn up again directly. What we ought to do is to send somebody to look for him in all the sailors' haunts: some sharp fellow, — dear me, what a knocking they keep up next door!"

"O, that is always the way when one wants a quiet chat. Drat the woman! I'll have her indicted."

"No, you won't, Miss Rouse: she is a poor soul, and has got no business except letting lodgings; she is not like you. But I do hope she will be so kind as not to come quite through the wall."

"Dear heart!" said Nancy, "go on, and never mind her noise, which it is worse than a horgangrinder."

"Well, then, if you can't find him that way, I say, — Advertise."

"Me!" cried Nancy, turning very red. "Do I look like a woman as would advertise for a man?"

"No, ma'am: quite the reverse. But what I mean is, you might put in something not too plain. For instance: If J. W. will return to N. R., all will be forgotten and forgiven."

"He'd have the upper hand of me for life," said Nancy. "No, no; I won't advertise for the fool. What right had he to run off at the first word? He ought to know my bark is worse than my bite by this time. You can, though."

"Me bite, ma'am?" said the old gentleman.

"Bite? no: advertise, since you 're so fond of it. Come, you sit down and write one; and I'll pay for it, for that matter."

Michael sat down, and drew up the following: "If Mr. Joseph Wylie will call on Michael Penfold, at No. 3, E. C., he will hear of something to his advantage."

"To his advantage?" said Nancy, doubtfully. "Why not tell him the truth?"

"Why, that is the truth, ma'am. Is n't to his advantage to be reconciled to an honest, virtuous, painstaking lady, that honors him with her affection — and me with her friendship? Besides, it is the common form; and there is nothing like sticking to form."

"Mr. Penfold," said Nancy, "any one can see you was born a gentleman; and I am a deal prouder to have you and your washing, than I should him as pays you your wages: pale eyes, — pale hair, — pale eyebrows, — I would n't trust him to mangle a duster."

"O Miss Rouse! Pray, don't disparage my good master to me."

"I can't help it, sir: thought is free, especially in this here compartment. Better speak one's mind than die o' the sulks. So shut your ear when my music jars. But one every other day is enough: if he won't come back for that, why he must go, and I must look out for another; there 's as good fish in the sea as ever came out of it. Still, I'll not deny I have a great respect for poor Joe. O Mr. Penfold, what shall I do! Oh, oh, oh!"

"There, there," said Michael, "I'll put this into the *Times* every day."

"You are a good soul, Mr. Penfold. Oh — oh, oh!"

When he had finished the advertisement in a clerkly hand, and she had finished her cry, she felt comparatively comfortable, and favored Mr. Penfold with some reflections.

"Dear heart, Mr. Penfold, how you and I do take to one another, to be sure. But so we ought: for we are honest folk, the pair, and has had a hard time. Don't it never strike you rather curious that two thousand pounds was at the bottom of both our troubles, yourn and mine? I might have married Joe and been a happy woman with him; but the devil puts in my head — There you go again hammering! Life ain't worth having next door to that lodging-house. Drat the woman, if she must peck, why don't she go in the churchyard and peck her own grave; which we shall never be quiet till she *is* there: and these here gimcrack houses, they won't stand no more pecking at than a soap-sud. — Ay, that 's what hurts me, Mr. Penfold: the Lord had given him and me health and strength and honesty; our betters had wed for love and wrought for money, as the saying is; but I must go again Nature, that cried 'Come couple'; and must bargain for two thousand pounds. So now I 've lost the man, and not got the money, nor never shall: and, if I had, I'd burn — Ah — ah — ah — ah — ah!"

This tirade ended in stifled screams of terror, caused by the sudden appearance of a human hand, in a place and in a manner well adapted to shake the stoutest laundress's nerves.

This hand came through the brickwork of the chimney-place, and there remained a moment or two: then slowly retired, and, as it retired, something was heard to fall upon the shavings and tinsel of the fireplace.

Nancy, by a feminine impulse, put her hands before her face, to hide this supernatural hand; and, when she found courage to withdraw them, and glare at the place, there was no aperture whatever in the brick-work; and, consequently, the hand appeared to have traversed the solid material, both coming and going.

"O Mr. Penfolds," cried Nancy; "I'm a sinful woman. This comes of talking of the devil arter sunset"; and she sat trembling so that the very floor shook.

Mr. Penfold's nerves were not strong. He and Nancy both huddled together for mutual protection, and their faces had not a vestige of color left in them.

However, after a period of general paralysis, Penfold whispered: —

"I heard it drop something on the shavings."

"Then we shall be all in a blaze o' brimstone," shrieked Nancy, wringing her hands.

And they waited to see.

Then, as no conflagration took place, Mr. Penfold got up, and said he must go and see what it was the hand had dropped.

Nancy, in whom curiosity was beginning to battle with terror, let him go to the fireplace without a word of objection, and then cried out, —

"Don't go anigh it, sir; it will do you a mischief; don't touch it whatever. *Take the tongs.*"

He took the tongs, and presently flung into the middle of the room a small oilskin packet. This, as it lay on the ground, they both eyed like two deer glowering at a piece of red cloth, and ready to leap back over the moon if it should show signs of biting. But oilskin is not preternatural, nor has tradition connected it, however remotely, with the Enemy of man.

Consequently, a great revulsion took place in Nancy, and she passed from fear to indignation at having been frightened so.

She ran to the fireplace, and, putting her head up the chimney, screamed, "Heave your dirt where you heave your love, ye Brazen!"

While she was objurgating her neighbor, whom, with feminine justice, she held responsible for every act done in her house, Penfold undid the packet, and Nancy returned to her seat, with her mind more at ease, to examine the contents.

"Bank-notes!" cried Penfold.

"Ay," said Nancy, incredulously, "they do look like bank-notes, and feel like 'em; but they ain't wrote like them. Bank-notes ain't wrote black like that in the left-hand corner."

Penfold explained.

"Ten-pound notes are not, nor fives; but large notes are. These are all fifties."

"Fifty whats?"

"Fifty pounds."

"What, each of them bits of paper worth fifty pounds?"

"Yes. Let us count them; 1, 2, 3, 4, 5, 6, 7, 8, 9, 10, 11, 12, 13, 14, 15, 16, 17, 18, — O Lord! — 20. Why, it is two thousand pounds — just two thousand pounds. It is the very sum that ruined me; it did not belong to me, and it's being in the house ruined my poor Robert. And this does not belong to you. Lock all the doors, bar all the windows, and burn them before the police come."

"Wait a bit," said Nancy, "wait a bit."

They sat on each side of the notes; Penfold agitated and terrified, Nancy confounded and perplexed.

CHAPTER LVIII.

Punctually at ten o'clock Helen returned to Frith Street, and found Mr. Undercliff behind a sort of counter, employed in tracing; a workman was seated at some little distance from him; both bent on their work.

"Mr. Undercliff?" said Helen.

He rose, and turned towards her politely, — a pale, fair man, with a keen gray eye and a pleasant voice and manner: "I am Edward Undercliff. You come by appointment?"

"Yes, sir."

"A question of handwriting?"

"Not entirely, sir. Do you remember giving witness in favor of a young clergyman, Mr. Robert Penfold, who was accused of forgery?"

"I remember the circumstance, but not the details."

"O, dear! that is unfortunate," said Helen, with a deep sigh; she often had to sigh now.

"Why, you see," said the Expert, "I am called on such a multitude of trials. However, I take notes of the principal ones. What year was it in?"

"In 1864."

Mr. Undercliff went to a set of drawers arranged chronologically, and found his notes directly. "It was a forged bill, madam, indorsed and presented by Penfold. I was called to prove that the bill was not in the handwriting of Penfold. Here is my fac-simile of the Robert Penfold indorsed upon the bill by the prisoner." He handed it her, and she examined it with interest. "And here are fac-similes of genuine writing by John Wardlaw; and here is a copy of the forged note."

He laid it on the table before her. She started, and eyed it with horror. It was a long time before she could speak. At length she said, "And that wicked piece of paper destroyed Robert Penfold."

"Not that piece of paper, but the original; this is a fac-simile, so far as the writing is concerned. It was not necessary in this case to imitate paper and color. Stay, here is a sheet on which I have lithographed the three styles: that will enable you to follow my comparison. But perhaps that would not interest you." Helen had the tact to say it would. Thus encouraged, the Expert showed her that Robert Penfold's writing had nothing in common with the forged note. He added, "I also detected in the forged note habits which were entirely absent from the true writing of John Wardlaw. You will understand there were plenty of undoubted specimens in Court to go by."

"Then, O sir," said Helen, "Robert Penfold was not guilty."

"Certainly not of writing the forged note. I swore that, and I'll swear it again. But when it came to questions whether he had passed the note, and whether he knew it was forged, that was quite out of my province."

"I can understand that," said Helen; "but you heard the trial; you are very intelligent, sir, you must have formed some opinion as to whether he was guilty or not."

The Expert shook his head. "Madam," said he, "mine is a profound and difficult art, which aims at certainties. Very early in my career I found that to master that art I must be single-minded, and not allow my ear to influence my eye. By purposely avoiding all reasoning from external circumstances, I have distanced my competitors in expertise; but I sometimes think I have rather weakened my powers of conjecture through disuse. Now, if my mother had been at the trial, she would give you an opinion of some value on the outside facts. But that is not my line. If you feel sure he was innocent, and want *me* to aid you, you must get hold of the handwriting of every person who was likely to know old Wardlaw's handwriting, and so might have imitated it; all the clerks in his office, to begin with. Nail the forger; that is your only chance."

"What, sir!" said Helen, with surprise, "if you saw the true handwriting of the person who wrote that forged note, should you recognize it?"

"Why not? It is difficult; but I have done it hundreds of times."

"Oh! Is forgery so common?"

"No: but I am in all the cases; and, besides, I do a great deal in a business that requires the same kind of expertise, — anonymous letters. I detect assassins of that kind by the score. A gentleman or lady, down in the country, gets a poisoned arrow by the post, or perhaps a shower of them. They are always in disguised handwriting; those who receive them send them up to me, with writings of all the people they suspect. The disguise is generally more or less superficial; five or six unconscious habits remain below it, and often these undisguised habits are the true characteristics of the writer. And I'll tell you something curious, madam; it is quite common for all the suspected people to be innocent; and then I write back, 'Send me the handwriting of the people you suspect *the least*'; and amongst them I often find the assassin."

"O Mr. Undercliff," said Helen, "you make my heart sick."

"O, it is a vile world, for that matter," said the Expert; "and the country no better than the town, for all it looks so sweet with its green fields and purling rills. There they sow anonymous letters like barley: the very girls wrote anonymous letters that make my hair stand on end. Yes, it is a vile world."

"Don't you believe him, miss," said Mrs. Undercliff, appearing suddenly. Then, turning to her son, "How can you measure the world? You live in a little one of your own, — a world of forgers and anonymous writers; you see so many of these, you fancy they are common as dirt; but they are only common to you because they all come your way."

"O, that is it, is it?" said the Expert, doubtfully.

"Yes, that is it, Ned," said the old lady, quietly; then after a pause she said, "I want you to do your very best for this young lady."

"I always do," said the Artist. "But how can I judge without materials? And she brings me none."

Mrs. Undercliff turned to Helen, and said: "Have you brought him nothing at all, no handwritings — in your bag?"

Then Helen sighed again. "I have no handwriting except Mr. Penfold's; but I have two printed reports of the trial."

"Printed reports," said the Expert, "they are no use to me. Ah! here is an outline I took of the prisoner during the trial. You can read faces: tell the lady whether he was guilty or not," and he handed the profile to his mother with an ironical look; not that he doubted her proficiency in the rival art of reading faces, but that he doubted the existence of the art.

Mrs. Undercliff took the profile, and, coloring slightly, said to Miss Rolleston, "It is living faces I profess to read: there I can see the movement of the eyes and other things that my son here has not studied." Then she scrutinized the profile. "It is a very handsome face," said she.

The Expert chuckled. "There's a woman's judgment," said he. "Handsome! the fellow I got transported for life down at Exeter was an Adonis, and forged wills, bonds, and powers of attorney by the dozen."

"There's something noble about this face," said Mrs. Undercliff, ignoring the interruption, — "and yet something simple. I think him more likely to be a cat's-paw than a felon." Having delivered this with a certain modest dignity, she laid the profile on the counter before Helen.

The Expert had a wonderful eye and hand; it was a good thing for society he had elected to be gamekeeper instead of poacher, detector of forgery instead of forger. No photograph was ever truer than this outline. Helen started, and bowed her head over the sketch to conceal the strong and various emotions that swelled at sight of the portrait of her martyr. In vain; if the eyes were hidden the tender bosom heaved, the graceful body quivered, and the tears fell fast upon the counter.

Mrs. Undercliff was womanly enough, though she looked like the late Lord Thurlow in petticoats; and she instantly aided the girl to hide her beating heart from the man, though that man was her son. She distracted his attention. "Give me all your notes, Ned," said she, "and let me see whether I can make something of them; but first perhaps Miss Rolleston will empty her bag on the counter. Go back to your work a moment, for I know you have enough to do."

The Expert was secretly glad to be released from a case in which there were no materials; and so Helen escaped unobserved except by one of her own sex. She saw directly what Mrs. Undercliff had done for her, and lifted her sweet eyes, thick with tears, to thank her. Mrs. Undercliff smiled maternally, and next these two ladies did a stroke of business in the twinkling of an eye, and without a word spoken; whereof anon. Helen being once more composed, Mrs. Undercliff took up the prayer-book, and asked her with some curiosity what could be in that.

"O," said Helen, "only some writing of Mr. Penfold. Mr. Undercliff does not want to see that; he is already sure Robert Penfold never wrote that wicked thing."

"Yes, but I should like to see some more of his handwriting, for all that," said the Expert, looking suddenly up.

"But it is only in pencil."

"Never mind; you need not fear I shall alter my opinion."

Helen colored high. "You are right; and I should disgrace my good cause by withholding anything from your inspection. There, sir." And she opened the prayer-book, and laid Cooper's dying words before the Expert; he glanced over them with an eye like a bird, and compared them with his notes.

"Yes," said he, "that is Robert Penfold's writing; and I say again that hand never wrote the forged note."

"Let me see that," said Mrs. Undercliff.

"O, yes," said Helen, rather irresolutely; "but you look into the things as well as the writing, and I promised papa—"

"Can't you trust me?" said Mrs. Undercliff, turning suddenly cold and a little suspicious.

"O, yes, madam; and indeed I have nothing to reproach myself with. But my papa is anxious. However, I am sure you are my friend; and all I ask is that you will never mention to a soul what you read there."

"I promise that," said the elder lady, and instantly bent her black brows upon the writing. And, as she did so, Helen observed her countenance rise, as a face is very apt to do when its owner enters on congenial work.

"You would have made a great mistake to keep this from *me*," said she, gravely. Then she pondered profoundly; then she turned to her son and said, "Why, Edward, this is the very young lady who was wrecked in the Pacific Ocean, and cast on a desolate island. We have all read about you in the papers, miss; and I felt for you, for one, but, of course, not as I do now I have seen you. You must let me go into this with you."

"Ah, if you would!" said Helen. "O madam, I have gone through tortures already for want of somebody of my own sex to keep me in countenance! O, if you could have seen how I have been received, with what cold looks, and sometimes with impertinent stares, before I could even penetrate into the region of those cold looks and petty formalities! Any miserable straw was excuse enough to stop me on my errand of justice and mercy and gratitude."

"Gratitude?"

"O, yes, madam. The papers have only told you that I was shipwrecked and cast away. They don't tell you that Robert Penfold warned me the ship was to be destroyed, and I disbelieved and affronted him in return, and he never reproached me, not even by a look. And we were in a boat with the sailors, all starved—not hungry: starved—and mad with thirst, and yet in his own agony he hid something for me to eat. All his thought, all his fear, was for me. Such things are not done in those great extremities of the poor, vulgar, suffering body, except by angels, in whom the soul rises above the flesh. And he is such an angel. I have had a knife lifted over me to kill me, madam,—yes: and again it was he who saved me. I owe my life to him on the island over and over again; and in return I have promised to give him back his honor, that he values far more than life, as all such noble spirits do. Ah, my poor martyr, how feebly I plead your cause! O, help me! pray, pray, help me! All is so dark, and I so weak, so weak." Again the loving eyes streamed; and this time not an eye was dry in the little shop.

The Expert flung down his tracing with something between a groan and a curse. "Who can do that drudgery," he cried, "whilst the poor young lady— Mother, you take it in hand; find me some material, though it is no bigger than a fly's foot, give me but a clew no thicker than a spider's web, and I'll follow it through the whole labyrinth. But you see I'm impotent; there's no basis for me. It is a case for you. It wants a shrewd sagacious body that can read facts and faces; and—I won't jest any more, Miss Rolleston, for you are deeply in earnest.—Well, then, she really is a woman with a wonderful insight into facts and faces. She has got a way of reading them as I read handwriting; and she must have taken a great fancy to you, for as a rule she never does us the honor to meddle."

"Have you taken a fancy to me, madam?" said Helen, modestly and tenderly, yet half archly.

"That I have," said the other. "Those eyes of yours went straight into my heart last night, or I should not be here this morning. That is partly owing to my own eyes being so dark and yours the loveliest hazel. It is twenty years since eyes like yours have gazed into mine. Diamonds are not half so rare, nor a tenth part so lovely, to my fancy." She turned her head away, melted probably by some tender reminiscence. It was only for a moment. She turned round again, and said quietly, "Yes, Ned, I should like to try what I can do; I think you said these are reports of his trial. I'll begin by reading them."

She read them both very slowly and carefully, and her face grew like a judge's, and Helen watched each shade of expression with deep anxiety.

That powerful countenance showed alacrity and hope at first: then doubt, and difficulty, and at last dejection. Helen's heart turned cold, and for the first time she began to despair. For now a shrewd person, with a plain prejudice in her favor and Robert's, was staggered by the simple facts of the trial.

CHAPTER LIX.

Mrs. Undercliff, having read the reports, avoided Helen's eye (another bad sign). She turned to Mr. Undercliff, and, probably because the perusal of the reports had disappointed her, said, almost angrily, "Edward, what did you say to make them laugh at that trial? Both these papers say that 'an Expert was called, whose ingenuity made the court smile, but did not counterbalance the evidence.'"

"Why, that is a falsehood on the face of it," said the Expert, turning red. "I was called simply and solely to prove Penfold did not write the forged note; I proved it to the judge's satisfaction, and he directed the prisoner to be acquitted on that count. Miss Rolleston, the lawyers often, do sneer at experts; but then four experts out of five are rank impostors,—a set of theorists, who go by arbitrary rules framed in the closet, and not by large and laborious comparison with indisputable documents. These charlatans are not aware that five thousand cramped and tremulous, but genuine, signatures are written every day by honest men, and so they denounce every cramped or tremulous writing as a forgery. The varieties in a man's writing, caused by his writing with his glove on or off, with a quill or a bad steel pen, drunk or sober, calm or agitated, in full daylight or dusk, etc. etc., all this is a dead letter to them, and they have a bias towards suspicion of forgery; and a banker's clerk, with his mere general impression, is better evidence than they are. But I am an artist of a very different stamp. I never reason *à priori*. I compare; and I have no bias. I never will have. The judges know this, and the pains and labor I take to be right, and they treat me with courtesy. At Penfold's trial the matter was easy; I showed the court he had not written the note, and my evidence crushed the indictment so far. How could they have laughed at my testimony? Why, they acted upon it. Those reports are not worth a straw. What journals were they cut out of?"

"I don't know," said Helen.

"Is there nothing on the upper margin to show?"

"No."

"What, not on either of them?"

"No."

"Show them me, please. This is a respectable paper too: the Daily News."

"O Mr. Undercliff, how can you know that?"

"I don't *know* it; but I think so, because the type and paper are like that journal; the conductors are fond of clean type; so am I. Why, here is another misstatement; the judge never said he aggravated his offence by trying to cast a slur upon the Wardlaws. I'll swear the judge never said a syllable of the kind. What he said was 'You can speak in arrest of judgment on grounds of law, but you must not impugn the verdict with facts.' That was the only time he spoke to the prisoner at all. These reports are not worth a button."

Helen lifted up her hands and eyes in despair. "Where shall I find the truth?" said she. "The world is a quicksand."

"My dear young lady," said Mrs. Undercliff, "don't you be discouraged: there must be a correct report in some paper or other."

"I am not so sure of that," said Undercliff. "I believe the reporters trundle off to the nearest public-house together, and light their pipes with their notes, and settle something or other by memory. Indeed, they have reached a pitch of inaccuracy that could not be attained without co-operation. Independent liars contradict each other: but these chaps follow one another in falsehood, like geese toddling after one another across a common."

"Come, come," said Mrs. Undercliff, "if you can't help us, don't hurt us. We don't want a man to talk yellow jaundice to us. Miss Rolleston must employ somebody to read all the other papers and compare the reports with these."

"I'll employ nobody but myself," said Helen. "I'll go to the British Museum directly.

"The Museum!" cried Mr. Undercliff, looking up with surprise. "Why, they will be half an hour groping for a copy of the *Times*. No, no; go to Peele's Coffee House." He directed her where to find that place; and she was so eager to do something for Robert, however small, that she took up her bag directly, and put up the prayer-book, and was going to ask for her extracts, when she observed Mr. Undercliff was scrutinizing them with great interest, so she thought she would leave them with him; but, on looking more closely, she found that he was examining, not the reports, but the advertisements and miscellanea on the reverse side.

She waited out of politeness, but she colored and bit her lip. She could not help feeling hurt and indignant. "Any trash is more interesting to people than poor Robert's case," she thought. And at last she said bitterly,

"Those *advertisements* seem to interest you, sir; shall I leave *them* with you?"

"If you please," said the Expert, over whose head, bent in dogged scrutiny, this small thunderbolt of feminine wrath passed unconscious.

Helen drove away to Peele's Coffee House.

Mrs. Undercliff pondered over the facts that had been elicited in this conversation; the Expert remained absorbed in the advertisements at the back of Helen's reports.

When he had examined every one of them minutely, he held the entire extracts up to the light, and looked through them; then he stuck a double magnifier in his eye, and looked through them with that. Then he took two pieces of card, wrote on them *Re* Penfold, and looked about for his other materials, to put them all neatly together. Lo! the profile of Robert Penfold was gone.

"Now that is too bad," said he. "So much for her dovelike eyes, that you admired so. Miss Innocence has stolen that profile."

"Stolen! she bought it — of me."

"Why, she never said a word."

"No; but she looked a look. She asked me, with those sweet imploring eyes, might she have it; and I looked yes: then she glanced towards you, and put down a note. Here it is."

"Why, you beat the telegraph, you two! Ten pounds for that thing! I must make it up to her somehow."

"I wish you could. Poor girl, she is a lady every inch. But she is in love with that Penfold. I'm afraid it is a hopeless case."

"I have seen a plainer. But hopeless it is not. However, you work your way, and I'll work mine."

"But you can't; you have no materials."

"No; but I have found a door that may lead to materials."

Having delivered himself thus mysteriously, he shut himself up in obstinate silence until Helen Rolleston called again, two days afterwards. She brought a bag full of manuscript this time: to wit, copies in her own handwriting of eight reports, the Queen *v.* Penfold. She was in good spirits, and told Mrs. Undercliff that all the reports were somewhat more favorable than the two she had left; and she was beginning to tell Mr. Undercliff he was quite right in his recollection, when he interrupted her, and said, "All that is secondary now. Have you any objection to answer me a question?"

She colored; but said, "O, no. Ask me anything you like"; then she blushed deeper.

"How did you become possessed of those two reports you left with me the other day?"

At this question, so different from what she feared, Helen cleared up and smiled, and said, "From a Mr. Hand, a clerk in Mr. Wardlaw's office; they were sent me at my request."

The Expert seemed pleased at this reply; his brow cleared, and he said, "Then I don't mind telling you that those two reports will bring Penfold's case within my province. To speak plainly, Miss Rolleston, your newspaper extracts — ARE FORGERIES."

CHAPTER LX.

"FORGERIES!" cried Helen, with innocent horror.

"RANK FORGERIES," repeated the Expert, coolly.

"Forgeries!" cried Helen, "Why, how can printed things be that?"

"That is what I should like to know," said the old lady.

"Why, what else can you call them?" said the Expert. "They are got up to look like extracts from newspapers. But they were printed as they are, and were never in any journal. Shall I tell you how I found that out?"

"If you please, sir," said Helen.

"Well, then, I looked at the reverse side, and I found seven misprints in one slip, and five in the other. That was a great number to creep into printed slips of that length. The trial part did not show a single erratum. 'Hullo!' said I to myself; 'why, one side is printed more carefully than the other.' And that was not natural. The printing of advertisements is looked after quite as sharply as any other part in a journal. Why, the advertisers themselves cry out if they are misprinted!"

"O, how shrewd!" cried Helen.

"Child's play," said the Expert. "Well, from that blot I went on. I looked at the edges, and they were cut too clean. A gentleman with a pair of scissors can't cut slips out of a paper like this. They were cut in the printer's office. Lastly, on holding them to the light, I found they had not been machined upon the plan now adopted by all newspapers; but worked by hand. In one word — forgeries!"

"Oh!" said Helen, "to think I should have handled forgeries, and shown them to you for real. Ah! I'm so glad; for now I have committed the same crime as Robert Penfold; I have uttered a forged document. Take me up, and have me put in prison, for I am as guilty as ever he was." Her face shone with rapture at sharing Robert's guilt.

The Expert was a little puzzled by sentiments so high-flown and unpractical.

"I think," said he, "you are hardly aware what a valuable discovery this may prove to you. However, the next step is to get me a specimen of the person's handwriting who furnished you with these. The chances are, he is the writer of the forged note."

Helen uttered an exclamation that was almost a scream. The inference took her quite by surprise. She looked at Mrs. Undercliff.

"He is right, I think," said the old lady.

"Right or wrong," said the Expert, "the next step in the inquiry is to do what I said. But that demands great caution. You must write a short civil note to Mr. Hand, and just ask him some question. Let me see: ask him what newspapers his extracts are from, and whether he has got any more. He will not tell you the truth; but no matter, we shall get hold of his handwriting."

"But, sir," said Helen, "there is no need for that. Mr. Hand sent me a note along with the extracts."

"The deuce he did. All the better. Any words in it that are in the forged note? Is Penfold in it, or Wardlaw?"

Helen reflected a moment, and then said she thought both those names were in it.

"Fetch me that note," said Undercliff, and his eyes sparkled. He was on a hot scent now.

"And let me study the genuine reports, and compare what they say with the forged ones," said Mrs. Undercliff.

"O, what friends I have found at last!" cried Helen.

She thanked them both warmly, and hurried home, for it was getting late.

Next day she brought Hand's letter to Mr. Undercliff, and devoured his countenance while he inspected it keenly, and compared it with the forged note.

The comparison was long and careful, but unsatisfactory. Mr. Undercliff could not conscientiously say whether Hand had written the forged note or not. There were *pros* and *cons*.

"We are in deeper water than I thought," said he. "The comparison must be enlarged. You must write as I suggested, and get another note out of Mr. Hand."

"And leave the prayer-book with me," said Mrs. Undercliff.

Helen complied with these instructions, and in due course received a civil line from Mr. Hand, to say that the extracts had been sent him from the country by one of his fellow-clerks, and he had locked them up, lest Mr. Michael Penfold, who was much respected in the office, should see them. He could not say where they came from; perhaps from some provincial paper. If of any value to Miss Rolleston, she was quite at liberty to keep them. He added there was a coffee-house in the city where she could read all the London papers of that date. This letter, which contained a great many more words than the other, was submitted to Undercliff. It puzzled him so that he set to work, and dissected every curve the writer's pen had made; but he could come to no positive conclusion, and he refused to utter his conjectures.

"We are in a deep water," said he.

Finally, he told his mother he was at a standstill for the present.

"But I am not," said Mrs. Undercliff. She added, after a while, "I think there 's felony at the bottom of this."

"Smells like it to me," said the Expert.

"Then I want you to do something very clever for me."

"What is that?"

"I want you to forge something."

"Come! I say."

"Quite innocent, I assure you."

"Well, but it is a bad habit to commence.

"All depends on the object. This is to take in a forger, that is all."

The Expert's eyes sparkled. He had always been sadly discontented with the efforts of forgers, and thought he could do better.

"I'll do it," said he, gayly.

CHAPTER LXI.

General Rolleston and his daughter sat at breakfast in the hotel. General Rolleston was reading the *Times*, and his eye lighted on something that made him start. He looked towards Helen, and his first impulse was to communicate it to her: but, on second thoughts, he preferred to put a question to her first.

"You have never told the Wardlaws what those sailors said?"

"No, papa. I still think they ought to have been told; but you know you positively forbade me."

"Of course I did. Why afflict the old gentleman with such a tale? A couple of common sailors! who chose to fancy the ship was destroyed."

"Who are better judges of such a thing than sailors?"

"Well, my child, if you think so, I can't help it. All I say is, spare the old gentleman such a report. As for Arthur, to tell you the truth, I have mentioned the matter to him."

"O papa! Then why forbid me to tell him? What did he say?"

"He was very much distressed. 'Destroy the ship my Helen was in,' said he: 'if I thought Wylie had done that I'd kill him with my own hand, though I was hanged for it next minute.' I never saw the young fellow fire up so before. But when he came to think calmly over it a little while, he said: 'I hope this slander will never reach my father's ears; it would grieve him deeply. I only laugh at it.'"

"Laugh at it! and yet talk of killing?"

"O, people say they laugh at a thing when they are very angry all the time. However, as you are a good girl, and mind what you are told, I'll read you an advertisement that will make you stare. Here is Joseph Wylie, who, you say, wrecked the Proserpine, actually invited by Michael Penfold to call on him, and hear of something to his advantage."

"Dear me!" said Helen, "how strange! Surely Mr. Penfold cannot know the character of that man. Stop a minute! Advertise for him? Then nobody knows where he lives? There, papa: you see he is afraid to go near Arthur Wardlaw; he knows he destroyed the ship. What a mystery it all is! And so Mr. Penfold is at home, after all; and not to send me a single line. I never met with so much unkindness and discourtesy in all my life."

"Ah, my dear," said the General, "you never defied the world before, as you are doing now."

Helen sighed; but, presently recovering her spirit, said she had done without the world on her dear island, and she would not be its slave now.

As she was always as good as her word, she declined an invitation to play the lion, and, dressing herself in plain merino, went down that very evening to Michael Penfold's cottage.

We run thither a little before her, to relate briefly what had taken place there.

Nancy Rouse, as may well be imagined, was not the woman to burn two thousand pounds. She locked the notes up; and after that night became very reserved on that head, so much so that, at last, Mr. Penfold saw it was an interdicted topic, and dropped it in much wonder.

When Nancy came to think of it in daylight, she could not help suspecting Wylie had some hand in it; and it occurred to her that the old gentleman, who lodged next door, might be an agent of Wylie's, and a spy on her. Wylie must have told him to push the £2,000 into her room; but what a strange thing to do! To be sure, he was a sailor, and sailors had been known to make sandwiches of bank-notes and eat them. Still, her good sense revolted against this theory, and she was sore puzzled; for, after all, there was the money, and she had seen it come through the wall. One thing appeared certain, Joe had not forgotten her; he was thinking of her as much as ever, or more than ever; so her spirits rose, she began singing and whistling again, and waited cunningly till Joe should reappear and explain his conduct. Hostage for his reappearance she held the £2,000. She felt so strong and saucy she was half sorry she had allowed Mr. Penfold to advertise; but, after all, it did not much matter; she could always declare to Joe she had never missed him, for her part, and the advertising was a folly of poor Mr. Penfold's.

Matters were in this condition when the little servant came up one evening to Mr. Penfold and said there was a young lady to see him.

"A young lady for *me?*" said he.

"Which she won't eat you, while I am by," said the sharp little girl. "It is a lady, and the same what come before."

"Perhaps she will oblige me with her name," said Michael, timidly.

"I won't show her up till she do," said this mite of a servant, who had been scolded by Nancy for not extracting that information on Helen's last visit.

"Of course, I must receive her," said Michael, half consulting the mite; it belonged to a sex which promptly assumes the control of such gentle creatures as he was.

"Is Miss Rouse in the way?" said he.

The mite laughed, and said: —

"She is only gone down the street. I'll send her in to take care on you."

With this she went off, and in due course led Helen up the stairs. She ran in, and whispered in Michael's ear, —

"It is Miss Helen Rolleston."

Thus they announced a lady at No. 3.

Michael stared with wonder at so great a personage visiting him; and the next moment Helen glided into the room, blushing a little, and even panting inaudibly, but all on her guard. She saw before her a rather stately figure, and a face truly venerable, benignant, and beautiful, though deficient in strength. She cast a devouring glance on him as she courtesied to him; and it instantly flashed across her, "But for you there would be no Robert Penfold." There was an unconscious tenderness in her voice as she spoke to him, for she had to open the interview.

"Mr. Penfold, I fear my visit may surprise you, as you did not write to me. But, when you hear what I am come about, I think you will not be displeased with me for coming."

"Displeased, madam! I am highly honored by your visit, — a lady who, I understand, is to be married to my worthy employer, Mr. Arthur. Pray be seated, madam."

"Thank you, sir."

Helen began in a low, thrilling voice, to which, however, she gave firmness by a resolute effort of her will.

"I am come to speak to you of one who is very dear to you, and to all who really know him."

"Dear to me? It is my son. The rest are gone. It is Robert."

And he began to tremble.

"Yes, it is Robert," said she, very softly; then turning her eyes away from him, lest his emotion should overcome her, she said, —

"He has laid me and my father under deep obligations."

She dragged her father in; for it was essential not to show Mr. Penfold she was in love with Robert.

"Obligations to my Robert? Ah, madam, it is very kind of you to say that, and cheer a desolate father's heart with praise of his lost son! But how could a poor unfortunate man in his position serve a lady like you?"

"He defended me against robbers, single-handed."

"Ah," said the old man, glowing with pride, and looking more beautiful than ever, "he was always as brave as a lion."

"That is nothing; he saved my life again, and again, and again."

"God bless him for it! and God bless you for coming and telling me of it! O madam, he was always brave, and gentle, and just, and good; so noble, so unfortunate."

And the old man began to cry.

Helen's bosom heaved, and it cost her a bitter struggle not to throw her arms around the dear old man's neck and cry with him. But she came prepared for a sore trial of her feelings, and she clenched her hands and teeth, and would not give way an inch.

"Tell me how he saved your life, madam."

"He was in the ship, and in the boat, with me."

"Ah, madam," said Michael, "that must have been some other Robert Penfold; not my son. He could not come home. His time was not up, you know."

"It was Robert Penfold, son of Michael Penfold."

"Excuse me a moment," said Michael; and he went to a drawer, and brought her a photograph of Robert. "Was it this Robert Penfold?"

The girl took the photograph, and eyed it, and lowered her head over it.

"Yes," she murmured.

"And he was coming home in the ship with you. Is he mad? More trouble! more trouble!"

"Do not alarm yourself," said Helen; "he will not land in England for years," — here she stifled a sob, — "and long ere that we shall have restored him to society."

Michael stared at that, and shook his head.

"Never," said he; "that is impossible."

"Why impossible?"

"They all say he is a felon."

"They all *shall* say that he is a martyr."

"And so he is; but how can that ever be proved?"

"I don't know. But I am sure the truth can always be proved, if people have patience and perseverance."

"My sweet young lady," said Michael, sadly, "you don't know the world."

"I am learning it fast, though. It may take me a few years, perhaps, to make powerful friends, to grope my way amongst forgers, and spies, and wicked, dishonest people of all sorts, but so surely as you sit there I'll clear Robert Penfold before I die."

The good feeble old man gazed on her with admiration and astonishment.

She subdued her flashing eye, and said with a smile, "And you shall help me. Mr. Penfold, let me ask you a question. I called here before; but you were gone to Edinburgh. Then I wrote to you at the office, begging you to let me know the moment you returned. Now, do not think I am angry; but pray tell me why you would not answer my letter."

Michael Penfold was not burdened with *amour propre*, but who has not got a little of it in some corner of his heart? "Miss Rolleston," said he, "I was born a gentleman, and was a man of fortune once, till false friends ruined me. I am in business now, but still a gentleman; and neither as a gentleman nor as a man of business could I leave a lady's letter unanswered. I never did such a thing in all my life. I never got your letter," he said, quite put out; and his wrath was so like a dove's that Helen smiled and said, "But I posted it myself. And my address was in it; yet it was not returned."

"Well, madam, it was not delivered, I assure you."

"It was intercepted, then."

He looked at her. She blushed, and said, "Yes, I am getting suspicious, ever since I found I was followed and watched. Excuse me a moment." She went to the window and peered through the curtains. She saw a man walking slowly by; he quickened his pace the moment she opened the curtain.

"Yes," said she, "it was intercepted, and I am watched wherever I go."

Before she could say any more a bustle was heard on the stairs, and in bounced Nancy Rouse, talking as she came. "Excuse me, Mr. Penfolds, but I can't wait no longer with my heart a bursting; it *is!* it *is!* O my dear, sweet young lady; the Lord be praised! You really are here alive and well. Kiss you I must and shall; come back from the dead; there — there — there!"

"Nancy! my good, kind Nancy," cried Helen, and returned her embrace warmly.

Then followed a burst of broken explanations; and at last Helen made out that Nancy was the landlady, and had left Lambeth long ago.

"But, dear heart!" said she, "Mr. Penfolds, I'm properly jealous of you. To think of her coming here to see you, and not me!"

"But I did n't know you were here, Nancy." Then followed a stream of inquiries, and such warm-hearted sympathy with all her dangers and troubles, that Helen was led into revealing the cause of it all.

"Nancy," said she, solemnly, "the ship was wilfully cast away; there was a villain on board that made holes in her on purpose, and sunk her."

Nancy lifted up her hands in astonishment. But Mr. Penfold was far more surprised and agitated.

"For Heaven's sake, don't say that!" he cried.

"Why not, sir?" said Helen; "it is the truth; and I have got the testimony of dying men to prove it."

"I am sorry for it. Pray, don't let anybody know. Why, Wardlaws would lose the insurance of £150,000."

"Arthur Wardlaw knows it: my father told him."

"And he never told me," said Penfold, with growing surprise.

"Goodness me! what a world it is!" cried Nancy. "Why, that was murder, and no less. It is a wonder she was n't drownded, and another friend into the bargain that I had in that very ship. O, I wish I had the villain here that done it, I'd tear his eyes out!"

Here the mite of a servant bounded in, radiant and giggling, gave Nancy a triumphant glance, and popped out again, holding the door open, through which in slouched a seafaring man, drawn by Penfold's advertisement, and decoyed into Nancy's presence by the imp of a girl, who thought to please her mistress.

Nancy, who for some days had secretly expected this visit, merely gave a little squeak; but Helen uttered a violent scream; and, upon that, Wylie recognized her, and literally staggered back a step or two, and these words fell out of his mouth: —

"The sick girl!"

Helen caught them.

"Ay!" cried she; "but she is alive in spite of you: alive to denounce you and to punish you."

She darted forward, and her eyes flashed lightning.

"Look at this man, all of you," she cried. "Look at him well: THIS IS THE WRETCH THAT SCUTTLED THE PROSERPINE!"

CHAPTER LXII.

"O Miss Helen, how can you say that?" cried Nancy, in utter dismay. "I'll lay my life poor Joe never did no such wickedness."

But Helen waved her off without looking at her, and pointed at Wylie.

"Are you blind? Why does he cringe and cower at sight of me? I tell you he scuttled the Proserpine, and the great augur he did it with I have seen and handled. Yes, sir, you destroyed a ship, and the lives of many innocent persons, whose blood now cries to Heaven against you; and if *I* am alive to tell the cruel tale, it is no thanks to you; for you did your best to kill me, and, what is worse, to kill Robert Penfold, this gentleman's son; for he was on board the ship. You are no better than an assassin."

"I am a man that 's down," said Wylie, in a low and broken voice, hanging his head. "Don't hit me any more. I did n't mean to take anybody's life: I took my chance with the rest, lady, as I 'm a man. I have lain in my bed many 's the night, crying like a child, with thinking you were dead. And now I am glad you are alive to be revenged on me. Well, you see, it is your turn now; you have lost me my sweetheart, there; she 'll never speak to me again, after this. Ah, the poor man gets all the blame! You don't ask who tempted me; and, if I was to tell you, you 'd hate me worse than ever; so I 'll belay. If I'm a sinner, I 'm a sufferer. England's too hot to hold me. I 've only to go to sea, and get drowned the quickest way." And with this he vented a deep sigh, and slouched out of the room.

Nancy sank into a seat, and threw her apron over her head, and rocked and sobbed as if her heart would break.

As for Helen Rolleston, she still stood in the middle of the room, burning with excitement.

Then poor old Michael came to her, and said, almost in a whisper, —

"It is a bad business; he is her sweetheart, and she had the highest opinion of him."

This softened Helen in a great measure. She turned and looked at Nancy, and said, —

"O dear, what a miserable thing! But I could n't know that."

After a while, she drew a chair, and sat down by Nancy, and said, —

"I won't *punish* him, Nancy."

Nancy burst out sobbing afresh.

"You *have* punished him," said she, bruskly, "and me too, as never did you no harm. You have driven him out of the country, you have."

At this piece of feminine justice Helen's anger revived. "So, then," said she, "ships are to be destroyed, and ladies and gentlemen murdered, and nobody is to complain, or say an angry word, if the wretch happens to be paying his addresses to you. That makes up for all the crimes in the world. What! Can an honest woman like you lose all sense of right and wrong for a man? And such a man!"

"Why, he is as well-made a fellow as ever I saw," sobbed Nancy.

"O, is he?" said Helen, ironically, — her views of manly beauty were different, and black eyes a *sine qua non* with her, — "then it is a pity his soul is not made to correspond. I hope by my next visit you will have learned to despise him as you ought. Why, if I loved a man ever so, I 'd tear him out of my heart if he committed a crime; ay, though I tore my soul out of my body to do it."

"No, you would n't," said Nancy, recovering some of her natural pugnacity; "for we are all tarred with the same stick, gentle or simple."

"But I assure you I would," cried Helen; "and so ought you."

"Well, miss, you begin," cried Nancy, suddenly firing up through her tears. "If the Proserpine was scuttled, which I 've your word for it, Miss Helen, and I never knew you tell a lie, why, your sweetheart is more to blame for it than mine."

Helen rose with dignity.

"You are in grief," said she. "I leave you to consider whether you have done well to affront me in your own house." And she was moving to the door with great dignity, when Nancy ran and stopped her.

"O, don't leave me so, Miss Helen," she cried; "don't you go to quarrel with me for speaking the truth too plain and rude, as is a plain-spoken body at the best; and in such grief myself, I scarce know what I do say. But indeed, and in truth, you must n't go and put it abroad that the ship was scuttled; if you do, you won't hurt Joe Wylie; he 'll get a ship, and fly the country. Who you 'll hurt will be your own husband as is to be, — Wardlaws."

"Shall I, Mr. Penfold?" asked Helen, disdainfully.

"Well, madam, certainly it might create some unworthy suspicion."

"Suspicion?" cried Nancy. "Don't you think to throw dust in my eyes. What had poor Joe to gain by destroying that there ship? you know very well he was bribed to do it; and risk his own life. And who bribed him? Who should bribe him, but the man as owned the ship?"

"Miss Rouse," said Mr. Penfold, "I sympathize with your grief, and make great allowance; but I will not sit here and hear my worthy employers blackened with such terrible insinuations. The great house of Wardlaw bribe a sailor to scuttle their own ship, with Miss Rolleston and one hundred and sixty thousand pounds' worth of gold on board! Monstrous! monstrous!"

"Then what did Joe Wylie mean?" replied Nancy. "Says he, 'The poor man gets all the blame. If I was to tell you who tempted me,' says he, 'you 'd hate me worse.' Then I say, why should she hate him worse? Because it 's her sweetheart tempted mine. I stands to that."

This inference, thus worded, struck Helen as so droll that she turned her head aside to giggle a little. But old Penfold replied loftily, —

"Who cares what a *Wylie* says against a great old mercantile house of London City?"

"Very well, Mr. Penfolds," said Nancy, with one great final sob, and dried her eyes with her apron; and she did it with such an air, they both saw she was not going to shed another tear about the matter. "Very well; you are both against me; then I 'll say no more. But I know what I know."

"And what do you know?" inquired Helen.

"Time will show," said Nancy, turning suddenly very dogged, — "time will show."

Nothing more was to be got out of her after that; and Helen, soon after, made her a civil, though stiff, little speech; regretted the pain she had inadvertently caused her, and went away, after leaving Mr. Penfold her address.

On her return home, she entered the whole adventure in her diary. She made a separate entry to this effect:—

Mysterious.—My letter to Mr. Penfold at the office intercepted.

Wylie hints that he was bribed by Messrs. Wardlaw.

Nancy Rouse suspects that it was Arthur, and says time will show.

As for me, I can neither see why Wylie should scuttle the ship unless he was bribed by somebody, nor what Arthur or his father could gain by destroying that ship. This is all as dark as is that more cruel mystery which alone I care to solve.

CHAPTER LXIII.

NEXT morning, after a sleepless night, Nancy Rouse said to Mr. Penfold, "Have n't I heard you say as bank-notes could be traced to folk?"

"Certainly, madam," said Michael; "but it is necessary to take the numbers of them."

"Oh! And how do you do that?"

"Why, every note has its own number."

"La! ye don't say so; then them fifties are all numbered, belike."

"Certainly, and if you wish me to take down the numbers, I will do so."

"Well, sir, some other day you shall. I could not bear the sight of them just yet; for it is them as has been the ruin of poor Joe Wylie, I do think."

Michael could not follow this; but, the question having been raised, he advised her, on grounds of common prudence, not to keep them in the house without taking down their numbers.

"We will talk about that in the evening," said Nancy.

Accordingly, at night, Nancy produced the notes, and Michael took down the numbers and descriptions in his pocket-book. They ran from 16,444 to 16,463. And he promised her to try and ascertain through what hands they had passed. He said he had a friend in the Bank of England, who might perhaps be able to discover to what private bank they had been issued in the first instance, and then those bankers, on a strong representation, might perhaps examine their books, and say to whom they had paid them. He told her the notes were quite new, and evidently had not been separated since their first issue.

Nancy caught a glimpse of his meaning, and set herself doggedly to watch until the person who had passed the notes through the chimney should come for them. "He will miss them," said she, "you mark my words."

Thus Helen, though reduced to a stand-still herself, had set an inquiry on foot which was alive and ramifying.

In the course of a few days she received a visit from Mrs. Undercliff. That lady came in, and laid a prayer-book on the table, saying, "I have brought it you back, miss; and I want you to do something for my satisfaction."

"O, certainly," said Helen. "What is it?"

"Well, miss, first examine the book and the writing. Is it all right?"

Helen examined it, and said it was: "Indeed," said she, "the binding looks fresher, if anything."

"You have a good eye," said Mrs. Undercliff. "Well, what I want you to do is—of course, Mr. Wardlaw is a good deal about you?"

"Yes."

"Does he go to church with you ever?"

"No."

"But he would, if you were to ask him."

"I have no doubt he would; but why?"

"Manage matters so that he shall go to church with you, and then put the book down for him to see the writing, all in a moment. Watch his face and tell me."

Helen colored up and said, "No; I can't do that. Why, it would be turning God's temple into a trap! Besides—"

"The real reason first, if you please," said this horribly shrewd old woman.

"Well, Mr. Arthur Wardlaw is the gentleman I am going to marry."

"Good Heavens!" cried Mrs. Undercliff, taken utterly aback by this most unexpected turn. "Why, you never told me that!"

"No," said Helen, blushing. "I did not think it necessary to go into that. Well, of course, it is not in human nature that Mr. Wardlaw should be zealous in my good work, or put himself forward; but he has never refused to lend me any help that was in his power; and it is repugnant to my nature to suspect him of a harm, and to my feelings to lay a trap for him."

"Quite right," said Mrs. Undercliff; "of course I had no idea you were going to marry Mr. Wardlaw. I made sure Mr. Penfold was the man."

Helen blushed higher still, but made no reply.

Mrs. Undercliff turned the conversation directly. "My son has given many hours to Mr. Hand's two letters, and he told me to tell you he is beginning to doubt whether Mr. Hand is a real person, with a real handwriting, at all."

"O Mrs. Undercliff! Why, he wrote me two letters! However, I will ask Mr. Penfold whether Mr. Hand exists or not. When shall I have the pleasure of seeing you again?"

"Whenever you like, my dear young lady; but not upon this business of Penfold and Wardlaw. I have done with it forever; and my advice to you, miss, is not to stir the mud any more." And with these mysterious words the old lady retired, leaving Helen deeply discouraged at her desertion.

However she noted down the conversation in her diary, and made this comment: People find no pleasure in proving an accused person innocent; the charm is to detect guilt. This day a good, kind friend abandons me because I will not turn aside from my charitable mission to suspect another person as wrongfully as he I love has been suspected.

Mem: To see, or make inquiries about, Mr. Hand.

General Rolleston had taken a furnished house in Hanover Square. He now moved into it, and Helen was compelled to busy herself in household arrangements.

She made the house charming; but unfortunately stood in a draught whilst heated, and caught a chill, which a year ago would very likely have gone to her lungs and killed her, but now settled on her limbs in violent neuralgic pains, and confined her to her bed for a fortnight.

She suffered severely, but had the consolation of finding she was tenderly beloved. Arthur sent flowers every day, and affectionate notes twice a day. And her father was constantly by her bedside.

At last she came down to the drawing-room, but

lay on the sofa, well wrapped up, and received only her most intimate friends. The neuralgia had now settled on her right arm and hand, so that she could not write a letter; and she said to herself with a sigh, "O, how unfit a girl is to do anything great! We always fall ill just when health and strength are most needed."

Nevertheless, during this period of illness and inaction, circumstances occurred that gave her joy.

Old Wardlaw had long been exerting himself in influential channels to obtain what he called justice for his friend Rolleston, and had received some very encouraging promises; for the General's services were indisputable; and, while he was stirring the matter, Helen was unconsciously co-operating by her beauty, and the noise her adventure made in society. At last a gentleman, whose wife was about the queen, promised old Wardlaw one day, that, if a fair opportunity should occur, that lady should tell Helen's adventure, and how the gallant old General, when everybody else despaired, had gone out to the Pacific, and found his daughter, and brought her home. This lady was a courtier of ten years' standing, and waited her opportunity; but when it did come, she took it, and she soon found that no great tact or skill was necessary on such an occasion as this. She was listened to with ready sympathy, and the very next day some inquiries were made, the result of which was that the Horse Guards offered Lieutenant-General Rolleston the command of a crack regiment and a full generalship. At the same time, it was intimated to him from another official quarter, that a baronetcy was at his service, if he felt disposed to accept it. The tears came into the stout old warrior's eyes at this sudden sunshine of royal favor, and Helen kissed old Wardlaw of her own accord; and the star of the Wardlaws rose into the ascendant, and for a time Robert Penfold seemed to be quite forgotten.

The very day General Rolleston became Sir Edward, a man and a woman called at the Charing Cross Hotel, and asked for Miss Helen Rolleston.

The answer was, she had left the hotel about ten days.

"Where is she gone, if you please?"

"We don't know."

"Why, has n't she left her new address?"

"No. The footman came for letters several times."

No information was to be got here, and Mr. Penfold and Nancy Rouse went home greatly disappointed, and puzzled what to do.

At first sight it might appear easy for Mr. Penfold to learn the new address of Miss Rolleston. He had only to ask Arthur Wardlaw. But, to tell the truth, during the last fortnight Nancy Rouse had impressed her views steadily and persistently on his mind, and he had also made a discovery that co-operated with her influence and arguments to undermine his confidence in his employer. What that discovery was we must leave him to relate.

Looking, then, at matters with a less unsuspicious eye than heretofore, he could not help observing that Arthur Wardlaw never put into the office letter-box a single letter for his sweetheart. He must write to her, thought Michael: but I am not to know her address. Suppose, after all, he did intercept that letter.

And now, like other simple, credulous men whose confidence has been shaken, he was literally brimful of suspicions, some of them reasonable, some of them rather absurd.

He had too little art to conceal his change of mind; and so, very soon after his vain attempt to see Helen Rolleston at the inn, he was bundled off to Scotland on business of the office.

Nancy missed him sorely. She felt quite alone in the world. She managed to get through the day, — work helped her; but at night she sat disconsolate and bewildered, and she was now beginning to doubt her own theory. For certainly, if all that money had been Joe Wylie's, he would hardly have left the country without it.

Now, the second evening after Michael's departure, she was seated in his room, brooding, when suddenly she heard a peculiar knocking next door.

She listened a little while, and then stole softly down stairs to her own little room.

Her suspicions were correct. It was the same sort of knocking that had preceded the phenomenon of the hand and bank-notes. She peeped into the kitchen and whispered, "Jenny — Polly — come here."

A stout washerwoman and the mite of a servant came, wondering.

"Now you stand there," said Nancy, "and do as I bid you. Hold your tongues, now. I know all about it."

The myrmidons stood silent, but with panting bosoms; for the mysterious knocking now concluded, and a brick in the chimney began to move.

It came out, and immediately a hand with a ring on it came through the aperture, and felt about.

The mite stood firm, but the big washerwoman gave signs of agitation that promised to end in a scream.

Nancy put her hand roughly before the woman's mouth. "Hold your tongue, ye great soft —" And, without finishing her sentence, she darted to the chimney and seized the hand with both her own and pulled it with such violence that the wrist followed it through the masonry, and a roar was heard.

"Hold on to my waist, Polly," she cried. "Jenny, take the poker, and that string, and tie his hand to it while we hold on. Quick! quick! Are ye asleep?"

Thus adjured, the mite got the poker against the wall, and tried to tie the wrist to it.

This, however, was not easy, the hand struggled so desperately.

However, pulling is a matter of weight rather than muscle: and the weight of the two women pulling downwards overpowered the violent struggles of the man; and the mite contrived to tie the poker to the wrist, and repeat the ligatures a dozen times in a figure of eight.

Then the owner of the hand, who had hitherto shown violent strength, taken at a disadvantage, now showed intelligence. Convinced that skill as well as force were against him, he ceased to struggle, and became quite quiet.

The women contemplated their feat with flushed cheeks and sparkling eyes.

When they had feasted a reasonable time on the imprisoned hand, and two of them, true to their sex, had scrutinized a green stone upon one of the fingers, to see whether it was real or false, Nancy took them by the shoulders, and bundled them good-humoredly out of the room.

She then lowered the gas and came out, and

locked the room up, and put the key in her pocket.

"I'll have my supper with you," said she. "Come, Jenny, I'm cook; and you make the kitchen as a body could eat off it, for I expect visitors."

"La, ma'am," said the mite; "he can't get out of the chimbley to visit hus through the street door."

"No, girl," said Nancy. "But he can send a hambassador; so Show her heyes and plague her art, as the play says, for of all the dirty kitchens give me hers. I never was there but once, and my slipper come off for the muck, a sticking to a body like bird-lime."

There was a knock at Nancy's street door; the little servant, full of curiosity, was for running to it on the instant. But Nancy checked her.

"Take your time," said she. "It is only a lodging-house keeper."

CHAPTER LXIV.

Sir Edward Rolleston could not but feel his obligations to the Wardlaws, and, when his daughter got better, he spoke warmly on the subject, and asked her to consider seriously whether she had not tried Arthur's affection sufficiently.

"He does not complain to you, I know," said he; "but he feels it very hard that you should punish him for an act of injustice that has already so deeply afflicted him. He says he believes some fool or villain heard him say that two thousand pounds was to be borrowed between them, and went and imposed on Robert Penfold's credulity; meaning, perhaps, to call again after the note had been cashed, and get Arthur's share of the money."

"But why did he not come forward?"

"He declares he did not know when the trial was till a month after: and his father bears him out; says he was actually delirious, and his life in danger. I myself can testify that he was cut down just in this way, when he heard the Proserpine was lost, and you on board her. Why not give him credit for the same genuine distress at young Penfold's misfortune? Come, Helen, is it fair to afflict and punish this gentleman for the misfortune of another, whom he never speaks of but with affection and pity? He says that if you would marry him at once, he thinks he should feel strong enough to throw himself into the case with you, and would spare neither money nor labor to clear Robert Penfold; but, as it is, he says he feels so wretched, and so tortured with jealousy, that he can't co-operate warmly with you, though his conscience reproaches him every day. Poor young man! His is really a very hard case. For you promised him your hand before you ever saw Robert Penfold."

"I did," said Helen; "but I did not say when. Let me have one year to my good work, before I devote my whole life to Arthur."

"Well, it will be a year wasted. Why postpone your marriage for that?"

"I promised."

"Yes, but he chose to fancy young Wardlaw is his enemy. You might relax that, now he tells you he will co-operate with you as your husband. Now, Helen, tell the truth, — is it a woman's work? Have you found it so? Will not Arthur do it better than you?"

Helen, weakened already by days of suffering, began to cry, and say, "What shall I do? what shall I do?"

"If you have any doubt, my dear," said Sir Edward, "then think of what *I* owe to these Wardlaws."

And, with that he kissed her, and left her in tears; and, soon after, sent Arthur himself up to plead his own cause.

It was a fine summer afternoon; the long French casements, looking on the garden of the Square, were open, and the balmy air came in and wooed the beautiful girl's cheek, and just stirred her hair at times.

Arthur Wardlaw came softly in, and gazed at her as she lay; her loveliness filled his heart and soul; he came and knelt by her sofa, and took her hand, and kissed it, and his own eyes glistened with tenderness.

He had one thing in his favor. He loved her.

Her knowledge of this had more than once befriended him, and made her refuse to suspect him of any great ill; it befriended him now. She turned a look of angelic pity on him.

"Poor Arthur!" she said. "You and I are both unhappy."

"But we shall be happy, erelong, I hope," said Arthur.

Helen shook her head.

Then he patted her, and coaxed her, and said he would be her servant, as well as a husband, and no wish of her heart should go ungratified.

"None?" said she, fixing her eyes on him.

"Not one," said he; "upon my honor."

Then he was so soft and persuasive, and alluded so delicately to her plighted faith, that she felt like a poor bird caught in a silken net.

"Sir Edward is very good," said he; "he feels for me."

At that moment, a note was sent up.

"Mr. Wardlaw is here, and has asked me when the marriage is to be. I can't tell him; I look like a fool."

Helen sighed deeply and had began to gather those tears that weaken a woman. She glanced despairingly to and fro: and saw no escape. Then, Heaven knows why or wherefore, — probably with no clear design at all but a woman's weak desire to cause a momentary diversion, to put off the inevitable for five minutes, — she said to Arthur: "Please give me that prayer-book. Thank you. It is right you should know this." And she put Cooper's deposition, and Welch's, into his hands.

He devoured them, and started up in great indignation. "It is an abominable slander," said he. "We have lost ten thousand pounds by the wreck of that ship, and Wylie's life was saved by a miracle as well as your own. It is a foul slander. I hurl it from me." And he made his words good by whirling the prayer-book out of window.

Helen uttered a scream. "My mother's prayer-book!" she cried.

"Oh! I beg pardon," said he.

"As well you may," said she. "Run and send George after it."

"No, I'll go myself," said he. "Pray forgive me: you don't know what a terrible slander they have desecrated your prayer-book with."

He ran out, and was a long time gone. He came back at last, looking terrified.

"I can't find it," said he: "somebody has carried it off. O, how unfortunate I am!"

"Not find it!" said Helen. "But it *must* be found."

"Of course it must be found," said Arthur. "A pretty scandal to go into the hands of Heaven knows who. I shall offer twenty guineas reward for it at once. I'll go down to the *Times* this moment. Was ever anything so unlucky?"

"Yes, go at once," said Helen; "and I'll send the servants into the Square. I don't want to say anything unkind, Arthur, but you ought not to have thrown my prayer-book into the public street."

"I know I ought not. I am ashamed of it myself."

"Well, let me *see* the advertisement."

"You shall. I have no doubt we shall recover it."

Next morning the *Times* contained an advertisement offering twenty guineas for a prayer-book lost in Hanover Square, and valuable not in itself, but as a relic of a deceased parent.

In the afternoon, Arthur called to know if anybody had brought the prayer-book back.

Helen shook her head sadly, and said, "No."

He seemed very sorry, and so penitent, that Helen said, —

"Do not despair. And if it is gone, why, I must remember you have forgiven me something, and I must forgive you."

The footman came in.

"If you please, miss, here is a woman wishes to speak to you; says she has brought a prayer-book."

"O, show her up at once," cried Helen.

Arthur turned away his head to hide a cynical smile. He had good reasons for thinking it was not the one he had flung out of the window yesterday.

A tall woman came in, wearing a thick veil, that concealed her features.

She entered on her business at once.

"You lost a prayer-book in this Square yesterday, madam."

"Yes."

"You offer twenty guineas reward for it."

"Yes."

"Please to look at this one."

Helen examined it, and said with joy it was hers.

Arthur was thunderstruck. He could not believe his senses.

"Let me look at it," said he.

His eyes went at once to the writing. He turned as pale as death, and stood petrified.

The woman took the prayer-book out of his unresisting hand, and said, —

"You'll excuse me, sir; but it is a large reward, and gentlefolks sometimes go from their word when the article is found."

Helen, who was delighted at getting back her book, and rather tickled at Arthur having to pay twenty guineas for losing it, burst out laughing, and said, —

"Give her the reward, Arthur; I am not going to pay for your misdeeds."

"With all my heart," said Arthur, struggling for composure.

He sat down to draw a check.

"What name shall I put?"

"Hum! Edith Hesket."

"Two t's?"

"No, only one."

"There."

"Thank you, sir."

She put the check into her purse, and brought the prayer-book to Helen.

"Lock it up at once," said she, in a voice so low that Arthur heard her murmur, but not the words; and she retired, leaving Helen staring with amazement, and Arthur in a cold perspiration.

CHAPTER LXV.

When the Springbok weighed anchor and left the island, a solitary form was seen on Telegraph Hill.

When she passed eastward, out of sight of that point, a solitary figure was seen on the cliffs.

When her course brought the island dead astern of her, a solitary figure stood on the east bluff of the island, and was the last object seen from the boat as she left those waters forever.

What words can tell the sickening sorrow and utter desolation that possessed that yearning bosom!

When the boat that had carried Helen away was out of sight, he came back with uneven steps to the cave, and looked at all the familiar objects with stony eyes, and scarce recognized them, for the sunshine of her presence was there no more. He wandered to and fro in a heavy stupor, broken every now and then by sharp pangs of agony that almost made him scream. And so the poor bereaved creature wandered about all day. He could not eat, he could not sleep, his misery was more than he could bear. One day of desolation succeeded another. And what men say so hastily was true for once, "His life was a burden." He dragged it about with him he scarce knew how.

He began to hate all the things he had loved whilst she was there. The beautiful cave, all glorious with pearl, that he had made for her, he could not enter it, the sight killed him, and she not there.

He left Paradise Bay altogether at last, and anchored his boat in a nook of Seal Bay. And there he slept in general. But sometimes he would lie down, wherever he happened to be, and sleep as long as he could.

To him to wake was a calamity. And, when he did wake, it was always with a dire sense of reviving misery, and a deep sigh at the dark day he knew awaited him.

His flesh wasted on his bones, and his clothes hung loosely about him. The sorrow of the mind reduced him almost to that miserable condition in which he had landed on the island.

The dog and the seal were faithful to him; used to lie beside him, and often whimpered; their minds, accustomed to communicate without the aid of speech, found out, Heaven knows how! that he was in grief or in sickness.

These two creatures, perhaps, saved his life or his reason. They came between his bereaved heart and utter solitude.

Thus passed a month of wretchedness unspeakable.

Then his grief took a less sullen form.

He came back to Paradise Bay, and at sight of it burst into a passion of weeping.

These were his first tears, and inaugurated a grief

more tender than ever, but less akin to madness and despair.

Now he used to go about and cry her name aloud, passionately, by night and day.

"O Helen! Helen!"

And next his mind changed in one respect, and he clung to every reminiscence of her. Every morning he went round her haunts, and kissed every place where he had seen her put her hand.

Only the cave he could not yet face.

He tried, too. He went to the mouth of it again and again, and looked in; but go into it and face it, empty of her — he could not.

He prayed often.

One night he saw her in a dream.

She bent a look of angelic pity on him, and said but these words, "Live in my cave," then vanished.

Alone on an island in the vast Pacific, who can escape superstition? It fills the air. He took this communication as a command, and the next night he slept in the cave.

But he entered it in the dark, and left it before dawn.

By degrees, however, he plucked up courage and faced it in daylight. But it was a sad trial; he came out crying bitterly after a few minutes.

Still he persevered, because her image had bade him; and at last, one evening, he even lighted the lamp, and sat there looking at the glorious walls and roof his hapless love had made.

Getting stronger by degrees, he searched about, and found little relics of her, — a glove, a needle, a great hat she had made out of some large leaves. All these he wept over and cherished.

But one day he found at the very back of the cave a relic that made him start as if a viper had stung his loving heart. It was a letter.

He knew it in a moment. It had already caused him many a pang; but now it almost drove him mad. Arthur Wardlaw's letter.

He recoiled from it, and let it lie. He went out of the cave, and cursed his hard fate. But he came back. It was one of those horrible things a man abhors, yet cannot keep away from. He took it up and dashed it down with rage many times; but it all ended in his lighting the lamp at night, and torturing himself with every word of that loving letter.

And she was going home to the writer of that letter, and he was left prisoner on the island. He cursed his generous folly, and writhed in agony at the thought. He raged with jealousy, so that his very grief was blunted for a time.

He felt as if he must go mad.

Then he prayed, — prayed fervently. And at last, worn out with such fierce and contending emotions, he fell into a deep sleep, and did not wake till the sun was high in heaven.

He woke; and the first thing he saw was the fatal letter lying at his feet in a narrow stream of sunshine that came peering in.

He eyed it with horror. This was then to haunt him by night and day.

He eyed it and eyed it. Then turned his face from it; but could not help eyeing it again.

And at last certain words in this letter seemed to him to bear an affinity to another piece of writing that had also caused him a great woe. Memory by its subtle links connected these two enemies of his together. He eyed it still more keenly, and that impression became strengthened. He took the letter and looked at it close, and held it at arm's length, and devoured it, and the effect of this keen examination was very remarkable. It seemed to restore the man to energy and to something like hope. His eyes sparkled, and a triumphant "Ah!" burst from his bosom.

He became once more a man of action. He rose, and bathed, and walked rapidly to and fro upon the sands, working himself up to a daring enterprise. He took his saw into the jungle, and cut down a tree of a kind common enough there. It was wonderfully soft, and almost as light as cork. The wood of this was literally useless for any other purpose than that to which Penfold destined it. He cut a great many blocks of this wood, and drilled holes in them, and, having hundreds of yards of good line, attached these quasi corks to the gunwale, so as to make a life-boat. This work took him several days, during which time an event occurred that encouraged him.

One morning he saw about a million birds very busy in the bay, and it proved to be a spermaceti whale come ashore.

He went out to her directly with all his tools, for he wanted oil for his enterprise, and the seal oil was exhausted.

When he got near the whale in his boat, he observed a harpoon sticking in the animal's back. He cut steps with his axe in the slippery carcass, and got up to it as well as he could, extracted it by cutting and pulling, and threw it down into his boat, but not till he had taken the precaution to stick a great piece of blubber on the barbed point. He then sawed and hacked under difficulties, being buffeted and bothered with thousands of birds, so eager for slices, that it was as much as he could do to avoid the making of minced fowl; but, true to his gentle creed, he contrived to get three hundred-weight of blubber without downright killing any of these greedy competitors, though he buffeted some of them, and nearly knocked out what little sense they had. He came ashore with his blubber and harpoon, and, when he came to examine the latter, he found that the name of the owner was cut deeply in the steel, — Josh. Fullalove, J. Fernandez. This inscription had a great effect on Robert Penfold's mind. It seemed to bring the island of Juan Fernandez, and humanity in general, nearer to him.

He boiled down the blubber, and put a barrel of oil on board his life-boat. He had a ship's lantern to burn it in. He also pitched her bottom as far as he could get at it, and provisioned her for a long voyage; taking care to lash the water-cask and beef-cask to the fore-thwart and foremast, in case of rough weather.

When he had done all this, it occurred to him suddenly, that, should he ever escape the winds and waves, and get to England, he would then have to encounter difficulties and dangers of another class, and lose the battle by his poverty.

"I play my last stake now," said he. "I will throw no chance away."

He reflected, with great bitterness, on the misery that want of money had already brought on him; and he vowed to reach England rich, or go to the bottom of the Pacific.

This may seem a strange vow for a man to make on an unknown island; but Robert Penfold had a powerful understanding, sharpened by adversity, and his judgment told him truly that he possessed wealth on this island, both directly and indirectly. In the first place, knowledge is sometimes wealth, and the knowledge of this island was a thing he could sell to the American merchants on the coast of Chili; and with this view, he put on board his boat specimens of the cassia and other woods, fruit, spices, pitch, guano, pink and red coral, pearl oysters, shells, cochineal, quartz, cotton, &c., &c.

Then he took his chisel, and struck all the larger pearls off the shells that lined Helen's cave. The walls and roof yielded nine enormous pearls, thirty large ones, and a great many of the usual size.

He made a pocket inside his waistcoat to hold the pearls safe.

Then he took his spade and dug into the Spanish ship for treasure. But this was terrible work. The sand returned upon the spade and trebled his labor.

The condition to which time and long submersion had reduced this ship and cargo were truly remarkable. Nothing to be seen of the deck but a thin brown streak that mingled with the sand in patches; of the timbers nothing but the uprights, and of those the larger half eaten and dissolved.

He dug five days, and found nothing solid.

On the sixth, being now at the bottom of the ship, he struck his spade against something hard and heavy.

On inspection it looked like ore, but of what metal he could not tell; it was as black as a coal. He threw this on one side, and found nothing more; but the next day he turned up a smaller fragment, which he took home and cleaned with lime-juice. It came out bright in places like silver.

This discovery threw light on the other. The piece of black ore, weighing about seven pounds, was in reality silver coin, that a century of submersion had reduced to the very appearance it wore before it ever went into the furnace.

He dug with fresh energy on this discovery, but found nothing more in the ship that day.

Then it occurred to him to carry off a few hundredweight of pink coral.

He got some fine specimens; and, while he was at that work, he fell in with a piece that looked very solid at the root and unnaturally heavy. On a nearer examination this proved to be a foreign substance incrusted with coral. It had twined and twisted and curled over the thing in a most unheard-of way. Robert took it home, and by rubbing here and there with lemon-juice, at last satisfied himself that this object was a silver box about the size of an octavo volume.

It had no keyhole, had evidently been soldered up for greater security, and Robert was left to conjecture how it had come there.

He connected it at once with the ship, and felt assured that some attempt had been made to save it. There it had lain by the side of the vessel all these years, but, falling clear of the sand, had been embraced by the growing coral, and was now a curiosity, if not a treasure.

He would not break the coral, but put it on board his life-boat just as it was.

And now he dug no more. He thought he could sell the galleon as well as the island, by sample, and he was impatient to be gone.

He reproached himself, a little unjustly, for allowing a woman to undertake the task of clearing him.

"To what annoyances, and perhaps affronts, have I exposed her," said he. "No, it is a man's business to defend, not to be defended."

To conclude: At high tide one fine afternoon he went on board with Ponto, and, hoisting his foresail only, crossed the bay, ranging along the island till he reached the bluff. He got under this, and, by means of his compass and previous observations, set the boat's head exactly on the line the ducks used to take. Then he set his mainsail too, and stretched boldly out across the great Pacific Ocean.

Time seems to wear out everything, even bad luck. It ran strong against Robert Penfold for years: but, when it had struck its worst blow, and parted him and Helen Rolleston, it relaxed, and a tide of good luck set in, which, unfortunately, the broken-hearted man could not appreciate at the time. However, so it was. He wanted oil; and a whale came ashore. He wanted treasure, and the sea gave him a little back of all it had swallowed; and now he wanted fine weather; and the ocean for days and nights was like peach-colored glass, dimpled here and there; and soft westerly airs fanned him along by night and day.

To be sure, he was on the true Pacific Ocean, at a period when it is really free from storms. Still, even for t[illegible]t latitude, he had wonderful weather for six days [illegible]nd on the seventh he fell in with a schooner, the [illegible]pper and crew of which looked over the bulwa[illegible] at him with wonder and cordiality, and, casting out a rope astern, took him in tow.

The skipper had been eyeing him with amazement for some hours through his telescope; but he was a man that had seen a great many strange things, and it was also a point of honor with him never to allow that he was astonished, or taken by surprise, or greatly moved.

"Wal, stranger," said he, "what craft is that?"

"The Helen."

"Where d' ye hail from? not that I am curious."

"From an unknown island."

"Do tell. What, another! Is it any ways nigh?"

"Not within seven hundred miles."

"Je—rusalem! Have you sailed all that in a cockle-shell?"

"Yes."

"Why, what are ye? the Wandering Jew afloat, or the Ancient Mariner? or only a kinder nautilus?"

"I 'm a landsman."

"A landsman! then so is Neptune. What is your name when you are ashore?"

"Robert Penfold. The Reverend Robert Penfold."

"The Reverend— Je—rusalem!"

"May I ask what is your name, sir?"

"Wal, I reckon you may, stranger. I'm Joshua Fullalove from the States, at present located on the island of Juan Fernandez!"

"Joshua Fullalove! That is lucky. I've got something that belongs to you."

He looked about, and found the harpoon, and handed it up in a mighty straightforward simple way.

Joshua stared at him incredulously at first, but afterwards with amazement. He handled the harpoon, and inquired where Robert had fallen in with it. Robert told him.

"You 're an honest man," said Fullalove, "you air. Come aboard." He was then pleased to congratulate himself on his strange luck in having drifted across an honest man in the middle of the ocean. "I 've heerd," said he, "of an old chap as groped about all his life with a lantern, and could n't find one. Let 's liquor."

He had some celestial mixture or other made, including rum, mint, and snow from the Andes, and then began his interrogatories, again disclaiming curiosity at set intervals.

"Whither bound, honest man?"

"The coast of Chili."

"What for?"

"Trade."

"D' ye buy or sell? Not that it is my business."

"I wish to sell."

"What 's the merchandise?"

"Knowledge, and treasure."

Fullalove scratched his head. "Ha'n't ye got a few conundrums to swap for gold dust as well?"

Robert smiled faintly: the first time this six weeks.

"I have to sell the knowledge of an island with rich products: and I have to sell the contents of a Spanish treasure-ship that I found buried in the sand of that island."

The Yankee's eyes glistened.

"Wal," said he, "I do business in islands myself. I've leased this Juan Fernandez. But [illegible] of them is enough at a time. I 'm monarch of al[illegible] survey: but then what I survey is a mixallaneou[illegible]lin' of Irish and Otaheitans, that it 's pizen to be [illegible]onarch of. And now them darned Irish has taken to converting the heathens to superstition and the worship of images, and breaks their heads if they won't: and the heathens are all smiles and sweetness and immorality. No, islands is no bait to me."

"I never asked you," said Robert. "What I do ask you is to land me at Valparaiso. There I 'll find a purchaser, and will pay you handsomely for your kindness."

"That is fair," said Fullalove, dryly. "What will you pay me?"

"I 'll show you," said Robert. He took out of his pocket the smaller conglomeration of Spanish coin, and put it into Fullalove's hand. "That," said he, "is silver coin I dug out of the galleon."

Fullalove inspected it keenly, and trembled slightly. Robert then went lightly over the taffrail, and slid down the low rope into his boat. He held up the black mass we have described.

"This is solid silver. I will give it you, and my best thanks, to land me at Valparaiso."

"Heave it aboard," said the Yankee.

Robert steadied himself, and hove it on board. The Yankee caught it, heavy as it was, and subjected it to some chemical test directly.

"Wal," said he, "that is a bargain. I 'll land ye at Valparaiso for this. Jack, lay her head S. S. E. and by E."

Having given this order, he leaned over the taffrail and asked for more samples. Robert showed him the fruits, woods, and shells, and the pink coral, and bade him observe that the boat was ballasted with pearl oysters. He threw him up one, and a bunch of pink coral. He then shinned up the rope again, and the interrogatories recommenced. But this time he was questioned closely as to who he was, and how he came on the island? and the questions were so shrewd and penetrating that his fortitude gave way, and he cried out in anguish, "Man, man! do not torture me so. O, do not make me talk of my grief and my wrongs! they are more than I can bear."

Fullalove forbore directly, and offered him a cigar. He took it, and it soothed him a little; it was long since he had smoked one. His agitation subsided, and a quiet tear or two rolled down his haggard cheek.

The Yankee saw, and kept silence.

But when the cigar was nearly smoked out, he said he was afraid Robert would not find a customer for his island, and what a pity Joshua Fullalove was cool on islands just now.

"Oh!" said Robert, "I know there are enterprising Americans on the coast who will give me money for what I have to sell."

Fullalove was silent a minute, then he got a piece of wood and a knife, and said, with an air of resignation.

"I reckon we 'll have to deal."

Need we say that to deal had been his eager desire from the first.

He now began to whittle a peg, and awaited the attack.

"What will you give me, sir?"

"What, money down? And you got nothing to sell but chances. Why, there 's an old cuss about that knows where the island is as well as you do."

"Then of course you will treat with him," said Robert, sadly.

"Darned if I do," said the Yankee. "You are in trouble, and he is not, nor never will be till he dies, and then he 'll get it hot, I calc'late. He is a thief and stole my harpoon; you are an honest man and brought it back. I reckon I 'll deal with you and not with that old cuss; not by a jugful! But it must be on a percentage. You tell me the bearings of that there island, and I 'll work it and pay five per cent on the gross."

"Would you mind throwing that piece of wood into the sea, Mr. Fullalove?" said Robert.

"Caen't be done, nohow. I caen't deal without whittlin'."

"You mean you can't take an unfair advantage without it. Come, Mr. Fullalove, let us cut this short. I am, as you say, an honest and most unfortunate man. Sir, I was falsely accused of a crime and banished my country. I can prove my innocence now if I can but get home with a great deal of money. So much for *me*. *You* are a member of the vainest and most generous nation in the world."

"Wal, now that 's kinder honey and vinegar mixed," said Fullalove; "pretty good for a Britisher, though."

"You are a man of that nation, which in all the agonies and unparalleled expenses of civil war, smarting, too, under anonymous taunts from England, did yet send over a large sum to relieve the distresses of certain poor Englishmen who were indirect victims of that same calamity. The act, the time, the misery relieved, the taunts overlooked, prove your nation superior to all others in generosity. At least my reading, which is very large, affords no parallel to it, either in ancient or modern history. Mr. Fullalove, please to recollect that you are a member of that nation, and that I am very unhappy and helpless, and want money to undo cruel wrongs, but have no heart to chaffer much. Take the island and the treasure, and give me half the profits you make. Is not that fair?"

Fullalove wore a rueful countenance.

"Darn the critter," said he, "he 'll take skin off my bones if I don't mind. Fust Britisher ever I met as had the sense to see *that*. 'T was ratther handsome, warn't it? Wal, human nature is deep; every man you tackle in business larns ye something. What with picking ye out o' the sea, and you giving me back the harpoon the cuss stole, and your face like a young calf, when you are the 'cutest fox out, and you giving the great *United* States their due, I 'm no more fit to deal than mashed potatoes. Now I cave: it is only for once. Next time don't you try to palaver me. Draw me a map of our island, Britisher, and mark where the Spaniard lies: I tell *you* I know her name, and the year she was lost in: larned that at Lima one day. Kinder startled me, you did, when you showed me the coin out of her. Wal, there 's my hand on haelf profits, and, if I 'm keen, I 'm squar'."

Soon after this he led Robert to his cabin, and Robert drew a large map from his models; and Fullalove, being himself an excellent draughtsman, and provided with proper instruments, aided him to finish it.

Next day they sighted Valparaiso, and hove to outside the port.

All the specimens of insular wealth were put on board the schooner and secreted; for Fullalove's first move was to get a lease of the island from the Chilian Government, and it was no part of his plan to trumpet the article he was going to buy.

After a moment's hesitation, he declined to take the seven pounds of silver. He gave as a reason, that, having made a bargain which compelled him to go to Valparaiso at once, he did not feel like charging his partner a fancy price for towing his boat thither. At the same time he hinted that, after all this, the next customer would find him a very difficult Yankee to get the better of.

With this understanding, he gave Robert a draft for £80 on account of profits; and this enabled him to take a passage for England with all his belongings.

He arrived at Southampton very soon after the events last related, and thence went to London, fully alive to the danger of his position.

He had a friend in his long beard, but he dared not rely on that alone. Like a mole, he worked at night.

CHAPTER LXVI.

Helen asked Arthur Wardlaw why he was so surprised at the prayer-book being brought back. Was it worth twenty pounds to any one except herself?

Arthur looked keenly at her to see whether she intended more than met the ear, and then said that he was surprised at the rapid effect of his advertisement, that was all.

"Now you have got the book," said he, "I do hope you will erase that cruel slander on one whom you mean to honor with your hand."

This proposal made Helen blush, and feel very miserable. Of the obnoxious lines some were written by Robert Penfold, and she had so little of his dear handwriting. "I feel you are right, Arthur," said she; "but you must give me time. Then, they shall meet no eye but mine; and on our wedding day — of course — all memorials of one —." Tears completed the sentence.

Arthur Wardlaw, raging with jealousy at the absent Penfold, as heretofore Penfold had raged at him, heaved a deep sigh and hurried away, while Helen was locking up the prayer-book in her desk. By this means he retained Helen's pity.

He went home directly, mounted to his bedroom, unlocked a safe, and plunged his hand into it. His hand encountered a book; he drew it out with a shiver, and gazed at it with terror and amazement.

It was the prayer-book he had picked up in the Square and locked up in that safe. Yet that very prayer-book had been restored to Helen before his eyes, and was now locked up in her desk. He sat down with the book in his hand, and a great dread came over him.

Hitherto Candor and Credulity only had been opposed to him, but now Cunning had entered the field against him; a master-hand was co-operating with Helen.

Yet, strange to say, she seemed unconscious of that co-operation. Had Robert Penfold found his way home by some strange means? Was he watching over her in secret?

He had the woman he loved watched night and day, but no Robert Penfold was detected.

He puzzled his brain night and day, and at last he conceived a plan of deceit which is common enough in the East, where Lying is one of the fine arts, but was new in this country, we believe, and we hope to Heaven we shall not be the means of importing it.

An old clerk of his father's, now superannuated and pensioned off, had a son upon the stage, in a very mean position. Once a year, however, and of course in the dog-days, he had a kind of benefit at his suburban theatre; that is to say, the manager allowed him to sell tickets, and take half the price of them. He persuaded Arthur to take some, and even to go to the theatre for an hour. The man played a little part, of a pompous sneak, with some approach to Nature. He seemed at home.

Arthur found this man out; visited him at his own place. He was very poor, and mingled pomposity with obsequiousness, so that Arthur felt convinced he was to be bought, body and soul, what there was of him.

He sounded him accordingly, and the result was that the man agreed to perform a part for him.

Arthur wrote it, and they rehearsed it together. As to the dialogue, that was so constructed that it could be varied considerably according to the cues, which could be foreseen to a certain extent; but not precisely, since they were to be given by Helen Rolleston, who was not in the secret.

But whilst this plot was fermenting, other events happened, with rather a contrary tendency; and these will be more intelligible if we go back to Nancy Rouse's cottage, where indeed we have kept Joseph Wylie in an uncomfortable position a very long time.

Mrs. James, from next door, was at last admitted into Nancy's kitchen, and her first word was, "I suppose you know what I 'm come about, ma'am."

"Which it is to return me the sass-pan you borrowed, no doubt," was Nancy's ingenuous reply.

"No, ma'am. But I 'll send my girl in with it, as soon as she have cleaned it, you may depend."

"Thank ye, I shall be glad to see it again."

"You 're not afeard I shall steal it, I hope?"

"La, bless the woman! don't fly out at a body like that. I can't afford to give away my sass-pan."

"Sass-pans is not in my head."

"Nor in your hand neither."

"I 'm come about my lodger; a most respectable gentleman, which he have met with an accident. He did but go to put something away in the chimbley, which he is a curious gent, and has travelled a good deal, and learned the foreign customs, when his hand was caught in the brick-work, somehows, and there he is hard and fast."

"Do you know anything about this?" said Nancy to the mite, severely.

"No," said the mite, with a countenance of polished granite.

"La, bless me!" said Nancy, with a sudden start, "Why, is she talking about the thief as you and I catched putting his hand through the wall into my room, and made him fast again the policeman comes round?"

"Thief!" cried Mrs. James: "no more a thief than I am. Why, sure you would n't ever be so cruel! O dear! O dear! Spite goes a far length. There, take an' kill me, do, and then you 'll be easy in your mind. Ah, little my poor father thought as ever I should come down to letting lodgings, and being maltreated this way! I am —"

"Who is a maltreating of ye? Why, you 're dreaming. Have a drop o' gin?"

"With them as takes the police to my lodger? It would choke me!"

"Well, have a drop, and we 'll see about it."

"You 're very kind, ma'am, I 'm sure. Heaven knows I need it! Here 's wishing you a good husband; and towards burying all unkindness."

"Which you means drounding of it."

"Ah, you 're never at a loss for a word, ma'am, and always in good spirits. But your troubles is to come. *I* 'm a widdy. You will let me see what is the matter with my lodger, ma'am?"

"Why not? We'll go and have a look at him."

Accordingly, the three women and the mite proceeded to the little room; Nancy turned the gas on, and then they inspected the imprisoned hand. Mrs. James screamed with dismay, and Nancy asked her drily whether she was to blame for seizing a hand which had committed a manifest trespass.

"You have got the rest of his body," said she, "but this here hand belongs to me."

"Lord, ma'am, what could he take out of your chimbley, without 't was a handful of soot? Do, pray, let me loose him."

"Not till I have said two words to him."

"But how can you? He is n't here to speak to, — only a morsel of him."

"I can go into your house and speak to him."

Mrs. James demurred to that; but Nancy stood firm; Mrs. James yielded. Nancy whispered her myrmidons, and, in a few minutes, was standing by the prisoner, a reverend person in dark spectacles, and a gray beard, that created commiseration, or would have done so, but that this stroke of ill-fortune had apparently fallen upon a great philosopher. He had contrived to get a seat under him, and was smoking a pipe with admirable *sang-froid*.

At sight of Nancy, however, he made a slight motion, as if he would not object to follow his imprisoned hand through the party wall. It was only for a moment; the next, he smoked imperturbably.

"Well, sir," said Nancy, "I hopes you are comfortable?"

"Thank ye, miss; yes. I 'm at a double sheet-anchor."

"Why do you call me miss?"

"I don't know. Because you are so young and pretty."

"That will do. I only wanted to hear the sound of your voice, Joe Wylie." And with the word she snatched his wig off with one hand, and his beard with the other, and revealed his true features to his astonished landlady.

"There, mum," said she, "I wish you joy of your lodger." She tapped the chimney three times with the poker, and, telling Mr. Wylie she had a few words to say to him in private, retired for the present. Mrs. James sat down and mourned the wickedness of mankind, the loss of her lodger (who would now go bodily next door instead of sending his hand), and the better days she had by iteration brought herself to believe she had seen.

Wylie soon entered Nancy's house, and her first question was, "The £2,000, how did you get them?"

"No matter how I got them," said Wylie, sulkily. "What have you done with them?"

"Put them away."

"That is all right. I'm blest if I did n't think they were gone forever."

"I wish they had never come. Ill-gotten money is a curse." Then she taxed him with scuttling the Proserpine, and asked him whether that money had not been the bribe. But Joe was obdurate. "I never split on a friend," said he. "And you have nobody to blame but yourself, you would n't splice without £2,000. I loved you, and I got it how I could. D' ye think a poor fellow like me can make £2,000 in a voyage by hauling in ropes, and tying true-lovers' knots in the foretop."

Nancy had her answer ready; but this remembrance pricked her own conscience and paved the way to a reconciliation. Nancy had no high-flown notions. She loved money, but it must be got without palpable dishonesty; *per contra*, she was not going to denounce her sweetheart, but then again she would not marry him so long as he differed with her about the meaning of the eighth commandment.

This led to many arguments, some of them warm, some affectionate; and so we leave Mr. Wylie under the slow but salutary influence of love and unpretending probity. He continued to lodge next door. Nancy would only receive him as a visitor.

CHAPTER LXVII.

HELEN had complained to Arthur, of all people, that she was watched and followed; she even asked him whether that was not the act of some enemy. Arthur smiled, and said, "Take my word for it, it is only some foolish admirer of your beauty; he wants to know your habits, in hopes of falling in with you; you had better let me go out with you for the next month or so; that sort of thing will soon die away."

As a necessary consequence of this injudicious revelation, Helen was watched with greater skill and subtlety, and upon a plan well calculated to disarm suspicion; a spy watched the door, and by a signal unintelligible to any but his confederate, whom Helen could not possibly see, set the latter on her track. They kept this game up unobserved for several days, but learned nothing, for Helen was at a standstill. At last they got caught, and by a truly feminine stroke of observation. A showily dressed man peeped into a shop where Helen was buying gloves.

With one glance of her woman's eye she recognized a large breastpin in the worst possible taste; thence her eye went up and recognized the features of her seedy follower, though he was now dressed up to the nine. She withdrew her eye directly, completed her purchase, and went home, brooding defence and vengeance

That evening she dined with a lady who had a large acquaintance with lawyers, and it so happened that Mr. Tollemache and Mr. Hennessy were both of the party. Now, when these gentlemen saw Helen in full costume, a queen in form as well as face, coroneted with her island pearls, environed with a halo of romance, and courted by women as well as men, they looked up to her with astonishment, and made up to her in a very different style from that in which they had received her visit. Tollemache she received coldly; he had defended Robert Penfold feebly, and she hated him for it. Hennessy she received graciously, and, remembering Robert's precept to be supple as a woman, bewitched him. He was good-natured, able, and vain. By eleven o'clock she had enlisted him in her service. When she had conquered him, she said, slyly, "But I ought not to speak of these things to you except through a solicitor."

"That is the general rule," said the learned counsel; "but in this case no dark body must come between me and the sun."

In short he entered into Penfold's case with such well-feigned warmth, to please the beauteous girl, that at last she took him by the horns and consulted.

"I am followed," said she.

"I have no doubt you are; and on a large scale; if there is room for another, I should be glad to join the train."

"Ha! ha! I'll save you the trouble. I'll meet you half-way. But, to be serious, I am watched, spied, and followed by some enemy to that good friend whose sacred cause we have undertaken. Forgive me for saying 'we.'"

"I am too proud of the companionship to let you off. 'We' is the word."

"Then advise me what to do. I want to retaliate. I want to discover who is watching me, and why. Can you advise me? Will you?"

The counsel reflected a moment, and Helen, who watched him, remarked the power that suddenly came into his countenance and brow.

"You must watch the spies. I have influence in Scotland Yard, and will get it done for you. If you went there yourself, they would cross-examine you and decline to interfere. I'll go myself for you, and put it in a certain light. An able detective will call on you: give him ten guineas, and let him into your views in confidence; then he will work the public machinery for you."

"O Mr. Hennessy, how can I thank you?"

"By succeeding. I hate to fail: and now your cause is mine."

Next day a man with a hooked nose, a keen black eye, and a solitary foible (Mosaic), called on Helen Rolleston, and told her he was to take her instructions. She told him she was watched, and thought it was done to baffle a mission she had undertaken: but, having got so far, she blushed and hesitated.

"The more you tell me, miss, the more use I can be," said Mr. Burt.

Thus encouraged, and also remembering Mr. Hennessy's advice, she gave Mr. Burt, as coldly as she could, an outline of Robert Penfold's case, and of the exertions she had made, and the small result.

Burt listened keenly, and took a note or two; and, when she had done, he told her something in return.

"Miss Rolleston," said he, "I am the officer that arrested Robert Penfold. It cost me a grinder that he knocked out."

"O, dear!" said Helen, "how unfortunate! Then I fear I cannot reckon on your services."

"Why not, miss? What, do you think I hold spite against a poor fellow for defending himself? Besides, Mr. Penfold wrote me a very proper note. Certainly for a parson the gent is a very quick hitter; but he wrote very square; said he hoped I would allow for the surprise and the agitation of an innocent man; sent me two guineas too, and said he would make it twenty but he was poor as well as unfortunate; that letter has stuck in my gizzard ever since; can't see the color of felony in it. Your felon is never in a fault; and, if he wears a good coat, he is n't given to show fight."

"It was very improper of him to strike you," said Helen, "and very noble of you to forgive it. Make him still more ashamed of it: lay him under a deep obligation."

"If he is innocent, I'll try and prove it," said the Detective. He then asked her if she had taken notes. She said she had a diary. He begged to see it. She felt inclined to withhold it, because of the comments; but, remembering that this was womanish, and that Robert's orders to her were to be manly on such occasions, she produced her diary. Mr. Burt read it very carefully, and told her it was a very promising case. "You have done a great deal more than you thought," he said. "*You have netted the fish.*"

CHAPTER LXVIII.

"I! NETTED the fish! what fish?"

"The man who forged the promissory note."

"O Mr. Burt!"

"The same man that forged the newspaper extracts to deceive you forged the promissory note years ago, and the man who is setting spies on you is the man who forged those extracts; so we are sure to nail him. He is in the net; and very much to your credit. Leave the rest to me. I'll tell you more about it to-morrow. You must order your carriage at one o'clock to-morrow and drive down to Scotland Yard; go into the yard, and you will see me; follow me without a word. When you go back, the other spies will be so frightened, they will go off to their employer, and so we shall nail him."

Helen complied with their instructions strictly, and then returned home, leaving Mr. Burt to work. She had been home about half an hour, when the servant brought her up a message saying that a man wanted to speak to her. "Admit him," said Helen. "He is dressed very poor, miss." "Never mind; send him to me." She was afraid to reject anybody now, lest she might turn her back on information.

A man presented himself in well-worn clothes, with a wash-leather face and close-shaven chin; a little of his forehead was also shaven. "Madam, my name is Hand." Helen started. "I have already had the honor of writing to you."

"Yes, sir," said Helen, eyeing him with fear and aversion.

"Madam, I am come" — (he hesitated) — "I am an unfortunate man. Weighed down by remorse for a thoughtless act that has ruined an innocent man, and nearly cost my worthy employer his life, I come to expiate as far as in me lies. But let me be brief, and hurry over the tale of shame. I was a clerk at Wardlaw's office. A bill-broker called Adams was talking to me and my fellow-clerks, and boasting that nobody could take him in with a feigned signature. Bets were laid; our vanity was irritated by his pretension. It was my fortune to overhear my young master and his friend Robert Penfold speak about a loan of two thousand pounds. In an evil hour I listened to the tempter, and wrote a forged note for that amount. I took it to Mr. Penfold; he presented it to Adams, and it was cashed. I intended, of course, to call next day, and tell Mr. Penfold, and take him to Adams, and restore the money, and get back the note. It was not due for three months. Alas! that very day it fell under suspicion. Mr.

Penfold was arrested. My young master was struck down with illness at his friend's guilt, though he never could be quite got to believe it; and I — miserable coward! — dared not tell the truth. Ever since that day I have been a miserable man. The other day I came into money, and left Wardlaw's service. But I carry my remorse with me. Madam, I am come to tell the truth. I dare not tell it to Mr. Wardlaw; I think he would kill me. But I will tell it to you, and you can tell it to him; ay, tell it to all the world. Let my shame be as public as his whom I have injured so deeply, but, Heaven knows, unintentionally. I — I — I — "

Mr. Hand sank all in a heap where he sat, and could say no more.

Helen's flesh crawled at this confession, and at the sight of this reptile who owned that he had destroyed Robert Penfold in fear and cowardice. For a long time her wrath so overpowered all sense of pity, that she sat trembling; and, if eyes could kill, Mr. Hand would not have outlived his confession.

At last she contrived to speak. She turned her head away not to see the wretch, and said, sternly, —

" Are you prepared to make this statement on paper, if called on ? "

Mr. Hand hesitated, but said " Yes."

" Then write down that Robert Penfold was innocent, and you are ready to prove it whenever you may be called upon."

" Write that down ? " said Hand.

" Unless your penitence is feigned, you will."

" Sooner than that should be added to my crime I will avow all." He wrote the few lines she required.

" Now your address, that I may know where to find you at a moment's notice." He wrote " J. Hand, 11 Warwick Street, Pimlico."

Helen then dismissed him, and wept bitterly. In that condition she was found by Arthur Wardlaw, who comforted her, and, on hearing her report of Hand's confession, burst out into triumph, and reminded her he had always said Robert Penfold was innocent. " My father," said he, " must yield to this evidence, and we will lay it before the Secretary of State, and get his pardon."

" His pardon! when he is innocent! "

" O, that is the form, — the only form. The rest must be done by the warm reception of his friends. I, for one, who all these years have maintained his innocence, will be the first to welcome him to my house, an honored guest. What am I saying? Can I? dare I? ought I? when my wife — Ah! I am more to be pitied than my poor friend is: my friend, my rival. Well, I leave it to you whether he can come into your husband's house."

" Never."

" But, at least, I can send the Springbok out, and bring him home; and that I will do without one day's delay."

" O Arthur!" cried Helen, " you set me an example of unselfishness."

" I do what I can," said Arthur. " I am no saint. I hope for a reward."

Helen sighed. " What shall I do? "

" Have pity on *me!* your faithful lover, and to whom your faith was plighted before ever you saw or knew my unhappy friend. What can I do or suffer more than I have done and suffered for you? My sweet Helen, have pity on me, and be my wife."

" I will; some day."

" Bless you: bless you. One effort more: what day? "

" I can't. I can't. My heart is dead."

" This day fortnight. Let me speak to your father: let him name the day."

As she made no reply, he kissed her hand devotedly, and did speak to her father. Sir Edward, meaning all for the best, said, " This day fortnight."

CHAPTER LXIX.

The next morning came the first wedding presents from the jubilant bridegroom, who was determined to advance step by step, and give no breathing time. When Helen saw them laid out by her maid, she trembled at the consequences of not giving a plump negative to so brisk a wooer.

The second post brought two letters; one of them from Mrs. Undercliff. The other contained no words, but only a pearl of uncommon size, and pear-shaped. Helen received this at first as another wedding present, and an attempt on Arthur's part to give her a pearl as large as those she had gathered on her dear island. But, looking narrowly at the address, she saw it was not written by Arthur; and, presently, she was struck by the likeness of this pearl in shape to some of her own. She got out her pearls, laid them side by side, and began to be moved exceedingly. She had one of her instincts, and it set every fibre quivering with excitement. It was some time before she could take her eyes off the pearls, and it was with a trembling hand she opened Mrs. Undercliff's letter. That missive was not calculated to calm her. It ran thus: —

" My dear Young Lady, — A person called here last night and supplied the clew. If you have the courage to know the truth, you have only to come here, and to bring your diary, and all the letters you have received from any person or persons since you landed in England. I am yours obediently,

" Jane Undercliff."

The courage to know the truth!

This mysterious sentence affected Helen considerably. But her faith in Robert was too great to be shaken. She would not wait for the canonical hour at which young ladies go out, but put on her bonnet directly after breakfast. Early as she was, a visitor came before she could start, — Mr. Burt, the Detective. She received him in the library.

Mr. Burt looked at her dress and her little bag, and said, " I'm very glad I made bold to call so early."

" You have got information of importance to communicate to me? "

" I think so, miss "; and he took out his notebook. " The person you are watched by is Mr. Arthur Wardlaw." The girl stared at him. " Both spies report to him twice a day at his house in Russell Square."

" Be careful, Mr. Burt; this is a serious thing to say, and may have serious consequences."

" Well, miss, you told me you wanted to know the truth."

" Of course I want to know the truth."

" Then the truth is that you are watched by order of Mr. Wardlaw."

Burt continued his report.

" A shabby-like man called on you yesterday."

" Yes; it was Mr. Hand, Mr. Wardlaw's clerk. And O Mr. Burt, that wretched creature came and confessed the truth. It was he who forged the note, out of sport, and for a bet, and then was too cowardly to own it." She then detailed Hand's confession.

" His penitence comes too late," said she, with a deep sigh.

" It has n't come yet," said Burt, dryly. " Of course my lambs followed the man. He went first to his employer, and then he went home. His name is not Hand. He is not a clerk at all, but a little actor at the Corinthian Saloon. Hand is in America; went three months ago. I ascertained that from another quarter."

"O, goodness!" cried Helen, "what a wretched world! I can't see my way a yard for stories."

"How should you, miss? It is clear enough, for all that. Mr. Wardlaw hired this actor to pass for Hand, and tell you a lie that he thought would please you.'

Helen put her hand to her brow, and thought; but her candid soul got sadly in the way of her brain. "Mr. Burt," said she, "will you go with me to Mr. Undercliff, the Expert?"

"With pleasure, ma'am; but let me finish my report. Last night there was something new. Your house was watched by six persons. Two were Wardlaw's, three were Burt's; but the odd man was there on his own hook; and my men could not make him out at all; but they think one of Wardlaw's men knew him; for he went off to Russell Square like the wind, and brought Mr. Wardlaw here in disguise. Now, miss, that is all; and shall I call a cab, and we'll hear Undercliff's tale?"

The cab was called, and they went to Undercliff. On the way Helen brooded; but the Detective eyed every man and everything on the road with the utmost keenness.

Edward Undercliff was at work at lithographing. He received Helen cordially, nodded to Burt, and said she could not have a better assistant.

He then laid his fac-simile of the forged note on the table, with John Wardlaw's genuine writing and Penfold's indorsement. "Look at that, Mr. Burt."

Burt inspected the papers keenly.

"You know, Burt, I swore at Robert Penfold's trial that he never wrote that forged note."

"I remember," said Burt.

"The other day this lady instructed me to discover, if I could, who did write the forged note. But, unfortunately, the materials she gave me were not sufficient. But, last night, a young man dropped from the clouds, that I made sure was an agent of yours, Miss Rolleston. Under that impression I was rather unguarded, and I let him know how far we had got, and could get no farther. 'I think I can help you,' says this young man, and puts a letter on the table. "Well, Mr. Burt, a glance at that letter was enough for me. It was written by the man who forged the note."

"A letter!" said Helen.

"Yes. I'll put the letter by the side of the forged note; and, if you have any eye for writing at all, you'll see at once that one hand wrote the forged note and this letter. I am also prepared to swear that the letters signed Hand are forgeries by the same person." He then coolly put upon the table the letter from Arthur Wardlaw that Helen had received on board the Proserpine, and was proceeding to point out the many points of resemblance between the letter and the document, when he was interrupted by a scream from Helen.

"Ah!" she cried, "he is here. Only one man in the world could have brought that letter. I left it on the island. Robert is here: he gave you that letter."

"You are right," said the Expert, "and what a fool I must be! I have no eye except for handwriting. He had a beard: and such a beard!"

"It is Robert!" cried Helen, in raptures. "He is come just in time."

"In time to be arrested," said Burt. "Why, his time is not out. He'll get into a trouble again."

"O, Heaven forbid!" cried Helen, and turned so faint she had to be laid back on a chair, and salts applied to her nostrils.

She soon came to, and cried and trembled, but prepared to defend her Robert with all a woman's wit. Burt and Undercliff were conversing in a low voice, and Burt was saying he felt sure Wardlaw's spies had detected Robert Penfold, and that Robert would be arrested and put into prison as a runaway convict. "Go to Scotland Yard this minute, Mr. Burt," said Helen, eagerly.

"What for?"

"Why, you must take the commission to arrest him. You are our friend."

Burt slapped his thigh with delight.

"That is first-rate, miss," said he: "I'll take the real felon first, you may depend. Now, Mr. Undercliff, write your report, and hand it to Miss Helen with fac-similes. It will do no harm if you make a declaration to the same effect before a magistrate. You, Miss Rolleston, keep yourself disengaged, and please don't go out. You will very likely hear from me again to-day."

He drove off, and Helen, though still greatly agitated by Robert's danger and the sense of his presence, now sat down, trembling a little, and compared Arthur's letter with the forged document. The effect of this comparison was irresistible. The Expert, however, asked her for some letter of Arthur's that had never passed through Robert Penfold's hands. She gave him the short note in which he used the very words, Robert Penfold. He said he would make that note the basis of his report.

While he was writing it, Mrs. Undercliff came in, and Helen told her all. She said, "I came to the same conclusion long ago; but when you said he was to be your husband —"

"Ah," said Helen, "we women are poor creatures; we can always find some reason for running away from the truth. Now explain about the prayer-book."

"Well, miss, I felt sure he would steal it, so I made Ned produce a fac-simile. And he did steal it. What you got back was your mother's prayer-book. Of course I took care of that."

"O Mrs. Undercliff," cried Helen, "do let me kiss you."

Then they had a nice little cry together, and, by the time they had done, the report was ready in duplicate.

"I'll declare this before a magistrate," said the Expert, "and then I'll send it you."

At four o'clock of this eventful day, Helen got a message from Burt to say that he had orders to arrest Robert Penfold, and that she must wear a mask, and ask Mr. Wardlaw to meet her at old Mr. Penfold's at nine o'clock. But she herself must be there at half-past eight, without fail, and bring Undercliff's declaration and report with her, and the prayer-book, etc.

Accordingly, Helen went down to old Mr. Penfold's at half-past eight, and was received by Nancy Rouse, and ushered into Mr. Penfold's room; that is to say, Nancy held the door open, and, on her entering the room, shut it sharply and ran down stairs.

Helen entered the room; a man rose directly, and came to her; but it was not Michael Penfold, — it was Robert. A faint scream, a heavenly sigh, and her head was on his shoulder, and her arm round his neck, and both their hearts panting as they gazed, and then clung to each other, and then gazed again with love unutterable. After a while they got sufficient composure to sit down hand in hand and compare notes. And Helen showed him their weapons of defence, the prayer-book, the Expert's report, etc.

A discreet tap was heard at the door. It was Nancy Rouse. On being invited to enter, she came in, and said, "O Miss Helen, I've got a penitent outside, which he done it for love of me, and now he'll make a clean breast, and the fault was partly mine. Come in, Joe, and speak for yourself."

On this, Joe Wylie came in, hanging his head piteously.

"She is right, sir," said he; "I'm come to ask your pardon and the lady's. Not as I ever meant you any harm; but to destroy the ship, it was a bad act, and I've never throve since. Nance, she have got the money. I'll give it back to the underwriters; and, if you and the lady will forgive a poor fellow that was tempted with love and money, why I'll stand to the truth for you, though it's a bitter pill."

"I forgive you," said Robert; "and I accept your offer to serve me."

"And so do I," said Helen. "Indeed, it is not us you have wronged. But O, I *am* glad, for Nancy's sake, that you repent."

"Miss, I'll go through fire and water for you," said Wylie, lifting up his head.

Here old Michael came in to say that Arthur Wardlaw was at the door, with a policeman.

"Show him in," said Robert.

"O no, Robert!" said Helen. "He fills me with horror."

"Show him in," said Robert, gently. "Sit down, all of you."

Now Burt had not told Arthur who was in the house, so he came, rather uneasy in his mind, but still expecting only to see Helen.

Robert Penfold told Helen to face the door, and the rest to sit back; and this arrangement had not been effected one second, when Arthur came in, with a lover's look, and, taking two steps into the room, saw the three men waiting to receive him. At sight of Penfold, he started, and turned pale as ashes; but, recovering himself, said: "My dearest Helen, this is indeed an unexpected pleasure. You will reconcile me to one whose worth and innocence I never doubted, and tell him I have had some little hand in clearing him." His effrontery was received in dead silence. This struck cold to his bones, and, being naturally weak, he got violent. He said, "Allow me to send a message to my servant."

He then tore a leaf out of his memorandum-book, wrote on it, "Robert Penfold is here; arrest him directly, and take him away," and, enclosing this in an envelope, sent it out to Burt by Nancy.

Helen seated herself quietly, and said, "Mr. Wardlaw, when did Mr. Hand go to America?"

Arthur stammered out, "I don't know the exact date."

"Two or three months ago?"

"Yes."

"Then the person you sent to me to tell me that falsehood was not Mr. Hand?"

"I sent nobody."

"O, for shame! — for shame! Why have you set spies? Why did you make away with my prayer-book; — or what you thought was my prayer-book? Here *is* my prayer-book, that proves you had the Proserpine destroyed; and I should have lost my life but for another, whom you had done your best to destroy. Look Robert Penfold in the face, if you can."

Arthur's eyes began to waver. "I can," said he. "I never wronged him. I always lamented his misfortune."

"You were not the cause?"

"Never! — so help me Heaven!"

"Monster!" said Helen, turning away in contempt and horror.

"O, that is it, — is it?" said Arthur, wildly. "You break faith with me for *him?* You insult me for *him?* I must bear anything from you, for I love you; but, at least, I will sweep *him* out of the path."

He ran to the door, opened it, and there was Burt, listening. "Are you an officer?"

"Yes."

"Then arrest that man this moment: he is Robert Penfold, a convict returned before his time."

Burt came into the room, locked the door, and put the key in his pocket. "Well, sir," said he to Robert Penfold, "I know you are a quick hitter. Don't let us have a row over it this time. If you have got anything to say, say it quiet and comfortable."

"I will go with you on one condition," said Robert. "You must take the felon as well as the martyr. This is the felon," and he laid his hand on Arthur's shoulder, who cowered under the touch at first, but soon began to act violent indignation.

"Take the ruffian away at once," he cried.

"What, before I hear what he has got to say."

"Would you listen to him against a merchant of the city of London, a man of unblemished reputation."

"Well, sir, you see we have got a hint that you were concerned in scuttling a ship; and that is a felony. So I think I'll just hear what he has got to say. You need not *fear* any man's tongue if you are innocent."

"Sit down, if you please, and examine these documents," said Robert Penfold. "As to the scuttling of the ship, here is the deposition of two seamen, taken on their death-bed, and witnessed by Miss Rolleston and myself."

"And that book he tried to steal," said Helen.

Robert continued: "And here is Undercliff's facsimile of the forged note. Here are specimens of Arthur Wardlaw's handwriting, and here is Undercliff's report."

The Detective ran his eye hastily over the report, which we slightly condense.

On comparing the forged note with genuine specimens of John Wardlaw's handwriting, no less than twelve deviations from his habits of writing strike the eye; and every one of these twelve deviations is a deviation into a habit of Arthur Wardlaw, which is an amount of demonstration rarely attained in cases of forgery.

1. THE CAPITAL L. — Compare in London (forged note) with the same letter in London in Wardlaw's letter.

2. THE CAPITAL D. — Compare this letter in "Date," with the same letter in "Dearest."

3. THE CAPITAL T. — Compare it in "Two" and "Tollemache."

4. The word "To;" see "To pay," in forged note and third line of letter.

5. Small "o" formed with a loop in the up-stroke.

6. The manner of finishing the letter "v."

7. Ditto the letter "w."

8. The imperfect formation of the small "a." This and the looped "o" run through the forged note and Arthur Wardlaw's letter, and are habits entirely foreign to the style of John Wardlaw.

9. See the "th" in connection.

10. Ditto the "of" in connection.

11. The incautious use of the Greek e. John Wardlaw never uses this e. Arthur Wardlaw never uses any other, apparently. The writer of

the forged note began right, but at the word Robert Penfold glided insensibly into his Greek e, and maintained it to the end of the forgery. This looks as if he was in the habit of writing those two words.

12. Compare the words "Robert Penfold" in the forged document with the same words in the letter. The similarity is so striking, that, on these two words alone, the writer could be identified beyond a doubt.

13. Great pains were taken with the signature, and it is like John Wardlaw's writing on the surface; but go below the surface, and it is all Arthur Wardlaw.

The looped o, the small r, the l dropping below the d, the open a, are all Arthur Wardlaw's. The open loop of the final w is a still bolder deviation into A. W.'s own hand. The final flourish is a curious mistake. It is executed with skill and freedom; but the writer has made the lower line the thick one. Yet John Wardlaw never does this.

How was the deviation caused? Examine the final flourish in Arthur Wardlaw's signature. It contains one stroke only, but then that stroke is a thick one. He thought he had only to prolong his own stroke and bring it round. He did this extremely well, but missed the deeper characteristic, — the thick upper stroke. This is proof of a high character: and altogether I am quite prepared to testify upon oath that the writer of the letter to Miss Rolleston, who signs himself Arthur Wardlaw, is the person who forged the promissory note.

To these twelve proofs one more was now added. Arthur Wardlaw rose, and, with his knees knocking together, said, "Don't arrest him, Burt; let him go."

"Don't let *him* go," cried old Penfold. "A villain! I have got the number of the notes from Benson. I can prove he bribed this poor man to destroy the ship. Don't let him go. He has ruined my poor boy."

At this Arthur Wardlaw began to shriek for mercy. "O Mr. Penfold," said he, "you are a father, and hate me. But think of my father. I'll say anything, do anything. I'll clear Robert Penfold at my own expense. I have lost *her*. She loathes me now. Have mercy on me, and let me leave the country!" He cringed and crawled so that he disarmed anger, and substituted contempt.

"Ay," said Burt. "He don't hit like you, Mr. Penfold; this is a chap that ought to have been in Newgate long ago. But take my advice; make him clear you on paper, and then let him go. I'll go down stairs awhile. I must n't take part in compounding a felony."

"O yes, Robert," said Helen, "for his father's sake."

"Very well," said Robert. "Now then, reptile, take the pen, and write in your own hand, if you can."

He took the pen, and wrote to dictation: —

"I, Arthur Wardlaw, confess that I forged the promissory note for £ 2,000, and sent it to Robert Penfold, and that £ 1,400 of it was to be for my own use, and to pay my Oxford debts. And I confess that I bribed Wylie to scuttle the ship Proserpine in order to cheat the underwriters."

Penfold then turned to Wylie, and asked him the true motive of this fraud.

"Why, the gold was aboard the Shannon," said Wylie; "I played hanky panky with the metals in White's store."

"Put that down," said Penfold. "Now go on."

"Make a clean breast," said Wylie. "I have. Say as how you cooked the Proserpine's log, and forged Hiram Hudson's writing."

"And the newspaper extracts you sent me," said Helen, "and the letters from Mr. Hand."

Arthur groaned. "Must I tell all that?" said he.

"Every word, or be indicted," said Robert Penfold, sternly.

He wrote it all down, and then sat staring stupidly. And the next thing was, he gave a loud shriek, and fell on the floor in a fit. They sprinkled water over him, and Burt conveyed him home in a cab, advising him to leave the country, but at the same time promising him not to exasperate those he had wronged so deeply, but rather to moderate them, if required. Then he gave Burt fifty guineas.

Robert Penfold, at Helen's request, went with her to Mr. Hennessy, and with the proofs of Arthur's guilt and Robert's innocence; and he undertook that the matter should go in proper form before the Secretary of State. But, somehow, it transpired that the Proserpine had been scuttled, and several of the underwriters wrote to the Wardlaws to threaten proceedings. Wardlaw senior returned but one answer to these gentlemen: "Bring your proofs to me at my place of business next Monday at twelve, and let me judge the case, before you go elsewhere."

"That is high and mighty," said one or two; but they conferred, and agreed to these terms, so high stood the old merchant's name.

They came; they were received with stiff courtesy. The deposition of Cooper and Welch was produced, and Wylie, kept up to the mark by Nancy, told the truth, and laid his two thousand pounds intact down on the table. "Now that is off my stomach," said he, "and I'm a man again."

"Ay, and I'll marry you next week," said Nancy.

"Well, gentlemen," said old Wardlaw, "my course seems very clear. I will undo the whole transaction, and return you your money less the premiums, but plus five per cent interest." And this he did on the spot, for the firm was richer than ever.

When they were gone, Robert Penfold came in, and said, "I hear, sir, you devote this day to repairing the wrongs done by your firm: What can you do for me?" He laid a copy of Arthur's confession before him.

The old man winced a moment where he sat, and the iron passed through his soul. It was a long time before he could speak. At last he said, "This wrong is irreparable, I fear."

Robert said nothing. Sore as his own heart was, he was not the one to strike a grand old man, struggling so bravely against dishonor.

Wardlaw senior touched his hand-bell.

"Request Mr. Penfold to step this way."

Michael Penfold came.

"Gentlemen," said the old merchant, "the house of Wardlaw exists no more. It was built on honesty, and cannot survive a fraud. Wardlaw and Son were partners at will. I had decided to dissolve that partnership, wind up the accounts, and put up the shutters. But now, if you like, I will value the effects, and hand the business over to Penfold and Son on easy terms. Robert Penfold has been accused of forging John Wardlaw's name; to prove this was a calumny, I put Penfold over my door instead of Wardlaw. The city of London will understand that, gentlemen, believe me."

"Mr. Wardlaw," said Robert, "you are a just, a noble — " He could say no more.

"Ah, sir," said Michael, "if the young gentleman had only been like you!"

"Mention his name no more to me. His crime and his punishment have killed me."

"O," said Robert, hastily, "he shall not be punished, for your sake."

"Not be punished? It is not in your hands to decide. God has punished him. He is insane."

"Good Heavens!"

"Quite mad; — quite mad. Gentlemen, I can no longer support this interview. Send me your solicitor's address; the deeds shall be prepared. I wish the new firm success. Probity is the road to it. Good day."

He wound up the affairs, had his name and Arthur's painted out at his own expense, and directed the painters to paint the Penfolds' in at theirs; went home to Elm Trees, and died in three days. He died lamented and honored, and Robert Penfold was much affected. He got it into his head that he had killed him with Arthur's confession, putting it before him so suddenly. "I have forgotten who said 'Vengeance is mine,'" said Robert Penfold.

The merchant priest left the office to be conducted by his father; he used the credit of the new firm to purchase a living in the Vale of Kent; and thither he retired, grateful to Providence, but not easy in his conscience. He now accused himself of having often distrusted God, and seen his fellow-creatures in too dark a light. He turned towards religion and the care of souls.

Past suffering enlightens a man, and makes him tender; and people soon began to walk and drive considerable distances to hear the new vicar. He had a lake with a peninsula, the shape of which he altered, at a great expense, as soon as he came there. He wrote to Helen every day, and she to him. Neither could do anything *con amore* till the post came in.

One afternoon, as he was preaching with great unction, he saw a long puritanical face looking up at him with a droll expression of amazement and half irony. The stranger called on him, and began at once, "Wal, parson, you are a buster, you air. You ginn it us hot, — *you* did. I'm darned if I ain't kinder ashamed to talk of this world's goods to a saint upon airth like you. But I never knowed a parson yet as couldn't collar the dollars."

After this preamble he announced that he had got a lease of the island from Chili, dug a lot of silver plate out of the galleon, sold ten tons of choice coral, and a ship-load of cassia and cocoa-nuts. He had then disposed of his lease to a Californian Company for a large sum. And his partner's share of net profits came to 17,247*l.* 13*s.* 3½*d.*, which sum he had paid to Michael, for Robert, Penfold in drafts on Baring, at thirty days after sight.

Robert shook his hand, and thanked him sincerely for his ability and probity. He stayed that night at the Vicarage, and by that means fell in with another acquaintance. General Rolleston and his daughter drove down to see the Parsonage. Helen wanted to surprise Robert; and, as often happens, she surprised herself. She made him show her everything; and so he took her on to his peninsula. Lo! the edges of it had been cut and altered, so that it presented a miniature copy of Godsend Island.

As soon as she saw this, Helen turned round with a sudden cry of love, "O Robert!" and the lovers were in each other's arms.

"What could any other man ever be to me?"

"And what could any other woman ever be to me?"

They knew that before. But this miniature island made them speak out and say it. The wedding day was fixed before she left.

Her Majesty pardoned this scholar, hero, and worthy, the crime he had never committed.

Nancy Rouse took the penitent Wylie without the £2,000. But old Penfold, who knew the whole story, lent the money at three per cent; so the Wylies pay a groundrent of £60 a year for a property which, by Mrs. Wylie's industry and judgment, is worth at least £400. She pays this very cheerfully, and appeals to Joe whether that is not better than the other way.

"Why, Joe," says she, "to a woman like me, that's afoot all day, 't is worth sixty pounds a year to be a good sleeper; and I should n't be that if I had wronged my neighbor."

Arthur Wardlaw is in a private lunatic asylum, and is taken great care of. In his lucid intervals he suffers horrible distress of mind; but, though sad to see, these agonies furnish the one hope of his ultimate recovery. When not troubled by these returns of reason, he is contented enough. His favorite employment is to get Mr. Undercliff's facsimiles, and to write love-letters to Helen Rolleston which are duly deposited in the post-office *of the establishment.* These letters are in the handwriting of Charles I., Paoli, Lord Bacon, Alexander Pope, Lord Chesterfield, Nelson, Lord Shaftesbury, Addison, the late Duke of Wellington, and so on. And, strange to say, the Greek e never appears in any of them. They are admirably like, though, of course, the matter is not always equally consistent with the characters of those personages.

Helen Rolleston married Robert Penfold. On the wedding-day, the presents were laid out, and amongst them there was a silver-box encrusted with coral. Female curiosity demanded that this box should be opened. Helen objected, but her bridesmaids rebelled; the whole company sided with them, and Robert smiled a careless assent. A blacksmith and carpenter were both enlisted, and with infinite difficulty the poor box was riven open.

Inside was another box, locked, but with no key. That was opened with comparative ease, and then handed to the bride. It contained nothing but Papal indulgences and rough stones, and fair throats were opened in some disappointment.

A lady, however, of more experience, examined the contents, and said, that, in her opinion, many of them were uncut gems of great price; there were certainly a quantity of jaspers and bloodstones, and others of no value at all. "But look at these two pearl-shaped diamonds," said she; "why, they are a little fortune! and, Oh!" The stone that struck this fair creature dumb was a rough ruby as big as a blackbird's egg, and of amazing depth and fire. "No lady in England," said she, "has a ruby to compare with this."

The information proved correct. The box furnished Helen with diamonds and emeralds of great thickness and quality. But the huge ruby placed her on a level with sovereigns. She wears it now and then in London, but not often. It attracts too much attention, blazing on her fair forehead like a star, and eclipses everything.

Well, what her ruby is amongst stones she is amongst wives. And he is worthy of her. Through much injustice, suffering, danger, and trouble, they have passed to health, happiness, and peace, and that entire union of two noble hearts, in loyal friendship and wedded love, which is the truest bliss this earth affords.

THE END.

www.ingramcontent.com/pod-product-compliance
Lightning Source LLC
LaVergne TN
LVHW021408110826
845150LV00007B/1840